A GREAT RESTLESSNESS

A GREAT RESTLESSNESS

THE LIFE AND POLITICS OF DORISE NIELSEN

FAITH JOHNSTON

UNIVERSITY OF MANITOBA PRESS

University of Manitoba Press
Winnipeg, Manitoba R3T 2N2 Canada
www.umanitoba.ca/uofmpress
Printed in Canada on acid-free paper by Friesens.

Cover: Doowah Design
Text design: Relish Design Studio
Cover images: Campaign poster (courtesy Eva Phelps); Peace Tower, Ottawa; Scattering of ashes of Dorise Nielsen (NAC); Dorise Nielsen with children Sally, John, and Christine (NAC); May Day parade, Winnipeg, 1930s (Communist Party of Canada, www.communist-party.ca).

Library and Archives Canada Cataloguing in Publication

Johnston, Faith
A great restlessness : the life and politics of Dorise Nielsen / Faith Johnston.

Includes bibliographical references and index.
ISBN 0-88755-690-6

1. Nielsen, Dorise, 1902-1980. 2. Communist Party of Canada–Biography.
3. Canada. Parliament. House of Commons–Biography. 4. Legislators–Canada–Biography.
5. Politicians–Canada–Biography. 6. Canada–Politics and government–1935-1948. I. Title.

FC581.N66J64 2006 328.71'092 C2006-903351-X

The University of Manitoba Press gratefully acknowledges the financial support for its publication program provided by the Government of Canada through the Book Publishing Industry Development Program (BPIDP), the Canada Council for the Arts, the Manitoba Arts Council, and the Manitoba Department of Culture, Heritage, and Tourism.

For Sally Nielsen and in memory of Christine

An adventure through the life of one woman who has been profoundly stirred by a great restlessness and you will comprehend more than from a library of theorizings.

—Ruth Benedict

TABLE OF CONTENTS

ACKNOWLEDGEMENTS

This book could not have been written without the collaboration of many witnesses, each with his or her own piece of the story. I am indebted to each and every one whose name appears in the list of those interviewed. Their generosity has warmed my heart and kept me going. Particular thanks to Sally Nielsen and Stewart Paul, to whom I have turned time and time again with questions. My gratitude also goes to other scholars who have included Dorise Nielsen in their studies of women on the left, including Elizabeth Smillie, Georgina Taylor, and Joan Sangster.

I was lucky to have friends and a few generous strangers who were willing to read the manuscript or parts of it at various stages. Their comments helped me enormously. Thank you Joan Thomas, Joan Givner, Sarah Klassen, Elizabeth Harvour, Stephen Endicott, Isabel Crook, Jim Mochoruk, John Groves, Jim Anderson, Arthur Ross, Julie Guard, and Franca Iacovetta. Particular thanks to the staff at the University of Manitoba Press (Pat Sanders, Cheryl Miki, and David Carr) for their skills and care and enthusiasm.

For assistance with research, thanks to Bonnie Bodnar at the Winnipeg Public Library, Larry Black at the Centre for Research on Canadian-Russian Relations, and Bob Ivanochko at the Great Plains Research Centre for responding so quickly to requests for information and materials. Thanks also to the Office of the Information Commissioner of Canada, whose investigators eventually retrieved Nielsen's CSIS files, and to the Manitoba Arts Council, which provided a travel grant for a research trip to Ottawa.

Particular thanks to Stephen Endicott for sharing his expertise on China, putting me in touch with people who knew Dorise there, and giving me advice and information in other areas; and to Diane Schmolka, for giving me a place to stay in Ottawa and, on occasion, playing chauffeur.

A GREAT RESTLESSNESS

PROLOGUE

ON MAY 16, 1940, a tall, blue-eyed woman with thick, dark hair took her place in the House of Commons as the member for North Battleford. Her appearance made heads turn, not only because she was the sole woman elected to the nineteenth Parliament of Canada, but also because of her height, her grace. Even those who remember her as an old woman remark on her appearance—elegant, they say, or stately, or, simply, attractive. When she entered Parliament, Mrs. Dorise Nielsen was thirty-eight years old. No one had expected the wife of a poor homesteader from northern Saskatchewan to cut such a figure.

If the honourable members had had the time and inclination to read the popular press, they would know that Nielsen had been born into a middle-class family in London, England, that she had immigrated to Canada as a teacher when she was twenty-four years old, and that she was the mother of three young children, whom she had brought with her to Ottawa. According to the editor of *Chatelaine*, Nielsen's election was "one of those thrilling true-to-life stories every editor longs for."[1] But all the hype failed to reveal the most interesting and pertinent fact of all—that Mrs. Nielsen was the first communist ever elected to Parliament in Canada.

The summer of 2002 I took the Yellowhead highway west from Winnipeg to Saskatoon. When I started out, the prairie fields were bright yellow with canola in blossom, green with half-grown wheat and rye and oats, occasionally blue with flax. But shortly after crossing the Saskatchewan border, I reached a desert zone. After three successive years of drought, the sloughs had dried up and their beds of cracked mud and clay were dusted with a white scum of salt. The fields were a wasteland of burnt tufts. On the radio, I heard the tale of a farmer who had shot over forty head of cattle because he had no hay left to feed them. At least he didn't put the gun to his own head, I thought.

Of course, all this was familiar. I knew about the Depression and the dust bowl. The dirty thirties (dirtier in Saskatchewan than anywhere else in Canada) were the catalyst for the tale I wanted to tell. It was the story of a woman who ran for Parliament in 1940. She was one of nine women who ran for election in Canada that year—all for reform parties—and she was a very unlikely candidate. Yet she won because she promised radical change. Just a few years before, a bachelor who lived on a farm not far from her home shot himself and left a suicide note (in Hungarian). "I leave my flesh to the capitalists," he wrote. "Let them make me disappear into their stomach."[2] Capitalism was not popular in Saskatchewan in the thirties (though the capitalists weren't doing very well, either). Radicalism thrived, and Dorise Nielsen was one of the most radical of them all.

Nielsen played an active role in one of the longest and most productive parliaments in Canada's history. In summing up Canada's nineteenth parliament, *Canadian Business* featured her as one of two "Parliamentary Personalities." She was a fine speaker, wrote Austin Cross, "the equal of three ordinary men and four cabinet ministers."[3] Nielsen's maiden speech was so impressive that Mackenzie King took the time, in the midst of Hitler's blitzkrieg on the Western Front, to try to solicit her support for the Liberals. She struck him as a woman of real ability, whose understanding of the effects of poverty was similar to his own. A month later, when he learned she was a communist, he ordered her investigated by the Department of Justice. From 1940 to 1942, when leaders of the Communist Party of Canada were either interned or underground, she was their public voice.

She continued to work for the party during the chilliest days of the Cold War. By 1957, when she left Canada for China, the RCMP had collected thirty volumes of material (over 4000 pages) on her.

Quite by accident, I made my way into Saskatchewan in 2002 on the 100th anniversary of Nielsen's birth, the summer of 1902, in London. If she had lived a long, long life, as more and more people do these days, she might have been willing to tell her own story, or at least answer a few questions. But more likely she would have told me to bloody well mind my own business. The *Globe and Mail* correspondent in Beijing was never able to get an interview with her. When she died in 1980, he had to piece together an obituary. "A former member of Parliament and pioneer of Canadian feminism died here last week," he wrote. "Reportedly bitter towards both her native country and the Communist Party of Canada, Mrs. Nielsen refused all interviews with foreign journalists and declined numerous invitations to the Canadian embassy."[4]

She died at seventy-eight, stubbornly silent to the end. During the early tumultuous days of the Cultural Revolution, when she had no work, she wrote a memoir that ended in 1928, shortly after her arrival in Canada. Although a good read, it was not much help in deciphering the next fifty years of her life. When her children asked her to write more, she said that the rest was too painful, and, in any case, she was more interested in the present than the past, always had been.

Unlike Nielsen, the past interested me enormously. Where were the women in Canadian history? Who came after Nellie McClung? In the 1980s my day job was teaching history and economics at an Ottawa school for girls. At the time, uncovering women's history in Canada was a new field, and little of it had reached the textbooks. I started to take graduate courses. One day, at the National Archives, I came across the name Dorise Nielsen. I wondered why had I never heard of this woman. That was the beginning of my quest. Soon I met Georgina Taylor, a feminist historian familiar with Nielsen's story. She introduced me to Nielsen's daughters, Christine and Sally. They had saved hundreds of letters and had dug through archives themselves. They were happy to share memories and insights and material with me, as long as I would do the same.

My first question, and the one that hooked me for a long time, was about the origin of her political allegiance. Had she brought left-wing politics with her from England, or had Saskatchewan provided her political education? In the thirties, was she a communist fellow-traveller or a bona fide member of the Co-operative Commonwealth Federation (CCF), as she said she was? If her allegiance shifted from the CCF to the communists, when did that happen and why? All these questions had nothing to do with my original feminist historical intentions. I felt as if I were inhabiting a novel by Le Carré.

Poverty was a radicalizing force in Saskatchewan in the thirties. But even there, associating with communists was a risky business. Yet Nielsen took that risk. "Whatever your problems are, tackle them," she advised a friend. "If needed do something desperate . . . but don't drift. Drifting is deadly and kills a woman by degrees."[5] She made daring leaps in her personal life, too. In 1940, the year of her election, she left her husband. She took the children with her to Ottawa that year, intending to give them a better life, but it didn't work out. By 1942, she had moved her children four times, from one boarding place to another. When she lost the election in 1945 and attempted to reconstitute her family, the damage had been done. The more I knew of the Nielsen family, the more I realized the cost of their mother's daring. Neither of the two women elected to Parliament before her had been raising children at the time. Nielsen bore the double burden more familiar to my generation than her own.

In the summer, when my own children were away on holidays with their father, I would step out of the National Archives late at night and think of Nielsen, leaving Parliament after an evening sitting, feeling the same dank heaviness of the evening air. She had a one-room apartment somewhere south of Parliament Hill, close enough to walk home for her supper. From her bathroom window she could see the Peace Tower clock. In a city crowded with troops and a burgeoning civil service, she was lucky to have such good accommodation, but she missed her children. She had thought that, somehow, she could do it all. She believed that women were not meant to be slaves to husbands and children, drudging all their lives. She wanted to change all that, but she discovered it wasn't so easy after all.

She had come of age in the 1920s, when anything seemed possible. In Canada and Great Britain, women had just gained the vote after long campaigns. Full equality, they believed, was just around the corner. Young women like Nielsen went to college, dated (without a chaperone), danced the tango, and smoked newfangled cigarettes. They had high expectations. They would marry, but their marriages would be collaborative adventures. Nielsen was exceptional—she was bright and amazingly energetic—but she was not unique. There were other women like her, women who had no intention of talking babies in the kitchen while the men talked politics in the parlour. Agnes Macphail and Martha Black, both elected before Nielsen, were the same.[6]

I could understand Nielsen's desire to be where the action was, but her love affairs were more of a problem for me. "I laughed when you said I was hard on men," wrote Nielsen to one of her daughters when she was an old woman. "Maybe those you knew, but I've known so many others. Actually I like men better than women, I think . . . they seem to have so many more interests than women."[7] But Nielsen was, indeed, hard on men, at least on the men who loved her. One of her partners, Robert Paul, who had organized her election campaign, later left his wife for her. In the 1950s Constant Godefroy, a Dutch mining engineer, shocked his family by taking off with her to Communist China, leaving yet another wife in the dust. But, in the end, she turfed both men out—quite decisively. "I shall welcome a break," she wrote when she separated from Con. "Freedom is such a sweet thing."[8]

"She was pragmatic when it came to people," said Robert Paul's eldest son. "She was a pretty tough cookie."[9] A "tough cookie"—a phrase to ring in my head and confound my vision of Nielsen. All those letters to friends, to her children and grandchildren, all those gifts mailed and received. The love poetry she sent Robert Paul. She wasn't always a tough cookie. Yet close relationships were never easy for her, and few people measured up to her standards for long.

Perhaps that is why the continuing thread in her life was not a relationship, or even a series of relationships, it was a cause. Better to work for the revolution, she believed, than to worry about one's personal happiness, which is such a fleeting thing. She was sure that capitalism would never survive another crisis like the thirties and it would never offer opportunities for all. In China in the 1960s, as in Saskatchewan thirty years before, she felt herself part of a great struggle for equality and social justice. She supported the north in the Vietnam War, donating part of her salary and attending huge demonstrations in Tiananmen Square. At the beginning of the Cultural Revolution in 1966, she joined a rebel regiment, believing that the dawn of the new era was just around the corner.

On my second day in Saskatchewan, I drove two hours straight north of Saskatoon to the village of Spiritwood. Charlie Szasz, who grew up on a farm adjacent to the Nielsens', was sitting at his kitchen table waiting for me. He had opened a book of local history to a one-column entry on Dorise Nielsen, the woman who became a Member of Parliament and left her husband. Both facts carried equal weight. She was an uppity woman, the article implied, one who couldn't be content with what she had but had to run off looking for something else. She was not the type of woman to be eulogized in a local history book. If it weren't for her stint in Parliament, she would not be in the book at all. It features the families who have remained in the area generation after generation, like the Szasz family. The transients who stayed a few years and moved on, who worked in the bank, or on the railroad, or taught school, the farmers like Pete Nielsen whose farms were foreclosed, did not appear in the book. They had vanished from history.

"That's really all I know," said Charlie, pointing to the entry on Dorise. A remarkably fit-looking man for seventy-eight, he was lean and tan and short on words. He was three when Dorise arrived in the area, sixteen when she was elected, and twenty-one when she left for good. Surely he knew more than he thought. And I knew that Charlie's parents had nine children living and three infants dead, and that his mother died at home after a three-day labour. At some point the doctor was sent for, but it was a long drive to Rabbit Lake to fetch him and he arrived too late. A needless death. One of many needless deaths that angered Dorise.

"What about Dorise and your mother? Were they friends?" I asked. We were driving south on a gravel road to the Szasz farm.

"Well, my mother didn't speak English, and Dorise didn't speak Hungarian. Mrs. MacMillan now, she learned some Hungarian."

We passed a cemetery on the right and soon after, we turned left down a dirt road to the farm, five farms originally, and now four of them belong to members of the Szasz family.

"That was MacMillans'," said Charlie, pointing to a house on the right (his niece lived there now, he would be going there for dinner). "Willards' was there." (Nothing now, just a field.)

A little further down, where the road curved left just before the Szasz place, was the Nielsen farm. Now there was a frame house hidden by trees. None of the original log buildings remained.

Charlie and I pulled into a yard that contained a hodgepodge of sheds, granaries, and machinery. Off to the side was the frame house his father built in 1933, now deserted. In the yard Charlie's brothers, Jim and Gordon, were building what appeared to be a playhouse. The two men put down their tools and we began to talk. They remembered the Nielsen children who were their playmates, how they all walked to school together, climbed trees, played tricks on Hallowe'en, how there was always a picnic in the summer, right over there in that field, with homemade ice cream, the works.

When I asked about Dorise, Jim, the outgoing one, full of jokes, hesitated only a second. "Dorise?" he said. "A shit-disturber!" And then there was a big guffaw of embarrassment. Perhaps he had gone too far. "No," he said suddenly, "she was an educated person. She had her own views and she stuck with them."

This sober second thought hung in the air as we scrambled into a shed to escape a shower. The playhouse, it turned out, was not a playhouse at all, but a miniature church being built as a memorial to their mother. In the shed were pews, a lectern, and a beautifully finished door that Jim had brought all the way from the coast. "Women were not meant to have so many children," said Charlie, who was eleven when his mother died. The memorial church was his idea.

Sophie Szasz died in 1935, the same year Dorise Nielsen made her first political speech. Two women, both products of a certain time, a certain place. I realized that in some ways Charlie and his brothers and I were bent on the same quest. As George Woodcock wrote in his biography of the Métis leader Gabriel Dumont, death and defeat are no excuse for forgetting.

SASKATCHEWAN

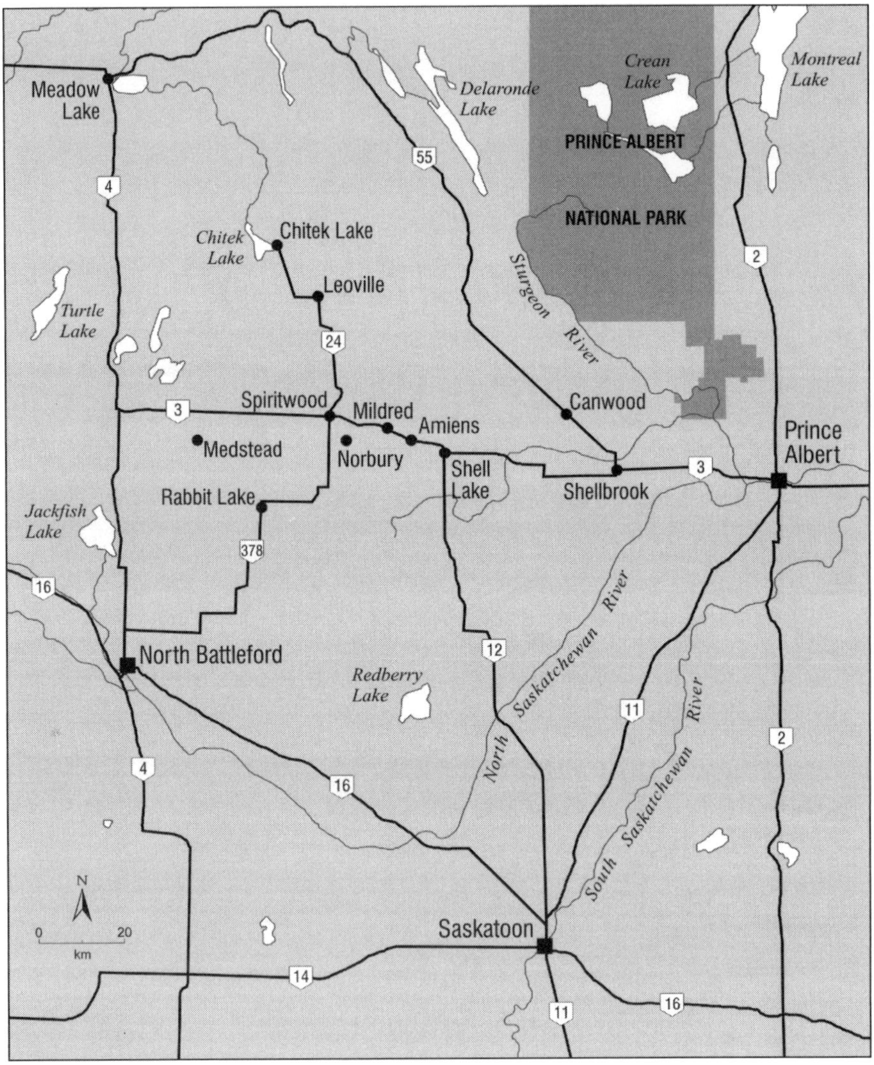

Central Saskatchewan

1

COMING TO CANADA

Canadian women knew what was ahead of them. They knew very well that if they got on a homestead they'd be working their fingernails to the bone.[1]

THE HOUSE IN WHICH DORISE NIELSEN, née Webber, was born still stands in an area of north London called Stoke Newington. An old Victorian row house, one of thousands in Britain, only two rooms up and two down but built to last. It is amazing to think of how many people lived in each unit a hundred years ago. The Webbers at 43 Defoe Road had a mere five children, but across the street in an identical row of terraced houses, the Baileys had ten and the Boffs nine. Despite the crowding, the terraced houses on Defoe bear the mark of distinction of that era. Each has a modest bay window on the first floor, a sign that its working-class inhabitants had certain aspirations. The occupations of the residents ranged from charwoman to clockmaker, with jobs such as cheesemonger's assistant, dressmaker, and lady cashier taking up the middle of the spectrum. Dorise's father was a master carpenter.

Born when her mother, Jessie Webber, was forty-four years old, Dorise was obviously an afterthought. According to family mythology (or perhaps Nielsen's own inventive imagination), Jessie concealed her pregnancy with the aid of corsets, and on the morning of July 30, 1902, presented her husband with a surprise package. John Webber, forty-nine himself, had come from Cornwall. Jessie's ancestors, the Styles, had been goldsmiths in London. By the time their last child was born, the Webbers had three grown daughters who lived at home, and a son, Harry, who was fourteen and still in school. John and Jessie named the new addition Doris Winifred (Doris would later add an "e" to her name). A month later she was baptized at the local Anglican church, St. Mary's Stoke Newington.

Nielsen remembered being lonely as a child. Either she was given too much attention or none at all. In a sense, she had three mothers but few playmates.[2] One of her sisters, Nell, taught her to read when she was very young, and she soon became an avid reader. When she started school, she was advanced two grades. Her mother was a rather stern and distant woman, dutiful but not demonstrative. From the time Dorise was old enough, she was given the task of brushing Jessie's hair, 100 strokes a night. It was long, black hair, very thick and with no sign of grey.

Memory is strange and selective. When Nielsen wrote a memoir sixty years later, she had a clear vision of her mother's hair (so much like her own) and no memory of her father at all. "He died when I was two," she wrote. In fact, he died in 1908 when she was six, probably of congestive heart failure. His bed had been set up in the living room because he was unable to climb the stairs. Almost daily, James Healey, a doctor who was also a family friend, dropped in to check on him. Nielsen called Healey "Deedoc" and became very attached to him. Then, one summer morning (according to another family story), John Webber woke early before the rest of the family. It was a beautiful morning, so fresh and new that he decided to get up by himself and go outside. When she woke up that morning, Jessie Webber found him sitting in a chair, dead, with a white rose in his hand. Nielsen turned to this story more and more often as she aged herself.

Her claim to have no memory of her father is not unusual. Young children can block out such early losses forever. It is possible she loved her father very much. She may have been closer to him than to her mother. Or perhaps she resented him for getting all the attention. In any case, the important male figure in her life disappeared early, and she turned quickly to another. James Healey, the doctor who attended her father, continued to pay visits to the family after John Webber's death. For Dorise, Deedoc's visit was the highlight of the day. Then, when she was about twelve, he died suddenly of a heart attack. It was his death, not her father's, that caused her great distress. She was now at an age to understand the permanence of death and to know that it comes to everyone. When Deedoc died, she says, "he left a big hole in my life that no one else ever filled." She cried every day for a long while.[3]

Surprisingly, the family fortunes did not decline with John Webber's illness and death. According to Nielsen, her father had established a construction business and had benefited from the rapid northward expansion of London.[4] He had purchased a lot for his own family near Clapton Common, where they relocated after his death. The Webber home and several of its neighbours on Kyverdale Road have been replaced by a block of apartments, but the rest of the street of semi-detached brownstones stands intact, all with prominent bay windows extending from the ground through the third floor. This is the twelve-room house with long back garden that Dorise remembered in her memoir, written many years later, when she lived in China during the Cultural Revolution. When she went to high school she was allotted the large attic room so that she could set up her paints. Apart from two years away at college, she lived at home until she left for Canada at the age of twenty-four.

Other people besides the Webbers lived in the house. Their names show up on the electoral rolls along with Jessie's.[5] Possibly the house was divided into two apartments. Dorise mentioned nothing of such arrangements when she wrote her memoir. She was an old woman then. The compound where she lived in China was almost deserted. Leaves fell in the courtyards and were never swept up. The ceiling of the dining room leaked. It took courage to walk out beyond the compound gate. The life she had led in England before World War I seemed particularly secure and luxurious. She remembered the food at Christmas, the nuts, the goose, the plum puddings and cakes, and all the shopping expeditions beforehand. If there were any struggles to make ends meet, like most children, she may not have been aware of them. In the memoir, she pictured her family as part of the bourgeoisie, enjoying a comfortable lifestyle built on the sweat of others. She had benefited, for a while, from British imperialism. The memoir is peppered with lessons in history from a Marxist perspective. "I was very proud of belonging to the empire," she wrote, "until I left England and began to learn a few things about what it was like to live in a colony."[6]

By the eve of World War I, the Webber household had achieved a certain stability. Two of Dorise's siblings, Maude and Harry, had married and moved out. Two others, Nell and Florry, were still unmarried and at home. Dorise was a tall, skinny twelve-year-old, with her hair braided in one long pigtail down her back. She was known as Dee and was accustomed to being treated as an adult in a household of adults. She was taught to play bridge and included in outings to concerts and the theatre. In the summer she was sent to Cornwall to stay with her Aunt Emmie, whom she loved (Emily was John Webber's youngest sister), or to family friends, Bill and Mabel Woodgate, in Devon. Bill Woodgate was a fisherman in his sixties.[7] Nielsen had fond memories of rowing out with the Woodgates' son, early in the morning, to fetch the lobster pots, and of being given a delicious crab for tea. She learned to swim and helped her Aunt Mabel sell the crabs. From her account, these were very happy times, with no thought of missing her mother.

Like most families in Britain and in so many other countries, the Webbers' equilibrium was severely unsettled by World War I and its aftermath. Dee began to read the newspapers and was horrified by the stories of German atrocities in Belgium. At home there was a struggle over her studying German at school. Nell's fiancé, Alfred Starr, was fluent in German and wanted to help her, but she refused. Already she had the reputation in the family of clinging to her loves and hates with a strong and stubborn passion. But before long, Jessie Webber had much more serious matters that drew her attention. Harry Webber's infant son died of meningitis, and then his wife of tuberculosis—all this while Harry was in the navy. At some point during the war, Nell married Alfred Starr, who had also joined up. The household was in almost constant flux with Alfred and Harry and various cousins passing through on leave. Sometimes the war moved even closer to home. There were zeppelin raids on London. Several bombs fell near the Lea River close by the house (apparently the Germans had mistaken the Lea for the Thames). Then in 1915 two Webber cousins died at the front.[8]

At school Dee endured weekly visits to a hospital with her schoolmates, where the girls read to soldiers and gave them sweets. She dreaded the smells, but the hardest part was seeing all the amputees. She tried to pretend that everything was normal, that she hadn't noticed anything missing at all. Apart from the hospital visits, she enjoyed school. It was a welcome break from home and all the talk of war. Her favourite subjects were history, geography, drama, and art. In secondary school she began to enjoy science, as well. Clapton County Secondary School for Girls was a new, progressive school with modern science labs, and it was the labs that stimulated her interest in botany and biology.[9] The school drew students from all over Hackney and even beyond. It was an area sprinkled with Jewish immigrants from Poland and Russia and central Europe.[10] Nielsen mentions nothing of this multiculturalism in her memoir. Still, the mixture of nationalities and religions was part of her environment, both at home and at school. This early immersion in a cosmopolitan community may account for her easy acceptance of the polyglot immigrant community in northern Saskatchewan, as well as her lifelong distain for racism.

The summer holidays in Devon and Cornwall continued throughout the war. At the Woodgates', the summer of 1916, she met a family called Gilchrist who took her sailing. There were two Gilchrist sons, Laurie, twenty, and Edward, sixteen.[11] Nielsen says she lied and told them she was sixteen, too, although she was barely fourteen that summer. In her memoir, those two summers during the war in the company of the Gilchrists are spun out for 150 pages and read like an old-fashioned romance novel. She fell in love with Laurie, the oldest son. Together they planned an adventurous future. She would go to university as he was doing; then they would travel the world. But all these hopes and dreams were dashed when he joined the RAF and crashed on his solo flight the summer of 1918.

According to her memoir, at fourteen Doris Webber met the love of her life and at sixteen she lost him. If only Laurie Gilchrist had lived, her life would have taken a very different course. Surely this dramatic story tells us more about the mind of the woman who wrote a memoir than it does about Dee as a young woman. But what it tells us is not easy to decipher. Was she seeking an explanation of why she had never had an enduring marriage like many of her contemporaries? In letters to friends she gave much more practical reasons. In one of them she speculated that women were no more suited to monogamy than men. But in the memoir, written for her children, she chose to expose her traditional, romantic side. Perhaps she was seeking their sympathy, and their forgiveness. "Little did I know that my whole life was to be ruined before the war was over," she wrote, placing the blame quite decisively on the imperialist warmongers, where she thought it belonged.[12] By the time Nielsen wrote her memoir, she had been a propagandist for over thirty years.

Meanwhile, as World War I ended, the drama in the Webber household continued. In the autumn of 1918, Dorise's brother-in-law, Alfred Starr, died of the Spanish flu. A few weeks later, Nell gave birth to their first child, a son.[13] Thus, the end of the war brought more turmoil and sadness. Dorise learned from those around her that life goes on, that one copes with grief by keeping one's chin up until eventually it feels like a natural posture. "My mother was a strong woman," she wrote. "She hid her grief and taught me that I should do the same. 'Never show your weakness,' was what she said."[14] It was Dorise's final year in secondary school. She buried herself in her studies and graduated in June 1919, a month before her seventeenth birthday.

At the end of the war, women over thirty were enfranchised in Great Britain. The campaign for women's suffrage had been a long one, and before the war it received wide publicity when hundreds of militant suffragettes were arrested. Despite all this, Nielsen says she never remembers her sisters bothering to vote, though her mother always voted Conservative "because Jack did." Harry, the brother she thought of as a genial giant, probably had similar inclinations. He lived at home for a few years after the war. Occasionally he took Dorise to Masonic dinners or tried to teach her to golf. Later he was horrified at her left-wing politics. Nielsen says she herself was more interested in the latest fashions and in learning the tango than she was in politics. Judging by the elaborate wardrobe she brought to Canada, she is probably telling the truth.

But she likely had a more developed sense of personal politics than she realized at the time. From the beginning, her speeches in Parliament showed a strong feminist bent. Like her contemporary, Simone de Beauvoir, she knew that women were capable of a whole range of accomplishments beyond housekeeping or raising children or supporting their husbands' careers. For as long as she could remember, she had lived in a household run by women. Her mother was a strong figure and so was her sister, Nell. And it wasn't only men who suffered in wartime. She knew that, too. The lives of Nell and all the other widows had been irretrievably changed by war, yet they were never lauded as heroes. Heroism seemed to be a man's prerogative. These were all issues she would raise in Canada's Parliament, during another war.

One of Dorise Nielsen's sisters had worked as a stenographer; another was a shop assistant before her marriage. These were considered genteel occupations in an era when the most common occupation for women was still domestic service.

But still, the precocious Dee, barely seventeen and just out of secondary school, aspired to something more exotic. She loved to paint and wrote reams of poetry. In 1919 her mother consented to send her to art school. Jessie's idea was that it really didn't matter too much what Dee did in the next few years, the choice of occupation would be a temporary thing—until the right man came along.

As usual, Dorise was the youngest in her group, but that fact wasn't obvious. She had spent most of her life so far negotiating the world of adults and she had become adept. But this was a new generation, with new values. "Hell bent on having a good time" is the way she describes herself and her friends in that period after the war. They made a point of casting off the Victorian values of their parents' generation. They smoked and danced the tango, went to plays by Bernard Shaw, and watched Charlie Chaplin at the movies. They believed there was nothing that couldn't be questioned (if you had the wit to do it wittily).

For Nielsen, it was a new world indeed, and the year in art school was her first taste of it. She became friends with some rather wild young men and dated several of them, but her feelings for them did not run deep. After a while, she says, she found them "irksome." "I was sick of the genteel middleclass conformity of my family," she writes, "but on closer acquaintance with the crowd I mixed with decided I didn't like them any better."[15]

She also discovered she didn't have the talent to go on with her art. She continued to sketch and paint, but knew she could not make a living at it. Influenced by a friend who had decided on teaching, she enrolled in a small, residential teachers' college for women north of London. It wasn't becoming a teacher that really interested her, she says, it was the chance to get away from home. Thus, the autumn of 1920, she and her friend, Westy, settled into a chilly dormitory at Hockerill College in Hertfordshire. They were part of a small contingent from London who considered themselves more sophisticated than the country girls, a snobbery she later regretted.

The gothic buildings and acres of lawn at Hockerill College still exist, but these days it is a posh private school with central heating. In Nielsen's day, the college offered a two-year teachers' training program for women and was associated with the Anglican Church. On Sundays all 120 students were expected to troop over the fields to the village of Bishop's Stortford for church. In their senior year they were required to take a religion course. Nielsen says she had already rejected the New Testament as a "mixture of myth and nonsense." She paid so little attention in class that she was the only student to fail the course.[16] She also found the teaching courses dull, and says she was mainly interested in botany and breaking rules, of which there were many. Nevertheless, after two years, she graduated from Hockerill with distinction in drawing and credits in botany and geography. She was proud to be among three graduates hired by the London County Council, which paid the highest teachers' salaries in England at the time.

Her memories of that first day at Eleanor Road Infants' School were still vivid when she wrote her memoir fifty years later. In a large assembly hall, the headmistress allotted her sixty-eight children in grade one. Even herding them along the hall to the classroom (and away from their mothers) was a challenge. Somehow she got them seated in their desks, but some children continued to howl; others quietly wet themselves. The janitor appeared with a bucket of sawdust to cover the puddles and sweep them up, while Dorise handed out plasticene. Her class was still not under control when she woke one day, the second week of school, with a blinding headache and dizziness. Her mother called the doctor, who immediately summoned a van to cart her off to a hospital for infectious diseases.

She had contracted a particularly serious case of scarlet fever and was in bed for seventeen weeks, so weak for part of the time that she had to be fed. No visitors were allowed, but her mother sent a parcel once a week. She shared her jam and fruit and other treats with other patients, most of them children, who did not receive parcels. The hospital was a great leveller. Everyone who contracted an infectious disease was confined in such a hospital and treated until they recovered. And the service was free. Dorise often thought of that hospital later in Saskatchewan where every family had to cope on its own with infectious diseases and other catastrophes. The London County Council provided better medical care and better schools than she encountered in Canada. Even if she had sixty-eight students, her cupboard at school was filled with paper and plasticene and other materials.

When she recovered, she had to decide whether to return to her job. Her mother was against the idea. The image of a stern, conservative, protective mother pervades Nielsen's memoir, but it was clearly the daughter who won most of the battles. Despite her months of illness, Nielsen discovered that she had been paid her regular salary. Having money of her own was such a treat that it took very little persuasion from the headmistress (who urged her not to waste her good training) to induce her to return. By this time her class had been whipped into shape by a strict substitute and was easier to handle. On her return, she found the students all sitting quietly with their hands behind their backs.

She remained teaching at Eleanor Road Infants' School for two more years. In that time she brightened up her cavernous classroom with posters from steamship companies, introduced her students to a variety of mice that proliferated in great numbers (and had to be disposed of by the sawdust-toting janitor), and generally caught on to teaching a horde of young children, or, at least, keeping them busy. With a friend from art school she painted large illustrations of fairy tales, then bound them into books. These were favourites with the children and were passed from class to class in the school. Still, Dorise did not derive a sense of satisfaction from teaching. She says she put in her five hours a day and lived for the evenings when she could go out with her friends. Her own home was not a lively one. Harry had remarried and moved out. By this time Jessie was over sixty, and Nell and Florry were in their forties. "A house of three sad old women," she writes (making no mention of Nell's little boy, Geoffrey.) At school the teaching was easier, but she had no passion for it and the routines bored her. She wanted something new, but didn't know what. "I seemed gripped in inertia when it came to choosing something else."[17]

Her mother thought she should marry a man called Jim Trevethick, a farmer from Cornwall who was twelve years her senior.[18] According to Nielsen, he began to court her and, despite her lack of interest, he was very persistent. It was an awkward situation because he was a family friend. Her dilemma was how she could escape her dreary job and even drearier home life without marrying him. Although she went dancing with friends, it was always in a group, and a group that was dwindling as members married or moved away. It seems there were no other serious suitors. Dorise was an attractive woman, but at five foot ten she was exceptionally tall for the times. And the cohort of men a few years older, from which she might have found a mate, had lost a quarter of its members to war. No wonder she was gripped with inertia. It would take an enormous effort on her part to change her prospects.

When Nielsen had been in teachers' training at Hockerill College, she had heard of the Fellowship of the Maple Leaf, a Church of England organization that sent British teachers to the Canadian prairies. She says that the idea of engaging in any sort of missionary effort to keep Canada British did not appeal to her, even then. But the summer of her twenty-fourth birthday, she decided to apply. It was one way of leaving home and being assured of a job. Although Dorise had heard that the only Canadian cities worth living in were Montreal and Vancouver, she was willing to give the prairies a try. Her summers in Cornwall and Devon had given her a taste of life in the country. She had a vision of small villages and picturesque paths through the woods. If she did not like the prairies, she thought she might go on to British Columbia and teach art. The Webbers knew a family whose daughter had married a Canadian soldier. They had sold their dairy business and retired to Vancouver. She wrote to them as well.

Jessie Webber did not approve of her daughter's plan to teach overseas. For an unmarried woman to travel such a long distance alone was far too perilous, she was sure. She called on Harry to talk his sister out of her wild idea. But by this time Dorise had been offered a position in Saskatchewan and she had decided to take it. Harry's words of caution had no effect at all. Later, she heard him tell her mother, "Maybe you'd better give her enough rope. She'll likely hang herself before she's much older and come running home again."[19] That made her angry and more stubborn than ever.

In the end Jessie Webber relented. She and Nell helped with the shopping for warm clothes and the packing of two cabin trunks for the voyage. Nielsen included a supply of cigarettes, her paints, and a portfolio of her best work. She threw away all her poetry.[20] She selected two costumes she had designed herself. One featured balloons and the other was a Cleopatra gown. Costume balls were all the rage and she was sure she would need them. For warmth, she bought a winter coat with a fur collar, a pair of fur-lined gloves, and a new pair of rubber overshoes that she thought would do for the winter. A week before Christmas 1926, her sister Nell accompanied her to Southampton where she boarded the *S.S. Marlock*. Her mother had said goodbye at the house, adding that she hoped to see her back home before long. There were no tears of farewell, for which Dorise was very glad.

The journey over—crossing the Atlantic in winter, arriving in Halifax, boarding the train for Saskatoon—all was an adventure. The *S.S. Marlock* took a southern route to avoid rough seas. During the first week it was warm enough to dance on deck. Dorise sat at the table of the Chief Engineer for dinner and flirted with a Scot on his way to Montreal. On the train west she met a couple from Winnipeg who told her she was welcome to stay with them if ever she came to town. She was amazed to receive such an invitation from strangers. That was only the beginning of her culture shock.

From Saskatoon she headed north to take up her teaching post in Norbury. The new school term began at the end of January. The first problem was getting there. Until 1930 no train passed remotely close to the hamlet of Norbury. She would have to get off at Canwood and then make a two-day trip by sleigh. When she arrived in Canwood, there had been a blizzard, and she had to wait several days for her ride. In the meantime, she was made very welcome by an English family that ran the hotel. Finally Seminar, the mailman from Shell Lake, arrived, gathered up Dorise, her trunks, and the waiting bag of mail, and took her home with him. He had a wife and eleven children crowded into a very dirty house. On the floor, near the stove, a haunch of deer was thawing in a bloody puddle. She was fed fried venison for dinner and could hardly choke it down. That night the children watched in amazement as she smoked a cigarette. She was put to bed with the eldest daughter.

Dorise was there a day and two nights, trying not to show her horror at the dirt, the diet of fried meat and potatoes, and the trips through the frigid air to the outhouse. The family was offering her hospitality and she tried to be a good guest. The second night, something truly astonishing happened—a pleasant surprise this time. A group of young men surveying for the railroad arrived for a concert. Seminar and his eldest son took out their fiddles. They played one tune after another as the grown daughter pumped away on a harmonium and another son played the flute. "Seminar himself kept time by tapping his feet while playing first fiddle, the eldest son played second fiddle and all the others whistled, tooted, twanged and piped their parts to the basic tune played by the girl on the harmonium. The concert, with short intermissions, went on for more than an hour. It was unbelievable."[21] Everyone knew the tunes but Dorise. It was her first encounter with Métis fiddling and she was impressed. Her own contribution to the evening was passing around her English cigarettes, and they were appreciated, too.

At noon the next day Peter Nielsen, one of the trustees at Tinson School, came to fetch her, and they set off for Norbury in a cutter. He was a tall, handsome man with a shock of thick, sandy hair. He was not very talkative, but she found he was quite interesting when he talked about something he liked. One of those things was horses. Also, he had been to Europe during the war so that was a common link. He said the only good thing about the war was that he'd been able to travel. His own parents had emigrated from Denmark, but he had been born in Canada. They continued past dark to reach her boarding place with a couple called Ambrose. It was a clear day and the sunset was the most magnificent she had ever seen.

Dorise would always remember those first days in great detail. Life in Canada was strange. The people were friendlier than in England, the houses, warmer (too warm for her), and the landscapes, vast and bleak, but sometimes beautiful. She had come to Canada's last frontier. The area known as parkland stretches north of the prairies to the pre-Cambrian rock of the boreal forests. It is a land of hills and light sandy soil more suitable for ranching than growing wheat, but during World War I and later in the 1920s, wheat prices were high enough to induce farmers north onto these marginal lands. A number of veterans like Pete Nielsen took up homesteads there after the war. There was no electricity, no telephones, and no railway until 1930. The roads were muddy ruts, passable only in dry weather or in the winter.

For the next few months Dorise did not see Pete Nielsen. When school started, Earle Ambrose saddled a horse for her and she set off across a frozen swamp and down a road marked by the tracks of a sleigh. She had never ridden a horse before. She was wearing woollen stockings instead of her usual silk, and moccasins in place of rubber overshoes. Still, her legs were painful with cold by the time she arrived and the children ran out to meet her. The school was new. In the spring of 1926, twenty-three settlers of the district had decided to build it. Pete Nielsen was at the meeting, and that summer he pitched in to build a one-room school. The first teacher, Arthur Lance Gordon, was not a success, though it's questionable if anyone could have made progress with such a wild group of unschooled children. Dorise described them as "rough little hooligans" and said she learned more from them than they did from her.

The new schoolhouse, painted white, stood alone in a field. Norbury, Dorise discovered, was not a town at all—it was simply a post office and store, which had operated from the home of an early settler, Alf Norbury, since 1912. After the war, settlers had built Winding Creek Hall to be a meeting place for church services, weddings, funerals, and dances. The hall, the post office, and the new school were all in different locations. When Dorise arrived in the midst of winter, social life in Norbury was negligible. Children went to school. Twice a week someone went to fetch the mail. Otherwise, people stayed put. Most families still lived in one- or two-room houses made of rough-hewn logs chinked with mud. There was not much space for entertaining.

Soon, the novelty of coming to Canada wore off, and Dorise's life settled into a rather grim reality. Eva Hunt, a twelve-year-old student at Tinson School, remembers Dorise riding to school that winter with her head scarf flying in the wind. Eva had to help her saddle up at the end of the day. According to Eva, Dorise was an extraordinary teacher. She introduced the children to stories by drawing scenes on large sheets of brown paper. "We did raffia and weaving, things we'd never thought of. And she was keen on composition—we had composition every day." Eva remembers Dorise wearing beautiful dresses and giving prizes for good work. One day the prize was a manicure set.[22]

But for Dorise, her six months' teaching at Tinson School were a nightmare. She had never taught anything but the early grades. Now she had seven students in grade one, and others ranging all the way to grade ten. The first day of school, a new family of children arrived. They were called Simon and none of them spoke English. She had to ask another Hungarian boy, Gabor Szasz, to translate. Some of the children came to school tired after doing chores on the farm, some were poorly clad for the cold weather, and all were behind in their studies. They had a lot to learn and so did she. She corrected all written work at home so that she could give lessons all day. The work seemed endless. Almost every night she cried herself to sleep. She was homesick, but she didn't want to give up.

Her social life improved that summer. There was a series of picnics and dances. At all the dances, the fiddle music went on through the night, and the last diehards packed up to leave at dawn. Dorise had never seen people so determined to have fun. At Willows Flats, a scrubby ranching area north of Norbury near Lake Witchican, the community roasted a whole steer at its picnic. Dorise perched on a fence to watch a rodeo there and caused a mild sensation by wearing a short, sleeveless dress and drinking a bottle of beer in public. (Years later, an old-timer would remember Nielsen as a woman who "wore short skirts and liked a drink.") Pete Nielsen began to visit her. He took her on an all-day outing to a picnic and dance at Rabbit Lake about thirty-five kilometres from Norbury.[23]

The Nielsens' courtship was short, not because of grand passion (at least not on Dorise's part), but a coincidence of wants. Peter Nielsen was a thirty-seven-year-old bachelor and eligible women were scarce. For him, it was now or never. And there is little doubt that he had fallen for Dorise. She was pretty and rather flirtatious. He must have thought he had some hope of success. For Dorise, the situation was not so simple. She had decided to leave Norbury at the end of July when the term ended, and she did. In fact, according to her memoir, she left hastily just before the end of term. One of her students, Mary Simon, had died from a mysterious fever.[24] There was not even a cemetery to bury her in—she was buried in the bush. Dorise was angry that no one in the community had taken responsibility for the family, and perhaps she felt guilty herself. The day before Mary's death, she had ridden out to the Simon homestead and discovered how ill the girl was. She advised calling the doctor immediately but was told he was too far away, and, in any case, there was no money to pay him. The family had just emigrated from Hungary, and the girl's father was away working in the coalfields in Alberta.

The next day, when she heard that Mary had died, Dorise packed her trunks and had a friend drive her to Canwood, where she stayed, once again, with the English family that ran the hotel. From there she sent her letter of resignation. She had not decided what to do or where to go. She was still hoping to go on to British Columbia but had had no word from family friends there. In the meantime, she helped out in the restaurant of the hotel. But Peter Nielsen did not give up easily. One day in August he appeared at the hotel and tried to persuade Dorise to return to Norbury. Teachers were hired from January to January. The Tinson school board was very upset that she had left. When she refused to come back, he offered to show her something of the prairies. He was on his way to his father's farm at Melaval, south of Moose Jaw, to help with the harvest. This time she said yes. They travelled by train and were met at the station by the father's second wife.

When they arrived at the farm, Dorise discovered that Nielsen's father was a tall, good-looking man in his seventies with white hair and a Danish accent. He lived in a decent house on what appeared to be a prosperous farm. Altogether, Nielsen senior made Dorise feel very welcome. Perhaps this is what Pete Nielsen had in mind when he suggested showing her the prairies. Soon he proposed. Again she said yes. On September 9, 1927, they were married in an Anglican church in Moose Jaw with two strangers as witnesses. It was a date she never could remember. In fact, thirteen years later, as part of a brief biography for the Parliamentary Guide, she gave her marriage date as September 24, 1927.

If the date of her marriage eventually faded from mind, the name she wrote in the register that day became a permanent fixture. Doris Webber became Dorise Nielsen. For some reason, she was not content with a new surname but felt the need for a new Christian name, too. A new name for a new life, was that her reason? In Canada, she had discovered, Jack was as good as his master. It was a new place with a whole new set of rules.

In the memoir written for her children, Nielsen says nothing of her name change, but goes to great pains to explain her decision to marry their father. Perhaps she had been mulling it over for years herself. Loneliness was part of it, she admits. She was in a strange land where she knew few people and had no plans, except that she did not want to give up and go home. "I made an impulsive decision ... believing that the longer I thought about it the more difficult it would be to make up my mind," she wrote. "I said very openly that although I'd do my best to be a good wife, I didn't love him and knew I never would because I loved another man and that was finished for me."[25] The other man, of course, was Laurie, the young man she had known during the war. Nine years is a very long time to nurse such a passion. But perhaps it was easier for her to love a man she had lost than a man in the flesh. Pete Nielsen was a gentleman, the best of the bachelors she had met. There were others, too obviously "hot with sexual excitement," who made her cringe. (Dorise may have criticized the mores of her Victorian mother, but she had also absorbed them.)

What she does not say, perhaps because it is so obvious, is that her options were limited. She did not want to give up and go home, but if she were to stay in Canada, she needed a job. Her six months' teaching in Norbury had been so difficult that she never wanted to teach again. What was she going to do? It seemed she either had to find a job or return to England. Both prospects appalled her. Marrying Nielsen solved her problems—temporarily.

Although there was a certain hard-headed logic in her choice, looking at it almost fifty years later, she had good reason to shake her head. She remembered Peter as gentle and considerate. Her first experience sleeping with a man was "not too bad," but afterwards she cried into her pillow, thinking of her lost love. Her brother had said, "Give her enough rope and she'll hang herself and come running home again." She knew she had pretty well hung herself, but at least she hadn't run home.

After the harvest was finished, Peter Nielsen returned to Norbury with his new bride. His neighbours were surprised. The English schoolteacher who had run off was back again. How long would she last as a farmer's wife?

Until that October day, Dorise had never seen the inside of Pete Nielsen's house. She had only seen a well-turned-out man who took her to dances and picnics. Perhaps she knew he was living in a typical one-room house made of squared-off logs chinked with mud, but when she entered it, the darkness surprised her. He had never whitewashed the interior walls, and very little light came in through the two windows. There were a stove and bedstead, kitchen table and chairs, a washstand—not much else. All Pete's possessions, all his clothes, his snowshoes, his moccasins, his ammunition belts, were hung from nails around the walls or suspended from the beams. His rifle and shotgun were balanced on a set of deer horns over the window. For Dorise, the thought of people coming in and seeing all her personal things openly displayed was embarrassing. Worse still was someone finding them in bed!

Back in England, Jessie Webber was so upset to hear about her daughter's marriage that she did not even write. Nell and Maude and Florry supported her by sending gifts. Maude gave her a Singer sewing machine and a cheque, and Florry, several embroidered tablecloths. Nell had packed a large crate full of finery she had saved for her own wedding and hardly used. When Dorise opened it, she wept. The blankets and sheets she could use, but what was she to do with table napkins and silver fish forks? The house already was crowded with the addition of her two trunks.

The memoir she wrote in China ends in the fall of 1928, a year after the wedding. According to Dorise, it was a year of trying hard and failing. She failed to persuade Pete to cut some logs that winter so that he could add an extra room to the house. (He said he would build a frame house—soon.) Having always lived at home, she knew little about cooking and baking. Her bread was soggy and her pastry, tough. She tried to make up in enthusiasm what she lacked in experience, but what an effort it was! She hated rising in the dark to stoke up the stove and make breakfast. Her only real successes came from her sewing. At a costume ball, she won first prize for her Cleopatra outfit. To spiff up the house, she made curtains and embroidered a floral bedspread. She curtained off one corner of the room and hung her clothes there—not such a bright idea, she discovered. In the spring she found that mice had eaten a hole in the crotch of her riding britches.

Her life improved when winter finally ended and she could work outside. She prepared a roughly ploughed space for her garden, hoeing and working some manure into the soil. But the garden was not a success, either. Almost everything except the potatoes was eaten by worms. Yet, the garden of her neighbour, Mrs. Szasz, flourished with beautiful lettuces and cabbages (Dorise carried an armload of them home one day). Occasionally, she would wander off to sketch or pick flowers and supper was late. Then Pete would lose his temper, though he was usually patient with her shortcomings. It was clear that winning a fancy dress ball didn't matter much in the long run, but having meals on time, and a cellar of vegetables to last the winter, did.

2

SLAVERY OR FREEDOM?

I started political work in the beginning to escape the prison walls of Norbury closing around me and burying me forever.[1]

NONE OF DORISE'S EARLY FAILURES at being a farmer's wife mattered for long. In time, she knew, she would learn—and she did. Canada, she would say, was her university, and she sopped up learning like a sponge. The real problem, the one that wouldn't go away, was something else altogether. Peter patiently woke her in the morning and taught her to light the stove and make bread, and all the other domestic skills he had acquired in years of living alone. Otherwise, he saw no reason for talk. In the winter evenings he sat in the only armchair, reading the *Western Producer* and the *Country Guide*, just as he had done when he lived alone. He had no desire to discuss what he read and little interest in the books Dorise devoured one after the other.[2] She had not expected this. She had a vision, it seems, of cosy evenings spent sharing thoughts and making plans for the future. Sometimes they would go out together, a tall, handsome couple, and dance up a storm, but most of the time, all they had together was work and silence and sex. "Maybe sex was the best thing between us," she wrote, "because all else seemed so little."[3]

Her other complaints about Peter (complaints likely muted by the time she wrote her memoir, thirty years after their separation) were that he had little ambition and that he drank. She believed he had had too many disappointments in life and that he was one of those people who did not bear up well to disappointment. The first setback was the war, which had started him drinking and left him too old to pursue his dream of becoming a veterinarian. During the 1920s he had laboured hard, grubbing out land to prove up two quarter sections,[4] but by the time the railway came through in 1930, wheat prices had plummeted. Farming in Saskatchewan had become a losing proposition no matter how hard you worked.

But the memoir ends a year before that disaster and all its repercussions. It ends with Dorise's and a hired woman's cooking for a threshing gang the autumn of 1928. They prepared five meals a day, taking two out to the fields. The house was so hot from the cooking that the two women, sleeping together, hardly got any rest at all. Dorise, as usual, tried her best to be a good sport, to fit in. Sometimes she was successful. She joked with the men, who liked to tease her about her cooking. When a whole pot of boiled potatoes ended up in the slop pail, she quickly fished them out and washed them off and no one knew the difference. But what she remembered most was the endless work and the heat of those days and nights when the stove never had a chance to cool off.

Eline Morrow, a distant neighbour who met Dorise the summer after her marriage, liked her immediately and was impressed by her sophistication: "Here she came. She was tall and stately, beautiful and poised. She had class, she had charisma. She had something that seemed to emanate from her—a charm."[5] But some closer neighbours thought her peculiar. "Mrs. Highpockets," they called her because of her long legs.[6] And when she got involved in politics, they wondered who was wearing the pants in that family.

About Pete Nielsen there were various opinions, but most of them confirm Dorise's portrait of him. Pete was a likable man, but in a community where most people worked from dawn to dusk, he was not considered a hard worker. Some time in the 1930s Pete sold off his equipment and gave up grain farming. He let his land to the neighbouring Szasz family for a third of the crop. He must have been in a desperate position to make such a move. With wheat prices so low, the income from one third of the crop from a half section could never come close to supporting a growing family. Such arrangements were not uncommon for elderly or ailing farmers, but Pete was only in his forties then, and he had a young family to support. His problems were partly a matter of timing. He had started his family late and had no sons to help him. From then on, Pete used his stud horse to earn some cash. He continued to cut logs for the fire, haul the water (the well was far from the house), milk the cows, mow hay, and prepare a large garden for planting. In 1937, when the family went on relief, he was required to work off the relief payments by working on the roads, grading and gravelling. And every fall he went hunting. He was known as an excellent marksman and always got his deer. But hunting was a social occasion, as well. Off he would go with his good buddies for a week at a time. The Scandinavians were known as heavy drinkers.

Altogether, Dorise was alone more than she wanted to be. Her closest friends were the English wives of other Scandinavians, Edith (Dolly) Gunderson and Eleanor Paulson, but when her children were young, she seldom saw them. In the space of three years, Nielsen gave birth three times. There was no more time to wander in the fields and paint pictures of tiger lilies, or saddle up Tony and go for a visit. Once again she was into something entirely new. Being the youngest in her family, she had no experience caring for infants. Their fragility frightened her. "I would just as soon pick up a stick of dynamite as a baby," she wrote.[7] But still she wanted a child to keep her company, and once she had her first, she wanted another.

In January 1929, Pete drove Dorise eighty-five kilometres by sleigh to a nursing home at Shellbrook to give birth to their first child, Christine. Most Norbury women gave birth at home with an untrained midwife in attendance. The nearest doctor, thirty-five kilometres away at Rabbit Lake, could be fetched if there were complications. But Dorise did not want to take any chances, so she insisted on the long, uncomfortable journey to Shellbrook. Fortunately, by the time her second child was born in February 1930, a branch line from Prince Albert to St. Walburg had been constructed. It passed through both Shellbrook and the new town of Spiritwood, twelve kilometres from the Nielsen farm, shortening the journey.[8]

The earliest picture we have of Pete and Dorise was taken in 1931. It is a clear day late in the summer. Pete has taken two chairs outside and placed them at the sunny side of the house. Dorise has dug out the family's box camera that was used sparingly, only on special occasions. Perhaps an Anglican priest arrived earlier that day and the community gathered for the christening of children in Winding Creek Hall.[9] Now, home again with a few friends, they decided to commemorate the day with a photo. There is Pete sitting straight in a clean shirt and overalls, proudly holding Christine on his lap. At two and a half, her blonde hair is already long. Beside Pete, in a high-backed rocking chair, sits Dorise, squinting into the sun. She is holding a swaddled infant, Thelma Fay

(Sally). The beauty and poise and charisma that so impressed Eline Morrow are starkly absent. The dark crêpe dress with its scooped neck and short sleeves, and the locket dangling from her neck, seem out of place on the body of a thin woman with lank hair, sitting in a field of weeds. It was less than a year since the Nielsens had buried their second child, Peter junior. He died, eight months old, in September 1930.

Later, Dorise wrote that "an epidemic of dysentery . . . swept through each farm and finally came to ours. My little boy fell sick one evening. I watched over him all night and roused my husband early. I told him to hurry to the nearest doctor, twenty-two miles away, but even as I told him how ill the baby was, the child died in my arms."[10] Her only consolation was that her child had not been buried in the bush, like Mary Simon. He had a proper gravesite in a new Anglican cemetery not far from Winding Creek Hall. Pete made a cross and a fence of white pickets to mark the grave. But it was poor consolation. "Even after the personal grief abated, I was still burning with anger that such things could happen," wrote Dorise.[11] Too many children died and, despite all her care and knowledge, now her own was one of the casualties.[12]

In time, her baby's death would become grist for her mill in her campaign to improve maternal and child health care. But it would always be more than that. Even in her old age, she would think of him and imagine how different life might have been if he had lived. Somehow she believed that having an older brother could have been a great help to her daughter, Sally. And certainly the death did not bring Pete and Dorise any closer. "Buck up," Nielsen told Dolly Gunderson at the funeral of one of her own children a few years later. "The show must go on."[13] And that was, no doubt, the advice she gave herself. It was a lesson Nielsen had learned in her own family—this was how to respond to loss. Keep busy, keep going, do not let on.

Eva Hunt remembers staying with Dorise the spring of 1931, eight months after Peter's death. Early in May Pete Nielsen had come over to the Hunt farm to fetch her. He was going away and did not want to leave Dorise and Christine alone while Dorise was pregnant. Eva has pleasant memories of that stay on the Nielsen farm. She was only sixteen, but Dorise shared confidences and made her feel like an equal. After her baby's death, Dorise and Christine had spent the winter in England with her family, but Dorise said that she was glad to be back in Canada.[14] The English, she told Eva, were rather backward. They had even made her leave the ship on a special plank for foreigners! One good thing, though, was having fresh fruit, all year round. There was always a bowl of fruit on her mother's table. That was one of the things she missed.[15]

Late in May the two women planted the garden together. Dorise was seven months pregnant, so Eva did most of the bending. When the lettuce was up, they used to walk out and pick a salad for their lunch. Nielsen obviously enjoyed having company. If intolerance of things foreign bothered her in England, in Canada her main problem was still isolation. She had discovered that the company of a child was not enough. She needed to talk to someone. "Loneliness can be a terrible thing in the country," she wrote soon after her election, and motherhood compounds a woman's isolation. "For a while, I sank into a strange state.... I had been used to cities and accustomed to having many people around me ... I still was not used to the tremendous silences of the farm." And what she really needed was not just company, but intellectually stimulating company. She could put up a good show of belonging, but, in fact, she still felt very out of place. "Even talking about babies I differed from the rest because I wanted to discuss scientific child welfare and they felt babies just naturally grew."[16]

So far she had met the challenges of being a farmwife, at least those that interested her. She could cook and can and plant a garden, nurse chicks, feed the broody hen, and gather the eggs. She had no intention of feeding the horses or milking the cows or working in the fields (if she started that, there would be no end to her labour). But she still needed something more. If she didn't find some interest, some project, she felt she would go mad.

One of Christine Nielsen's early memories is of a group of women coming to the Nielsen home to hook a rug. It was black with bright red maple leaves. Dorise had probably designed it. The rags had been dyed in pots on the Nielsen stove. It was to be used for a raffle to raise funds for Tinson School.

By this time the Nielsen home had an additional room where all members of the family slept, while the original room served as living room, kitchen, and general workroom. Like most farm kitchens, it was a hive of activity. In the winter it was often strung with laundry. In the summer and fall Dorise canned vegetables, wild berries, and chicken. She made soap and butter, and sewed all the family clothes except for heavy outerwear and the shoes, which were ordered from Eaton's catalogue. Pete milked two cows. Dorise raised chickens for eggs and meat. With wheat prices so low, it made sense to feed livestock. Essentially, the Nielsens, like many others in northern Saskatchewan, had become subsistence farmers. There was little cash involved, though sometimes Dorise sold butter for ten cents a pound.[17] With that and a bit of money from the stud horse, and the parcels from Dorise's family in England, they appeared to be getting by, although the farm was mortgaged and the payments more and more difficult to meet.

About the financial woes of the family, the children knew very little. Everything is relative, of course, and the Nielsen children, on the surface at least, were no worse off than their neighbours. Their early childhood was predictable and in some ways even rich. They went to school. They worked alongside their parents. Before bedtime their mother read them a story from an endless book of stories her sister had read to her when she was a child. They seldom saw their father drunk or heard their parents argue. In the winter evenings, if he could afford to get the radio battery charged, Pete liked to stretch out on the daybed for *Crimebusters.* On Saturdays Dorise shooed the children out to play so that she could sit in Pete's armchair and listen to the Metropolitan Opera undisturbed.

Months before the first snowfall, she had the children go through the Eaton's catalogue and choose one gift. With her help they wrote letters to Santa, dropped them in the fire, and imagined them going up the chimney and on to the North Pole.[18]

From the time the Nielsen children can remember, Christmases were always celebrated in style and with friends. There was always a tree with candles lit on Christmas Eve, and on Christmas Day, crackers to pull at the table, each with a prize inside and a funny hat. All these trimmings, as well as gifts, arrived in a box sent from England by their grandma and Auntie Nell. The friends who came for Christmas were Cecil and Bob Paul and their two boys, and sometimes the Nielsens travelled by sleigh to the Pauls' homestead further north near Leoville. The two families had become acquainted in the early 1930s when Bob and Cecil taught at local schools. They moved to the Leoville homestead in 1933. Whenever the Nielsens and the Pauls got together, there was a great deal of talk and teasing and general merriment. Some of the talk was about politics, but in the mid-thirties politics had not yet become Dorise's full-time preoccupation. Her central concerns were providing for a growing family and keeping herself sane. For the moment, she seemed to be holding the line on both fronts.

Two photos taken in 1935 show a family with a certain pride. The first, taken in early summer, is of three children sitting on a blanket by the bush. In the middle, a fat, bald baby, eight months old, grins into the camera. On either side are his sisters, Christine and Sally, each holding a kitten. Pete has cut their hair in fashionable bobs and they are pleased. The baby, John Kay Nielsen, was born in October 1934, and baptized the next spring by a visiting Anglican bishop. The photo may have been taken to celebrate his baptism—he appears to be wearing a dress.

The second picture was taken in the fall of that year, November probably, after hunting season. As usual, Pete got his deer. The deer has been set on the snow with its head up, as if it were alive and amazingly docile. On either side, each holding an antler, are Christine and Pete. Pete is long and lean in his knickers and high boots. Christine, almost six but small for her age, is wearing a coat and leggings and a warm wool hat with flaps and tassels. Already, despite her size, she thinks of herself as her father's helper. On the back of the photo, Dorise has written, "With best wishes for a Happy Xmas, 1935, from all of us at Norbury."[19]

By 1935, when both photos were taken, Dorise was already known as a political activist, but she seems to have made an effort to shelter the children from that portion of her life. They remember few strangers coming to the house. Dorise would sometimes go away, but never for long. Occasionally, in the winter, Bob Paul would arrive unexpectedly in a sleigh pulled by a team of Shetland ponies. He would store the fish he was peddling under a mound of snow in the yard. At this point Bob Paul, with his fish, and Pete, with his hunting and his stud horse, probably had more political contacts in the district than Dorise.

The Nielsen children were too young to realize that the world around them was crumbling. There were families right in their district who did not have food on the table or shoes to go out in the cold. Most of these people were refugees from the south who had left their farms in the dust bowl and migrated north to start again. The government had given them homesteads and a relief allowance of approximately five dollars a month per couple, ten dollars for a whole family. All through northern Saskatchewan where the rains still fell, such people came, living in tents the first summer, then in dirt-floored shacks.[20] They sent their children to schools that were going bankrupt because so few people had the money to pay their taxes. The Nielsens themselves were poor. They had no hope of getting ahead. By 1932 average wheat prices were a third of what they had been in 1929, and there would be no real recovery until 1943.[21] But these newcomers were destitute beyond belief. The worldwide depression had landed on the Nielsens' doorstep. And it was clear to Dorise that raffling a rug to raise funds for Tinson School would not solve the problem.

There is a joke in Saskatchewan that whenever two or three farmers gather together, they form a political party. In the early 1920s farmers from the prairies and Ontario supported the meteoric rise of the Progressives. In the 1930s it was Social Credit and the CCF. In 1931, the United Farmers of Canada (Saskatchewan Section) decided to enter politics. By 1932 it had allied itself with Saskatchewan's Independent Labour Party as the Farmer-Labour Party.[22] The same year the new Saskatchewan party joined with other provincial farmers' groups and regional labour parties to form the Co-operative Commonwealth Federation. The ideas of democratic socialism were not new on the prairies. The radical farm movement, peppered with Marxists and Christian socialists, had been advocating cooperation rather than capitalist competition for years. In 1932, with capitalism in crisis, the time had surely come. The same year as the founding of the CCF, the Swedish Labour Party formed a government that would establish the first welfare state. New Zealand followed in 1935.

Pete and Dorise Nielsen were involved in the Farmer-Labour Party (the new CCF) from at least 1934. In the provincial election that year, Pete was a poll captain in the new constituency of Meadow Lake. The campaign manager that year could think of only twelve men he could really rely on, and Pete Nielsen was one of them.[23] A neighbour remembers Dorise making her first political speeches in that campaign. She was amazed. Here was a woman who had the courage to speak out and somehow she did it with such passion and such style that she was able to make her point.[24]

During the campaign that spring, the provincial CCF leader, M.J. Coldwell, flew north to address a meeting at Shellbrook. It may have been on that May weekend that Coldwell first met Dorise. In his memoirs, Coldwell tells of meeting her early on, "when she was quite unknown," near her home at "Spirit River" (sic):

> The area was desperately poor. … She had two children and when I met her was living in the direst of circumstances on a homestead. She was, however, a good neighbour, and when I first met her at a public meeting, she had just come from a confinement case near Spiritwood, where she had delivered a baby, and found nothing to wrap it in except the well-worn coat of the father.[25]

Coldwell and Nielsen probably found much in common at first. Both were English immigrants, both were teachers, and both were engaged in the CCF campaign for economic reform and social justice. Eventually they would be enemies, but in the beginning there was mutual admiration.

The CCF did not do as well as it hoped in the 1934 provincial election. It elected only five members to the Saskatchewan legislature. The people of Saskatchewan had decided to oust a Tory government by giving the Liberals a whopping forty-nine seats. The only comfort was that the Tories had been so completely shut out that the five CCF members formed the official opposition. Also, there would be a federal election in 1935. Members of the CCF immediately began to organize for the new contest.

At this point Dorise appeared to have no particular political ambitions. Like most women at the time, she accepted her role on the sidelines. Still, her determination was remarkable. On October 5, 1934, she sent a long handwritten letter—and such beautiful handwriting it is, not a smudge, not a biff (as Dorise would say)—to Frank Eliason, general secretary of the CCF of Canada. It was written only a few days before her trip to the nursing home at Shellbrook for Johnny's birth. She was wrapping up loose ends, preparing for the siege, first the twelve kilometres to Spiritwood, then the train to Shellbrook, and, after the birth, the weeks of near sleepless nights.

In her letter she was looking ahead to the spring, thinking of the federal election, how the CCF could put on a better show, and what part she could play in the process. She proposed a rally for the whole district to take place the following summer. The district proposed would be from Leoville in the north to Rabbit Lake in the south, and from Shell Lake in the east to Bapaume in the west. Various locals would have to put on entertainments throughout the winter in order to raise funds for the rally. "Do you think this is feasible?" she asked.[26]

Her plans and requests were very specific and fully stated, as if several heads had been at work, anticipating just how much money would be required for the rally and how it should be spent. (Surely one of those heads was Bob Paul, whose homestead near Leoville was the northern boundary of the area proposed for the rally.) It seems that the CCF supporters in Nielsen's part of the provincial constituency of Meadow Lake were determined to do better next time, and she had become their spokesperson. "We should like to be assured four speakers for purposes of advertisement," she wrote, "1) the federal candidate, 2) Mr. Coldwell, preferably, or another well-known speaker, 3) Mrs. Lucas, or other well-known woman speaker, and 4) a good French Catholic speaker, as there are many French-speaking people in the northern portion of the district." The funds raised would be used for the speakers' transportation and for prizes for sporting events such as baseball and horse racing to draw the crowd. Did Mr. Eliason know of other such rallies? Would he pass on any names to whom they could apply for a little help?[27]

If there was a frenzy of fundraising in Norbury that winter, or a district rally the summer of 1935, no news of it appears in the CCF files or in the weekly *Spiritwood Herald*. However, during this period, the CCF files are sparse and the *Herald* was more inclined to report meetings of the Women's Missionary Society, involving, always, the serving of a dainty lunch, than it was news of the CCF.

In the 1935 federal campaign, Peter Nielsen once more served as a poll secretary, and Dorise spoke in support of the CCF candidate for North Battleford, the Rev. Hill Hamilton.[28] His serious, bespectacled face appears on the official CCF stationery (think of Trotsky without beard or moustache) and beneath the face is his slogan: "What say you: Slavery or Freedom?"

The rhetoric may seem inflated, but it was not. According to Tommy Douglas, another CCF candidate in the 1935 federal election, the Saskatchewan Liberals were a breed apart, a bunch of reactionary rednecks, he called them—much further to the right of the political spectrum than the Conservatives.[29] And because of the Depression, the corrupt Liberal machine in Saskatchewan became more entrenched than ever. There were relief inspectors to appoint and public works jobs to distribute. If you wanted a job working on the roads, you'd better keep your politics to yourself, or, better still, declare yourself a Liberal. You might be called a "heeler" for kowtowing to the establishment, but at least you could put food on the table.

But people were growing desperate and, as Dorise discovered, desperation can foster rebellion as well as fear. Everyone with a conscience was thinking about politics in 1935, and those with enough courage were scraping up a dollar to join the CCF or another new reform party that had swept in from Alberta called Social Credit. Even the rabble-rousing communists were gaining supporters. Some hardly souls were going all the way and letting their names stand as candidates. People such as Tommy Douglas, Sandy Nicholson, and Hill Hamilton, all rural ministers, had never thought of running for election, but they'd seen the poverty first-hand and couldn't turn their backs. In North Battleford federal constituency, where the Nielsens lived, the Liberal incumbent, Cameron McIntosh, had been the MP since 1925. He owned three newspapers in the constituency and could still call in a lot of favours. But with a little luck and a lot of work, the CCF hoped to shut him out.

North Battleford was a huge, sprawling constituency, one of the largest in Canada at the time. It was this constituency that Nielsen would win in 1940. In 1935, the CCF campaign manager had a great deal of work to do, organizing polls, raising funds, bringing key men on board. Once again Coldwell flew north on a speaking tour. But in September 1935, Social Credit pulled the carpet out from under the CCF by winning a stunning victory in the Alberta provincial election.[30] A month later, in the federal election, the opposition to Cameron Ross McIntosh was so evenly divided between CCF and Social Credit that he won again with less than half the votes cast.[31] The lesson of the campaign was clear: if McIntosh were to be defeated by the new protest parties, they would have to combine their forces.

In May 1936, Bob Paul wrote an important letter to the CCF provincial office. "Please send a map of the constituency boundaries," he typed, "and the names, numbers and boundaries of the polls." The CCF had a system of organizing a constituency, but what good was it if no one kept records and passed them on?

"The provincial organization in this, the Meadow Lake constituency, seems to have completely vanished," he pegged out. "The information would be used in a little pre-convention work we are doing."[32]

The Pauls had been living on a homestead near Leoville, about thirty kilometres north of Spiritwood, since their youngest son, Douglas, was born in 1933. In the summer Bob worked on the farm and in the winter he bought fish from the Aboriginal people and peddled it to Catholic families for their Friday dinners. He barely made enough to feed the family and keep his Shetland ponies alive.

Everyone was pretty well in the same boat. Some of the folks under re-establishment were even worse off. They had walked away from farms in the dust bowl and started all over again, built log cabins and started breaking the soil for the first time, and it wasn't the greatest soil at the best of times. Bob had seen these people come up, hopeful at first on account of the rain. Then they'd learned what it was like to live on relief for a year or two. They'd experienced the class struggle intimately, the capitalist class in this case being the bankers and the Liberal machine with all its hangers-on.

And the problems weren't just on the prairies, they were everywhere. There were no jobs to be had in the cities. A quarter of the labour force was unemployed. Men were hopping freight trains from town to town, looking for work. In 1932 Prime Minister Bennett had concocted a scheme of sending single men off to relief camps in the wilderness, where they worked for their board and got twenty cents a day. By 1935 these men wanted something better—a chance to earn some real money for their labour building roads and cutting trees. In British Columbia, where half the camps were located, men flocked to the communist-led Relief Camp Workers Union. Early in 1935 they went on strike. Then, in May, over a thousand of them had started a trek to Ottawa to state their grievances.

In June 1935, the Nielsens and the Pauls were among many Canadians who followed news of the On-to-Ottawa trek on their radios. The trekkers made the national news day after day and sympathy for them mounted. By most accounts, they were a well-disciplined group of young men. On they went, from Vancouver to Kamloops to Calgary, riding on top of freight cars, suffocating from smoke through the long tunnels, pelted by rain. There were so many men on the cars that the trains resembled giant caterpillars with every section in motion. Some men had never ridden the rails before. Others were old hands. But in the summer of 1935 they were not just drifting from place to place, they were rolling on with a purpose. They sent emissaries ahead to make arrangements for provisions. They held tag days to raise funds. In each town where they camped, ad hoc groups of citizens, including members of the CCF and the Young Communist League, formed to support them. The trek soon became the *cause célèbre* of the Canadian left in all its manifestations.

By the middle of June, the trek had reached Regina. There the trekkers remained for two weeks, camping at the fairgrounds, playing baseball, and holding public meetings, while eight of their leaders were transported to Ottawa (first class this time) to meet with Bennett. None of the men were optimistic about the meeting, and they were right. Bennett rejected the trekkers' demands. In fact, he was not willing to negotiate at all. He had determined to halt the march in Regina. Already warrants for the arrest of the leaders were being prepared on the grounds that they belonged to an illegal organization, the Relief Camp Workers Union. Military and RCMP contingents were moving into Regina. Apparently, none of the trekkers knew for sure when the arrests would take place, but plans were made to get the leaders to safe houses. One of those was the Nielsens', another was the Pauls'.

The crackdown came on Canada Day, July 1. Trek leader Arthur Evans had started to address a public meeting in Regina's Market Square when a police whistle blew and plainclothes police moved quickly to arrest him. The ensuing Regina Riot saw trekkers, armed with stones and bats, take on the city police and RCMP, who fired several rounds, wounding an estimated forty people. Officially, one policeman and one trekker died (though the trekkers say there were others).[33] A hundred people were arrested that night. Downtown Regina looked like a war zone.

At some point late on July 1 or early on July 2, 1935, Pete Nielsen got word to prepare for a visitor. He hustled Dorise and the three children to a neighbour's and waited for a knock on the door. It was dark when a Model T Ford pulled up and delivered a young man known as Doc Savage. The youngest of the trek leaders, Savage was one of the eight who had gone to Ottawa to meet Bennett. The night of the Regina Riot, he had encountered two well-dressed gentlemen (cops, he thought at first) who turned out to be members of the

CCF. They took him to a freight yard, where he was hidden in the cab of a train going north. The train, he says, was searched by the RCMP, but the engineer and fireman were in sympathy and kept him hidden.

According to Savage, Pete was not happy to see him. Pete treated him as a young whipper-snapper, too cocky for his years. The dislike was mutual. Where was Mrs. Nielsen? Savage wondered. He had heard about her from Arthur Evans and when he realized he was at the Nielsen home, he wanted to meet her. He didn't know if she was communist or CCF, but certainly she was already known as being in favour of a united front (something the Communist Party was pushing in 1935). She was, as the communists would say, someone in the left wing of the CCF, someone you could trust. At least, that was her reputation. About her husband, he wasn't so sure. In any case, he was exhausted and there wasn't much conversation. Most of that day he lay on the couch while Pete sat at the kitchen table, watching over him. On the second morning, three men arrived with a telegram from Arthur Evans (who was out on bail), saying there was no warrant out for the arrest of Savage. He left immediately for Alberta.[34]

Further north at Leoville, the Pauls also sheltered two trekkers. Stewart, the Pauls' eldest son, remembers his dad's anger when he heard their stories first-hand, "Dad was wild ... he had this British sense of fairness. He taught me I couldn't hit first—I took some awful beatings."[35] It was after the Regina Riot, Stewart believes, that Bob decided to devote more of his time to politics. The summer of 1936 they rented out the farm and moved even further north to Chiteck Lake, where Cecil had found a job teaching at Spruce Creek School. From that time on, it was Cecil's work that provided the family with a steady income. Bob occasionally took a teaching job, but most of the time he travelled, drumming up support for the CCF, the united front, and other left-wing causes.

The letter Bob Paul wrote to CCF leader George Williams that May evening in 1936 was the beginning of Paul's intense two-year effort to win Meadow Lake provincial constituency for the CCF. His attempt to form an alliance between the CCF, the communists, and the Social Credit would ultimately fail, but the campaign's lessons would not be lost. In 1940 Paul would go on to help Dorise

Nielsen win the federal election because of this earlier fight. By then he knew dozens of people on whom he could rely. He was a stubborn man. If he believed in something, he wouldn't give up.

Bob Paul was thirty-six years old, as old as the century. He had grown up near Prince Albert in a Scots Presbyterian family. His father was a farmer who belonged to the Conservative Party. He was the reeve of the rural municipality of Prince Albert for over twenty years, and knew both Prime Minister Mackenzie King, who was Prince Albert's Member of Parliament, and a future prime minister, the up-and-coming young lawyer, John Diefenbaker. Thus, politics came naturally to Bob Paul. Like his father, he was a man who could strike up a conversation with anyone and usually find some common ground. And although he would never induce any of his family to join the left wing, he never stopped trying.

Bob had always had a mind of his own. In 1915 he deliberately failed high school so that he could go off and fight the Germans. He began the year with astonishingly high grades—97 in chemistry, 93 in physics, 96 in algebra—then plummeted to an average of less than 20.[36] As soon as he turned sixteen, he joined the army.

On his return to Saskatchewan, he accepted the teaching certificate offered to veterans (even veterans who had not finished high school themselves) and began teaching at country schools outside Prince Albert. He soon discovered he didn't like teaching, but he would have to do it off and on for the next twenty years. Perhaps he found the routines boring, for he was always looking for ways to spice things up. His eldest son remembers his writing the timetables on the soles of his shoes, then sitting with his feet up on his desk. "The kids loved him," he said, "but Dad didn't like to teach."[37]

Not long after the war, Bob met Cecil Simpson, another young teacher whose family had immigrated to the Prince Albert area from Nebraska. They were married in the early 1920s and moved to Portland, Oregon, where they ran a small confectionery along the shore. Their first baby was stillborn. When Cecil became pregnant again, Bob decided they must move back to Canada so that their child would be a British subject. They sold their business and in 1928 Bob became part-owner of a general store at Mildred, Saskatchewan, a village not far from Norbury. When the store failed to turn a profit, the Pauls took teaching jobs nearby. It was while living in the Tinson teacherage near Norbury that the Pauls became good friends of the Nielsens.

Stewart Paul remembers intense political discussions whenever the two families got together. Books were passed around and the air was thick with words like "dialectical materialism" and "qualitative versus quantitative change." Although he was only nine when the family left Leoville, he picked up some of the jargon himself. "What are you feeding that kid?" the merchant in Leoville asked Bob one day. "He's in my store talking politics."[38]

Bob Paul was obviously either part of the left wing of the CCF or he was already a communist. His ideas came from Marx rather than the social gospel. He was a man looking for solutions. He wanted some explanation of the current crisis in the world. Every community in Saskatchewan had its "old Bolshevik" who was more than willing to give you his take on the situation. In the case of Bob Paul and Dorise Nielsen, that person was likely Bob Bowie, a German settler who lived on a homestead near Lake Witchekan, between Norbury and Leoville. Much later, during the Cultural Revolution in China, Nielsen wrote a brief account of her life (probably for official purposes) and named Bowie as her mentor:

> An old German organized a group of seven poor farmers into a party club and made contact with the party in the provincial city of Regina. The old comrade, walking 20 miles to see me and 20 miles home again, made many visits to encourage me to join the struggle for relief, food and clothing. He introduced me to Marxism and taught me all I knew about the revolutionary struggle in Europe. … Early in 1932 I joined this small party group secretly. It was decided by the provincial committee of the party, which still operated under cover, that I was to openly join the CCF which had just been formed.[39]

If this account is true, Dorise Nielsen certainly fooled a lot of people who believed that she was CCF first and only became a communist in the late thirties or early forties. Yet, Bob Bowie was a friend of Nielsen's, and he was active in the communist-led Farmers' Unity League in the early 1930s.[40] Both Dorise's daughters remember his name. He was the person who gave their mother a terrier pup that became Tootsie, the family pet. And once, when the family was on the way home from the Pauls' on a wintry day, they stopped at Bowie's farm. Christine was surprised to find that her mother knew this strange man so well.

It is likely, then, that both Nielsen and Paul were influenced by Bowie; however, the timing of Nielsen's conversion is problematic, and so is her assertion that she was essentially a communist from the very beginning of her political activity.[41] It is possible that Nielsen and Paul both started out with the CCF and subsequently were courted by communists who recognized their ability and their legitimacy in the English-speaking community. This period of courtship may have occurred early in the 1930s, but more likely it took place in 1934 or 1935 when the communist push to unite the left began.

Apart from supporting a united front, the particular issues that led Bob Paul and Dorise Nielsen to choose communism over democratic socialism can be only a matter of speculation. Later, Nielsen would say that the communists she met had been of a very high calibre. And, like many thoughtful people at the time, Nielsen and Paul were interested in learning from the socialist experiment in the USSR. A number of first-hand accounts were being published and most were favourable. One was written by George Williams, leader of the Saskatchewan CCF, who had visited the Soviet Union in 1931.[42]

What is clear is that by 1936 both Paul and Nielsen were strongly sympathetic to the communists, that they were known for those sympathies by at least some of the communist leadership (all eight leaders of the trek, including Doc Savage, were communists), and that Bob Paul was ready to put his political ideas into action by taking over the CCF organization in the provincial constituency of Meadow Lake. The friendship between the Pauls and the Nielsens was about to turn into an intensively active political alliance between Dorise Nielsen and Bob Paul. Pete Nielsen and Cecil Paul, although sympathetic to the cause, would be left more and more on the sidelines.

3

THE UNITED PROGRESSIVES

Never under ordinary circumstances would I have agreed to participate in such a life. But the 30's were not ordinary and I was more or less forced by circumstances to play the role I did in North Battleford.[1]

IN JULY 1936, on the eve of the CCF provincial convention, Tim Buck, the general secretary of the Communist Party of Canada (CPC), spoke before a large audience in Regina Park. He was a slightly built man who looked as though he could use a good meal. Many people had come just to have a look at him.

Everyone knew the name Tim Buck. In 1931 the Tory government of Ontario had attempted to douse worker discontent by sending Buck and seven other leading communists to the Kingston Penitentiary. They had been charged under Section 98 of the Criminal Code of Canada, which had been passed in 1919 during another "red scare." It declared unlawful any association that advocated the use of force or violence, or any other unlawful means, to bring about governmental, industrial, or economic change in Canada.

But now, after three years in prison, Tim Buck was out on the hustings again. His release, late in 1934, was the result of a national campaign that had gathered 459,000 signatures on a petition to free the prisoners and repeal Section 98.[2] Even Mackenzie King, then leader of the opposition, had taken up the cause. When the Liberals won the 1935 election, King fulfilled his promise and repealed Section 98. Once again, the Communist Party of Canada could operate freely, and in 1936 it had an important message to deliver.

"We must unite," urged Tim Buck that day in Regina. "We must present a united front, first to drive the Liberals and Conservatives together, and then to drive them into the garbage can of history."[3] Buck was proposing a coalition between the CPC and the CCF. He wasn't in Regina on the eve of the CCF convention by accident.

Like all other major policies of the CPC, the push for a united front of communists and social democrats was a worldwide drive authorized by the Communist International (Comintern). As the editor of *Saturday Night* pointed out a few years later, "The members of the CPC always sing in a chorus, and the tune is composed elsewhere."[4] But from the point of view of the CPC, "singing in a chorus" made sense. Hadn't Marx urged the workers of the world to unite?

And the new united front policy was not hard to justify. In Germany the parties of the right had managed to put Hitler in power in 1933. Everywhere the economic crisis was causing a similar political polarization. If the left failed to unite, more countries would fall to fascism. In Europe, popular front coalitions of communists and social democrats were beginning to stem the fascist tide. Already, by the summer of 1936, popular front governments had won elections in France and in Spain.

The message of uniting the left had a lot of appeal in Saskatchewan, too. Not many people were prepared to compare the Liberals or the Conservatives to Hitler, but those parties sure hadn't done much for Saskatchewan lately. It was this message of uniting the left that Nielsen and Paul would preach in northern Saskatchewan for the next two years. That summer of 1936 was only the beginning, and, so far, Bob Paul had had little success. He had attended the constituency convention at the end of June but it was a poor affair. There were less than a dozen CCF memberships in the whole constituency and no money to send a delegation south for the provincial convention that summer. He had to be content with following developments on the radio.[5]

The day after Buck's speech in Regina Park, the united front issue was fought out on the floor of the CCF convention. The party's national leader, J.S. Woodsworth, wanted nothing to do with the communists. He was sick of their slavish following of Soviet policies. He viewed them as thoroughly unreliable and devious. One day they denounced the CCF and the next day they wanted to join them! As if the CCF didn't have enough problems proving its competence and respectability, without taking a bunch of communists on board. "We cannot have Soviet methods here," he told the convention. "We cannot cooperate with the Communist Party which believes in dictatorship."[6]

But the Saskatchewan branch of the CCF did not agree. Woodsworth was followed by delegate after delegate who pointed out that he did not understand the situation facing the province. Even the provincial leader, George Williams, stood against his leader. "Whether we like it or not," he said, "the people of this province are demanding unity. How can we ignore the demand of our members?"[7] After years of drought and declining wheat prices, delegates were not content to build their organization slowly. They wanted their voices heard in Regina and in Ottawa, and they didn't want to wait. Uniting the left was the only way.

At the end of the debate, the delegates voted overwhelmingly (306 to 8) for a resolution requesting the provincial organization "to call upon all progressive organizations to unite on the immediate issues that are facing the people of Saskatchewan." Tim Buck had not gained the formal coalition with the CCF that he had sought, but he hadn't lost the battle, either. The convention vote showed how keen CCF members were on working alongside communists and the Social Credit, and, essentially, they had been given free rein to do so.

According to Communist Party records, there were approximately 600 members of the Communist Party in Saskatchewan in January 1936. By the next year, its membership had more than doubled.[8] The numbers were small, even when compared with the nascent CCF, but every member of the CPC was expected to be active and to contribute to the party financially. Several organizers travelled the prairies, shoring up support, and once in a while a speaker would come through northern Saskatchewan, but for the most part, communist clubs operated pretty much on their own. Directives would come from Winnipeg or Regina, and clubs would study them and try to follow them as best they could.

In the early thirties, despite being under attack, the party had formed both the Farmers' Unity League (FUL) and the Workers' Unity League (WUL). The FUL helped farmers fight for relief and better prices, and resist evictions. The WUL led a miners' strike in the Estevan coalfields and the On-to-Ottawa trek by relief camp workers that had resulted in the Regina Riot. No one in Saskatchewan was ignorant of the work of communists, despite their small numbers. And many people saw them as sincere and dedicated workers on behalf of the poor.

Now, with the new policy of a united front, both known communists and fellow-travellers flocked to work with local CCF organizations. Sometimes they ended up on constituency executives and even on the CCF Provincial Council. On the CCF Provincial Council, elected at the 1936 convention, at least two members, Nelson Clarke and Minerva Cooper, were communists. Nelson Clarke would later become the leader of the Saskatchewan section of the Communist Party.

Bob Paul and Dorise spent most of 1937 and 1938 organizing the Meadow Lake provincial constituency for the CCF, and it is likely that Pete Nielsen also played a supportive role in the process. But most of the time, it was Dorise and Bob, going from town to town and farm to farm, preaching the socialist gospel and promoting a united front. On the surface they were working solely for the CCF, setting up study clubs and trying to collect the one-dollar CCF membership fee.

Meadow Lake was one of three provincial constituencies that composed the federal constituency of North Battleford, but it was the largest one geographically, and to the north it included the newly settled Meadow Lake area. Sometimes Dorise and Bob travelled by train, sometimes by car or sleigh, but everywhere she went in 1937 and 1938, Dorise appeared in a dress she had sewn herself and her galoshes. Her pumps were so cracked and worn, she was ashamed of them. She hoped people would think it had rained somewhere along the way and she hadn't had time to remove her galoshes.[9] In the cold weather she wore the coat with the fur collar she had worn when she arrived from England ten years before.

By the summer of 1937 even the conservative *Spiritwood Herald* was taking note of Mrs. Nielsen and the CCF. On July 7, 1937, it mentioned that "Mrs. Nielsen has gone to Maidstone, St. Walburg, and other points." A month later it noted that "several Norbury people attended an anti-war conference at Meadow Lake"[10] and, in October, Mr. Coldwell came to speak to a CCF meeting in Spiritwood.[11] The local RCMP detachment had also taken note of Nielsen's activities, and it is likely its assessment was closer to the truth. "Mr. and Mrs. Pete Nielsen," they reported, "are known as local organizers for the

Communist Party." They went on to describe Pete (whom they assumed was the real leader of the pair) as "a man with a sandy moustache, about 46," who was known to have induced a number of settlers to join the Communist Party.[12] But in their next entry in the Nielsen file a year later, it was only Dorise whom they reported as "an active member of the C.P."[13]

Like others on the left, Nielsen worked for several causes that year. One of the burning issues in 1937 was the Spanish Civil War. Stewart Paul remembers his parents and Dorise collecting money to help send a group of Canadians, the Mackenzie-Papineau Battalion, to Spain, and to support Dr. Norman Bethune's mobile blood service. When Bethune made a cross-country tour that summer, Nielsen missed hearing him speak in Prince Albert because of muddy roads, but someone did get him to autograph a picture for her. Bethune was on his way to China that summer to set up another mobile hospital for the army of Mao Zedong. In 1937 the Japanese had attacked China in force. Soon Dorise and other members of the League Against War and Fascism added another item to their agenda—a petition to stop the sale of Canadian scrap iron to Japan.[14]

In the fall of 1937, Dorise slipped on a street in Spiritwood and fractured her shoulder. Pete took over making the bread. Dorise kept going to meetings, her arm in a sling. After harvest she and Bob Paul started a local study club.[15] A group of like-minded people would make their way to each other's houses Wednesday nights to discuss socialism and world events and exchange books. Then they would wake their children and trundle home by wagon or sleigh or on foot. They often met at Polaskis' or Wakefields' or Hunts' and it was Bob or Dorise who led the discussions. One of the members, Willard Block, remembers that the meetings were always more interesting when Dorise was present. She was the one people turned to for answers.[16]

Another of Nielsen's tasks, starting in 1937, was writing a series of letters to the *Western Producer*, a popular, left-leaning farm weekly. She used the pseudonym Judy O'Grady, which she had taken from Rudyard Kipling's poem "The Ladies." Strange, one might say, for a woman to choose a poem that anyone today would call misogynist. It's about a man who has "taken his fun where he found it" with women of all colours and creeds, and how he's learned through experience that "the Colonel's lady and Judy O'Grady are sisters under their skins." But it was likely the class issue that interested her. To throw off the

Victorian distinction between a lady and a woman of ill-repute was to move forward, as far as she could see.

Judy is a name she may have chosen quickly for the purpose of writing letters to the *Western Producer*, but soon it became her party name. Officially she was still Dorise, the ladylike woman who knew her manners. But her aspirations had changed since 1927. Now she was also Judy, the revolutionary, engaged in saving not just herself but the world.

The Judy O'Grady letters appeared, often monthly, on the *Western Producer's* women's page. Nielsen was one of many women who wrote to the *Western Producer* in the 1930s and who concealed their identities with such homespun pseudonyms as Smiling Pal, Another Believer, Never Say Die. They did this not just for fun, though they needed some fun in their lives. The more pressing reason not to reveal their identities was that, in their letters, they dared to take stands on the divisive political issues of the day. Only a few people knew that Judy O'Grady was actually Dorise Nielsen. One was her close friend Dolly Gunderson (who occasionally wrote under the name of Cinnamon Top) and another was the *Producer's* women's editor, Violet McNaughton.

Not all the letters on the women's page were overtly political. There was more than one recipe for baked beans. There was an explanation of the nutritional value of thistles, and a claim that wheat, alone, contained all the elements necessary for the human body. Stomachs had to be filled. Was it possible to live on bread and potatoes? What about bread and thistles? "In a few years," wrote Old Timer, "we will have a cultivated thistle that will be valued as much as spinach for its healthful properties."[17]

But Nielsen was impatient with the exchanges on nutrition. She was among the writers who were far more interested in recipes for a workable economic and political system. Did Russia have the answer? At least everyone there was working. What about the Scandinavian countries or New Zealand, which had elected socialist governments? They had old-age pensions at sixty in New Zealand, why couldn't Canada do that? The sides lined up and laid on the rhetoric, hoping to win readers to their cause. Violet McNaughton nudged her readers towards democratic socialism (the Scandinavian model) while Nielsen pumped for the Russian model.

In one of her early letters, Nielsen urged women to clear the cobwebs from their minds and "study the USSR where over one sixth of the world's people are busy constructing a new society," while, in Germany, women were being excluded from higher education and relegated to the kitchen. She recommended particular pamphlets published by the League Against War and Fascism, and books by leading Marxist popular writers John Strachey, Palme Dutt, and Anna Louise Strong.[18]

Before 1937, she had had only one letter published. In it she defended the CCF despite its disappointing showing in the 1935 federal election. No, she wrote, the CCF was not sunk, as some people said it was.[19] The letters beginning in 1937 show an important change in Nielsen's political awareness and her proselytizing activity. She had moved from simply defending the CCF to a new mission—uniting the left. And she had taken on the role of defending communism and the Soviet experiment, even though she still claimed not to be a communist herself. "I am still a church-goer and a member of the CCF," she wrote, "but I'm willing to join hands with all those who mean business."[20] Sometimes she went even further, praising Canadian communists as "working among the lowest strata of our society, stretching out a helping hand, and showing them how to help themselves. . . . " She maintained that "the communists alone, because of their analysis of the cause, can supply us with the solution to our present difficulties. They are the real comrades and helpers of the destitute and hungry, proving by their actions their real love of humanity."[21]

The year of 1937 was a hard one in northern Saskatchewan. It was the first year of drought in the north. In the small community of Norbury, the school was closed in June on account of measles and again in September because of four cases of infantile paralysis (polio).[22] It was also in 1937 that the Nielsens first went on relief. By that time, they had come to the end of their resources. In 1936 both Johnny Nielsen and Pete had been rushed to the Rabbit Lake hospital for appendectomies and the doctor had to be paid. They had no money and had to sell one of their two cows. Until 1937 they had been able to live from the garden, but because of the drought they had no homegrown vegetables. Even potatoes had to be purchased. With the cash provided by relief, they were able to eat, but not to eat well. Most of the time they lived on bread and potatoes. Soon four-year-old Johnny showed sign of rickets.

"May I ask why Mary Jane goes to Russia for pictures of starving children?" wrote Dorise to the *Western Producer* that summer. "What about Spain? What about every country governed by capitalists?" she wrote. "Why right here in northern Saskatchewan I could show you some starving children. Perhaps not hungry, but children who have lived through a very hard winter on the most unappetizing unvaried diet, who have suffered epidemics of infectious diseases one after the other, and whose little wasted forms certainly show it."[23]

In July 1937, Dorise was part of a small delegation from Meadow Lake provincial constituency to the CCF provincial convention in Regina. By this time she was vice-president of the local constituency and Bob Paul was campaign manager. Both were already well known in the area. In fact, Dorise had been advertised as "a prominent speaker" at the constituency convention that June (the other speaker was A.J. Macauley, an MLA).[24] As usual when travelling to meetings, they packed a suitcase of sandwiches to last the trip and Dorise wore her galoshes. They called themselves the hicks, the bush rats, and had a good laugh.

The best part of the convention in 1937 was hearing the new whiz kid, the CCF's first National Secretary, David Lewis.[25] He had recently returned from studying on a Rhodes Scholarship in England and knew all about the fascist menace in Europe. Dorise and Bob practically cheered when he addressed convention delegates as "comrades."

Once again the convention approved a resolution on unity (339 for, 7 against). "Whereas we believe that a victory for democracy and progress can only be won by cooperation with various progressive organizations in Saskatchewan," it read, "[we resolve] that it is most desirable that the initiative to secure this unity should be taken by the CCF."[26] That was worth another cheer from the bush rats. Already there was a declared communist serving on the CCF Meadow Lake executive committee. Wass Turple was particularly knowledgeable and articulate. He was a hard worker, too, and well respected in the community. He had been elected to the executive with sixty-four out of sixty-seven votes cast.[27] Getting Social Credit on board was proving a harder nut to crack, but Bob Paul was working on it.

It was Nielsen's first convention and she had achieved her goals. Mrs. Nielsen was recognized as a rising star in the CCF. Only a few of the delegates had met her before that convention. Coldwell knew her and some others had heard about her. Now they could see for themselves. Here was a woman who could hold her own with the best speakers of the day. Despite her British accent, she had a common touch and a very good sense of humour. It seems that no one (except the RCMP) questioned her loyalty to the CCF. She was elected a member of the CCF Provincial Council. For the next year she would attend meetings in Regina and Saskatoon to develop CCF policy between annual conventions.

Strangely, as Nielsen's personal life disintegrated into dire poverty and increasing strife with her husband, her political life grew to fill the spaces. Being on relief was not a disadvantage when it came to politics—half the people in Meadow Lake constituency were on relief. And at least she knew she was on the right side of history. She was part of a worldwide movement to oppose fascism and usher in a new age of equality and racial tolerance. It was not such a bad place to be. When her own role in the process weighed heavily (and it did sometimes when there was simply too much to do), she remembered that there were people counting on her. They had chosen her to deliver a certain message and she didn't want to let them down.

On the plus side, both personally and politically, was Bob Paul's move back to the Norbury area. The fall of 1937, he managed to get a school at Amiens, a village west of Norbury. Most weekends he came to the Nielsens' to plot strategy or take Dorise to meetings. Eva Hunt, Nielsen's former student, was home again, too. She had come to help care for a younger brother who'd been stricken with polio. By late fall Dorise was able to hire her for five months under a government work plan.[28]

Throughout the winter of 1937–38 Bob and Dorise devoted all their energies to the provincial campaign. Bob scheduled a series of zone meetings leading to the nomination meeting in April 1938. He brought his typewriter to the Nielsens' and they set up a primitive machine, called a hectograph, to duplicate letters and circulars. The communists sent a full-time organizer, Maynard Woollard, to help with the work. He was a bright young man from Weyburn who had started out working in Tommy Douglas's campaign in 1935. But he had become impatient with the social democrats who seemed to do nothing but talk. At some point before 1938, he had jumped to the Communist Party. He was still only twenty-three. A little wet behind the ears, Dorise thought. However, he had lots of enthusiasm and knew how to write a letter.

They still had no candidate. Bob was the obvious one but he was not willing. He was much better at organizing behind the scenes. But if the unity idea caught on, they'd have a good chance of winning, and then they'd have no trouble finding a candidate. And so they worked through the winter, sending out missives that the children helped pump out on the old hectograph. Occasionally, the adults took a break to play bridge, but even then the talk was of politics. Locally, this small group of radicals led by Nielsen and Paul had some success. They helped elect Lee Wakefield reeve and Bill Polaski school trustee. Their confidence and influence were growing. But the big test would be the provincial election, expected to be called for June 1938.

In 1938 northern Saskatchewan entered its second year of drought. Once again Dorise planted her garden only to watch the sprouts collapse and wilt. Without water she couldn't even grow potatoes. The wild berries failed that year, too. The best she could do was harvest the leaves of wild strawberries and dry them to make tea.[29]

While the local scene was grim and unrelenting, the international scene continued to move from crisis to crisis. In March 1938 the Nazis marched into Austria and, by the summer, they were threatening Czechoslovakia. And for the Canadian left, it wasn't much of a stretch to lay these crimes at the door of the hated Liberals. Hadn't Mackenzie King opposed sanctions against Italy when it invaded Ethiopia in 1935? Hadn't he met with Hitler in 1937 and declared him a harmless peasant?[30]

Even in Canada the prolonged depression had fostered the growth of fascism. Canadian fascists held their first national convention in July 1938. At a meeting in Toronto's Massey Hall attended by 1500 persons, Adrien Arcand, the leader of the New National Unity Party, flanked by his blue-shirted lieutenants, declared that fascism would enable Canada to "reconquer its own territory from the red clutches of Moscow and international Jewry within three years."[31] At the same time, in Maple Leaf Gardens, an anti-fascist rally sponsored by the Canadian League for Peace and Democracy (the new name for the League Against War and Fascism) attracted 12,000 persons. Both left and right were lining up, each one calling for unity. At this point it seems that the left had far more support than the right, but even if the Canadian fascists were weak in numbers, it was hard to discount them in view of how quickly fascism had snowballed abroad. In 1930 Hitler and his Nazis had been regarded as the lunatic fringe. By the summer of 1938, after five years in power, they had brought Europe to the brink of war.

It was in such an atmosphere that the Saskatchewan CCF held its annual convention in July 1938, a month after the provincial election. Dorise and Peter Nielsen made the trip to Regina with Bob Paul in his old Nash. As they drove south, the land was transformed, so green, so lush, such a contrast to previous trips in which they had driven from the green of the northern bush into a wasteland. The rains had come to the south at last and a bumper crop was possible.

The contrast in landscape mirrored the gap growing between the Meadow Lake CCF and the provincial executive of the party. The constituency organization had had its knuckles rapped in the spring when its nomination slate included a communist (Wass Turple) and a Social Crediter (James Hatton). Provincial Council had quickly produced a ruling that members of other political parties could not run for the CCF. Then George Williams, the provincial CCF leader, had written a courteous letter to Wass Turple, asking him to resign from the Communist Party so that he could run for the CCF, but Turple had refused. There was no way, he wrote, that he could shed his membership "as a snake sheds its skin. ... I can only conclude that you ... fail to understand what the C.P. means to its adherents."[32]

Bob Paul and Dorise were furious with the last-minute interference. Williams had indicated earlier that they had carte blanche to negotiate cooperation with other groups. "I'm pleased with the way you are working things out in your constituency," he had written. It was fine to cooperate with the communists, he said, as long as they were not allowed to take over.[33] Then, less than three months before the election, he had vetoed their candidate. At this point Bob was still teaching at Amiens and Pete Nielsen was in a Prince Albert hospital, recovering from surgery.[34] Neither Bob nor Dorise wanted to run. Perhaps they drew straws and Bob lost. He became the candidate and Dorise acted as campaign manager.

"Don't experiment with new forms of government and economic systems," read the Liberal ads in the 1938 campaign, "let other countries do the experimenting.

DON'T SWAP HORSES MIDSTREAM. VOTE LIBERAL." But most people did, in fact, want to swap horses. The Liberals won again only because the protest vote split once again between Social Credit and the CCF. The CCF gained nine seats, however, almost doubling its previous representation.[35]

In the constituency of Meadow Lake, Bob Paul came in a respectable third and kept his deposit.[36] Nevertheless, for Bob and Dorise, and for most of the Meadow Lake CCF, the provincial election campaign of 1938 was a turning point. All their confidence in promoting a united front through the CCF evaporated. In 1938 they had gone all out to unite the protest vote. They had held card parties and dances and picnics to raise money for pamphlets, gasoline, and the election deposit. The CCF provincial organization provided no funds. Bob Paul was constantly receiving bills from George Williams's secretary, Georgina Mathers. At one point, late in the campaign, she refused to send him any more pamphlets until the Meadow Lake bill was paid in full.[37] Bob and Dorise managed to collect a hundred CCF memberships that year, and every dollar went to the provincial office. There was no doubt the CCF needed the money, but it was becoming a tough sell in the north. With gardens failing for the second year in a row, more and more people like the Nielsens were ending up on relief. If they were going to put their precious money into an organization, they wanted to see some results.

The delegates driving south for the CCF convention that summer of 1938 had learned a lot in the past year and they had come up with a new plan. Previously, they had attempted to unite the left under the CCF banner. Now, for the upcoming federal election in North Battleford, they would form a coalition of equal partners with Social Credit and communists. By stressing that the unity coalition was not a new party, they hoped for CCF endorsement, but with or without central CCF approval, they would go ahead. The plan, Bob Paul said later, was to get a unity candidate into the field early, before the CCF could nominate, and, if the CCF did nominate, to label them splitters.[38]

It was an extremely bold move, a gamble, really, to think that a small group of CCFers and communists from one provincial constituency organization could convince a motley crew of populists from the two other provincial constituencies that made up the sprawling federal constituency of North Battleford to go along with them. At the CCF convention that summer, they got little support. In fact, the convention backtracked on the unity issue and passed a resolution recommending to "all constituency organizations the advisability of seeking the cooperation of all *former* supporters of other political parties."[39] Williams had learned his lesson, too. He was not going to have the reputation of the CCF sullied by the possibility of having a communist nominated under the banner of the CCF. This time he was determined to run straight CCF candidates in all ridings.

Once more Dorise was elected to the CCF Provincial Council. In September she travelled south to Regina for a meeting and again made an eloquent plea for permission to form a coalition of reform parties in Meadow Lake. Again she was turned down. A month later, George Williams was flabbergasted to receive a press notice that on October 8, 1938, a United Progressive Committee had been formed in North Battleford with a view to running one progressive candidate in the federal election. The notice was signed by Maynard Woollard, who was one of three communists on the nine-person committee. Nielsen and Paul were listed as CCF members of the committee. The meeting had been held at Medstead in the presence of Joseph Needham, Social Credit MP from The Battlefords and president of the Saskatchewan Social Credit Association.[40]

Between the provincial election in June 1938 and the formation of the United Progressives (UP) in October, Dorise had no time to catch her breath, but in some ways political work was what she needed. It gave her something to think about. It often got her out of the house, away from her personal worries, which were mounting.

"I have recently taken over secretarial work for the United Progressives up here," she wrote to Violet McNaughton in November 1938, "and I am certainly going to have my hands full." She expected to have little time to write letters to the *Western Producer*. "In our tiny shack this winter there will be two grown-ups, three children and a pup, two kittens, a radio and a typewriter if I can get one."[41] As usual, Dorise was presenting her chin-up, plucky self. At the age of thirty-six, she had just had all her teeth out, and once her gums had healed, she would have to make do with an ill-fitting set of store-bought teeth, but when she told McNaughton, she made light of that, too.

The Nielsen household with its kittens and pup and three children sounded happy enough, but there was much going on beneath the surface. It had been a very difficult year, personally as well as politically, and having all her teeth out was the least of Dorise's problems. That summer of 1938, the Nielsens were threatened with the loss of their farm. "I have been losing a bit of my beauty sleep lately," Dorise wrote McNaughton in August. "The Debt Adjustment Board has advised my husband that he must release the one quarter section on which we are living to the Mortgage Company." She apologized for imposing on McNaughton's good nature, but said she knew no one else in Canada who could give her advice.[42] The letters flew back and forth. Somehow the foreclosure was staved off for a few years.

How did all the personal anxiety affect Dorise's political path? It seems to have made her even more determined, more bitter, some would say, and certainly more radical. This time she did agree to run for election. Whether she had to be pressured into it, we will never know. It was logical, though, that she should stand, even if she were a woman. By this time she was well known as a member of the CCF, an outstanding speaker, the wife of a veteran and a homesteader. And, like everyone else, she was poor. Everything about her gave her a legitimacy that the United Progressives needed. That she was willing to work with the communists troubled few CCF voters in her constituency, and was never a problem for her chief correspondent, Violet McNaughton, who (though neither CCF or communist) supported a similar united front movement in Saskatoon.

There was, however, one problem when it came to respectability. "What are people saying?" Dorise asked Eva in 1938. Already rumours were circulating that Dorise was having an affair with Bob Paul. It is possible they were true, though, so far, the two of them had had very little opportunity. Certainly, it was evident to all observers that Paul was in love with Dorise. (She seems to have been much better at camouflaging her feelings.) Both Cecil Paul and Peter Nielsen suspected something, but they were too devoted to the socialist cause themselves to broadcast their suspicions. At home it was a different matter.

What is going on? Pete would ask. Nothing, Dorise would say. In the Paul household, Cecil was asking the same question and getting the same answer.[43]

It is not surprising that a marriage between two such different characters as Pete and Dorise Nielsen would crack under the stress of prolonged hardship. Long before 1938, Dorise regretted her impulsive decision to marry Pete Nielsen. "How many years I tried to find a way in which your father and I could find common ground, but failed," she wrote later, "my own lacks in some directions being as great as his in others."[44] And now here was Bob Paul, a man with whom she could share all her ideas and hopes, a true partner in life. But, of course, he had come along too late.

The whole dilemma of how she could leave Pete weighed on her even more than her fears about reputation or her affection for Paul. If she left the farm, what could she do to make a living? She could not imagine teaching in a country school as Cecil Paul did, and she was probably too well known as a radical to get a teaching job in any case. The only other job she might do was office work, in Saskatoon, perhaps. But these were thoughts she shared with no one at the time, except, perhaps, Bob Paul. Being Mrs. Nielsen, wife of a veteran and homesteader, was an important part of her persona. There was no way that Judy O'Grady (or any single woman with a questionable reputation) could lead the United Progressives to victory.

By this time, Nielsen had a small circle of neighbours who supported her politically and were prepared to ignore any rumours that would sully her reputation. The largest group was the study club. They could always be counted on to put personal differences aside and work for the cause. Even Bob's wife, Cecil, was a faithful supporter. Then there were Dorise's friends, Dolly (Edith) Gunderson and Eleanor Paulson, whom she'd known from the beginning, and a new teacher who had arrived in Norbury in 1937. Heide Vockeroth had heard of Nielsen before she came. "You will meet an interesting woman in Norbury,"[45] someone had told her, and she did. Soon the two were close friends and political allies. Heide Vockeroth was an interesting woman herself. She taught in rural schools while bringing up her two sons, for the most part, on her own. Her husband was a watchmaker whom she saw only occasionally. Like the Pauls and the Nielsens, the Vockeroths agreed on politics but on little else.

In the fall of 1938 the CCF did everything in its power to persuade Nielsen and Paul and the rest of the Meadow Lake CCF executive committee to withdraw their support from the United Progressive coalition, but they stood firm. When George Williams ordered Bob and Dorise to resign from the CCF executive, they refused. The rest of the executive committee backed them up—if Nielsen and Paul are forced out, they said, we will all resign.[46] In January 1939 the Meadow Lake CCF executive was formally declared disbanded,[47] but it continued to function in defiance of the declaration.

The provincial CCF knew it was in trouble. In the other provincial constituencies that composed the federal constituency of North Battleford, its organization was very weak. If it couldn't win back Meadow Lake from the United Progressives, there would be no hope at all of running a candidate. That spring, George Williams attempted to reorganize Meadow Lake for the CCF. He hoped that by sending prominent CCFers north to hold meetings, he could rally support for a straight CCF candidate. Bob Paul was furious. He felt that the party was investing far more to destroy the unity movement than it had ever done to support the CCF in the area before. In Saskatoon, a similar unity coalition had formed, but there the CCF was backing off. It was hard not to take the interference in Meadow Lake personally. He paced the floor night after night, trying to control his anger.[48]

In April 1939, two provincial MLAs, Brockelbank and Valleau, held four CCF meetings in the Spiritwood area and found them all pro-unity. Altogether, straight CCF supporters seemed to be in short supply. In fact, Brockelbank and Valleau found themselves shunned by many former CCF supporters for trying to break up the unity movement. One night they were forced to accept "the offered hospitality of Mr. and Mrs. Wass Turple for there was no other place to go." They noted that Mr. Turple, a known communist, carried "a lot of weight in the district."[49]

Later that month George Williams came north himself to address meetings. He also went on radio to denounce the United Progressives in North Battleford and the United Reform group in Saskatoon as "undoubtedly communist-controlled, having been engineered, organized and directed by communists." He predicted that "a communist-directed organization cannot win an election, most certainly anywhere in Saskatchewan and probably anywhere in Canada."[50] Williams was right on one count—both the United Progressives and United

Reform were, indeed, organizations engineered by communists. But, in this instance, the communist strategy of a united front made sense to a majority of the electorate.

Once the roads opened that spring of 1939, Dorise was on tour, speaking to a series of meetings for the UP. In late July, at Medstead, the United Progressives held their nominating convention. Guest speakers were S.A. Berg, a Social Credit MLA from Alberta, and Joseph Needham, a Social Credit MP. Dorise ran against two other candidates representing the Communist Party and Social Credit. She won on the first ballot.[51] As far as most voters knew, Mrs. Nielsen was still CCF, and her party had treated her badly.

4

A MIGHTY EFFORT

They have pushed me into the soup! I could not escape,
and so I'm doomed to a few months of strenuous stumping....
There is, in my opinion, a dog's chance of a win. Only by
the most mighty effort can it be done.[1]

THERE IS LITTLE ABOUT NIELSEN'S CAMPAIGN in the local or regional press. The silence could be construed as a Liberal effort to squelch her campaign, for the sympathies of the *Saskatoon Star-Phoenix*, the *Regina Leader-Post*, and the *North Battleford News* were with the established political parties. In fact, the *North Battleford News*, as well as the *Turtleford Sun* and the *St. Walburg Times*, were weeklies owned by the Liberal incumbent, Cameron McIntosh.

A man in his sixties, Cameron McIntosh had first been elected to Parliament in 1925 and was fighting his fifth campaign. His nomination (by acclamation) in August 1939 was reported at length in the *North Battleford News*, with the hall at Medstead described as being full of enthusiastic supporters despite the lack of contest. Nielsen, nominated in the same hall a month before, had merited a small notice on the front page, "Nomination Accorded Norbury Woman." There was no picture, no explanation of the United Progressive platform, and no description of Nielsen apart from her being the mother of three children and wife of a veteran. In that edition, a much bigger splash was made by a Mr. Percy Mark, who was nominated by the National Socialist Party "No, I'm not a fascist," he declared. "We just thought it was a good name so we chose it."[2]

The big news in 1939, according to the *North Battleford News*, was all in the air. The country inaugurated a national airline, Trans-Canada Airlines, in April, and North Battleford would officially open its own airfield, to be called McIntosh Field, on September 4 that year. It was to be a grand event with twenty planes arriving and Prime Minister Mackenzie King in attendance. In the meantime, the airport in North Battleford was operational, and the names of all persons arriving and departing appeared in a weekly column called "Airport News."

But for Nielsen there were no flights, just the lurch of the railway or the jostle of Paul's old Nash along dirt roads that made driving as hazardous as flying. Often that summer they were accompanied by Paul's eleven-year-old son, Stewart. There was gossip about Nielsen and Paul and they were determined to squelch it by taking along a chaperone. Campaigning was intense throughout the summer, for Mackenzie King was expected to call the election for October. In the constituency of North Battleford, it was essentially a two-way race. Of Percy Mark's National Socialist campaign, there is no record. Presumably, his supporters ran for cover once Canada declared war on Hitler's National Socialist government that September. When the election was finally called, his name did not appear on the ballot.

Only on the eve of the election did the *Spiritwood Herald*, Nielsen's local weekly, deign to print an article about the United Progressive campaign: "United Progressive Candidate Visits Meadow Lake." In it Nielsen was described as "a courageous woman and a good speaker" who spoke to filled halls at Four Corners, St. Cyr, Pierceland, Good Soil, Meadow Lake, Makawa, Loon Lake, and Sandy Ridge. "Her reception went beyond the most optimistic hopes of the supporters of the United Progressive Movement."[3] By then, even the *Leader-Post* in far-off Regina seems to have got wind of a possible upset in North Battleford. An article called "Whose Who and Where in 21 Saskatchewan Seats" featured the pictures of only six candidates, and Nielsen, "born in London, and wife of an ex-soldier" was one of them.[4]

For a fuller account of her campaign, we must rely on scraps of memory, none of them from Nielsen herself. If she wrote anything at the time, she did not keep it and, later on, she said she preferred to forget her political career. In the 1970s, when tourism to China began to open up, she was visited by journalists from Canada and by former colleagues Tommy Douglas and Sandy Nicholson. They urged her to write her memoirs or record them on tape but she refused, explaining to Nicholson that "I don't consider that my life has been so very interesting. There were many years of hardship followed by years of political life for which I was not by nature fitted . . . never under ordinary circumstances would I have agreed to participate in such a life."[5] But the few accounts of her campaign show a tough, confident woman, at the top of her game. Even breaking her nose in an auto accident that fall hardly slowed her down. Before the bruises had faded, she was off to Saskatoon, stumping for another unity candidate.

She spoke in dozens of schoolhouses and community halls to largely male audiences. Sometimes she was the only woman in the room. These were critical audiences who expected a good show. They sat, astonished at first, to see a woman in politics, but by the end she had them in the palm of her hand. She seemed to be talking right to you, people remember, and she never read a speech.[6] There was always a joke and often an extended metaphor to drive a point home. Here was a woman with a patrician English accent poking fun at racial pretensions—people so proud of their ancestors, she said, reminded her of potatoes, the best part of them was underground.[7] She had a flair for the dramatic. A wagon full of Hansards (the official transcripts of debates in the House of Commons) would be pulled on stage. She would reiterate the problems of her constituency, then ask, "What did your honourable member have to say about that?" She would leaf through one of the Hansards and, inevitably, she would find that the incumbent, Cameron McIntosh, had said nothing.[8]

The eight-point United Progressive platform covered issues that anyone from Social Credit or CCF or the Communist Party could support. It promised an improved Wheat Board, with prices based on the cost of production, old-age pensions at age sixty, unemployment insurance, "general health services," and "the issuance and control of currency and credit to be in terms of people's needs." It advocated the "the socialization of those industries which are essential to a national planned economy and which are monopolistic in character." An election pamphlet was printed with the platform on the second page and, on the first page, a picture of Dorise in her coat with the fur collar, and the slogan "Unity Means Victory."[9]

Nielsen and Paul made a powerful team. They had been working together for years, and both had found their forte. He was busy making the contacts and plotting strategy, or "making the snowballs," as he liked to say, and Nielsen was throwing them. There were, however, outside developments that affected their campaign, and the first was the splintering of the Conservative Party.

The Conservatives had been in the doldrums since their overwhelming defeat in 1935. In 1938 R.B. Bennett, a Calgary businessman who had won the West in 1930 and lost it in 1935, resigned as leader. In choosing his successor, the party passed over W.D. Herridge, Bennett's energetic ambassador to the United States, who had become convinced of the need for sweeping government intervention in the economy along the lines of Roosevelt's New Deal. In order to placate Bay Street businessmen and win Quebec, the convention chose instead a mild-mannered, middle-of-the-road, Catholic physician, Dr. R.J. Manion. Herridge, a man brimming with ideas, was not content to let matters rest. In the spring of 1939, he proposed to the members of the CCF and Social Credit parliamentary caucuses, as well as dissident Conservatives, that they unite their forces to defeat the Liberals in the next election. He called his movement New Democracy.

The unity idea was not new. By this time the communists had been on a united front campaign for five years, and the idea of running one "progressive" candidate against the all-powerful Liberals had already won some support among Social Credit and CCF supporters at a grassroots level. In both North Battleford and Saskatoon, unity movements, largely engineered by communists, had been formed in the fall of 1938, months before Herridge launched New Democracy.

Still, in the spring and summer of 1939, a vital time in Nielsen's campaign, it was the New Democracy movement that kept both Social Credit and the Conservatives from nominating candidates in North Battleford. In fact, Social Credit leader William Aberhart, premier of Alberta, gave his full support to the Herridge movement. In Alberta, all the incumbent Social Credit MPs ran under the New Democracy label, and in Saskatchewan, by the end of the summer, four New Democracy candidates had been nominated.[10] In a speech given in Meadow Lake early in her campaign, Nielsen used the Herridge campaign to her own advantage. The United Progressives, she explained, were part of a larger movement with W.D. Herridge as national leader.[11]

Although New Democracy was ultimately a flash in the pan, the debate over New Democracy in that summer just before the war vividly illustrates the political polarization of western Canada. For many Westerners, be they Social

Credit, CPC, or CCF, it was clear that the economic system had failed and needed radical reform. They were equally sure that under the Liberals, if reform came at all, it would be slow and grudging. The King government, in power since 1935, had done little apart from repealing Section 98 of the Criminal Code and disbanding federal relief camps for the single unemployed. So far, the new Wheat Board had done very little to support prices.[12]

There was anger and urgency in the debates among the left that summer. In Europe, war loomed—a war that everyone knew would involve Canada in some way. It would be a war against fascism, and hadn't the rise of fascism been caused, ultimately, by the failure of capitalism to deal with the Depression? That much was clear to Herridge and to all reformers, no matter what stripe. The government, he said, must not just tinker with the old order, but build a new order. Production could not be regulated by profits alone. Russia and her economic system had stood the test. According to Herridge, Canada, like Russia, must develop its own new system to suit its own people and to "employ, justly and fully, the natural wealth within our territories."[13]

Is it any wonder that the communists endorsed New Democracy? The support was not unconditional, stated Walter Wiggins, speaking in Regina's Market Square, but the idea of nominating just one progressive candidate was key. Finally, the united front was becoming a reality. In Saskatchewan, by the end of the summer, not only were there four New Democracy candidates, but one of them was T.G. McManus, leader of the Communist Party in Saskatchewan. As well, there were four straight communist candidates, and three candidates bearing labels Unity, United Reform, and United Progressive.[14] All this before the federal election had even been called. The prospect of such widespread communist influence made at least some of the establishment quake in their boots. In August, at a Kiwanis convention in Regina, delegates were warned that there were more communists in western Canada than in Russia at the time of the Bolshevik Revolution.[15]

Like New Democracy and its supporters, the CCF stood for a new social and economic order, but it was having no truck with shifting alliances at this point. Under the leadership of George Williams, the 1939 provincial convention that ousted Nielsen and her Meadow Lake delegation for throwing in their lot with the United Progressives also soundly rejected cooperation with Herridge.[16]

Still the debate continued as war clouds darkened. On August 23, as France mobilized to face a possible German invasion, 1200 people gathered in Regina's Market Square to hear CCF leader M.J. Coldwell debate Mayor Ellison on the issue of a united front in the coming federal election.[17] Regina's popular mayor repeated the same message that crowds had been hearing from Herridge, from Nielsen, and from Aberhart: "Unite where we agree and let us tolerate where we disagree." One way or another, the Liberals had to go.

A week later Germany invaded not France, but Poland, and Great Britain declared war. Mackenzie King summoned Parliament. The grand opening of McIntosh Airfield was postponed as Cameron McIntosh and other MPs scrambled to make their way to the capital. On September 10, Canada, too, was at war. There would be no election that fall, after all.

Canadians took up the war effort with very heavy hearts. The glory of war was a myth and they knew it. Canada had suffered heavy casualties in World War I. The survivors were middle-aged men, many of them like Pete Nielsen, who still bore the scars of battle and were inclined to be cynical about government promises that sacrifices would be evenly distributed.

Nevertheless, all but two members of Parliament bowed to the inevitable and supported the declaration of war. Although a French-Canadian nationalist and the pacifist leader of the CCF, J.S. Woodsworth, were the only MPs who spoke against the war, reservations abounded. The prime minister, whose greatest fear was dividing the country (and the Liberal Party) over the issue of conscription, promised that the mobilization of manpower would be for home service only; overseas service would be left to volunteers. The CCF insisted that any mobilization of resources must include conscription of wealth as well as manpower. This war was not to be fought on the backs of the poor, with manufacturers growing rich on war contracts.

Earlier in the year, during debate on the Defence Production Act, the CCF had managed to secure a 5 percent profit-limitation clause. Once Canada declared war, this limit was considered too low to induce the necessary production and was removed. From the beginning, massive appropriations for the war dwarfed the government's appropriations to work programs during the

Depression. Tommy Douglas (CCF Weyburn) recalled how, during budget debates in the thirties, the finance minister of the day had lectured him that "money doesn't grow on gooseberry bushes." Now, it appeared that the government had suddenly discovered a very fertile gooseberry bush.[18] The problem was how to hold the government accountable without appearing to be unpatriotic. In fact, holding the Liberals accountable for anything would become a major problem. After calling the brief session to declare war and vote appropriations at the beginning of September 1939, King gave Parliament no opportunity to debate either foreign or domestic issues until May 1940.

The problems the war caused the CCF and the Liberals were minor when compared to its effect on the Communist Party. Communists had been in the forefront of anti-fascist activities in Canada since 1934. They had supported a strong stand against Mussolini's invasion of Ethiopia and sanctions on Japan because of her war on China. They had fought and died in the Spanish Civil War. They had condemned the Munich Agreement as a sellout, and pushed for a mutual assistance treaty between the Soviet Union, France, and Great Britain. Many of these activities had been coordinated through a communist-led League Against War and Fascism, which had considerable support from the non-communist left.

After all this effort in the battle against fascism, communists throughout the world were stunned when news of the Soviet-German Non-Aggression and Mutual Assistance Treaty hit the papers on August 22, 1939. After failing to secure a mutual assistance pact with France and Great Britain, and fearing a German attack, the Soviet Union had pulled a quick about-turn and negotiated with the devil himself. A little more than a week later, on September 1, Hitler, now assured that the Soviets would stay out of his way, invaded Poland, and World War II began.

The initial reaction of both the British and Canadian communist parties was to support the war against Hitler. Tim Buck, in a telegram to Mackenzie King, urged an all-out effort to support the Polish people. There was some fear on the part of Canadian communists that Britain and France, given their record of appeasement, might not be willing to open up a second front against Germany and would let Poland fight it out alone. In fact, Poland did fight it out alone, and not only against Nazi Germany. Soon the Soviet Union joined the attack on Poland to regain territory it had lost in the previous war.

This dramatic shift in Soviet foreign policy caused some leading communists in Britain and elsewhere to leave the party. For those who remained, it was a matter of digesting the Communist International's interpretation of the new alignment. According to Comintern, the war was not a fight against fascism. It was an imperialist war, like World War I, with Germany and the other west European powers alike in their drive for empire. The lack of fighting on the Western Front for the first seven months of the war tended to support this theory. Perhaps France and Britain were not serious about beating Hitler, after all; perhaps they would come to terms. Why, then, should Canadians divert their wealth and energies and lose their lives to help Britain?

Obviously, a double standard was being applied here. Communists did not criticize the Soviet Union for invading Poland and later Finland. These actions were attributed entirely to self-defence. Nevertheless, by October 1939, the bitter pill handed down by the Comintern had been digested and the Communist Party of Canada was adamantly against the war. It would have been so much easier to support the war, but communists were used to suffering for their allegiance and they were about to do so again, and in greater numbers than ever before.

Soon certain communist publications were banned, only to spring up again under new names. Publishers and distributors of anti-war literature were arrested and sentenced to short terms in prison. In the Manitoba legislature, the lone communist member, James Litterick, took over an hour to explain his stand on the war, despite shouts of disapproval.[19] On the streets, there was less tolerance and less protection. In November a number of people were arrested for distributing pamphlets signed by Tim Buck, which attacked the Chamberlain government. The Defence of Canada Act, Section 39 (a) allowed for this broad sweep: "No one shall . . . make statements, false or otherwise, intended or likely to cause disaffection to His Majesty's forces or to interfere with the success of His Majesty's forces or the forces of any allied or associated power."[20]

In the Regina civic election that fall, the entire Labour slate, including long-time Mayor Ellison, was defeated. "Communist Fear Was a Big Factor," declared the *Leader-Post*, quoting one of the defeated aldermen.[21] Between August 1939 and the federal election the following spring, three New Democracy candidates and three communist candidates withdrew from the race in Saskatchewan. Because of the war and the communist stance on the war, the electoral chances of any candidate tinged with red were clearly on the wane.

But the effect of the war on Nielsen's campaign was probably mixed. At the end of September 1939, a letter to the editor of the *Western Producer* reported a recent meeting of the coordinating committee of the United Progressive Movement in North Battleford at which a resolution supporting Canada's declaration of war on Germany was passed unanimously. At the time, support for the war was still official policy of the Canadian Communist Party.[22] Later that winter, after the election was actually called, the United Progressives put out a three-page election brochure outlining the UP platform. Its stand on the war could be described as lukewarm. It called for control of war profiteering and "defence of democracy, both at home and abroad," including "freedom of speech, press, assembly, religion, and the right of labour to bargain collectively." The only other reference to the war called for a referendum "if conscription becomes an issue." This cautious approach to the war seems designed to appeal to both those who viewed it as a bitter pill to be swallowed and others who saw it as a genuine fight for freedom. In any case the UP platform could not be construed as a statement "likely to cause disaffection for His Majesty's forces."

Actually, the cautious policy of the UP on the war may have increased Nielsen's chances of election. If the UP had continued with all-out support of the war as declared in September, it may have lost support of certain ethnic groups, heavily represented in the riding, who were not in support of the war. In his later analysis of Nielsen's win, Bob Paul cited the votes of French Canadians, Ukrainian Nationalists, and Germans coming to the UP because it did not fully support the war.[23] As for the WASP vote, Nielsen's Britishness was undoubtedly an asset. Who would question the loyalty of a woman from London, especially in the wake of a triumphal royal visit the previous summer, and with the papers full of pictures of doughty Londoners digging trenches in the public parks?

Nielsen's campaign was given another boost on December 18, 1939, when a united front candidate won a federal by-election in Saskatoon. Like the United Progressives in North Battleford, the United Reform group in Saskatoon had formed in the autumn of 1938 in the wake of the provincial election, months before Herridge and his New Democracy movement. And, as in North Battleford, communists had played a prominent role in a movement that included Social Credit and grassroots CCF supporters as well. The candidate was Rev. Walter George Brown, a Presbyterian minister and former moderator of the Presbyterian Church of Canada, who had been fighting battles on behalf of the unemployed since 1936. As in North Battleford, it was a two-way race with the Liberals.

The by-election, called after the Liberal incumbent died of a brain tumour, became a populist crusade. Brown was described as a people's candidate who would stand up to powerful and privileged interests. As well as monetary and fiscal reform, he pledged unemployment insurance and other social benefits, elimination of patronage, and control of war profits. His opponent charged Brown with being a tool of the communists, but despite the fact that Brown's campaign manager, Nelson Clarke, was a communist, and other communists campaigned for him, the juggernaut could not be stopped. The majority of people in Saskatoon, including Violet McNaughton and her husband, wanted Brown and they were willing to fraternize with communists to get him elected. "Unity Means Victory" was their slogan. They held rallies and teas and meetings addressed by Brown and Nielsen and three Saskatchewan MLAs who supported unity. On election day Brown won a resounding victory, gaining 10,766 votes compared to his opponent's 5757. At that moment, surely, it was possible to believe that unity really did mean victory, that whenever a general election were to be called, the Liberal empire would be shaken.[24]

The exhilaration of Brown's win probably helped to carry Nielsen through the final months of a long campaign. She had been involved with the United Progressive campaign from the beginning, and before that she had been Bob Paul's campaign manager in the provincial election—over two years of putting politics first, but somehow coping on the domestic front, as well. It was during these years of intense political activity, for example, that Heide Vockeroth's sons walked the four kilometres from the Tinson teacherage to the Nielsen farm so that Dorise could cut their hair.[25] The Vockeroths spent Christmas at the Nielsens', eating well and singing Spanish Civil War songs. "We used to eat so much at Christmas—it was the best food we had all year," remembers one of Heide's sons.[26]

These memories of children, focussing on their own well-being, their full stomachs, their long walks through the fields to a friend's house, give one picture of the Nielsen household on the eve of its disintegration. The Nielsen children, too, tend to view that time as Eden before the fall. They had playmates nearby, trees to climb, and a school picnic with ice cream every summer. When they first went on relief, Christine was allowed to choose a brand-new snowsuit (that would be passed down, like all her clothes, to sister Sally). She went through the Eaton's catalogue with her father, trying to make the momentous decision. She remembered her father as a gentle man, most of the time.[27] Dorise was the strict one, though she seldom raised her voice. In the midst of the campaign, the family was lucky enough to receive a crate of pears. In Dorise's absence, they ate the whole thing, fresh, without thought of canning. When she arrived home, she was furious. What were they going to eat that winter? After fifty years, these incidents still stick in the children's memory.[28] There was no great row, no harbinger of catastrophe. Life was predictable. Home was home.

The weather was mild that Christmas of 1939, one of the warmest Christmases on record. Altogether, it was a strange year with more surprises to come. On January 24, 1940, 10,000 people gathered in Regina to see the troops march down Elphinstone Street to the railway station on their way to Britain.[29] Canada had been at war for five months but so far none of her troops had seen combat. The next day Parliament resumed, and the Rev. W.G. Brown attended the shortest parliamentary session in history. Mackenzie King, smarting from criticism that he was a slacker when it came to the war, allowed no debate whatsoever. Instead, he called a spring election.

One February evening, in the midst of the election campaign, Christine and Sally were fetching the wood when they heard a great roar. Suddenly the trees north of the house were lit like daylight. They dropped their wood and ran for home. A few seconds later, a giant, wingless insect swung through the gate and stopped in front of the house, and two men climbed out. One was a lawyer whom Dorise recognized as a Liberal supporter. He had come from Spiritwood by snow-plane to deliver a final writ of foreclosure on the Nielsen homestead, and he had made a big mistake.

The threat of eviction soon became a campaign issue. It was raised in the Saskatchewan legislature by Mr. A. Stewart, one of two unity MLAs. Mrs. Nielsen, he said, was being unduly harassed. In response, the Liberal government promised the Debt Adjustment Board would look into the matter. Consequently, eviction procedures were dropped.[30] The threat of eviction was publicized in both the *Western Producer* and in Nielsen's election pamphlet. No doubt, it gained her a good deal of support as an underdog taking on the local Liberal machine.

By this time, CCF leader George Williams had decided to give some support to Nielsen's campaign. A month before the election, he wrote Nielsen that he would like to give her some unofficial assistance, but needed a guarantee from her that such support "would be reciprocated later on" in the form of support for the CCF in Ottawa, and assistance to the Saskatchewan CCF in the next provincial election. He had not had a good experience with unity candidates elected provincially in 1938—they had formed a sort of opposition to the opposition—but then, they were not socialists like Nielsen, he said. He ended this plea for future cooperation by saying he was "looking forward to the day" when Nielsen would "be able to be elected as a straight CCF candidate."[31]

A month later, having received no reply, Williams wrote once again, saying that, with or without a commitment from her, he intended to declare his support for her in a radio broadcast on the eve of the election.[32] There is no evidence that Nielsen made any deal with Williams, but, shortly after her election, when she responded to his letter of congratulations, she said she did not anticipate any trouble in regards to cooperation at Ottawa because of the similarity in the platforms.[33]

What difference Williams's last-minute support made is difficult to gauge. Already, in January 1940, the communists believed her chances of winning were very good.[34] And on March 26, win she did, by a margin of over 2000 (10,500 to 7867). News of the victory was slow in coming to Norbury. The election took place on a Tuesday. The next day, on the radio, Nielsen heard that a unity candidate had won, but there were several unity candidates running, so she wasn't sure whether to celebrate. Her first news of the win came in a telegram of congratulations from her mother, who had read the news in a British paper.[35]

Nine women ran in the 1940 federal election, five of them from the prairies and all of them candidates for reform parties. The big upset was the defeat of Agnes Macphail in Ontario. Macphail had been the first woman to be elected to Parliament in 1921 and had been re-elected ever since. On April 5, in the midst of what must have been a domestic whirlwind, Nielsen sat down to write her a letter. "A great deal of the pleasure we felt up here over the victory of the United Movement was certainly dimmed when we heard that you would not represent your constituency."[36] Nielsen encouraged Macphail to run in

Saskatoon, for the Rev. Brown had died suddenly a week after the election, leaving Saskatoon without a member and Nielsen without a colleague in the House.

It was a congenial letter to Macphail, and Dorise received several of her own. Coldwell and Woodsworth, still hopeful of her cooperation, wrote letters of congratulation. Coldwell advised her of her right to a rail pass and suggested that any bank would be willing to loan her some money until she began to receive her parliamentary salary.[37] Perhaps, then, there was a brief and hopeful honeymoon on both the political and the domestic front. She would be able to buy new shoes for the children in either Prince Albert or Saskatoon, their first shoes not ordered from Eaton's catalogue. At last, she would not have to worry about money or about her children's education. She would be living in a city and would find housing close to a good school. (Tinson School has been closed since January due to lack of funds.) If Peter Nielsen were mourning the loss of his wife and departure of his children, he had had months to prepare himself for this moment. Perhaps he told himself that they would be back for the holidays, that they would be better off, really, in the city. Perhaps he had already decided to join the Veterans Guard and rid himself of the farm for good.

At the end of April, the whole Nielsen family travelled to Saskatoon, where Dorise addressed a May Day rally. Photographs mark the event. Here is Pete in a suit and Dorise in a matronly dark crêpe, posing for a picture with the children on Minerva Cooper's ramshackle porch, and there they are again, having their pictures taken on the station platform. Christine, eleven, Sally, eight, and Johnny, five, all blonds like their father, all euphoric and exhausted. For the first time, they have taken a bath in a porcelain tub with running water. They have heard a telephone ring. And tonight they will sleep on a train and go all the way to Ottawa. They will have bunk beds and eat fancy meals and everyone will know that their mother is famous. It is very early in the morning, but Violet McNaughton has come to see them off and brought them each a package of cookies and books to read on the way. From Pete there is an awkward hug. It is such a strain to mind their manners. They are anxious to be off.

Dorise, too, is anxious to be off and on her way. She has much to learn, much to do, and many new people to meet. Her contact in the Communist Party will be A.A. MacLeod in Toronto. Already, he is passing the word to those who can be trusted: one of our own is in the House of Commons—at last![38]

OTTAWA

5

FIGHTING FOR THE WEST

I wanted to meet Mrs. Nielson [*sic*] to get her sympathy with our party before she gets too quickly antagonistic to it by association with other groups. So sent her a note to see if I might see her this evening.[1]

THE FIRST WEEK IN MAY, Dorise and her children boarded the CNR train in Saskatoon for the forty-eight-hour journey over the prairies and through the boreal forests and rocky outcroppings of the Laurentian Shield to Ottawa. At night she tucked the two girls between the starchy white sheets of the upper berth while she and Johnny settled into the lower. During the days she tried to interest them in books, or in looking out at the wall of dense bush in search of a bear or a moose, but only Christine was amenable to reading for long. Like her mother, she had been able to read before she started school and was now into Dickens. Sally had had six different teachers in her first year at Tinson School and still found reading a painfully slow process. Dorise simply hadn't had the time to teach her, but she had hopes that the school in Ottawa would make up for this deficiency. During the trip Sally was train-sick off and on and had no use for books. There was nothing to be done but have her lie down with a pillow and a cold cloth on her forehead. Johnny caught his fingers in a car door during a short stop in Winnipeg. But soon he was off again, lurching down the aisles, investigating. All minor problems, Dorise wrote Violet McNaughton, but a tiring trip nonetheless.[2]

In the spring of 1940, Ottawa was a sleepy town on the brink of a growth spurt. Soon, temporary government buildings would sprout like mushrooms in parks and on empty lots, and any kind of housing would be hard to find. The sight to see in Ottawa was the new memorial to the Great War (World War I), finished just the summer before. It stood on an island amid the traffic, only a stone's throw from the rail lines that followed the Rideau Canal into town. Dorise caught a glimpse of it when she arrived. One day she walked over to take a longer look before boarding her bus home. Two mounted soldiers and many others on foot pulling a gun carriage struggled through its monumental arch. The weariness of war was etched on every face.

In Ottawa, Nielsen and her children had been met at the train by Muriel Kerr, a good friend of Agnes Macphail's, who put them up for several nights in her Cooper Street apartment.[3] Dorise was given the office on the sixth floor of Parliament (next to the dining room) that had been occupied by Macphail for all her eighteen years in Parliament. Since the twenties, when the first progressives and labour MPs had been elected, the sixth floor had been known as "socialist alley." The offices of J.S. Woodsworth and other CCF members, most of them Westerners, were just down the hall. Dorise was also assigned Macphail's private secretary, Lilla Bell, so she did not have to rely on the secretarial pool like other backbenchers. Lilla Bell's advice on routines and procedures was invaluable. And if Lilla didn't know, Dorise could call on Coldwell, or Angus MacInnis, or Tommy Douglas, all CCFers who'd held seats since 1935.

Soon Dorise rented a furnished house on Fulton Street in Ottawa South and registered all three children at Hopewell School. She chose the suburbs so they would have space to play. The Rideau Canal with its broad boulevard was close by, and the Experimental Farm, only a short walk. In June and July they would be able to swim in the Rideau River near Hog's Back. Yes, Nielsen wrote Violet McNaughton, the children were happy. They still found the flush toilet and the telephone "nothing short of miraculous."[4]

In the 245-seat House of Commons, Dorise was one of eighty-five new members, most of them Liberal backbenchers. The Liberals, back in power since 1935, had once more swept the country, this time with a plea for national unity to fight the war. The 184-member Liberal caucus spilled over from the government side of the House and took up half the backbenches on the opposition side. Nielsen occupied a desk at the very bottom of the House near the door. To her right was a crew of CCF and New Democracy (Social Credit) members, mainly from the West, eighteen in all, and, finally, nearer the Speaker and opposite Mackenzie King's cabinet, sat the official opposition, the Conservative (or National Government) Party, reduced to only thirty-nine members, most of them from Ontario. By profession, the House consisted of seventy-six lawyers, forty-eight businessmen, thirty-seven farmers, eighteen doctors, ten teachers, nine engineers, four clergymen, and one housewife.[5]

Like Nielsen, most third-party members in the House had been nominated and elected on domestic issues that had nothing to do with the war. The prairies had suffered longer and harder from the Depression than any other part of the country. Wheat prices were still rock bottom. In 1940, net farm income in Saskatchewan was half of what it had been in 1928, and in 1941 it was even worse.[6] Municipalities had gone bankrupt, schools had closed, teachers and doctors had gone unpaid. As far as the prairie people were concerned, the Depression was not over.

It was Monday evening after the second day of debates that Nielsen took the floor for the first time. It was growing late, probably close to ten o'clock. That afternoon R.B. Hanson, the Conservative House Leader, had responded at length to the Throne Speech, and when the session had resumed at eight o'clock in the evening, Prime Minister Mackenzie King had answered Hanson at even greater length. Then it was the turn of M.J. Coldwell. The CCF leader, James Shaver Woodsworth, had just suffered a stroke and, for the first time, Coldwell spoke in his place.

Coldwell was eloquent and to the point. He managed to say twice as much as either Hanson or King, and in half the time. He reiterated the CCF's stand on no conscription for overseas service, and criticized the Defence of Canada Regulations that allowed the government to imprison, without trial, anyone who encouraged opposition to the war effort. But the heart of his speech dealt with two serious blows that had just struck Saskatchewan: the first, a drastic cut in federal relief grants; the second, a crash in wheat prices. The King government, after refusing to peg the price of wheat during the Depression, had finally intervened just two days before and set the price of number one Northern at the low level of seventy cents a bushel. All these were concerns of Nielsen, as well.

Speaking after Coldwell and before Nielsen was John Blackmore from Lethbridge, Alberta, leader of the New Democracy (Social Credit) movement.

The fifty-year-old Blackmore, a Mormon teacher and father of twelve, was not at his best. He stumbled from praising both the British Empire and William Aberhart (the Social Credit premier of Alberta) to quoting Ezekiel on the evils of usury. It was a muddy-minded, inarticulate speech. Members who had no reason to linger probably made for the exit. Finally, the speaker informed Mr. Blackmore that his time had expired, and it was Nielsen's turn.

Her speech that evening was both clever and heartfelt. Clever because she managed to mask her opposition to the war, heartfelt because she spoke from the core of her concerns. She mentioned her position as the sole woman in the House. All through history, she said, women had been regarded as the property of men, and even now they were expected to "reflect their ideas and echo their sentiments." But women had ideas peculiar to themselves that should be reflected in Parliament. Her predecessors Agnes Macphail and Martha Black "have contributed greatly," she said, "and I very much regret that they are not sitting on these benches this evening."[7]

So far, she said, the war had received more attention than anything else, but she proposed to speak from a woman's point of view, not about death but about the protection of life. She described the destitution in the West and urged that a fair price be established for farm products so that farmers could once more be self-supporting. She cited her own struggle to feed a family of five on the $11.25 a month provided by relief ("a dirty shame" shouted one honourable member), and now relief was to be cut, condemning people to "slow and agonizing death, both mental and physical." The deprivation of poverty goes beyond hunger "of the belly kind," she said, quoting Robert Service. There is loneliness and boredom, and a whole generation of children who may never reach their potential because their schools have been closed, or their parents have been unable to buy textbooks. Then there is the desperation of a parent with a sick child who "has had to travel twenty miles or more in sub-zero weather, not to fetch a doctor, but like a whipped dog to beg of a relief officer permission to get a doctor." How could such people be asked to make more sacrifices on account of the war? And what about the plight of veterans of the last war? Saskatchewan was full of such men, "cast like driftwood on desolate homesteads."

"I should like to bring some of these men here," she said, "in all their rags and tatters, and stand them around your great monument, to form a living monument to the ingratitude of Canada."[8]

By now, no doubt, everyone in the House was listening, and some were wondering just how far she would go. Here was another Agnes Macphail, another bleeding heart, this one with a queenly bearing and posh British accent rather at odds with what she was saying. Bitter, one journalist would say. If only she hadn't been so bitter. She was a good speaker, he wrote, one of the best, though she made the same speech over and over again.[9] But that night was the first speech; she had not yet worn out her welcome. She ended by calling on the government, in its concern to protect Canada from subversive elements, to recognize "the most subversive element of all—poverty."

After a final speaker and the tabling of business for the following day, the debate adjourned at 11:10. Members of the CCF caucus and others gathered around to congratulate her. She knew most of them already—George Castleden, Percy Wright, Sandy Nicholson, M.J. Coldwell, and Tommy Douglas were all from Saskatchewan, but Angus McInnis (BC) and Clarence Gillis (Cape Breton) also came over to shake her hand, and so did Conservative opposition leader Richard Hanson, and John Blackmore and Victor Quelch from New Democracy, and John Diefenbaker, a well-known Conservative lawyer from Prince Albert, Saskatchewan, who had been trying to get into politics for the last fifteen years and had finally made it. There were others, too, whom she didn't know. As the only woman, she was instantly recognizable, but, like a teacher on the first day of school, she still had many names and faces to learn.

Right from the beginning, Dorise had far more work than she had anticipated. The war, at a stalemate for months, would be all but lost that summer. After securing Denmark and Norway in April, Germany began its blitzkrieg into Holland, Belgium, and France on May 10. By the time the Canadian Parliament met on May 17, Holland had capitulated and near-panic reigned in the Canadian House of Commons. Each speaker who rose to respond to the Throne Speech acknowledged the gravity of the situation. James Sinclair, a new Liberal member from BC (later, father of Margaret Trudeau), called these "the darkest days since our nation was born."[10]

According to some reports, Holland had been betrayed by a group of German agents among the many Germans (some of them Jews) taking refuge in Holland. Could there be a similar "fifth column" in Britain? In Canada? During

World War I, Canada had interned more than 8000 German and East European nationals, but in 1939 she had chosen a more cautious and humane path. So far there had been no wholesale internments. But in the atmosphere of war hysteria, that policy could change at any moment.

Dorise's stand on the war continued to be cautious. Unlike the Communist Party, she never openly advocated withdrawal from the war. Her private thoughts can only be guessed. Perhaps she had come to believe, like many communists, that Britain would continue her appeasement policies and come to terms with Hitler without much of a fight. Then Germany would be free to continue her incursions on the Eastern Front. Whatever her thoughts on the war, Dorise saw herself as part of a great revolutionary movement that required disciplined collective action from all its members. Her first year in Parliament would be a severe test.

A few days after making her maiden speech, Nielsen was amazed and somewhat amused to receive an invitation to chat with the prime minister, himself, in private. A page brought her the note in the afternoon. "If you are to be in the House this evening till after 9, it would be a great pleasure to me to have the opportunity of visiting you personally." Should they meet in her office or his? He would leave that up to her. "I'm afraid all this sounds very much like an 'adventure'! I am only too sorry not to have had the chance to meet you at the beginning of the session."[11]

That evening she took the elevator down to the second floor and knocked on King's door at exactly nine-thirty. He answered the door himself and shook her hand very warmly. He was sorry to lose McIntosh, he said, but otherwise was very happy to have her in the House. He indicated two leather easy chairs where they could sit comfortably. It was a large room with long windows looking south over the lawn (though the drapes were closed now). She thought of her own cubbyhole on the sixth floor under the eaves. She had the same view—through a window the size of a porthole.

First he wanted to know about her background. Had she gone to university? No, she told him, nothing so grand. She had been a teacher. It was a training college for teachers she had attended. The papers must have given him the wrong impression. But she had learned a lot since then. Life experience was the best university, he agreed. He wanted to know about her experience living on relief. "You were the only candidate on relief in the whole election,"[12] he told her, and he listened attentively, occasionally nodding his head as she told him about the devastating effects of poverty and handouts. How a relief inspector had power to cut you off for any misdemeanour, how people suffered, sometimes died, for lack of a doctor.

Then he told her about his own experiences as a young man working at Hull House. He promised to send her a copy of his book, *Industry and Humanity*. And he would appreciate Nielsen's support in the House, he added, as if the thought had just occurred to him. Surely there was no point in antagonism when they clearly had so much in common. If she could see her way to an alliance with the Liberals, he believed he could use his influence to secure her a permanent position in some worthy organization, possibly the YWCA. Now she understood, very clearly, the reason for the visit. She was astonished. How smooth he was at co-opting any opposition! And what possible difference could it make if she supported the Liberals or not? They had a whopping majority as it was. What he wanted to do was buy her silence.[13]

That evening, when King dictated his thoughts on the day to his secretary, he mentioned that he had had a very pleasant talk with Mrs. Nielsen and that she struck him as a woman of real ability. He did not mention the offer to secure her a permanent position, but he recorded his promise to send her a copy of his book. A week later, he retrieved a copy of his book and inscribed it "To Mrs. D.W. Nielsen, M.P. on the occasion of her maiden speech in the House of Commons of Canada and with best wishes for her endeavours on behalf of *Industry and Humanity*."[14] He had not given up.

The House sat from three in the afternoon until eleven at night. In the mornings there was mail to answer and committee meetings to attend. Nielsen was receiving forty to sixty letters a day. The days were long and hot and she was exhausted. Once, as she left Parliament late after an evening sitting, a man standing outside at the bottom of the steps greeted her rather warmly. She smiled and said hello, thinking maybe she should know him—there were far too many faces to remember. He could be a journalist or another member, waiting for his ride. The next thing she knew, he moved closer and whispered: "Are you lonesome, sister?" She wanted to laugh. No, not lonesome, she thought, and not in the mood for anything but sleep. And she tucked the story away for Heide and the others at home.[15]

Through the summer of 1940, having no caucus to rely on, Dorise seldom missed a sitting. She was there for the announcement on June 10 that Norman Rogers, the Minister of National Defence, had just died in a plane crash on his way back from Toronto. She had sympathy for Mackenzie King that day as he broke the news, and then there was the family, the woman left with three children. She went down with the others a few days later when the coffin was set in the front lobby for a short memorial service. The sitting was shortened half an hour that day, otherwise they ploughed on as the Liberals pushed through bill after bill, granting the government massive appropriations and unheard-of power to fight the war.

Even worse than Mackenzie King's long-winded speeches were the constant "verbal spitballs" shot between the Liberal and Tory benches. The grimmer the war news, the more the Tories harped for King's resignation and demanded that the government crack down on "the fifth column." Some wanted all 16,643 Germans and Czechs who had registered as enemy aliens to be put in camps.[16] On June 10, when Italy entered the war, Italians were added to the list. How Dorise hated all this stirring-up of racial hatred and all the time wasted on useless quibbling.[17] The Liberals had a mandate to manage the war, to manage the country, just as they saw fit. There was no getting around that fact.

The earnestness of the western progressives often seemed out of place in Ottawa. Sandy Nicholson showed his snaps of children shoeless in the snow.[18] Dorise read snippets from letters she had received: the couple whose relief had been cut to four dollars a month, teachers describing conditions she knew so well—salaries unpaid, half a dozen books for the whole school—childhood accidents, and illnesses unattended until the parents feared imminent death.[19] What did this world have to do with war contracts and points of order and points of privilege? Poor George Castleden, the new member for Yorkton, was censured for reading his first speech.[20] Indeed, there were always some smirks on the opposite benches when the bumpkins spoke, and often many absentees.[21] It seemed the only way to accomplish anything here was by lobbying individual ministers.

"I had a short interview with Norman McLarty, Minister of Labour, the other day," Nielsen wrote to Violet McNaughton three weeks into the session. "He is going to send a federal and provincial inspector ... to see what things are really like in the northern part of my constituency."[22] Otherwise, she wrote, she found herself "letting things slip without expressing an opinion" because she was not yet used to the procedure. However, with some help from more experienced members of the CCF caucus, she soon learned. In four months of parliamentary debates that year, she rose fifteen times either to ask questions or to debate bills. And already she had discovered the advantages of having a secretary. Her letters to McNaughton were neatly typed on House of Commons stationery by Lilla Bell. Her parliamentary salary of $4000 was another boon. She was able to hire a housekeeper, and to repay a "little loan" from McNaughton and a much larger one taken several years before from her sister in England.

On the surface she was adjusting to life in Ottawa as well as any greenhorn, and better than some. Right from the beginning, she exuded a certain coolness that passed for confidence. "She has a calm assurance that fits her into the Ottawa scene as neatly as if she had always been there," observed a *Toronto Star* reporter.[23] But beneath the surface she must have been anything but calm. The Communist Party was under siege and any contacts she had were in jeopardy.

Despite police harassment for its anti-war stand, the party had run ten candidates in the March 26 election.[24] Soon after, communist leader Tim Buck, short of funds and unable to get material printed in Toronto, moved his base of operations to New York City.[25] Meanwhile, three communists were found guilty of distributing subversive materials in Toronto, and, as a result of their trial, in mid-May the Communist Party became illegal in Ontario. As the German army advanced into western Europe, more and more citizen groups demanded national action against all groups and individuals who opposed the war effort. Organizations such as the Lions Club, the Canadian Legion, and the Knights of Columbus demanded the arrest and detention of long lists of "subversive elements" from the German Bund to the Jehovah's Witnesses to the communists.[26] Dorise sat in the House, day after day, waiting for the axe to fall.

Finally, on June 6, using the War Measures Act, the federal government declared the Communist Party and its related organizations illegal. Under the Order-in-Council, any person who attended a meeting, distributed literature, or spoke in advocacy of such an organization could be arrested and interned without trial. Warrants for the arrest of known members were issued immediately. Some escaped the net, but before long 110 communists were picked up and interned in several camps where they shared premises with Germans,

Italians, domestic fascists, and some Quebecois who were also opposed to Canada's participation in the war.[27] Soon the most prominent internee would be the flamboyant mayor of Montreal, Camille Houde, who objected to the government's national registration program, declaring it a precursor of conscription for overseas service.

Canada was the only Western democracy to ban the Communist Party because of its opposition to the war. The British cabinet considered such a move but decided against it on the grounds that trade unionists would revolt just at a time when the war effort required all-out production. But in Britain, communists were not considered a foreign element as they were in Canada. Therefore, they did not suffer from the stirring-up of ethnic prejudice that accompanied the war here.

Of the Canadian communists who escaped arrest, a few took refuge in the US but most had already gone underground in Canada, where they moved from house to house for the next two years. Groups in Quebec were particularly adept at operating underground because they had experienced frequent persecution under Quebec's Padlock Law and had their networks ready. It was the underground leadership in Montreal, probably Leslie Morris and Stewart Smith, who kept in contact with Nielsen that first summer. Several times she was visited by a young woman who brought missives from the Montreal group.

Louise Harvey, née Smith, was twenty-eight, ten years younger than Dorise. Born into a wealthy family in Montreal, Louise had studied English at Wellesley College in Boston, and married a Montreal lawyer, Reg Harvey-Jellie. In the late 1930s the couple attended meetings of the Civil Liberties Association in Montreal and, through that group, secretly joined the Communist Party. Louise was the ideal courier for the CP's missives to Dorise. In Montreal it was the "foreign element" (largely Jewish) that the RCMP and provincial Red Squad pursued. She visited Nielsen at her home and sometimes stayed overnight. The two women became friends and kept up a correspondence until Nielsen's death, forty years later.[28]

What were the instructions that Nielsen received that summer of 1940? The only clues come from her parliamentary speeches. Her strategy that summer was to focus on issues of domestic welfare, particularly the plight of farmers facing low wheat prices and constituents who had had relief payments cut. And it was not difficult to find examples of other domestic needs, such as child and maternal health, areas that had been neglected for years and were now facing funding cuts to pay for the war. Essentially, her criticisms of government legislation, whether it was on relief payments, the budget, or emergency powers, were similar to those of the CCF. She demanded that no one should profit from the war and she opposed conscription without a plebiscite, even conscription for work on the domestic front. Like the CCF, she talked of equality of sacrifice—if labour were to be conscripted, wealth should be conscripted, too. No one should be making profits while others died. She repeated this mantra in speech after speech.

Did the Liberals dozing on the opposite benches, or the CCF sitting to her right, realize how far to the left she leaned? Probably not at this point. Several times, CCF members referred to her speeches favourably, and, during the budget debate in July, after Nielsen had taken her strongest stand yet, declaring that "this government has passed legislation to subjugate the Canadian people and to force them into both political and economic bondage,"[29] the Rev. Daniel McIvor, a sixty-seven-year-old Liberal backbencher from Fort William, remarked, "I count it an honour to be allowed to follow the lone, yet happy and brilliant lady member of this House." He went on to say there should be more of her kind, "provided that increase in numbers would not cause some of us to lose our seats."[30]

It is possible, of course, that McIvor had not been listening to Nielsen's speech at all and was simply in the habit of paying tribute to the ladies. Still, it's difficult to imagine his making such a remark if he suspected she were one of a band of subversives currently being rounded up by the RCMP. But it is also possible that the Rev. McIvor was not one of the more astute members of the Liberal caucus. He went on to praise the Minister of Finance for delivering the budget address "in such splendid form" that "very few members were reading their newspapers" and "very few members were sleeping."

According to Tommy Douglas, CCF member from Weyburn, Saskatchewan, who knew Nielsen as well as anyone in the House, she "was a woman of very considerable ability and in her first few months in Parliament made a good impression." It was only as time went on that he realized she was a committed communist. He cites her opposition to the war as being the telling clue to her allegiance.[31] No doubt, as the CCF warmed to the war effort, Nielsen's outspoken criticism of everything connected to the war became more obvious.

But by this time Mackenzie King, who had a deep hatred for communism and communists, had already turned against Nielsen. On June 20, a month after their very pleasant talk, he changed his mind about her. That day his Minister of Agriculture, Jimmy Gardiner,[32] handed him a note from one of his contacts in Saskatchewan. Mrs. Nielsen was a communist, it said, and so was her husband. King said he was not surprised to hear that—all her going on about living on relief had raised his suspicions. He had the letter sent to the Department of Justice for investigation.[33]

It was a long hot summer, with the session lasting until August 7. Even in June Dorise found the weather abominable and told Violet McNaughton that she was always sleepy. Although she added that the children were doing well, it is hard to imagine that family life was blissful with Dorise absent until close to midnight four nights a week and exhausted the rest of the time. Getting and keeping a housekeeper to play the role of mother as well as maid was not easy.

By the end of July, Nielsen realized that she could not manage the daily care of her children any longer. For the next school year, she arranged to board the children with Anne and Bill Polaski on their farm at Norbury. The children's holiday that summer would be a leisurely drive to Saskatchewan in the car Nielsen had just purchased from her secretary, Lilla Bell, with Lilla herself as chauffeur. Nielsen had no time for holidays. Agnes Macphail was running for Parliament in the Saskatoon by-election and Dorise had promised to campaign for her.

A souvenir of the brief time the children spent in Ottawa is a family photo taken by Yousuf Karsh on a hot afternoon in late July. Karsh, at thirty-two, was on the verge of making his reputation with a widely reproduced photo of Winston Churchill. That spring he had photographed all eighty-five new Members of Parliament. Dorise liked his work, but she was not in the mood for a photo that day. She had to dress and the children had to be dressed and then marched down the street to a scenic spot along the canal. It was too hot for all that fuss. She decided not to wear a bra. Who would know the difference? Christine, eleven years old, but already playing mother, was appalled. She knew you didn't wear a good dress without a bra. It simply wasn't done.[34]

There were standards, obviously, that she had learned from her mother, standards of correct behaviour, of what to do and how to dress, of thank yous to be said, and letters answered promptly. And now her mother was breaking her own rules. Years later Christine would look at the photo and laugh about the bra—Dorise got away with it, after all, and no one knew the difference. But it would be a long time before she could take her mother's behaviour so lightly. For years she would hold Dorise accountable for the unhappiness of those years, in the desperate way children have of searching out the source of their pain and discovering that parents are flawed and weak, sometimes hypocritical, and only human, after all. The summer of 1940, the process was only beginning.

Dorise took the train west immediately after the session ended early in August. Agnes Macphail was waiting in Saskatoon, impatient for her to arrive. The United Reform executive had refused to begin Macphail's campaign without Nielsen. Macphail had been impressed by the executive at first, but was beginning to suspect that the three people who were holding everything up were communists.[35] She had had quite enough of communists in the Ontario CCF, and wondered how on earth she would work with this group if she were elected. But she realized that winning the election was unlikely. The United Reform group had hardly a cent to its name (this was its third campaign in less than a year) and this time the Conservatives had decided to run a candidate, so she wouldn't have the Reverend Brown's advantage of a strictly two-way race. Besides, she was a flown-in candidate, and even if everyone knew her by reputation, that did matter.

At this point Agnes Macphail was fifty years old and jobless. She had been a rural schoolteacher in Ontario before becoming the first woman elected to Parliament in 1921. Since then she had been an outstanding crusader for social justice. She had run first for the United Farmers of Ontario (UFO), and had brought that organization into the CCF. When the UFO withdrew from the CCF, she had continued on as an independent. Everyone in Saskatoon knew of Macphail, and many admired her. On August 19 she lost to the Conservative candidate by only 741 votes, far ahead of the four other candidates. The loss was a mixed blessing—she still had no job and no pension, but at least she could say goodbye to the United Reformers. By this time she was certain members of the executive were communists, and, although she liked Nielsen personally, "it was obvious that she was a communist, too."[36]

Nevertheless, Macphail and Lilla Bell agreed to tour Nielsen's riding before they headed off for a holiday on the west coast. Bob Paul drove Lilla Bell's old Ford from farm to farm so that they could see local conditions for themselves. The poverty was worse than anything Macphail had ever imagined. She described the Nielsen house as "no better than a henhouse." Stewart Paul remembers the two women coming home with his dad. Macphail was weeping and trying to give money to the children who crowded into the house to see her.

The thrill of meeting Agnes Macphail was one bright spot in a summer of desperate activity for Bob Paul and Dorise and other communists in northern Saskatchewan. Despite having the popular Macphail as candidate, they had lost the election in Saskatoon. Further north, Maynard Woollard, the communist organizer, was moving from house to house (and sometimes from barn to barn), just one step ahead of the RCMP. Then Nelson Clarke and Harold Miller were expelled from the CCF for being communists.[37] Dorise continued to deny she was a communist, presenting herself as a grassroots socialist, accountable only to the people who elected her, but it was obvious from the searches of her friends' homes that the RCMP was gathering material to use against her.[38] In the pursuit of Woollard, they had seized two books: *The Teachings of Karl Marx* and *Women Under Communism and Socialism.* Both, unfortunately, bore the inscription "Please return to D.W. Nielsen."[39] But the police seemed to be more interested in a one-page flier she had had printed in the thousands, entitled *Why I Opposed the Budget.* Copies of it were being confiscated from coast to coast.

In the constituency, Bob Paul worked furiously to hold together the United Progressive coalition. A number of meetings that fall focussed on the wheat problem, all of them a buildup to two conferences in October, one in Saskatoon, the other in Regina. Percy Wright (CCF MP) and O.W. Valleau (CCF MLA), both of Melfort, were listed as sponsors of these events along with Nielsen. So were Frank Eliason and George Bickerton of the United Farmers of Canada (UFC), but there is no evidence that the CCF or any farm organizations participated officially in the conferences or supported the eight resolutions passed.[40] It is likely that the word was out that the conferences were a new forum for the communists. Even if the wheat crisis was real, the CCF was determined to distance itself from such initiatives.

Still, the small band of communists ploughed ahead and garnered a good deal of grassroots support. Dorise estimated she travelled 8000 kilometres that fall.[41] In Medstead, some farmers came more than 150 kilometres to hear her at the largest rally ever held in that district.[42] In Biggar the RCMP reported that the majority of the 200 people who came to her meeting "were of British descent and fairly well-to-do farmers" who stomped their feet and clapped whenever she criticized the government.[43] This should not have come as a surprise. Late in the summer of 1940, the government had fuelled the flames of protest by announcing its latest solution to the wheat surplus: farmers would be allowed to market only five bushels per acre. The rest would have to be stored on the farm for sale later.

In response to protests from all sectors of the grain trade, the minister responsible came west to make a personal survey of the situation and ended up raising the quota to eight bushels per acre and promising cash advances against farm-stored grain. His announcement may have taken some of the wind out of Nielsen's sails. Still, in October Nielsen presided over wheat conferences in Saskatoon and Regina. After long deliberations delegates called for a moratorium on all secured debt (no more foreclosures on farms), open trials for all those interned, parity prices for farm products, and $1.25 a bushel for the first 3000 bushels of wheat delivered by each farmer.

The *Western Producer* carried a detailed account of the Saskatoon conference, but the mainstream media was not impressed. The *Star-Phoenix* criticized the Saskatoon conference, saying "no adequate remedy for the farm emergency was suggested, save … the adoption of stock resolutions"[44] and the *Winnipeg Free Press* went even further, saying "it is wrong to believe that the solution lies in government hand-outs (for that is what $1.25 a bushel would be)." Already, in one year, the government had increased taxes by 66 percent. "Imagine what would happen," the *Free Press* article said, "if we diverted $200 million [from the budget] and gave it to Canadian agriculture."[45]

Later, when she spoke to a Winnipeg rally, Nielsen used the *Free Press* editorial to good advantage. "Yes," she said, "I can imagine what would happen. I can imagine these men and women who have toiled for years to build a home would have a feeling of security, would have a feeling that they could carry on. They could pay their taxes. They could help to keep their schools going. They could maintain themselves as decent Canadian citizens. That is what would happen."[46]

Indeed, in the summer of 1940, with wheat pegged at seventy cents a bushel, it was a stretch to imagine it selling for $1.25, and perhaps even whispering the words in wartime made some people feel downright unpatriotic. But the inspiration for much farm militancy throughout the thirties and forties came not from Moscow but from the US, where, in 1933, Roosevelt's Agricultural Adjustment Act had incorporated the idea of parity prices for farm products. What this meant was that as the price index for other products increased, so should the price for agricultural products. Thus, farmers would be assured of an adequate and stable living. In 1936, researchers at the University of Saskatchewan decided that the parity price for wheat was actually $1.06.[47] The issue of parity prices had been around for over ten years, and had been supported by many organizations including the Wheat Pools, the United Farmers of Canada, and the CCF. If the price Nielsen and her friends advocated seemed outrageously high, it is significant that no one in the West thought seventy cents a bushel was adequate. All farmers agreed that a farm emergency existed.

As Percy Wright (CCF Melfort) explained in the House that fall, only the really big farmers could exist on seventy-cent wheat. In fact, he called it fifty-cent wheat because it was worth seventy cents a bushel only once it was delivered to the port of Fort William (Thunder Bay). Wright and Nielsen, both representing constituencies in northern Saskatchewan, were concerned about all those farmers on quarter- and half-sections who couldn't make a living under current conditions and whose municipalities were too broke to provide even the most rudimentary services. Percy Wright cited a case of an indigent man who had once been a homesteader. In 1940 he was badly in need of medical care, but his municipality already owed the local hospital thousands of dollars, so the man remained alone in his shack, unable to care for himself. "If I had a dog or a horse who was starving to death and this were reported by a neighbour," said Wright, "they would have me reported for cruelty to animals."[48]

Many of the farmers in Wright's constituency and in Nielsen's were still going further into debt each year. These were the families whose plight made Agnes Macphail weep. When the wheat surplus ended in 1943 and the government was forced to offer $1.25 a bushel in order to fulfil its export commitments, some of these families had given up farming for good. The young had joined the armed services while their parents had found work in other provinces. But in the fall of 1940, Nielsen's solutions to saving the family farm appeared too stale to some and too radical to others. "The West is entitled to better leadership than it is getting from Mrs. Nielsen and her friends," said the *Winnipeg Free Press* in October.

Records on the Communist Party of Canada available through the Soviet Archives do not mention Nielsen until early in 1941. In January 1941 William Ross, a young communist living underground in Winnipeg, typed a four-page report on "The Anti-War Role of Mrs. Dorise Nielson [*sic*], United Progressive Member of the Canadian Parliament from the West." In it he summarized the platform on which she was elected, quoted her maiden speech and favourable newspaper reports, and noted that "outside Parliament Mrs. Nielson has been extremely active in developing a mass movement for the needs of the toilers." He went on say that "from a number of indirect indications, there seems to be absolutely no question that the CP forces are directly, although quietly co-operating with Mrs. Nielson."[49] The same themes were picked up in a Comintern report on Canada, written a few months later, which described Nielsen as the only voice raised in Parliament "on behalf of the workers and the farmers.... In the industrial centers she speaks at meetings in the largest halls seating 18 to 20 thousand people. The CCF, naturally, regrets the day it gave her support in elections."[50]

The Comintern report may have exaggerated the numbers present at Nielsen's meetings and ignored other voices raised on behalf of workers and farmers, but it was correct about the CCF regrets. The CCF press had begun to ignore Nielsen and to warn members to avoid her meetings.[51] Now, even if she were willing to cooperate with the CCF, she had lost that opportunity. She was fully in the communist camp now, and that camp was largely underground, with only a few brave or foolhardy groups operating on the surface. Nielsen and her United Progressive group in Saskatchewan were one. Another was the staff of the *Canadian Tribune*, a weekly newspaper published in Toronto since January 1940, a month after the Communist Party's *Clarion* had been closed down for violating the Defence of Canada Regulations (DOCR).

The RCMP had been watching the *Tribune* since its inception, but so far it had been steering a very careful course. Calling itself "a journal of democratic opinion," the paper had six names on its list of editors, only one of whom had been clearly identified with communist causes before, and that was Alexander Albert MacLeod, former head of the League Against War and Fascism. The paper reprinted articles from Britain and the US as well as from Canadian papers, publicized arrests under the DOCR, and published, in full, all Nielsen's speeches in the House of Commons. It even gathered all the speeches together into a booklet called *Democracy Must Live*, available for only ten cents. Printing Nielsen's speeches was one way to get the word out without fear of contravening the DOCR. All speeches in Parliament are privileged—one cannot be sued or prosecuted for something said in the House of Commons. So the two groups of communists operating on the surface were closely linked, and the whole underground system, whether it was William Ross moving from house to house in Winnipeg, or Leslie Morris holding clandestine meetings in Montreal, or Tim Buck sending missives from New York, was depending on Nielsen to deliver its message.

But by the end of October, she had done her best and it was time to return to Ottawa for another session. She left Bob Paul in charge of the riding. In addition, along with the communists in Saskatoon, he was writing for a new monthly newspaper called the *Western Farmer*.

One day Bob drove her out to the Polaskis' so she could say goodbye to the children. The Polaski house was more crowded than ever now that the Nielsen children had moved in. At night, when the daybed was spread out for them to sleep (all three together in one bed), there was hardly space for the Polaski sons to climb the ladder to their attic bedroom. But it was the best Dorise could do for the moment. The Nielsen farm was gone—sold for taxes that summer—and Pete Nielsen was gone, too. He had joined the Veterans Guard. The house had been hastily cleared out before school started. Each child had grabbed a treasure, and Dorise had arranged to store a few pieces of furniture. Already the house and all its contents smelled of mice and mildew.[52]

That fall she had seen her children less than she would have liked and now there would be a long separation until Christmas. Still, it was a brusque goodbye, no lingering, no tears. She hated emotional goodbyes; she didn't trust emotions that could not be turned into actions. She had provided for the children as best she could, and the Polaskis would be better off this year because of their boarders. She would write to the children and to Annie Polaski, and hope that someone would take the time to write back. There were no telephones nearby, so letters would have to do.

Defoe Road, Stoke Newington, where Dorise was born. (Courtesy: Elizabeth Kerstetter, 2003)

Kyverdale Road, Stoke Newington, where Dorise lived until emigrating to Canada. (Courtesy: Robert Wong)

Dorise Nielsen with Sally, and Peter Nielsen with Christine, beside their homestead with its additional room. Norbury, 1931. (Courtesy: Sally Nielsen)

Peter Nielsen with Christine. Norbury, c. 1935. (Courtesy: Sally Nielsen)

Christine, John, and Sally Nielsen, with kittens. Norbury, 1935. (Courtesy: Sally Nielsen)

Dorise Nielsen's election pamphlet, 1940. (Courtesy: Eva Phelps)

Tommy Douglas, a rural minister elected to Parliament in 1935. He later served as premier of Saskatchewan from 1944 to 1960, and then as federal leader of the New Democratic Party from 1961 to 1972. On extreme left, M.J. Coldwell, CCF federal leader from 1942 to 1960. (Saskatchewan Archives Board, R–B28772–2)

James Shaver Woodsworth, a Methodist minister, social worker, and politician, who served as federal leader of the CCF from 1933 to 1941. (Saskachewan Archives Board, R–B5801–1)

George Williams, one of the founders of the Saskatchewan CCF, who served as its leader from 1935 to 1941. (Saskatchewan Archives Board, R–A723–2)

Dorise Nielsen with Sally, John, and Christine. Colonel By Drive, Ottawa, 1940. (National Archives of Canada, Karsh Collection, E1913587)

Peter Nielsen was a member of the Veterans Guard from 1941 to 1945. (Courtesy: Robert Wong)

Dorise Nielsen. Ottawa, 1940. (National Archives of Canada, Karsh Collection, E000945410)

Leaders of the Communist Party of Canada who gave themselves up in Toronto, September 1942. Front row: Henri Gagnon, Fred Rose, Tim Buck, Emery Samuel, Sam Lipshitz. Back row: Gus Sundqvist, William Kashtan, Evariste Dubé, Jim Litterick, Sam Carr, Willie Fortin, Stewart Smith, and Stanley Ryerson. (University of Toronto Library, Thomas Fisher Rare Book Library, Kenny Collection F3218)

The Paul family: Douglas, Cecil, Stewart, and Bob, at the Polaski farm. Norbury, c. 1944. (Courtesy: Sally Nielsen)

Violet McNaughton, farm activist and women's editor of the Western Producer, c. 1935. (Chambury Studio, Saskatoon. Courtesy: Saskatoon Public Library, Local History Room)

Heidi Vockeroth, a friend of Dorise Nielsen's and supporter of the United Progressive campaign, Saskatoon, 1947. (Courtesy: Robert Vockeroth)

6

ESCAPING THE NET

As you are aware, every endeavour is being made to obtain the necessary evidence against Dorise W. Nielson [*sic*] to support a charge under the Defence of Canada Regulations.[1]

NIELSEN RETURNED TO OTTAWA in November 1940, fully conscious of her responsibilities. All summer the RCMP had been rounding up party members. Over a hundred were interned in a camp near Petawawa, a short distance from Ottawa. In the West, leaders of the Ukrainian Farmer-Labour Temple Association (UFLTA), a party affiliate, were interned in Kananaskis, Alberta. The UFLTA had been careful not to campaign against the war, fearing massive deportations, but its caution had got it nowhere. The UFLTA properties had been seized, its leadership put out of commission, and a major source of funds for the underground Communist Party had dried up overnight.[2]

Dorise knew she had become the chief spokesperson for an increasingly unpopular group. She must have realized that her own activities might lead to prison or internment, but it's doubtful she knew just how close she came. That summer the RCMP discovered it would be difficult to present definitive evidence that Nielsen was a member of the Communist Party. Some informants said she was; others said she was not.[3] The most damning evidence they could come up with was a document, likely written by the leader of the Saskatchewan branch of the CPC, that had been seized during the arrest of a CP member. Written in January 1940, before the election, it described Nielsen as being a thoroughly reliable member, although her membership was secret. This document was quoted again and again in reports passed on to RCMP Commissioner

Wood, to Justice Minister Lapointe, and to Mackenzie King himself. Still, it was considered not quite damning enough. They would have to find another way.

By the end of the summer, the attorneys-general of both Alberta and Saskatchewan were amassing evidence to prosecute her under the Defence of Canada Regulations. The Department of Justice concurred that Nielsen's leaflet, *Why I Opposed the Budget*, breached the DOCR because it went beyond her speech in the Commons by calling on Canadians to protest the budget. All that was needed was a clear indication that she had been involved in the printing and distribution of the leaflet. On October 26, as she was making her way back to Ottawa, the police raided a printing firm in Toronto and found evidence that she had ordered the leaflet and paid for it. This was not information she had ever tried to hide. In fact, the police already possessed a letter, seized in another raid, in which Dorise had written that she was having 100,000 more copies of her leaflet printed and she would send them to Edmonton as soon as possible.[4]

It was a short session that fall. Mackenzie King had not wanted to call Parliament back at all. He and his ministers had been working overtime since the spring to mobilize Canada's war industries, put in place the Commonwealth Air Training Plan, and negotiate a defence agreement with the United States. That summer a furious air battle had raged over Britain and the German invasion of Britain appeared imminent. If Britain were to fight on, she would have to replace pilots and air crew. If she were defeated, Canada would need the American alliance for self-defence. It was only under heavy pressure from the opposition that King called for a parliamentary session in November.

The session lasted only a month, but its timing could not have been better for Dorise. Parliament gave her a platform, and soon the RCMP pursuit of Mrs. Nielsen was making headlines. In her one opportunity to speak that session, she began by lambasting the DOCR. Her speech relied heavily on a recent editorial by B.K. Sandwell, editor of *Saturday Night*. Fifteen hundred people had been interned under the DOCR. Surely they had a right to know what their offences were? Surely they should have the right to confront the witnesses against them? What had happened to British justice? Nielsen even quoted Colonel George Drew, the Tory opposition leader of Ontario: "If we are prepared to shed our blood to preserve democracy, we should try to make it work under stress of war."

And then came the surprise. Nielsen had decided on a pre-emptive strike in her own defence. "Certain people," she said, "have been arrested merely because they have in their possession literature of a certain kind." A bookstore owner in BC had been charged. Possibly she would be next. "During the recess reports were brought to me that the provincial police were going round the country looking for a certain little leaflet I had had printed.... I would have given it to them with the greatest pleasure, because it was nothing but an open letter to the Canadian people giving in condensed form what I had said in the debate on the budget," but, instead of coming to her, the police "travelled miles through the north country, visiting house after house asking for leaflets, and stirring up fear and apprehension."

"Shame," called out one honourable member. She had gained some sympathy. Perhaps she would be able to persuade the Department of Justice to back off. Her speech picked up steam and she grew less cautious. "In Germany ... the cry of 'Jew, Jew' was raised. In Canada, if certain people want to discredit anyone, they do not raise the cry of 'Jew', they raise the cry of 'red, red'."[5] It would not be the last time she would compare Canada to Nazi Germany, but she was not the only one pumping up the rhetoric. A few days earlier Coldwell had castigated both Mackenzie King and opposition leader Hanson for collusion in attempting to avoid calling Parliament: "I would remind them both that this is still a free parliament and not a fascist grand council or a nazi reichstag, to be assembled or dismissed at the will of any member of this house no matter how high the office he may hold."[6]

Soon, the wrangle between Mrs. Nielsen and the RCMP had made the front pages. "Woman Fights for Freedom" read the *Globe and Mail.* Mrs. Nielsen, it said, had performed a valuable public service that no male MP had dared to do. It commended her for her "effective exposé of the wrong-headed obscurantism of the police authorities and of the methods employed by them."[7]

But even before Nielsen's exposé, the plan to prosecute her was beginning to flag. The agent of the Attorney-General of Saskatchewan, it seems, was not content with the evidence amassed so far. He wanted a watertight case before charging her. A search of Mrs. Nielsen's parliamentary office, he believed, might turn up even more evidence to connect her to the leaflet. The request was passed from the RCMP in Saskatchewan to headquarters in Ottawa. There, someone scrawled in the margin, "nothing more likely to bring a hornet's nest down on our heads." Any pursuit of Nielsen would have to be authorized right from the top, he wrote, from the Director of Criminal Investigation.[8] And that never happened. Soon all the documents seized from the Toronto printers (and from the office of the weekly *Canadian Tribune*) were returned. Even the copies of *Why I Opposed the Budget* were carefully given back to the various individuals and organizations from whom they had been seized. Orders were issued that copies of a longer booklet containing several of Nielsen's speeches, called *Democracy Must Live* (already in its third printing), were not suspect and should not be confiscated. In her own defence, Mrs. Nielsen had obviously won the first round.

But there were still a hundred communists in detention and the campaign against the DOCR continued. In December Dorise skipped the last two days of the session and took the train to Montreal. She wore a new dress with lace-trimmed cuffs and a felt hat set at a jaunty angle. Unlike Agnes Macphail, who had initially been criticized for her dowdiness, Dorise needed no advice on how to dress well. All she needed was a bit of money. And she knew from the beginning that if you are a woman, no matter how important your message, the audience will still take note of your clothes.

The party had been busy activating its usual networks of support in civil rights and labour circles. The first evening in Montreal, Nielsen spoke at a banquet for 250, sponsored by the Canadian Civil Liberties Union, Montreal Branch. The following night, she was one of two featured speakers for a larger public meeting held in the Atwater Market and sponsored by the same group. Over 2000 people, thirty-four of them plainclothed police officers,[9] turned out to hear Nielsen and J.L. Cohen, a well-known left-wing Toronto lawyer who had taken on the defence of both the communist internees and the Jehovah's Witnesses.[10]

The next day it was on to Toronto, where she took tea with society women at the University Club, appropriately decorated for the occasion with pink mums. It was a gala occasion. All the leaders of women's organizations turned up. The list of guests took up several columns in the *Toronto Star*. That evening she was greeted by more than 8000 people at Maple Leaf Gardens. It was clear the majority had come to hear Nielsen. Though they had to wait two hours while other speakers held the floor, she was still given a rousing welcome.[11] The thrust of all these meetings (the next day there was another in Oshawa) was to rally those opposed to the DOCR into a new organization, a grassroots "people's movement" for the defence of democracy. A similar campaign was being launched by the Communist Party in Britain.

While in Toronto, Nielsen stayed in the home of A.A. MacLeod, editor of the *Canadian Tribune*, who had chaired and organized the meeting in Maple Leaf Gardens. Nielsen and MacLeod had much to discuss. The "people's movement" was to be a national campaign. MacLeod was the organizer and Nielsen, the featured speaker. A series of mass meetings had to be arranged in the West before the next parliamentary session began in late February.

MacLeod was a more seasoned hand than Nielsen, and others in the party speculate that he became her mentor.[12] Certainly Nielsen became a close friend of A.A. and his wife, Virginia, and she and A.A. cooperated on a number of ventures, particularly while the leadership of the party was underground. Both Albert and Virginia MacLeod were originally from Cape Breton, but, at the time of their marriage in 1930, they were living in the United States. After service in World War I, MacLeod had worked for the YMCA in Halifax and then Chicago. Later he moved to New York City as executive editor of a socialist-pacifist magazine called the *World Tomorrow*. Among its editors was the theologian Reinhold Niebuhr, with whom MacLeod exchanged philosophical letters after his return to Canada.[13]

While working in New York, A.A. had met once again the vivacious Virginia MacLean. Both A.A. and Virginia were pacifists and supporters of the Socialist Party in the US at that time. Several factors soon pushed them into the communist camp. One was the case of the Scotsboro Boys. In 1931, two white American women claimed to have been raped on a train by twelve black men. In short order, nine black youths were arrested, tried, and found guilty. Eight of them, two only fourteen years old, were condemned to death. The Communist Party of the USA became heavily involved in the campaign for a retrial. Virginia joined the communist-sponsored Defence League for the Scotsboro Boys.[14] The other issues pushing the MacLeods further left were poverty and anti-fascism. MacLeod first appears in the RCMP files the summer of 1933 when he campaigned for J.B. McLachlan, veteran union leader among Cape Breton miners and candidate of the Nova Scotia legislature.[15] By 1934, when A.A. became involved in setting up the League Against War and Fascism in Toronto, both he and Virginia were party members.

Dinners in the MacLeod household were formal affairs, even though guests other than Nielsen were rare. They were very much an orderly, middle-class, Canadian family, settled comfortably in a semi-detached house near Bathurst and Bloor. Nielsen would sit at the dining-room table, a queenly figure, always perfectly groomed and controlled. If there was any tension, any worry about police raids, the MacLeod children remained unaware of it. Nielsen was simply a friend of their parents who liked to talk about her own children.[16]

Like Nielsen, the MacLeods were never in the inner circle of the party, but their talents and their credibility in the Anglo community made them useful public figures. As well as heading the Canadian League Against War and Fascism, MacLeod also played an important role in the Committee to Aid Spanish Democracy. He was instrumental in getting Norman Bethune and the volunteers in the Mackenzie-Papineau Battalion to Spain and home again. In 1940 his assignment was to navigate the perilous waters of the Defence of Canada Regulations and keep the *Canadian Tribune* afloat, and so far he'd pulled it off. In all his efforts, Mac was a superb organizer and speaker. He also had a notable ability to raise funds. The night of Nielsen's speech in Maple Leaf Gardens, he managed to cajole $1700 from the crowd.

Despite her worries about arrest, this was a heady time for Nielsen and her growing friendship with the sophisticated MacLeods was only part of it. The press was still on her side. In Toronto and Montreal the crowds had come out and listened and cheered her. In Montreal, a furrier had presented her with a raccoon coat. But, most importantly, she was doing the big job she had been assigned, and so far she was doing it surprisingly well.

When Dorise arrived at the Polaskis' in December 1940, smelling of lavender and wearing her amazing fur coat, her children expected, somehow, that all would be well. Christine, almost twelve and at constant loggerheads with Annie Polaski, was particularly anxious to see her parents. I met Christine in Ottawa almost fifty years after that Christmas, but she remembered it well—the feel of that fabulous coat, the hopes, the disappointments. She had raised five children herself by the time I met her, and had some sympathy for her mother.

The first calamity that December happened shortly after Dorise's return from the East. One cold afternoon, when Annie had shooed the children out of the house so that she could rest, they headed off to the fields to slide down a haystack with their pieces of cardboard. Johnny ran ahead, clambered up to the top, and dropped three metres to the frozen ground on the other side. He had fractured his right thigh. Getting help took a long time. From Spiritwood, Bill Polaski managed to reach Dorise by phone. She, in turn, phoned a doctor in Prince Albert and set out for the Polaski farm. They both arrived after midnight to find a feverish six-year-old with a badly swollen leg. Over the next three months, John would have two surgeries, one to reset his leg, the other to remove a metal plate.[17]

But Johnny's accident wasn't the only problem that Christmas, at least not as far as Christine was concerned. Dorise was set on sending her to a convent school in Prince Albert, and Annie Polaski agreed. She simply couldn't handle a girl who was twelve going on twenty, so determined to skip out and have fun with her friends. Christine dug in her heels. She was sure her father would take her side. But he wasn't there—that was the problem. He came only for a day, carefully avoiding Dorise, and then was off again. Christine promised she'd behave. She'd rather stay at the Polaskis' any day than be sent so far away from home. But it was a problem that had to be settled, and Dorise didn't have the patience for fusses when there were so many other matters needing her attention. She thought there was nothing wrong with a good boarding school. So what if it were Catholic? Christine could take the religious part with a grain of salt and get a far better education than she was getting at Tinson School, she was sure.

"I was a difficult child," Christine admitted, thinking back to that year. "I was unhappy, and I blamed my mother." After Christmas in 1940, she went to the convent in Prince Albert, and she hated it. "In hindsight, I realize that they took good care of me, but I didn't see it that way at the time."[18] For Christine, a search for love and security began that Christmas and continued for a very long time. When I met her, she was living in Ottawa and working as a counsellor to women with addictions. On her dining-room table she'd stacked several sets of her mother's letters. I read through them while she made scrambled eggs for our lunch. Then she played me a tape of Dorise giving a lecture in a lovely musical voice, much like her own.

In January 1941, Dorise took Christine to Prince Albert for the opening of the school term. She had time for one more visit there that term. She was involved in a speaking tour that began on the west coast and wound back to various points in Saskatchewan and on to Winnipeg. Then she was off to Ottawa for the opening of the session in mid-February. Christine remembered spending that one-day visit with her mother at Holy Cross Hospital where Johnny was still in traction. Dorise was in a whirlwind of activity that winter, and the RCMP was still hot on her heels. All she could do was deal with each problem as it came along. She was being pulled in too many directions at once. If she thought for a moment that her children faced, for the first time, separation not only from their parents but from each other, she likely figured she had no choice. And hadn't she been sent off for months every summer when she was younger than Christine? The one she worried about was Johnny, barely six years old, alone and in pain. She supposed that Sally, who was more docile than Christine, would manage well enough at the Polaskis'.

Nielsen's speaking tour, which had been carefully arranged by A.A. MacLeod, was a great success. She visited nine cities in three weeks, speaking on local radio stations and in theatres and halls that were jammed to overflowing. At Winnipeg's Walker Theatre, she spoke for two hours to an estimated 2500 people. Two hundred had to be seated on the stage and many were turned away.[19]

Several RCMP constables were present at every meeting. A.A. was quick to point them out, in a joking way, and Dorise tried to take it all in the same spirit. The tour began with a widely advertised meeting sponsored by the Civil Liberties Union, which attracted about 2000 people to the Vancouver auditorium. MacLeod had placed an empty chair on the stage to emphasize the absence of Wilfed Ravenor, the Vancouver bookseller who had been arrested under the Defence of Canada Regulations. His dramatic ploy worked. Members of the audience pulled $591 from their pockets for the Ravenor Defence Fund.[20] At another meeting in Vancouver, sponsored by the Housewives League, the RCMP reported that 200 or more Housewives were so excited at entertaining such a distinguished visitor that they forgot to take up the customary collection. After meetings in Nanaimo and Victoria, Nielsen made her way to Edmonton, where over 1500 people jammed the Grand Theatre. The RCMP reported that "representatives of every class of citizen were present . . . though judging by the appearance and enthusiasm of those in attendance . . . the great majority were of the radical element."[21] However, the meeting did open with "O Canada" and close with "God Save the Queen," and the mayor himself was on the platform to welcome Nielsen.

MacLeod chaired all the major meetings and, unlike the Housewives, he never forgot the customary collection. Other fundraisers were the sale of Nielsen's pamphlet *Democracy Must Live* and of the January 4 edition of the *Canadian Tribune*, which featured a full-page New Year's message from Nielsen to the Canadian people. It appears that sales of these items were brisk, with 300 copies of the pamphlet sold at the Edmonton meeting alone and another 5000 placed with an Alberta distributor. The RCMP noted that Nielsen said nothing in her speeches that was more subversive than what she had already written in her pamphlet and New Year's address. The gist of all her speeches was the same—criticism of the Defence of Canada Regulations and a call for a national "people's movement" to preserve democracy in Canada.

With numerous reports forwarded to Ottawa from points west, RCMP officials realized that Nielsen was attempting to reconstitute the Communist Party under a new name. And there was great concern that she was gaining support from people who had no idea of her "communist leanings." The RCMP chief for Saskatchewan, who had recently ordered that under no circumstances were Nielsen's pamphlets to be confiscated, had a new suggestion for her entrapment. "Could not this woman be asked in the House of Parliament as to whether she is or has been a member of the Communist Party?" Then, he suggested, when she denied the accusation, certain documents could be produced that would prove her wrong. But higher authorities in the RCMP and the Department of Justice did not agree.[22] Perhaps they realized that criticizing the government, even in wartime, would not be viewed as treasonous by most Canadians. (The newspapers were full of other critics and none of them were prosecuted.) Or perhaps exposing Nielsen was not worth the risk of exposing their own informants within the communist movement.

Meanwhile, in northern Saskatchewan, some of Nielsen's non-communist supporters were not happy with her role as national spokesperson for "the radical element." In February Heide Vockeroth wrote Nielsen of this and other things from her current teaching post at Blaine Lake. Nielsen replied from Ottawa in a handwritten letter. It was after nine on Monday evening, February

24. C.D. Howe, Minister of Munitions and Supply, was answering a question on the Bren gun contract and Nielsen, obviously bored by the very dry debate, decided to make use of her time to raise Heide's spirits and shore up her political alignmnent. "Don't ever write me such a pessimistic letter again," she wrote, and she went on to give the numbers of people who had attended her meetings in the East before Christmas and more recently in the West. "They didn't come just to see what hat I was wearing," she assured Heide. "They are tired of poverty, meager meals, poor clothes, anxiety and destitution, especially when they hear of 3¼ billion being spent on the armaments of death." It was worth all the fatigue to see "the conscience of the people stirring," but maybe "in the backwaters of Saskatchewan these things are difficult to realize."[23]

The letter is typical of Nielsen. It is a guarded letter, a letter that deliberately strikes an optimistic note, as if she has assigned herself the role of cheerleader. Even when she turns, just for a moment, to her personal life and confides her own worry about Johnny ("That leg is going to hurt plenty when he starts to walk on it.") and goes on to say how much she misses her children, she is essentially giving herself a pep talk. "Buck up woman, the show must go on," she seems to be telling herself. And the show she refers to, first and always, is the political show. If the personal must be set aside for the moment—so be it.

The next Monday, another letter from home arrived. It was postmarked Meadow Lake and written by James Hatton, the man who led the Social Credit faction in the United Progressive coalition. It was a letter of warning. In it Hatton cited threats from two local RCMP officers.

"Sergeant Major Hill is quite astonished at the attitude you take regarding the war regulations," wrote Hatton. "He thinks you are very foolish to proceed as you are doing. In fact he got quite hot and said: 'The D. fool can't she see that the same law will put her behind the wires ... she'll be there before long if she keeps up the pace she's hitting for they'll frame up something somehow.... She should remember she's not a lawyer and she may leave a loop hole somewhere and if she does, in she goes.... First thing she knows she'll be down there keeping Houde of Montreal company.'" According to Hatton, a younger officer also told him that "while in training they were told to keep their eyes and ears open for anything on Nielsen."

Hatton himself warned Nielsen that she was losing prestige among some of her most ardent supporters because people were becoming more war-minded.

He thought she should tone down her criticisms of the DOCR, or, he feared, the movement would crumble and all their efforts would have been in vain. "If we lose you we lose all," he wrote. "You are the one and only person to put our program over."[24]

Nielsen was not surprised, but now she had it on paper. No less than two officers had admitted she was being watched. They had even gone so far as to mention a frame-up. One more piece of evidence that the RCMP, backed by the government, were determined to crush all opposition. The week before, just after she wrote to Heide, she received the news the *Canadian Tribune* had been suspended. One of the Communist Party's bubbles had burst. How long would the other remain afloat?

By March 1941, the crisis of the previous summer had passed. Apart from the night bombing of British cities and the constant submarine attacks on the ships crossing the north Atlantic, there had been no significant German initiatives for months. Thousands of Canadian troops stationed in Britain had not yet seen action. At home the Commonwealth Air Training Plan was underway. In the United States, Congress was debating a massive plan to provide material aid to Britain and her allies. Why, then, had the Canadian government chosen such a time to suppress a newspaper that had been publishing the same sort of anti-war propaganda for over a year?

Dorise's immediate reaction to the *Canadian Tribune*'s suspension was to fire off hundreds of telegrams, asking individuals to send their protests to the Secretary of State. A list of their names was quickly available to the police through wartime censorship. Soon an analysis of their political connections appeared on the desk of RCMP Commissioner Wood.[25]

A week after the suppression of the *Canadian Tribune*, a bill to set up a special parliamentary committee to investigate the implementation of the controversial Defence of Canada Regulations came up for debate in the House. Appointing a committee was, of course, a way of deflecting growing criticism of the regulations by the press and civil libertarians of all stripes, as well as the parliamentary opposition, but first the government had to endure a debate on the bill itself. Ernest Lapointe, Minister of Justice, was on the hot seat and the opposition wanted answers. Was it justified, even in wartime, to suppress a newspaper, seize the property of an ethnic organization, and incarcerate people indefinitely without trial? How many people were presently interned? Was the government rounding up labour leaders to appease its business buddies? Why had the RCMP raided homes and confiscated pamphlets containing the speeches of the MP for North Battleford? At first, M.J. Coldwell and Tommy Douglas of the CCF led the charge. Then it was the turn of Nielsen herself and she did not back down. On March 17, *Time* magazine characterized the exchanges between Nielsen and Lapointe as "two of the hottest sessions in recent history" and credited Nielsen with sending the House "into a howling dither."

The first speaker on the DOCR debate, M.J. Coldwell, raised three issues: the *Tribune*'s suspension; the internment of Pat Sullivan, president of the Canadian Seaman's Union; and the confiscation of Nielsen's pamphlet, *Why I Opposed the Budget*. "Make no mistake about it," he said. "I have nothing but the utmost contempt for communist activities in relation to the war." He agreed that special regulations were, indeed, needed in wartime, but they must be administered impartially and at the moment that did not seem to be the case. The RCMP Commissioner S.T. Wood had gone on record, saying he was more concerned about the reds than about the fascists. But the communists' criticisms of the war effort were no more scurrilous than those of the *Ottawa Citizen* and the *Financial Post* and the government seemed to have no intention of suppressing those newspapers, Coldwell maintained.[26]

In fact, the most pointed criticisms of the war effort, whether they came from the mainstream newspapers, the CCF, or the communists, had focussed on profits and war contracts. Profiteering had been scandalous during World War I and critics were determined it wouldn't happen again. "We are not supporting the struggle," said Coldwell, "in order that the system which allowed men to acquire ... vast amounts of profit should be perpetuated."[27]

Lapointe, like an old warhorse, rose to reply to Coldwell's criticisms. A burly giant of a man, first elected in 1904, he had served the Liberal party faithfully ever since. Now, near the end of a long career, he was bearing the double burden of keeping Quebec in the Liberal fold and serving as Minister of Justice. At this point in history, Quebec nationalists had a strong right-wing bent, and keeping them on board in the war effort without offending the left was an impossible task. Already Lapointe had outraged the left when he refused to disallow Quebec's anti-communist Padlock Law. Now he was ultimately responsible for the execution of the Defence of Canada Regulations, and had the final say in all internment cases.

Lapointe assured Coldwell that the trade unionists were interned not because they were trade unionists but because they were communists and were spreading "communist ideas." As for the RCMP commissioner's remarks, Lapointe believed that he was correct. It was, indeed, the communists who were giving the most trouble. Despite the confiscation and destruction of printing presses in Montreal, "we are flooded all the time with communist circulars." In the meantime, the fascists were either interned or they were being "good boys and ... keeping peaceful." He said nothing about Nielsen's pamphlet and referred the matter of the *Canadian Tribune* to the Secretary of State, who was in charge of censorship.[28]

But whether the issue was censorship or internment, it was the RCMP gathering the evidence and its chief commissioner making the recommendations. Since 1919, when the RCMP intelligence wing had been created during the first red scare, tracking communists and communist-led activities had been one of its preoccupations. In response, the communists had developed their own tactics of operating under siege, and now that war hysteria had subsided, they were putting them into action. In a sense Dorise Nielsen was not a new phenomenon; she was a tactical blip in an ongoing battle between the communists and the RCMP. For a brief time the RCMP had faltered; now they had caught up. They had realized that the People's Movement campaign was part of the communist anti-war strategy, and the woman leading it was either a communist or a dupe. For confirmation, they could look to Britain, where a recent People's Convention in London had so alarmed the government that they had decided to suppress the *Daily Worker* and the *Week*. Coldwell was right. When it came to censorship, it wasn't so much a matter of what was said, but of who said it.

A few days after Lapointe's defence, the scrappy Tommy Douglas once again lit into the DOCR, and defended the *Tribune* with the words of Voltaire: "I disagree most heartily with what you say but I defend your right to say it." In a hard-hitting speech frequently interrupted by heckling, he defended the communists, the Jehovah's Witnesses, and the Ukrainian Farmer-Labour

Temple Association. Referring to Nielsen's pamphlet, he asked why no explanation had been forthcoming. "When a home can be raided and a pamphlet containing speeches, all of which can be found in the records of the Canadian House of Commons, are seized as though it were some piece of vile or salacious literature ... surely this house has a right to some sort of explanation."[29]

When her turn came, Nielsen chose to treat the confiscation of her pamphlets lightly. It was an attempt at intimidation, she said, but it didn't work. "In fact, I think I should thank the government for some good advertising." And she wasn't joking. The second collection of her speeches, *Democracy Must Live*, had gone into a fourth printing. As she spoke, copies of it were on sale at the Chateau Laurier newsstand.[30]

After raising individual cases of internment, Nielsen went further than Douglas and accused the government of acting like a fascist state in trying to silence all protest. "In Italy and Germany you find the Red bogy was brought out to scare and intimidate people, and here in Canada you find the same thing happening.... If these regulations continue in their present form I, for one, feel that this government will no longer have any right to call itself a democratic government of the Canadian people."[31]

Her words finally provoked a response from Lapointe. Considering the "very bad company" she kept and the inflammatory things she was saying to meetings across the country, he said, he thought her adopted country was treating her pretty well. Did members realize that on platforms across the country she had referred to the DOCR as the Defence of Capitalism Regulations? She certainly wouldn't have such freedom of expression in Germany or Italy, or even in Russia. "If ... the police have searched for those leaflets," he said, "it is because my honourable friend keeps very bad company, very bad company indeed." If only he were "at liberty to say what there is on the files of the Royal Canadian Mounted Police!"[32]

Nielsen happened to be absent the evening of Lapointe's remarks, but the next afternoon she rose on a point of privilege to refute his charges. "Yesterday the Minister of Justice insinuated that I had some connection with the communist party.... A few years ago the Prime Minister went to Germany where he had conversations with Hitler and was lauded in the German press. But how indignant he would be if I or anyone else were to insinuate that he were a fascist."[33] She proposed to read a letter from a constituent maintaining the RCMP were looking to frame her. Despite shouts of "order" from various members, and the Speaker's request that she either reveal the writer's name or take her seat, she remained on her feet. "She's a law unto herself," muttered Lapointe. "The lady has not finished yet," interjected Hanson, Leader of the Opposition.

Finally Nielsen agreed to table the letter, and the Speaker ruled that she could continue her statement. Despite continuing shouts for order from the Liberal side of the house, she called the RCMP "this Canadian version of the Gestapo," and cleverly wrapped up her defence using Lapointe's own words: "I will do what I think is right whatever may be the consequences. Neither inducement, blackmail or threat will have any influence."[34] A few days later she wrote to Lapointe, saying she was not at all curious to know what his files contained. "I have always mingled very freely with all kinds of people; neither race, religion, nor politics has been a bar."[35]

Although Nielsen had certainly lied in denying her communist connections, she believed wholly in what she was doing and would not be deterred. Once again her outspoken defence had garnered some good publicity. The suppression of the *Tribune* was only temporary—a sort of rap on the knuckles. It was publishing again within a month and its first issue featured Nielsen's reply to Lapointe. In the *Time* magazine article, the Defence of Canada Regulations were called "the reddest rag that can be waved in front of any liberal-left Canadian," and Nielsen's campaign against them was lauded as "simple, non-political, and effective." The caption beneath her picture repeated one of her favourite slogans: "poverty is subversive." What did it matter if the *Winnipeg Free Press* realized she wasn't non-political at all and labelled her a communist fellow-traveller?[36] Publicity always cut both ways.

Without the children, Dorise found that the late-night sessions were no longer so exhausting and the cold weather was more conducive to work than the sultry summer heat. On March 12, 1941, there was yet another snowstorm. The next day Dorise wrote to Violet McNaughton that she had, at last, had occasion to wear a Chinese shawl McNaughton had lent her. "If you would like a laugh—Look up *Time* March 17th page 36," she scribbled at the bottom. The joke was a description of her as a woman who had arrived in Ottawa "tired, badly dressed, with broken nails and an ill-fitting set of store teeth. ... an unpleasant reminder that all is not well on the farms of Canada's great west."

"I suppose they felt they must fit you into their picture of a farm woman from the north country, something you never looked," replied McNaughton. "However I guess you can take it, as well as a good many other things." She was concerned, though, that Nielsen was working too hard and might burn out. She included a little verse by Edna St. Vincent Millay, beginning "My candle burns at both ends, it will not last the night." She had sent the same verse to Bob Paul. The poor man had had a bad cold all winter but still continued to work as hard as ever.[37]

The exchange between Nielsen and McNaughton makes no mention of a very embarrassing episode that occurred just before the *Time* article appeared. Perhaps McNaughton was not aware of it, though she usually followed the news very closely. Possibly her comment about Nielsen's ability to stand up to pressure is an oblique reference to the incident. The letter to Nielsen from James Hatton, warning her that the Mounties were seeking to frame her, had been investigated immediately. The RCMP found that only part of the letter was the truth. There was indeed a young constable, fresh out of training college, who had let slip that the police were watching Nielsen. In Ottawa he had an instructor who had told the recruits about her. Who was that instructor? He refused to say. His superior concluded that the young man was suffering from some sort of complex and his prospects in the force were not promising. In the end, his penalty for "discussing certain instructions he had received" was a ten-dollar fine, and a warning not to discuss political matters with civilians.[38]

But the information about the young recruit's confession never saw the light of day. Instead, a mere eleven days after James Hatton's letter had been tabled, Lapointe announced in the House that Hatton had lied. He presented the House with a statement Hatton had signed in the presence of an RCMP inspector in Saskatchewan. According to the document, Hatton admitted putting into the mouth of another, more senior, RCMP officer the words of warning he, himself, had for Nielsen, because he thought they would carry greater weight. He believed that Nielsen should give up on her advocacy for freeing the communist internees, or she would find herself among them.[39]

It is painful to imagine the humiliation of James Hatton signing his recantation in the presence of Inspector Spriggs, and of Nielsen sitting in the House as Lapointe read the full text of the signed confession. Still, only three days later, she was writing McNaughton of other, lighter things. Perhaps the overdue thank-you for the Chinese shawl was a way of mending her fences, of shoring up support. And, indeed, if Nielsen's credibility was plummeting in some circles, the response from Violet McNaughton shows that it was holding in others. There would be no more flowery references to her charm and beauty in the House of Commons. But she was still considered a champion by enough people to make all the work meaningful.

For several weeks she had been preparing her speech on the war appropriations bill. It would be an opportunity to speak, not about the distribution of war contracts, but about the need for a national health insurance program. She didn't have to look far for ammunition. She was well-versed in the problems of maternal and child health. In Quebec, one child in ten died before his first birthday. And she had found an even more startling way to present the case. During the Great War, 60,000 Canadians died in battle. During four years of the Depression (1931 to 1935), 71,000 infants died in Canada. And those who survived were not necessarily healthy. Recently, the Minister of National Defence for Air, Chubby Power, had told the House that one third of young men applying to enlist had been found medically unfit for military service.[40]

McNaughton's warning about burning out was one Nielsen often gave herself. In some ways, the coming Easter recess would be more tiring than the session. Two speaking engagements on the way home—one in Winnipeg, where Bill Kardash, a young communist who'd fought in Spain, was running in the provincial election, and then, on the way back to Ottawa, a foray to Timmins and Kirkland Lake and several other stops in northern Ontario, with more speeches to be made—and while she was home, Bob was sure to have some meetings lined up. She knew she would be exhausted from near-sleepless nights on the train and she would be lucky to spend even a few days with the children.

Then, on March 21, Dorise arrived on the Hill to learn that another member from the West, Fred Casselman, had died the night before. He had attended the Thursday evening session as usual, made his way home, and collapsed at the door of his apartment. He was fifty-six. That day the corridors were full of the solemn faces of middle-aged men, a number of them older than Casselman. When the session opened at three, someone had placed a bouquet of flowers on his empty desk. For an hour the partisan rhetoric was stilled and members sat silent while each political leader delivered his tribute. A year ago it had been Brown, then Woodsworth (though he lived on). The strain of war and politics, and long trips back and forth across the country, was taking its toll.

By this time the feisty Nielsen had become an important issue in the Liberal caucus. How could the government shut her up without incurring even more criticism? She'd gotten her comeuppance on the James Hatton letter, but no one believed that would keep her quiet for long. The solution, urged Mackenzie King, was to get another woman in the House. And the death of Fred Casselman provided the perfect opportunity.[41]

7

SUPPORTING THE WAR

Her new V for Victory clubs may say they're out to promote the war effort, but actually they'll be teaching revolutionary ideology.[1]

DORISE MOUNTED THE PLATFORM of the Alberta Avenue Community Hall in Edmonton to address the smallest audience she had encountered since her election. It was May 26, 1941. She had skipped the last three weeks of the parliamentary session to support A.A. MacLeod in his bid for the late Fred Casselman's seat in Edmonton East. With the party being illegal, he was running as a People's Movement candidate. In the hall that could easily hold several hundred people, about two dozen were sitting on folding chairs in the first few rows, and two of them, sitting well apart, were obviously RCMP constables. She had noticed one of them writing in his notebook as she came in.[2]

Everyone there, including Albert and Virginia MacLeod, the local organizers, perhaps even the RCMP constables, was aware that in a few minutes President Roosevelt would begin a radio address that was expected to have an important impact on the war. What initiative would Roosevelt take now? Dorise wanted to know, too, but she was committed to this campaign even if Mac's chances were dimming by the moment. In April Bill Kardash had managed a substantial win in Winnipeg and now sat as a MLA in the Manitoba legislature. She had spoken to a meeting of 3000 people in his support. Edmonton, as it turned out, was a different kettle of fish. Not only did the Liberals find an ideal candidate, the grieving widow, but Social Credit had joined the fray and would split the reform vote.

And then, there was the war. Britain had just delivered the first cheery news in a long time. The German battleship *Bismarck* had been sunk that morning. And tonight, Roosevelt's address. Not an easy job, at this moment, to focus on domestic issues. But, as Bob Paul liked to say (and she liked to remember in trying times)—if the going gets easy, you'd better ask yourself if you're in the vanguard of the proletariat after all.

Her push for the rest of that summer, like the last one, was to focus on the problems of small farmers. She began her meetings in the towns and villages near Edmonton, and then made her way through Saskatchewan for the rest of June. Federal wheat policy was once more the outstanding economic and political issue in Saskatchewan. The federal government had come through, at the last moment as usual, with a plan to reduce wheat acreages by paying farmers a bonus for fields left fallow. Otherwise, seventy-cent wheat and delivery quotas would remain. There was still no way to make a living on a small acreage. Dorise explained it this way: Not so long ago, after the last war, it had been government policy to settle veterans on those small acreages. "Go west, young man" had been the thrust of government policy then. Now, after years of toil, the whole process had been reversed. People who had carved communities out of the wilderness were being forced to migrate once again, this time to take up jobs in the war industries in the East or on the west coast. "Go east, old man," was how Dorise put it. Her remedies included, once again, $1.25 per bushel for the first 1000 bushels delivered from each farm. It was a message she would deliver again and again. And in the summer of 1941, it was still a very powerful message in Saskatchewan.

A week after the Edmonton meeting, A.A. MacLeod lost the election to Cora Casselman. Cameron McIntosh, owner and editor of the *North Battleford News*, whom Nielsen had defeated the year before, was overjoyed. He praised Casselman as "one of the busiest, best informed, most courageous women in the Dominion … a patriotic lady, not a paid agent of Moscow," and said she was "the best-looking woman Canada has ever had in Parliament." He rejoiced that MacLeod had lost his deposit and declared the People's Movement "dead right from its illegitimate birth."[3]

Mackenzie King's plan seemed to have worked. Nielsen was no longer the sole woman in Canada's House of Commons. The two women sat on opposite sides of the House and were opposites in other ways, too. Cora Taylor Casselman, at fifty-three, was a city woman, mother of a grown daughter, and active in such conservative circles as the IODE and the University Women's Club. Perhaps, if their politics had not divided them so decisively, these two women could have found some support in each other's company, but there is no indication that they ever collaborated at all. They sat opposite each other for over three years, divided not only by different life experiences and paths to politics, but also by the discipline of party allegiance. And, despite the high hopes of Mackenzie King and Cameron McIntosh, it was Nielsen, not Casselman, who continued to attract press attention.

Roosevelt's announcement that May evening before the by-election in Edmonton East was, indeed, significant. He vowed that the American navy would defend supply lines to Britain, which had been seriously threatened by German U-boats. But soon, there would be an even more important check to Nazi fortunes, and one that arrived completely unheralded. In the early hours of June 22, Hitler threw the might of the German army and air force into a massive invasion of the Soviet Union. When Canadians woke that Sunday morning, the invasion was already hours old and German divisions were deep into Russian territory. Suddenly the focus of the war had changed from Britain and the United States to the Eastern Front, where an estimated nine million men were engaged in a fight to the finish. And it was soon apparent that the Russians were putting up a gallant fight—their prowess was applauded in all the papers. The *Winnipeg Free Press* called them "the hope of the free nations."[4] Churchill offered all possible aid. "Russia's danger is our danger," he said.[5] Sir Stafford Cripps, a communist fellow-traveller who had been ousted from the Labour Party in 1939, became British ambassador to Moscow.

In Canada, the Communist Party used its underground press and the flagship *Canadian Tribune* to call for an all-out war against Hitler. Within a week, Tim Buck returned from New York and conferred with his underground colleagues at a cottage in St. Janvier, near Montreal.[6] How did communists throughout Canada receive the news of this sudden reverse in party policy? By most accounts, they were relieved. It seems that many who had dutifully accepted the party's stand against the war had always been uncomfortable with it. They did not need Tim Buck's explanation that the invasion of the Soviet Union had "changed the possibilities for the outcome of the war," or his assurance that after June 22 there could be no compromise, no question of a conditional peace, that either socialism or fascism would be victorious.[7] Now, once again, the path was clear. Britain and Canada were on the side of the Soviet Union, which was fighting for its life. That was enough.

Since none of its aims could now be considered subversive, the underground party was able to distribute materials more freely and to activate an organization to spearhead the campaign for freeing communist internees. A.E. Smith and Becky Buhay, one of the party's leading women, were instructed to set up an office on Bay Street in Toronto for the National Committee for Democratic Rights. A seventy-year-old former Methodist clergyman politicized during the Winnipeg General Strike in 1919, Smith was a veteran of many battles on behalf of his communist friends. Expecting to be swiftly dislodged by the RCMP, he waited two weeks before having a phone installed at the Bay Street office.[8] Soon, the National Committee for Democratic Rights was organizing public meetings in Toronto, Montreal, and Winnipeg.

Like other Canadians, Dorise received the news of Germany's invasion of the Soviet Union over the radio. It was the beginning of a hot, dry summer in Saskatchewan. She was not in St. Janvier for the meeting of the party leadership, or at Maple Leaf Gardens for the first pro-Soviet rally. Until mid-August she was in the midst of the usual round of meetings of the United Progressives, as well as at rallies to protest the government's wheat policy. The annual UP convention, held in the middle of July at Medstead, was the largest ever. Five hundred people came out from all parts of the North Battleford constituency. At the end of the convention, delegates from Meadow Lake provincial constituency elected Art Doucet as candidate for the next provincial election, which could come as soon as the following summer.[9] From the high attendance at the convention, it would seem that Hitler's invasion of the Soviet Union, and the anticipated legalization of the Communist Party, had once more legitimized the UP's idea of uniting the left.

After the convention Dorise had a brief respite from travel and meetings. For two weeks she and the Pauls rented a cabin on Emma Lake, north of Prince Albert. The woods towered above them; white spruce and poplar hugged the shore, nourished year after year by the waters of the huge sinkhole. The five children played in the shallow water and enjoyed the novelty of having a boat. They rowed each other around and Bob took them fishing. But it is hard to imagine that the recreative powers of a cottage holiday had much effect on the adults. Cecil Paul, intensely unhappy, still hoped that her husband's fascination with Nielsen was a passing fancy.[10] Bob and Dorise continued to pretend that their relationship was all business.

The Paul children, eight and thirteen that summer, remember their parents constantly quibbling over something or other. Cecil was not as adept as Dorise at presenting a happy face to the world, but in some ways they were similar. Both women had ambitions beyond the traditional raising of a family. Cecil wrote short fiction and sent it off for publication in the *Family Herald*. Like Nielsen, she believed in sharing the housework and taught her boys to mend socks and cook. Neither Cecil nor Dorise could be described as an accommodating type of woman. But Bob Paul had fallen for each of them in turn. He obviously wanted a woman to whom he could talk.

It was, indeed a strange ménage, and Emma Lake was not the last of it. A few years later, when Cecil came to teach in Spiritwood, she and Dorise lived together for several months. And while Dorise was in Ottawa and her children needed something, she would wire Bob or Cecil and they always came through. Was Cecil's loyalty to a man or to a cause? A bit of both, perhaps. Like James Hatton, she may have believed that Dorise was the only person who could "put the message across." And the children had to be cared for one way or another. That was a duty she took very seriously.[11] In any case, she chose not to make a fuss. Appearances were important. As long as she played the role of faithful wife, people might believe she had a faithful husband.

After the sojourn at Emma Lake, Dorise took her children back to the Polaskis', where all three would go to school in September. Christine had not adjusted to the convent school and Dorise had given up that battle.

Following a final conference in Regina, she worked with Minerva Cooper on a brief to the federal wheat committee. According to the brief, more than 15,000 people attended the regional conferences that summer, and, even allowing for some optimism in the figure, such participation is impressive. Eventually the ideas advocated by Nielsen (and by other groups as well), ideas of stabilizing farm income through government marketing boards and other supports, did become government policy and, although they did not save the small homestead from extinction, such supports helped raise the standard of living for those who had been able to weather the storm and stay in business. The work of a small group of communists who organized meetings throughout Saskatchewan during the summers of 1940 and 1941 ultimately played a role in that process.

That fall, Nielsen set off for her first speaking tour of Nova Scotia. In Glace Bay, Sydney, and New Waterford, she shared the stage with her friend A.A. MacLeod, but she was the featured speaker. Then it was back to Ontario, where on Labour Day she spoke at a rally in Hamilton. Steel workers in both Ontario and Nova Scotia were on a militant path for union recognition through the Congress of Industrial Organization (CIO) and Canadian communists were determined to play a key role in the drive. Dorise described steel workers as a civilian army that had to be in top form if the war were to be won. With inflation over 12 percent since the war started, no one should be expected to hold the line on wages. The officials urging workers to tighten their belts, she said, had no idea what a tight belt felt like.[13] In Toronto she urged a thousand striking steel workers to hold fast by quoting Dolores Ibarruri, heroine of the Spanish Civil War: "Better to die standing than to live kneeling."[14]

From Toronto, Nielsen went to Winnipeg to begin her second western tour—this one with the party's new pro-war message. Nevertheless, the RCMP continued to monitor all her meetings. Mrs. Nielsen, some of them believed, was still a threat to the war effort. "Her new V for Victory clubs may say they're out to promote the war effort, but actually they'll be teaching revolutionary ideology," reads one report.[15] She was becoming a very irksome personality, as far the police were concerned. Her effectiveness was part of the problem. "Mrs. Nielsen has considerable personal charm of dress and manner and knows how to use it," wrote an officer reporting on a strike meeting in St. Catherine. "She is short on logic, deductions and facts, but long on emotional appeal, and enjoys a marked success in her role as crusader on behalf of the 'poor down-trodden workingman'."[16] Another irksome quality was her increasing boldness in taking shots at the police. In Winnipeg she arrived shortly after a Chief Constables Convention. She told her audience that if only she had known about the RCMP convention, she would have attended and taken notes.[17] She carried that joke with her across the prairies and got laughs all along the way.

On September 26, 1941, Dorise mounted the stage of the Empire Theatre in Edmonton to speak to a crowd of 700 to 800 people (approximately 75 percent were of either Russian or other Slavic racial origin, noted Constable Ozarko, who was already taking notes). She had just held two meetings in Calgary, and in a few days would begin a round of meetings on the west coast. She was already weary and she missed the banter and support of MacLeod, who had fallen and broken his wrist just as they were to set out.

On stage were pictures of Roosevelt, Churchill, and Stalin, together with their national flags. When the chairman called for an appreciation of the three great leaders, Stalin got by far the most applause. Then it was Nielsen's turn to give a lesson in the history of appeasement, starting with the Japanese invasion of Manchuria in 1931 and ending with the mysterious flight of Rudolph Hess to Great Britain just a few weeks before.[18] Hilter's hope, she said, was that Hess would be able to rally the fascist appeasers there and gain England's support in a "holy war" against Russia. But the era of appeasement was over, she said. Now the first real fight was being made against fascism. Fifteen million Russian soldiers were showing their courage daily. It was time for the Canadian people to throw all their strength into the war effort. She urged the formation of a People's Victory Party to rally support towards that goal.[19]

Fatigue became a way of life for Dorise. Back and forth across the country on trains full of uniformed men, always carrying a fat briefcase of reading and correspondence. She was greeted at railway stations, taken to tea in someone's home, where she met other women, and then to dinner, often in a restaurant, and while the others were still on dessert, she was expected to say a few words. And then, it was on to an evening meeting. Even finding time to listen to the latest radio news was a challenge, and she was always hopping off the train to buy a newspaper.

Nielsen's western tour the fall of 1941 picked up momentum in Vancouver, where she addressed 4000 people in Hastings Park Forum and shared the stage with Harold Winch, the provincial CCF leader. The meeting endorsed a resolution to "strain our resources to the utmost in assisting our Soviet ally" and to open a second front against Hitler.[20] On that, the communists and the radical

CCFers of BC agreed. News from the Russian front was growing worse by the day. It was rumoured that Russian casualties were in the millions. The city of Leningrad was already under siege and German armies were nearing Moscow.

But, despite the agreement on aid to Russia, there was competition between the CCF and the communists for the allegiance of the Canadian left. Discontent with the federal government was building. The cost of living had risen rapidly since the war began and, in the cities, housing shortages were becoming pressing.[23] How could all this restiveness be harnessed for the socialist cause? Since Mackenzie King had cleverly called a federal election early in the war, before shortages and inflation could take hold, the first signs of eroding Liberal support showed in provincial elections. In October 1941, shortly after Nielsen's visit, the CCF in BC doubled its seats in the provincial house, leaving the Liberals there with a minority government. An unprecedented five women were elected, three of them for the CCF.

On her return from the coast, Dorise held her first meeting in North Battleford. Here she was impinging on Cameron McIntosh's home territory, for, although her constituency was called North Battleford, it did not include the town itself. The meeting was chaired by Reeve George Edwards and attracted about 300 people, a "meager number," according to the *North Battleford News*. On the editorial page McIntosh went even further. "Two propaganda peddlers held forth their worthless wares in North Battleford Tuesday night," he wrote. "They were never here before and those who had the misfortune of hearing them are beseeching high heaven they may never come again." He referred to Nielsen and A.A. MacLeod as "squealing swine," and "anti-Fascist flame-eaters." The problem was, of course, that MacLeod had not been present at all. McIntosh prefaced his editorial by admitting he had written it before the meeting, but (obviously pleased with his rhetoric) had decided to run it anyway.[22]

In the rest of the country, Dorise was soon in the thick of the competition between the CCF and the Communist Party. With the upsurge of industries such as ship building, aircraft, and automobiles, as well as munitions, and impressive gains of the Congress of Industrial Unions south of the border, Canadian workers were flocking to unions. Membership was already up an amazing 60 percent from pre-war figures.[23] So far, all the federal government efforts to diffuse industrial disputes through conciliation boards and other measures had failed miserably. What workers wanted was not only more pay, but legislation that compelled an employer to negotiate with the union chosen by his employees. Once again, unions and left-wing politicians could point to Britain and the United States, where such legislation was already in place. Meanwhile, in Canada, by the time of Nielsen's western tour, the federal government had sent troops to end a strike at Alcan in Arvida, Quebec, and thousands of workers were on strike against General Motors in Ontario.[24]

The world of union organization, a male world rife with factional struggles, was new to Nielsen. That fall she attended, as an observer, the annual conventions of both the Trades and Labour Congress and the new Canadian Congress of Labour.[25] Before the brief parliamentary session that November, she travelled up to Kirkland Lake, a gold-mining centre in northern Ontario, where one of the longest and most bitter strikes in Canadian history was about to begin. Gold mining was a leading industry when the war broke out. Mine owners like Sir Harry Oakes had made huge profits during the 1930s when the price of gold bullion had gone up, while miners' pay stagnated. Organizers for the International Union of Mine, Mill and Smelter Workers, some of them communists, had big hopes. If they were successful at Kirkland Lake, they would go on to organize Sudbury, Timmins, and a number of other northern mining towns where mine owners had stubbornly opposed unions for years. Both union and management had too much at stake to back down.

"The eyes of all Canada are on Kirkland Lake," said Nielsen, addressing a thousand women of the town who had assembled at the Strand Theatre. "The whole future of organized labour in Canada depends on the battle you are waging here."[26] She was scarcely exaggerating. Kirkland Lake was a test not only of the miners' determination but also of the federal government's labour policy. Despite the unanimous recommendation of a government-appointed conciliation board, the mine owners refused to negotiate with the Mine-Mill union. Mackenzie King had the power to use coercive measures. Would he use them on behalf of the miners or the owners?

For Nielsen, the people of Kirkland Lake had a particular appeal. Here was an isolated northern community where various ethnic groups such as Scandinavians, Slavs, and French Canadians had united to fight for their rights. Just as the United Progressives in northern Saskatchewan had banded together to fight a corrupt and right-wing Liberal machine that had ruled their lives for too long, the workers of Kirkland Lake had finally mustered their strength against the mine owners. She returned to Kirkland Lake several times during the strike, and so did sympathizers in the CCF, Clarence Gillis and Angus MacInnis. All three spoke on behalf of the miners in the House that November, but the government refused to act and the strike dragged on through the winter.

Parliament met for only two weeks the fall of 1941. If anyone needed a lesson in courage and determination, it was provided by J.S. Woodsworth. Partly blind, and with his right arm and leg semi-paralyzed, he hobbled into the House to take his seat for the first time in over a year. Members of the House rose in thunderous applause.[27] Otherwise, the session was an exercise in frustration for all concerned. There was no business, no legislation—the real business of government was being done by Orders-in-Council issued by the cabinet. In a Saturday night broadcast less than two weeks before the session, King had announced a comprehensive wage-price freeze. To cushion the blow for wheat farmers and employees caught with low wages, there would be a compulsory cost-of-living bonus for employees and an acreage bonus for wheat.[28] Having taken the wind of out the opposition's sails on the most pressing issues, Mackenzie King allowed Members of Parliament to question the government and generally let off steam for two weeks. He told the House that, having considered the dearth of accommodation in Ottawa, he thought it best to keep the session as short as possible. Thus, members were able to stay in hotels and leave the search for rooms until January, when the new session would begin in earnest.

Across the river in the Hull jail, seventy-eight communist internees swore affidavits of loyalty to Canada and awaited news of their fate. They had been moved from Petawawa in the summer and had the jail all to themselves, but there was still no sign of their release. On November 9, A.E. Smith and his National Committee for Democratic Rights (NCDR) held a mass meeting in Toronto to celebrate the twenty-fourth anniversary of the Bolshevik Revolution. Blazoned across the stage were the slogans "Restore Production to Defeat Hitler," "Create a Second Front," "Release All Anti-Fascists and Let Them Fight Hitler."[29] In the House Nielsen read the text of a telegram she had sent to the Russian people on behalf of the workers and farmers of Canada, praising the Russians' bravery and promising Canada's continued support.[30]

On the same day Dorise presented a petition to Parliament, signed by communist internees who offered their services in the war effort wherever it might be deemed most useful.[31] Now the communists, in the words of Lapointe, were being "good boys." Their hidden presses and underground leaders were busy churning out pro-war propaganda and preaching labour unity. But so far, their efforts at good behaviour had failed to move the Liberal government.

After the session wrapped up in the middle of November, Dorise made her way home to Spiritwood, to her children and to Bob Paul. High on her agenda, politically, was the provincial election still expected to be called that June. All their plans had to be settled before Nielsen returned to Ottawa in January. Already the UP had nominated Art Doucet in Meadow Lake. A battle was warming up between "the Saskatoon group" (probably Nelson Clarke, Harold Miller, and Minerva Cooper), who wanted to run a candidate in Turtleford, and Nielsen and Paul, who were opposed. They felt that if the UP opposed the CCF in both Meadow Lake and Turtleford, the CCF would surely run a candidate against Nielsen in the next federal election. This was one of the issues that required her attention as she took up headquarters once more in the little house she had rented in Spiritwood. It was, very likely, a life of unrelenting politics, with no time to think of her personal future beyond the next campaign.

But, as usual, there was a pause for Christmas with the Pauls and the Polaskis. Five adults and seven children crowded into the Polaskis' house. Dorise brought all the trimmings and the women shared the cooking. They all made the effort to celebrate, as parents do, for the sake of the children. Annie Polaski was already ailing from Bright's disease (she would die a few years later of kidney failure), and the news from overseas was increasingly gloomy. The Japanese attack on Pearl Harbor in early December was the beginning of a long string of Japanese successes. Both the American and the British fleets in the Pacific had been struck hard. Hong Kong was under siege with two Canadian regiments fighting a desperate defence, their families at home waiting for news. It was a time of great peril, a time when it seemed possible that the Axis powers might soon control much of the world. Later, historians would view the attacks on Russia and the United States as turning points in favour of the Allies, but the turn was not immediate. Christmas 1941 was a low point in Allied fortunes. On Christmas Eve Churchill made the long, gruelling flight over the Atlantic to confer with Roosevelt.

Amidst the feasting and singing in the farm that Christmas, it is likely that the radio was tuned in to the CBC evening news. On December 30, 1941, Churchill spoke to Canada's Parliament. Like all MPs and senators, Dorise had received a telegram inviting her to attend, but there had been no hope of getting to Ottawa in time, and no point, really, with the session not starting until late January, so she had to be content with the radio. She was not there, watching Churchill flash the victory sign, do a pirouette, move the crowd to laughter and tears, to courage and hope, all in a short address. He must have been weary—the overseas flight, the conferences with FDR, and then the train ride up to Ottawa. But he still knew just what to say and where and when to say it. He knew enough to turn the surrender of Hong Kong into praise for the gallant Canadians who had slowed the Japanese advance. That was the job of a politician. It was, perhaps, as important as the work of miners and the work in munitions plants and aircraft factories, and even the work of the men on the front lines.

Three times a week, when the train arrived in Spiritwood, there was mail and newspapers with detailed maps of the battle areas, and, somewhere further in, a list of casualties. Casualties were light so far, most of them Canadian airmen flying out of Britain or involved in training accidents in Canada. The list from Hong Kong was still not available. Dorise could also read the results of the new Gallup poll, which promised to "make the people's voice continually heard." It was clear that Canadians were warming to the idea of conscription, and the Conservatives were pushing hard for it. That would be the burning issue of the next session. The Liberals had promised a vote, a plebiscite, before introducing conscription for service overseas. It would be a hard sell in Quebec and not an easy one in northern Saskatchewan, where disaffection with the Liberals ran so deep. If there were a plebiscite, and it seemed more and more likely, she would need all the energy she could muster. She would make no apologies. Her original platform had called for no conscription without a plebiscite, and now conscription was clearly necessary. The boys overseas must be reinforced. For once she could support the Liberals. The question was—would her constituents follow her?

With war news growing grimmer daily, the opening of Parliament in January 1942 was particularly sober. There was no honour guard for the arrival of the Governor General, and, in keeping with the reduction in formal wear in wartime, the ladies in attendance wore simple afternoon dresses. Of course, most of the ladies present were seated in the gallery. Seated on the floor of the Senate Chamber were two women, Cairine Wilson and Iva Fallis, and standing among the throng of over 200 Members of Parliament gathered near the door were Dorise Nielsen and Cora Casselman. As expected, King used the Throne Speech to announce his intention to hold a nation-wide plebiscite on conscription for overseas service.

The session was expected to be a long one, and attendance that first day was almost full. Senators and MPs scrambled to find rooms in a capital becoming so crowded with civil servants that apartments were scarcer than ever before. Daniel McIvor, who had once praised Nielsen as "the lone and brilliant lady in the House," declared that every last house in Ottawa was rented and that the city should provide better accommodation.[32] Ottawa's mayor, Stanley Lewis, tired of all the criticism, suggested that the problem would be improved if MPs simply went home and stopped wasting everyone's time.[33]

It is likely that Dorise settled for whatever shelter she could find, probably a rooming house in either Centre Town or Sandy Hill, within easy commuting distance of Parliament. In a later session she would comment on her good luck in having a one-room apartment with a bathroom and shower to herself. But in 1942, it was a scramble, and it hardly mattered, anyway. She spent most of her evenings on Parliament Hill and many weekends travelling to out-of-town meetings.

Twice, the meetings came to her. In early February, 400 farmers from Saskatchewan marched up Parliament Hill to lobby for an increase in wheat prices for the 1942 crop. It was the largest farm delegation to Ottawa in thirty years.[34] Mr. King received the delegation and indicated that he recognized the problem. Although Saskatchewan had remained Canada's third-largest province, the 1941 census had shown a remarkable fall in its population. Per capita income figures for 1940 showed the reason why. In Ontario, per capita income was $505 a year, but in Saskatchewan, it was only $261.[35]

By 1942 the demand for wheat exports was growing. Surely the government could increase wheat prices from the seventy cents per bushel it had paid for the last two years? The Wheat Pools, which sponsored the march, were asking for a one-dollar initial payment with a final payment based on purchasing parity. Nielsen must have felt vindicated. Her earlier proposal of $1.25 per bushel was not out of line with the Wheat Pools' proposal, which had garnered such widespread support.

For Dorise, the presence of 400 Saskatchewan farmers in Ottawa was a chance to relax and be herself. She met several old friends and found it "wholesome to have honest guys to talk to again and not to watch every damn." In a letter to Heide Vockeroth, Dorise referred to the "honest guys" as "Tom, Dick, and Harry."[36] To give their actual names would not be wise. Even Coldwell and Richard Hanson, the Tory House Leader, had complained of their parliamentary mail's being read by the censors.[37]

Later in February, the National Committee for Democratic Rights, the organization leading the fight to free the communist internees, held a weekend conference at the Chateau Laurier. The group intended to cap its efforts by lobbying the Minister of Justice. Its timing could not have been worse. Freeing a few communists languishing in the Hull jail was not high on the government's list of priorities. The burning issues of the day were preparing for the April plebiscite on conscription (already there had been anti-conscription rioting in Montreal), and financing, in addition to Canada's own war effort, a massive billion-dollar credit to Great Britain, which had run out of foreign currency. And now there was the problem of what to do with the Japanese population in BC. The day after Pearl Harbor, King had ordered the confiscation of Japanese fishing vessels and the registration of all the Japanese people in Canada. So far, thirty-eight persons of Japanese origin had been interned.[38]

But the rapid advance of the Japanese in the Pacific was causing problems in Canada. Already there was fighting in the Philippines and the Dutch East Indies, and Australia feared it would be next. The rumour was that Japanese communities in Malaya and elsewhere had aided the Japanese advance by providing intelligence. The fall of Singapore on February 15 had caused fresh alarm on Canada's west coast. King's assurances that the country was safe from invasion were beginning to ring hollow. On several occasions German submarines torpedoed ships within sight of the Atlantic coast, and in February an oil refinery in California was shelled by a Japanese sub.[39] In BC there was a clamour to intern all 21,000 Japanese residents.

All this, and King was without the wise advice, the solid judgment, of Ernest Lapointe, his Quebec lieutenant, who had died of a heart attack just after the fall session. Lapointe had been his Minister of Justice since 1924 and his experience was badly needed now. Whether the new fellow, Louis St. Laurent, could eventually fill his shoes remained to be seen. He was an influential corporate lawyer from Quebec who had never held elected office before.

No, freeing the communists and lifting the ban on the party were not high on King's list, but he bowed to increasing agitation from the communists, the CCF, and civil libertarians of all stripes, and sent his new Minister of Justice to meet with a delegation from the NCDR that claimed to represent 140,000 people from thirty-one cities.[40] A hundred or so delegates had conferred at the Chateau Laurier all weekend. On Monday night they had ended their conference with a mass meeting at which Mrs. Nielsen had given her usual fiery speech. She urged the government to let the anti-fascists go and fill the Hull jail, instead, with Japanese fifth columnists and the "subversive influences fomenting disunity in French Canada."[41] Why, she asked, were Canadian anti-fascists still in jail, when in Britain "the genius of Mr. Churchill" had appointed Sir Stafford Cripps, who held similar views, to his war cabinet?[42]

Nielsen must have watched Cripps's rise with great interest and hope. Like Nielsen, he had been expelled from a socialist party (the British Labour Party) for supporting a united front with the communists, but since the invasion of the Soviet Union a year before, he had been welcomed into Churchill's coalition government, first as ambassador to Moscow and next as Britain's negotiator with the Indian independence movement. Her remarks that night show that she shared, to some extent, the prejudices of her time and was willing to play on those prejudices to achieve her goals. Only a year before, the communists themselves could have been described as "a subversive influence fomenting disunity." She would have argued, no doubt, that the situation had fundamentally changed.

On Wednesday morning, February 25, the NCDR sent its representatives to meet with King's new Minister of Justice. If St. Laurent looked distracted or a little weary, it was with good reason. He, too, had been conferring all weekend, and, following the American example, had just been given the authority to remove all Japanese residents from the coast. All the previous day, he and King and other cabinet ministers had endured a day-long question period during Parliament's first secret session. Although the proceedings of that session were not recorded, news reports speculated that coastal defence and the removal of Japanese-Canadians from the coast were high on the agenda. The big question of where to put them had not yet been settled. Townspeople in the interior of BC had already expressed alarm at the numbers of Japanese Canadians trying to rent or buy property there.[43]

The political ramifications of security issues were indeed complex, perhaps more complex than Louis St. Laurent had anticipated. Even the communists had advocates in high places. The delegation he met that day was accompanied by four Members of Parliament: Charles Johnston and Victor Quelch, both Social Crediters from Alberta; Mrs. Nielsen, who had already presented a petition to Parliament on behalf of the internees and whose sympathies were well known; and the heavyweight of the group, the Hon. Arthur W. Roebuck, former Attorney-General of Ontario, a liberal-Liberal who, not long before, had been ousted from the Ontario cabinet for failing to support Premier Mitchell Hepburn in his struggle against industrial unions.[44] The Liberal party was a minefield in itself. St. Laurent said very little in the meeting. According to A.E. Smith, who led the delegation, the minister listened to all that was said, "but it was impossible to judge what wheels were turning in his mind."[45]

For Dorise, that week was particularly hectic. Three days of meeting NCDR delegates, plus the long-awaited secret session, and then, on the day of the conference with St. Laurent, she received a telegram from Sudbury. In the continuing battle between the mine owners and the International Union of Mine, Mill and Smelter Workers, the owners had struck an unexpected blow. A dozen men had wrecked the Mine-Mill office in Sudbury and had severely beaten two union organizers. What did the government propose to do? she asked that afternoon. She was told it would do nothing. Preserving law and order was a provincial responsibility. Angus MacInnis (CCF Vancouver) followed up her question and pointed out that the federal government had sent the RCMP to keep order in other cases of disorderly conduct. The two MPs got nowhere. The following weekend, both Nielsen and MacInnis set off to Kirkland Lake to investigate another case of injustice in the ongoing battle for union recognition.

Like the NCDR, the miners of Kirkland Lake had chosen a very poor time to assert their rights. Gold exports had plummeted during the first years of the war. The mine owners persisted in refusing to recognize the Mine-Mill union and ignored a government request to submit the issue to arbitration. They were thus able to use the strike as an excuse to cut their costs and cull their labour force.[46] On their return from Kirkland Lake, Nielsen and MacInnis reported to Parliament that, although the strike was over, older miners and those involved with the union were not being rehired, and the owners' claim of non-discriminatory rehiring was an absolute falsification.[47]

On her return Dorise also received a letter from Heide and hurried to reply because "letters from home are like a breath of fresh air in this foetid atmosphere." That remark was to be taken literally as well as figuratively. She had a deskmate—a Liberal backbencher from Quebec who had crossed the floor to protest conscription for overseas service. He now occupied that other half of Dorise's double desk. They had become the butt of many jokes, she told Heide, but the worst of it was that he "suffers from perspiring feet—or should I say I suffer?" She tried to turn her back to him and write small.

She described her trip to Kirkland Lake. After urging the men to "stick with it weeks ago," she felt she had to be with them "in the hour of their retreat." Nielsen had wondered if she had the guts to go up there, but once she was on the platform and saw the faces of the men and women, she felt better. It was a huge meeting: 1000 people were turned away. "It is impossible to doubt the ultimate victory of Democracy when you are among the people," she wrote.[48]

That letter to Heide, written Monday evening, March 2, 1942, was a long one, begun in the afternoon and spilling over into the evening session. At eight o'clock, after the dinner break, when the House was being treated to a long and boring debate, Nielsen wrote that "most everybody is amusing themselves as best they can—I am writing to you." After the account of her trip to Kirkland Lake, she turned to personal matters: what a fine job Heide was doing of raising two sons, pretty much on her own, and how their friend, Dolly Gunderson, was about to have another child ("Sometimes when I'm snowed under with petty work, when I can't seem to accomplish anything—I have often got a second wind by reminding myself of Dolly's guts!"). Nielsen's own children were still at Polaskis', but Annie didn't have much experience with adolescent girls and Christine was going through a difficult period. Dorise said she would like to get her into a high school somewhere (she was finishing grade eight), but who would take in three children? At Easter she would hardly have time to see them. She had to give a speech in Toronto and then "stump for the pleb" in her own constituency.

What comes across in this letter, and others, is Nielsen's great impatience with the dreariness and futility of Parliamentary debates, her longing to be with more ordinary folk. Whether she was as isolated as she portrays herself is questionable. Politically, at least, she had formed several alliances with other Westerners in the CCF and the Social Credit. Frequently her questions were followed up by supplementary questions from CCF members and vice versa. Sandy Nicholson and Tommy Douglas, both CCF MPs from Saskatchewan, knew her well enough to contact her later when they visited China.

It is possible she was also a friend of Angus MacInnis, with whom she travelled to Kirkland Lake on several occasions and who supported her in presenting a petition from the communist internees. MacInnis, almost twenty years older than Dorise, a former streetcar conductor and the son of a poor potato farmer, had been involved in socialist politics on the west coast for many years. He was a close friend of Woodsworth and had married his daughter Grace, who was one of three CCF women elected to the British Columbia legislature in 1941. Whether his occasional assistance to Nielsen was out of friendship or chivalry, or some sort of political trade-off, is hard to say. Nielsen had little to offer when it came to political trade-offs. More likely, MacInnis and others felt that on most issues they were simply workers in a common cause. There were many issues on which Westerners on the left could agree. And as Tommy Douglas liked to say, why should one withhold support for a good cause just because the communists were supporting it too?[49]

Victor Quelch (Social Credit, Alberta) was probably Nielsen's closest friend on the Hill.[50] Not only did he support some of her political initiatives, he and his wife shared a cottage with Nielsen and her children one summer. Ten years older than Nielsen, Quelch had been born in British Guiana and educated in England before taking up a homestead in Alberta, so they had their Britishness in common. Like Agnes Macphail (and many others), Quelch obviously liked Nielsen personally, but, unlike so many others (including Macphail), he did not let her politics interfere with friendship.

And Nielsen made an effort to cooperate with other MPs where she could. She commended Cora Casselman's strong pitch for an increase in old-age pensions, which at that time were paid only to the indigent and had remained a measly twenty dollars a month since they were introduced in the 1920s.[51] On the death of J.S. Woodsworth, she was among the first of many backbenchers to pay tribute to him in the House of Commons. "In years gone by, when pioneers in new social thought were few, Mr. Woodsworth worked untiringly." She went on to pay tribute to his wife for supporting her husband and forgoing many hours of his companionship for the cause. "Many a year he might have spent with his wife and family had he not given so unstintingly of his health and strength in the cause so dear to his heart."[52] It was just two years from the date of her own election, but already Nielsen was acutely aware of the sacrifices involved in the political life.

On the surface, at least, she was becoming more and more part of the mainstream. Now that the communists were on board for a total war effort, she could stump for a "yes" in the plebiscite with a clear conscience and with the support of such diverse groups as the Trades and Labour councils and Canadian clubs. In a Toronto plebiscite rally, she shared a stage with Paul Martin, Sr., the young Liberal MP from Windsor who had pummelled her for her lack of patriotism just a year before.[53] Meanwhile, in Toronto, the Tim Buck Plebiscite Committee campaigned for a "yes" to conscription, but Tim Buck and other underground communist leaders were still lying low. Throughout the winter of 1942, communist internees were released in dribs and drabs; however, the party remained illegal and the arrest warrants issued in June 1940 were still being enforced.[54]

During the Easter break that year, even the Conservatives, who thought the plebiscite an unnecessary waste of time and money, were out "stumping for the pleb." They might have disputed the need for a plebiscite, but they were determined that the government should have no more excuse to postpone conscription for overseas service. The fact that results would be recorded by constituency gave MPs an added incentive. For Dorise and other rural MPs, simply getting people out to vote was a problem. Gas rationing had just started on April 1.

Dorise had the added challenge of a huge area settled by diverse ethnic groups who had no particular interest in saving Britain. Thankfully, with the Russians still taking the brunt of the action, she could often play the Russian card, except with the Ukrainian nationalists, who were consistently anti-communist and anti-

Soviet. She and Bob debated whether she should even go to the village of Krydor, where the nationalists made up the majority. She might be hooted or pelted or run out of town. On the other hand, there was no point in just preaching to the converted.

It was indeed, a busman's holiday that Easter. Sometime during the three-week break, she moved her children from the Polaski farm to the home of Vi Miller in Saskatoon. It was the only place that would accommodate all three children and she was determined not to separate them.[55] Harold and Vi Miller lived a block from the end of Avenue C on the east side of Saskatoon and their house had none of the amenities of city living. The Nielsen children helped fetch water from a community tap a few blocks away. It was like living in the country, except they knew no one, not even the Millers. There were two Miller children, both younger than the Nielsens, and the house was in chaos most of the time. Years later, in weighing the experience, all that Christine put on the positive side of the scale was that Dorise bought her a bicycle (to be shared with her sister). Sally felt abandoned. She could no longer turn to Cecil Paul or Annie Polaski for affection. Once again she was ashamed that she failed her grade at school. The only pleasure she can remember is that she helped take care of the baby.[56]

Before returning to Ottawa, Dorise held a meeting in Krydor and put on such a good show that for years Bob Paul would tell the tale of how she moved the nationalists to tears over the plight of their red brothers.[57] When the vote was counted, North Battleford voted two to one in favour of conscription, a figure that was close to the average for Saskatchewan. Although Nielsen now stood with the majority of English-speaking Canadians, her fervour for the war effort disgusted M.J. Coldwell. But Coldwell was warned by CCF in his home province that many people "took exception" to his criticism of Mrs. Nielsen. She was still popular in Saskatchewan and it wasn't just the communists who supported her.[58]

Nielsen's support of the war went further than stumping for a "yes" vote in the plebiscite. Earlier that year, she had tried to enlist in the Canadian Women's Army Corps (CWAC), which had recently been formed to free more service-men for combat roles. Many public figures were enlisting in the military. In Saskatchewan, George Williams had abandoned his posts as CCF leader and leader of the opposition to enlist. The mayors of Ottawa and Hull had enlisted on the same day. It was a matter of setting an example, but more than that, it was a matter of doing useful work. Nielsen was disappointed to be refused. Women with dependent children were not eligible. "Personally I think it's one of the most idiotic regulations made by men," she told the House.[59]

She was sure that women could be doing a thousand and one things, but instead they were being asked only to manage their households economically and buy war savings stamps. An ad in *Chatelaine* was a perfect example of the government's chauvinism. "There's one job you alone can do," it said. "It concerns the man you love. He has a terrific task ahead of him." Just keep him happy, keep him fit, it said. "This is the job of every woman who cherishes the love of a man and deserves his esteem."[60] That was certainly not Nielsen's idea of women's role. One can almost hear her say, "What bilge!"

8

PARENTING

Whenever we acted up, it was always
'Don't you know there's a war on?'[1]

WITH THE PARLIAMENTARY SESSION lasting half the summer of 1942, and her children running wild at the Millers' in Saskatoon, Dorise devised a new approach. Christine and Sally were old enough, she thought, to be with her while she worked. In June, as soon as school finished, Christine boarded the train for Ottawa. She would spend the month of July helping out Lilla Bell in the sixth-floor parliamentary office, stuffing envelopes, filing, running errands. At thirteen, she caught on to everything quickly and got to know the Centre Block so well it almost felt like home, or, at least, as much like home as the Miller place in Saskatoon. The real holiday was an excursion to Niagara Falls and a ride on the *Maid of the Mist*, but that was just one weekend. Otherwise, it was a "weird" summer, as she remembered it. So embarrassing to have her mother always trying to find her a friend, someone she could do things with, trying to manage her life as if she were a kid.

Many years later, after Dorise's death, her daughters made a list of events. It was a bare-bones sort of outline of what they knew about their parents and about their own lives, a long time ago. They titled it "Things We Agree Upon" (for they didn't always agree). The left-hand column is about their father, Peter: where he was born, how he served in the army in World War I, then farmed, and joined the Veterans Guard in World War II. It ends with the date of his death from a heart attack in 1956. There isn't much on Pete's side of the page. After 1940 there is just the odd line—"Dad visited us in Saskatoon," "Dad gave

Chris a watch," "Dad visited us all."[2] They remembered how they came home from school one day in Ottawa and found him sitting on the back step. The next day, he took them all to a movie.[3] In June 1940 he was training for the Veterans Guard near Petawawa, not far from Ottawa. After that he guarded internees and German POWs at various camps scattered on the prairies. They saw him only a few times a year, and never for long.

In composing their list of the things they agreed upon, the two women tried very hard to be objective and keep to the facts. "Summer '42," Sally wrote, "Chris to Ottawa, Johnny to Coates, & Sally 2 wks in rumble seat on Mom and Bob's speaking tour." This cryptic information was recorded in the right-hand column that had begun a few pages before, under the heading "Mother." Now their own lives were in that column, too, snippets of Christmases and summer holidays and where they went to school, all in a long, skinny list.

What did Sally think of her two weeks in the rumble seat of Bob Paul's car that summer of 1942? Was she pleased, at last, to get some share of her mother's attention or was she jealous of her sister's month in Ottawa? Did she even manage to get much of her mother's attention at all? The list says nothing of this. And now she has forgotten many of the details, except that she was there, bouncing over the rutted roads of Dorise's constituency, being teased by Bob Paul, who was always a tease, and sleeping beside her mother in a series of strange beds. And though it didn't register at the time, she sat through some of the most acrimonious political meetings Dorise had faced so far.

At the end of August 1942, the United Progressives encountered stiff opposition from the CCF when they attempted to nominate a candidate in the provincial riding of Turtleford. The whole speaking tour that summer had been a buildup to that moment. At local meetings UP delegates were selected to attend the final convention in Turtleford. The plan was to nominate Minerva Cooper, but the delegates chose, instead, by a narrow margin of seventy-one to sixty, to support Robert Wooff, who had already been nominated by the CCF. Instead of letting the decision of the Turtleford convention stand, the UP (meaning, at this point, its communist leaders, including Paul, Nielsen, and Cooper) called another convention two weeks later, and at last were able to nominate Cooper.

Years later, Bob Paul would remember the whole episode with shame. He would say that he had been following orders with which he basically disagreed.[4] And this dubious exercise in democracy was fodder for Cameron McIntosh, Dorise's arch-rival and editor of the *North Battleford News*. The split in the left boded well for his chances in the next federal election. He mustered all his rhetorical powers and, in several editorials, dismissed the United Progressives as "Win the War wrigglers," "double-crossers and inveterate falsifiers," "an aggregation of agitators," "gamblers with people's souls," and "godless gangsters."[5]

As McIntosh anticipated his comeback, Nielsen and Paul struggled to regain credibility. They blamed the Saskatoon communists for the mess. Bob Paul wrote a long letter to the party brass in the East, explaining his differences with the "DC" (district committee) in Saskatchewan. The United Progressive Movement was never intended to be provincial, he said, and even though Minerva Cooper was a candidate of Mrs. Nielsen's calibre, the whole campaign had been a disaster. In his opinion "the correct thing to do would be for the DC to get down to work and organize (the) withdrawal" of Minerva Cooper's candidacy. But he and the DC did not agree. The DC thought Paul was trying to run a one-man show and that he was "politically undeveloped." On his part, Paul felt that his job had grown too big and that he had lost contact with the people. After offering more advice about the predicament, including a strong suggestion that the Alliance (i.e., the communists) would stand to gain most by throwing Mrs. Nielsen's support behind the CCF candidate in Turtleford, Paul offered his resignation. "I have no heart left for the work and getting out seems to be the quickest corrective force."[6]

At this point Bob Paul had been working for six years to build a united front on the left. He had begun work with limited goals and much grassroots support from people who were sick of political rhetoric and corruption, people who could perhaps best be described as populist reformers. But along the way, the success of the UP movement had led to inflated expectations. The communists from Saskatoon, who had once placed their hopes on the Rev. Brown, had transferred their attention to Nielsen and her sprawling constituency. Obviously the pressures on Paul, the man-on-the-spot, had escalated. He was expected to be the key man to organize three provincial constituencies and win them for the UP, when he believed he had more than enough to do just getting Nielsen re-elected. And he realized that the times had changed. The CCF was gaining the confidence of more and more people on the left. This time it was determined not to back down.

All these developments were on Bob Paul's mind as he typed out the letter that began "Dear friends" and ended "BP." He and Dorise had carried out the decisions of the Saskatoon group for a whole year without being in agreement. Now was the time for a showdown. Paul kept a carbon copy for his own files and sat back to catch his breath and await a response.

It had been a busy and, in his estimation, a futile summer. They had driven from meeting to meeting, trying to drum up support for Minerva Cooper's nomination. And Sally's presence in the rumble seat was a constant reminder of another problem. "Mrs. Miller is rather anxious to know your future plans about the children," wrote Violet McNaughton on August 20, "if she is to have them next term she wants to get a maid."[7] McNaughton believed that getting a maid would not improve the situation for the children. Miller was simply too busy with outside responsibilities. Already Nielsen had decided to move the children from Millers' if she could possibly find another place. The only prospect thus far was the home of Sophia Dixon, a woman who had just moved from the farm to the city so that her own four children could attend high school and university.

Like Nielsen, Dixon was a former teacher married to a farmer, and she had been active in left-wing politics through the United Farmers of Canada and the CCF. Many years later she would win one of the first Person's Awards for her work among women, but in 1942 she was struggling to feed and educate her children on a pittance. She had rented a large house and planned to board several university students to help pay her way.

Sophia Dixon hesitated to take the Nielsen children because they were young and would take more care, but if Christine would help with the housework, she said she was willing to give it a try.[8] It was, no doubt, with some relief that Dorise settled her children into Dixon's house on Temperance Street and registered them once again in new schools that fall. There were magpies cawing from the trees and grassy spaces to play along the quiet street not far from the University of Saskatchewan. The four young Dixons, though not young enough to be playmates, were serious students who could provide a good example for the Nielsen children and, perhaps, even help them a little with their homework. And it would do Christine no harm to wash a few socks and make beds for the boarders.

At the end of the third page of "Things We Agree Upon," Sally has written, "Sept 42 to Mrs. Dickson's, high side of Saskatoon, Chris went to high school called Nutana." Did the two sisters have any happy memories at all of those months spent at Sophia Dixon's? Did Christine think of the permanent she finally extracted from her mother that Christmas, of the compliments paid her for her blonde curls? Did they remember tobogganing down the steep bank of the South Saskatchewan River just a few blocks from the Dixon house? Or have the memories of any good times in Saskatoon been obliterated by the stain of the way their sojourn on Temperance Street ended? There was no need to write any of that down. Sally wrote simply, "Chris ended up in Winnipeg . . . Cecil Paul rescued S&J, returned us to Polaskis' until mom could come." That was enough.

While the Saskatchewan communists fought over the wisdom of Minerva Cooper's nomination, important developments were taking place in the East. On September 25, 1942, Tim Buck and fourteen other leading communists gave themselves up to the RCMP in Toronto. They had been underground for over two years. According to Buck, the surrender was a boldly calculated gamble that paid off. He judged that the Ontario premier, Mitchell Hepburn, was softening on communism. That summer three communists had been picked up in Toronto and charged, not with being communists, but with failing to present their national registration cards. They had been held briefly in the Don Jail instead of being sent to internment in Hull.[9]

Buck and his comrades also ended up in the Don Jail for a short stint. In October, after pledging to refrain from political activity, they were released. Shortly after his release, Tim Buck joined Premier Hepburn in a rally at Maple Leaf Gardens to call for the unity of all classes and parties for the war effort.[10] At the same time, the fifteen internees who remained in the Hull jail were freed. Most of the younger men enlisted immediately, while the older men and women[11] quickly took up political work under the guise of the Communist-Labour Total War Committee. The group was monitored by the RCMP but there were no further arrests. In a peculiar way, the government of Mackenzie King, nudged by Hepburn, the Liberal premier of Ontario, had achieved an ad hoc peace with the communists that served its purposes very well. Communists in the labour movement worked for a "no strike" pledge to speed war production. Meanwhile, to appease the anti-communist Liberals in Quebec, the Communist Party remained officially illegal.

But despite its illegal status, the party essentially picked up where it left off before the war began. It had been gaining popularity then and, by the end of 1942, it was once more on a roll. Sympathy was strong for the Russians who, that fall, were fighting the desperate Battle of Stalingrad. When three Soviet war heroes spoke in Toronto, thousands lined the streets to welcome them and Eaton's hoisted the Russian flag. This pro-Soviet enthusiasm began to translate into votes for communists who ran as independents or labour candidates. By the time Parliament met at the end of January 1943, Jacob Penner, recently released from internment, had been re-elected to Winnipeg's city council, while in Toronto, Stewart Smith and Joe Salsberg had won seats on the city council for the first time. Plans were already in the works to nominate leader Tim Buck and Montreal organizer Fred Rose for federal seats.

Now that all the old boys were back, Nielsen's work on the national scene was not essential. She spent the fall of 1942 in Saskatchewan. One day towards the end of September, about the time Tim Buck and the other leaders gave themselves up, Nielsen and Bob Paul were on the road from Turtleford to Spiritwood. It was a long, straight road, bordered with clumps of bush and fields of golden stooks. Both of them were tired from work and worry about the future. They had just managed, in a second nomination meeting, to follow their instructions and get Minerva Cooper nominated as a candidate in Turtleford. It had been a tremendous effort, and a futile one, they were almost sure. They could see the United Progressive movement, the enterprise that had engaged their passion and ingenuity for the past four years, sinking like a stone. But the day itself was a gift (a sunny, warm day in late September is always a gift), and so they took a reprieve from work, from the winter to come, and most of all from the need to present an appearance of rectitude. They turned north on a dusty track through a thick forest of spruce and golden poplars to the shores of Turtle Lake.

Like Emma Lake and other lakes in the northern Saskatchewan, Turtle Lake is a wonder. There is no river running through, just a huge lake with a sandy bottom waiting for the swimmers and boaters and fishermen to appear. For Dorise, the experience was worthy of a poem.

There it was, the great lake
Remote and beautiful
From the liquid sky dropped down
Into these soft sands
Where only bird footprints
Trace their faint filigree.

That day in 1942, there was no one else. Bob Paul and Dorise Nielsen had the shore to themselves and they lingered there through the afternoon. Perhaps Dorise was already jotting a few notes in her head as they shook the sand out of their shoes and headed to Spiritwood. It is not a love poem, exactly, and certainly not an ode to Bob Paul. In fact, his presence is barely acknowledged. It is really a poem about Nielsen, and how the natural beauty of that day, that place, revived her "old longings," "soothed her worries," and "washed away her doubts." She is too guarded (or possibly too determinedly poetic) to reveal just what those longings and doubts were all about. But when I read the poem, I hear Dorise's later words, "We were happy once," and I am inclined to believe that the stolen afternoon in the autumn of 1942 was part of that happiness. Here are the last three stanzas of Nielsen's poem, "Turtle Lake":

There was no sound of man
Just the high wheeling note of gulls
And, oldest of all sounds
The wind-whipped water.
Primaeval music
Finding deep within me
Response
Twanging half forgotten chords
Letting loose soft sounds
Calling long buried impulses
Shutting out Time

Lifting me up
Into the gentle arms of space.

White feather-tipped
Wind wafted waves
Lapping with gentle insistency
Upon the wall of my reserve
Breaking down the high tension bastions
Dissolving fear's grey rocks
Into nothingness.
Washing away doubts
Soothing out the deep creases
Of fretful worry
Shutting out the clamor
Ebbing and flowing
Into deep bosomed water
Sweeping over me with its own serenity.

We stayed so long
And yet so short a time.
While lazily the waves uncurled themselves
And rolled in play
Around our feet
While gulls at leisure
Made trips around the sun
Till the shadows of the trees grew spindly long
On saffron-shell encrusted sands.
As a thirsty man drains the cup
We took one last long look
And went back to the road
The dusty winding road
And all that lay ahead.
But
Someday we shall go back.[12]

By mid-October the harvest was finished and Dorise was on the road once more. Throughout Alberta and Saskatchewan, she spoke on current farm issues and advocated the opening of a second front in Europe to relieve the beleaguered Soviets. The police continued to attend her meetings, estimating the proportion of "the foreign element" and noting that certain meetings ended with the "Internationale," as well as "God Save the King," but at the end of each report there was always a clear message—"Nothing subversive said."

Farming in Saskatchewan had emerged from depression and drought, but just at a time when it was possible to turn a profit, farmers were short on manpower. From the village of Mayfair, south of Spiritwood, Nielsen wrote a note to Violet McNaughton, requesting an extra copy of the *Western Producer* for a "progressive farm woman" who had intended to save an article on collective farms in the USSR, "but someone lit the fire with it!"[13] Collectivization, cooperation, the pooling of farm machinery, none of these were new ideas, but for Nielsen and others they seemed particularly relevant for small farmers who faced growing production quotas with their sons in the army and without the cash or credit to buy new machinery. As usual, the problems were felt more keenly on the marginal northern farms. On her return to Parliament, Nielsen promoted a long list of suggestions to ease the labour shortage. These included a moratorium on voluntary enlistments in the West, the use of army recruits at harvest time, and the formation of a women's land army to help with farmwork.[14]

Shortly before Christmas Nielsen went to Saskatoon to fetch the children. She had spent much of the last month travelling from one hamlet to another, and possibly knew nothing of the drama that awaited her. Christine had been counting the days until her mother's arrival. She believed she had suffered an injustice at the hands of Sophia Dixon and expected Dorise to take her part. Mrs. Dixon was accusing her of being a bad girl, of doing things she shouldn't with one of the boarders and with soldiers in the park. When she heard the news, Dorise promptly burst into tears. It was the first time Christine had ever seen her mother cry. It was clear that Dorise took Mrs. Dixon's accusations seriously.

For Christine, her mother's betrayal left a gaping wound. She had not quite reached her fourteenth birthday and she felt alone in the world. None of the attention she got from men (and there would be more, Saskatoon was only the beginning—she was a very pretty girl and a vulnerable one) could ever make up for the lack of attention from her parents. We can only surmise Dorise's own feelings. By all accounts, she was proud of her self-possession. Showing anger or sorrow or regret were aberrations for her, but there is no doubt she carried a great deal of guilt when it came to her children. "I neglected you," she would say later, "but what else could I have done?"

What could she have done? Once she had decided to run for election and once she had won, could she have played out her role of mother any differently? The months of separation and the hours of work were daunting for any MP during the war. But in addition, as a spokesperson for the party, she was bound to follow party directives. So, during the Parliamentary recess, she was seldom available to her children, either, and when she was, her mind was often somewhere else.

Soon, Dorise would settle on the idea that her children had been sacrificed for the cause of socialism. Later, she would blame the party for demanding too much work from her while failing to help with her children. Later still, she would blame herself for bottling up her emotions and not letting her children know how much she loved them. The fallout would go on for years, years of letters and arguments and reconciliations, of gifts given and received, of family rifts and reunions. It would go on even after Dorise's death in the events that Sally and Christine could not agree upon and the things that Johnny preferred to forget. Never would Dorise acknowledge that her life on the stage, with hundreds of people hanging on her every word, gave her any satisfaction at all. She had a natural gift. She was a master teacher and entertainer rolled into one. No one who heard her speak ever forgot the experience (not even the RCMP). And though she would not admit it, her children sensed that her work was all-absorbing and that they were simply obstacles in her path.

The Christmas of 1942, as usual, the family returned to Spiritwood. Dorise quickly regained her composure and scrambled to arrange another boarding place for Christine. If she needed any assurance that her own worries were small compared to others', she had only to read, with the rest of the world, that the rumours of the mass slaughter of European Jews had been confirmed by the Inter-Allied Information Committee. Already two million people were believed dead by electrocution and lethal gas poisoning.[15]

After Christmas Nielsen returned her two younger children to Sophia Dixon's in Saskatoon and boarded the train for Winnipeg with Christine. She had decided that her daughter had fallen into bad company and needed a fresh start in a good progressive household.[16] Bill and Mary Kardash had agreed to take her for the rest of the year. Dorise knew the Kardashes well enough to vouch for their politics. She had supported Bill's election to the Manitoba legislature in 1941, and, on several occasions since, they had travelled together to meetings in Toronto.

On her way to Ottawa she stopped, as usual, for a meeting in Toronto. For the first time she could meet openly with veteran leaders Tim Buck, Sam Carr, Leslie Morris, Stewart Smith, and Joe Salsberg, and with the party's rising young intellectual, Stanley Ryerson. Annie Buller was there, out of prison at last, and so was Becky Buhay, who had been working for the party underground since the war began. Nielsen was finally able to sort out the problem of Minerva Cooper's candidacy in Turtleford. "Bob and I have received the verdict," she wrote Heide in February 1943. "We were correct and the Sask(atoon) group incorrect."[17] She had waited a long time for the party's decision. Once more, Bob had prepared the snowballs, and she had thrown them. Bob and Dorise had won the battle within the party and Minerva Cooper withdrew. What would happen in the constituency was another matter. It would not be easy to build support again after such a mess. But if anyone could do it, she was confident that Bob could.

When Dorise wrote to Heide, she was once again in the House, enduring a long evening session. Another item on her mind (and on the minds of everyone interested in politics) was the growing popularity of the CCF. The tide had turned in the war. In eastern Europe and in North Africa, German armies were being pushed back and, in the far east, the Japanese advances had been stopped short of India and Australia. The Allied invasion of Hitler's "fortress Europe" was expected sometime in 1943. Then the war would wind down and so would the Canadian economy. Many voters expected the return of depression and, therefore, turned to the CCF. It was the only party (apart from the communists) that had consistently advocated a planned economy and comprehensive system of social security. In the course of 1942, CCF support nationally had increased from 10 to 25 percent. They had already surpassed the Tories and were closing in on the Liberals.[18] In a Toronto by-election that year, an unknown CCF high school teacher, Joe Noseworthy, had defeated the leader of the Conservative Party, Arthur Meighen.

"The CCF is so cocky these days," Dorise wrote Heide. "My friend Joe Noseworthy is holding forth and I'm listening with one ear. He is not a bad speaker but very slow—I want to push him along."[19]

The CCF had a right to feel cocky—their popularity was pushing the established parties further to the left. The Conservatives had just chosen as their new leader the former Progressive premier of Manitoba, John Bracken, and had changed their name to the Progressive Conservative Party. In the Speech from the Throne that year, Mackenzie King promised a national scheme of social insurance that was to include health insurance. He would begin by appointing a committee to decide on the steps to be taken.

Yes, the inhabitants of socialist alley on the sixth floor were cocky enough, but no more confident than the communists, who were sure they would win in the end. "Social reformism ... is a natural development through which we have to pass," wrote Dorise. "It is not, however, the end—only the beginning of the real fight, and they [the CCF] have not the scientific knowledge to go on to the real issue! Oh well, we all have a lot to learn."[20] So what if she sometimes felt about eighty and was plagued with worries over her children and the constituency. She was sure she was on the right path politically, the only true path to socialism.

Now that she had met all the party leaders, Nielsen was even more confident of her choice. Many of them were working-class men who had been educated by the party. But they came from all classes and all ethnic groups, Jews and Gentiles, workers and intellectuals, united in their devotion to a common cause. They were erudite talkers and loved to explain the finer points of Marxism, including the equality of women under socialism. Meanwhile, Mackenzie King had the temerity to leave women out of a speech on his hopes for a more representative Parliament. "He mentioned labour and the farmers ... men with broad human sympathies ... but he never mentioned anything about women. I cannot let that pass," said Dorise in the House. "I believe that every honorable member and every person in Canada will acknowledge that during these war years the women of the country have proved by their deeds what capable people they are. They have gone into practically every one of the industries that are vital to war production. They have undertaken heavy physical labour. They have also taken on types of work requiring executive ability." She said that she hoped the prime minister's failure to mention women "was not intentional but occurred merely because for the moment he failed to think."[21]

Though her remarks made the news,[22] few people in Parliament had been listening that night. It was a Thursday evening and she had counted only fifteen on the Liberal benches. "God it's terrible to get up and talk to a House like that," she told Heide. Those MPs closer to home could cut the Thursday night session and spend a long weekend with their families. Home for Dorise was a long way off and becoming hard to define. Her room down the hill with hot plate for making tea or boiling an egg was one of many she had occupied—each session, there was a change. Home was definitely not Ottawa. And the little house in Spiritwood was more like an office. With the children in Saskatoon and Winnipeg, she was more of a nomad than ever. "Please write," she asked Heide, "and tell me everything. I long for news of home . . . I seem so far away from everybody while I'm here."[23]

In 1943 the parliamentary session was another long one. On July 1 Nielsen was still in Ottawa. That day she spoke on federal support for day nurseries, a cause very dear to her heart. She believed that such facilities should not be viewed as temporary wartime measures and that they should be available to all working mothers. The need for day nurseries had existed before the war and would continue to grow. "The emancipation of women as wage-earners has come to stay," she maintained. After the war there would be no return to "kirchen, kuchen, kindern." And she thought that children would benefit from the experience, provided that childcare workers were well-paid and properly trained, and the centres were bright, airy places with adequate space to play outdoors. The preschool nursery, she believed, was the answer to training children in good social habits. Even the children from wealthy homes would benefit, for children should not be "petted too much and given an exaggerated sense of their own importance."[24]

But the Minister of Labour, Humphrey Mitchell, disagreed. He believed that her ideas were not in sync with the rest of the country. "Our people are a little wary about giving their children up to what some may consider institutional care," he maintained.[25]

Despite Nielsen's apparent confidence, her speech that day was one of the most difficult she ever delivered. She was frantic for the safety of her own children. Was it possible, she wondered, for a mother ever to leave her children in the care of others with any assurance at all? That morning she had received an airmail letter from Sophia Dixon, saying that she would not keep Sally and Johnny another twenty-four hours. She had discovered they had been systematically stealing from her. If they were not taken off her hands immediately, she threatened to put them in a home for delinquents.

As soon as she read the letter, Nielsen phoned Spiritwood and left a message for Bob Paul to fetch the children from Saskatoon. That evening, after delivering her speech on day nurseries, she wrote to Violet McNaughton. Nielsen said she thought Sophia Dixon must be "on the verge of a very serious nervous breakdown," and asked McNaughton, who was a friend of Sophia's, to phone and check on her. "She is such a fine person, and so conscientious. I am terribly upset to think she is working herself into a breakdown."[26]

As for the children and what the whole experience had done to them, she hated to think. "My children are very ordinary little children and to be tempted to steal is something to which all children are subjected sometime in their lives, I guess. I have seldom known of cases properly handled where a good lesson could not be taught and the trouble stopped." She had sent Mrs. Dixon a telegram earlier that day, saying that on no account should the children be put in a home. Bob Paul would come to fetch them as soon as possible. In fact, it was Cecil Paul, already in Saskatoon to attend summer school, who came to the rescue and returned John and Sally to the Polaski farm. It was the only place they felt safe and truly at home.

But when Dorise delivered her speech and wrote McNaughton, she had no idea whether her children would be rescued. Still, she was willing to give Sophia Dixon the benefit of the doubt. She knew well enough the stresses of overwork. "I hope . . . that she takes things a little easy," wrote Nielsen, because undoubtedly the woman had "more than she could manage."

Months before the accusations against her younger children, Dorise had begun to wonder if Sophia's accusations against Christine had been exaggerated. The reports from the Kardashes in Winnipeg had been quite normal. But even if Dorise were prepared to confess her own mistake, Christine was not in a mood to forgive her mother. That summer, when Dorise stopped in Winnipeg, Christine refused to go on a family holiday.

Dorise and the two younger children spent the first two weeks in August at a cottage on Lake Edith near Jasper. The lake was glacial but still they swam. Dorise would remember Lake Edith for the rest of her life as one of the most beautiful places on earth—the snow-capped mountains, turquoise lake, the pure air. They watched in awe as antlered elk grazed as tame as cows and they fed bear cubs near the cabin door. Before bed, Dorise read to Sally and Johnny from a stack of books she'd brought with her. "We enjoyed every minute of the time together," she wrote McNaughton, though it took a while to become acquainted again and she could have done with a month.[27]

It was during the holiday that she told the children they would be moving again, this time to Winnipeg. After the holiday, she deposited her two younger children at the Kardashes' home on Redwood Avenue. Once again, Sally and Johnny were living with strangers and attending new schools. And, because of limited space there, Christine moved in with another family called Hollenberg, where she shared a room with the only son, a six-year-old boy. At least, for once, there was no disruption of her schooling or her social life.

The Nielsen children lived in Winnipeg until the summer of 1945. In many ways, this was an interval of peace and stability and acceptance, particularly when compared to their experience in Saskatoon. Still, it was difficult for anyone to make up the traumatic losses they had already suffered. Dorise worried that Christine was boy crazy and that Sally suffered from low self-esteem,[28] but apart from finding them places to live and footing the bills, there was little she could do. She tried to see the children once a month, but even when she managed that, her visits were often rushed. On one short visit, Christine spent the whole time begging her mother for money to buy a particular jacket. Dorise resisted until just before her departure and handed the money over on the station platform. Another time Dorise bought a Sally a mandolin so that she could take lessons at the Labour Temple. And the summer of 1944, she enrolled John Nielsen at St. John's College School, a venerable Anglican school for boys that took a few boarders. The Kardashes had a new baby, their second child. That made two adults and four children sharing two bedrooms and a sun porch. So this time it was nine-year-old Johnny who would have to move.

In the House of Commons Nielsen held her own. She did not back down when heckled and she did not give up. She spoke with an authority that did not come easily to women of her generation. Years later, Liberal MP Sheila Copps would say that her best training for Parliament was playing on her high school basketball team. You have to throw yourself into the game, give it all you've got, and, if you lose, put it all away and come out smiling, ready for the next round. The competitive, game-playing world of politics traditionally belonged to men, but Nielsen mastered it quickly.

With her children, Nielsen's voice of authority was not so effective. Despite all her wise pronouncements on raising children, when it came to her own children she ran out of patience. She gave ultimatums and they either obeyed or rebelled. There seemed to be no room for negotiation. The first to take on her mother was Christine, but each would follow in turn. Their rebellions would be spectacular, life-altering events. Was Nielsen an unreasonable mother? Were her children particularly difficult? Certainly, at the time, other parents sympathized with Nielsen's problems with her children.[29] But, of course, it was not only Nielsen who suffered through the problems, it was her children, too.

9

WORKING FOR A NEW WORLD

> Are the government and employers going to say to these women, 'Well girls, you have done a nice job: you look very cute in your overalls and we appreciate what you have done for us; but just run along; go home; we can get along without you very nicely'?[1]

AT THE END OF AUGUST 1943, Nielsen stood chatting with veteran labour organizer Joe Salsberg in the lobby of the King Edward Hotel in Toronto.[2] In the ballroom, 500 delegates had assembled to choose a new name for the Communist Party of Canada and to settle on a platform. It was almost a year since its leaders had been released. Communists had been running for office as labour candidates with surprising success. But if the party were to reap the benefits of this upswing in support, it needed the ease of operating openly as a legitimate political party.

The decision to create a new party had been made early in the year. From February to April, Tim Buck had toured the country, hitting even the smallest of villages, wherever there was any grain of support.[3] It helped that the party had dropped its revolutionary rhetoric and once more adopted the reformist stance of the popular front period. At the founding convention, delegates declared their opposition to "violence, conspiracy and secrecy" and their determination to educate and organize Canadians in the cause of socialism. More specifically, they proposed such reforms as medicare, a full employment policy, protection of the family farm, pensions at the age of sixty, and the abolition of the Senate. They also wanted Canada to make anti-Semitism a punishable offence and to adopt a distinctive national flag.[4] The name they chose was the Labour Progressive Party (LPP).

Hopes were high that the party's image as a clutch of foreign-directed radicals would fade. It was advocating many of the same reforms that had just brought the Ontario CCF within four seats of winning a provincial election. And the newspapers, full of tales of Soviet heroism on the battlefield and successes on the home front, were doing no harm. Foreign correspondents in Moscow were sending home detailed and usually complimentary accounts of a socialist economy in action. (In Moscow, for example, a 2400-bed hospital was run by women alone. Surely the communists were doing something right!)

It was the right moment, the party had decided, for Dorise Nielsen to declare her allegiance. Her introduction as a new member of the LPP would be one of the highlights of the convention. But several events intervened that would make her first appearance on a stage with Tim Buck and the others an anti-climax. A few weeks before, Fred Rose, a seasoned communist organizer in Quebec, won a by-election in the federal riding of Montreal-Cartier. And only a few days before that, A.A. MacLeod and Joe Salsberg had been elected to the Ontario legislature. Although Nielsen had campaigned hard for both Rose and MacLeod, these men, fresh from victory, were the obvious stars of the occasion. Nevertheless, the convention gave Nielsen a very hearty welcome ("they went almost haywire," wrote the RCMP).[5] She went on to speak in support of a resolution that the new party affiliate with the CCF.[6] Later that weekend, she was elected to the seventeen-member National Executive of the LPP. She had come out of the closet at last.

"We had a most inspiring convention in Toronto," wrote Nielsen to Violet McNaughton, two weeks later. "I have felt more assured all the time about the correctness of the decisions made. I find myself in most resolute company and among kindred spirits.... I find among these people a much higher calibre than anything I ever found in the CCF and I am very proud to have become one of them."[7]

But only a few months before, Nielsen had fought hard against openly joining the new party. She was sure it would ruin her chances of being re-elected in North Battleford, and Bob Paul agreed. So far, many of her supporters in the CCF had chosen to ignore the evidence that Mrs. Nielsen was a communist. If she confirmed those rumours herself, there would be a great falling-off of support. And her support from Hungarians and French Canadians was bound to plummet. She would be condemned from every Roman Catholic pulpit in the riding. According to Stewart Paul, who was fifteen at the time, Dorise and his father tried unsuccessfully to convince the leadership that she should remain a secret party member, but in the end they bowed to a command from the centre. Obviously, the party wanted Nielsen as a national spokesperson for the new party. Secrecy may have helped her in North Battleford, but as far as the LPP was concerned, she would be far more useful out in the open.

In her letter to McNaughton, it is clear that Nielsen had decided to put a positive spin on her new situation and plough on. The past was the past. She had lost the battle but still hoped to win the war. And once she mounted the stage at the convention, she felt caught up in a heroic struggle that almost swept her away. Surely she was part of something much greater than the plotting and planning that went on in Spiritwood and Turtleford. "In the silence of a moment I heard the thundering roar of battle, Madrid and Stalingrad; a Chinese wail. Felt crowds waiting in Calcutta while I straightened my notes."[8] At heart, then, Dorise Nielsen was a romantic, and all her pragmatism was harnessed to an heroic ideal of devotion to a cause.

By mid-September Dorise was back in Spiritwood, awaiting the end of harvest so that her meetings could begin. It is clear, on looking back, that her links with Saskatchewan were in jeopardy from the moment she openly joined the LPP, if not before. The core strength of the Communist Party was the larger cities, such as Winnipeg, Montreal, Toronto, which had significant Jewish populations. In other cities and in rural areas, it remained a party of particular ethnic minorities such as Finns and Ukrainians. But in the euphoric days of 1943, when even Stephen Leacock had declared himself in favour of a planned economy,[9] and when *Saturday Night*'s business page maintained, in mincing words, that "private enterprise cannot possibly be evil in itself, even though ... evil may come from it,"[10] it was, perhaps, possible to believe that the LPP could lose its alien stigma and ride the wave.

There were torrents of rain that October. Dorise and Bob slithered over muddy roads to meetings where attendance varied from passable to poor, while others were cancelled. But, considering the weather, she didn't do badly. At all her meetings she rallied support for the government's fifth victory loan campaign, and advocated a petition to Mackenzie King on the opening of a second front. Then it was on to the issue of post-war reconstruction, an issue on the tip of every political tongue. So far the Liberals had done nothing but talk. "Post-war reconstruction must be in the hands of the people," she urged, "not the financial magnates."[11] And then she pitched the crowd to support one Progressive candidate in the next federal election. It was a matter of defeating the Liberals. Cameron McIntosh, editor of the *North Battleford News* and staunch supporter of capitalism, was hovering in the wings, ready to run again. So far the CCF had not nominated.

In November, when the roads were drivable once again, she toured the constituency with Tim Buck, who always drew a good crowd. "If we can produce for war, we can produce for peace," he said. "If it is worth $1B to destroy German cities, it is worth $1B to maintain a decent standard of living." The old parties would not carry out the necessary policies, he warned. Government reconstruction plans favoured the big capitalists. It would be up to the LPP to change the system.[12]

That series of meetings culminated with the first convention of the Saskatchewan Labour Progressive Party, held in Regina. Once more Tim Buck spoke, urging the defeat of the old parties. He announced that the LPP would support CCF candidates in the next Saskatchewan provincial election, except in ridings where the LPP was in a better position to represent the working class. That was just what Nielsen wanted to hear. By supporting the CCF in the provincial election, she hoped to gain a clear field in the federal election.

But as she looked over the group at the Saskatchewan LPP convention, Dorise must have found it difficult to be truly optimistic. The war had shifted the composition of her meetings (of all political meetings, perhaps) from the young to the old. Many of the men who had worked so energetically in her own campaign were in the armed forces now, with younger women following their men from one training centre to another, or staying home with more responsibility than ever before. Only the old guard was left to carry on. Florence Theodore had agreed to be provincial leader of the LPP. Her husband, Alex, would be provincial organizer and Walter Wiggins would serve as president. All three had been active through the twenties and thirties and were on the verge of retiring and moving to the coast, but they would hang on until after the war. Dorise became vice-president, and Bob Paul was elected to the executive committee.[13]

While Dorise was reflecting on her chances in Saskatchewan, another conference was taking place halfway round the world in Tehran. For the first time, in December 1943, all three great war leaders were meeting. With the end of the war in sight, plans for the post-war world were high on the agenda. Until the war, the Soviet Union had been isolated by the Western powers, but the Tehran Agreement, negotiated at that meeting, promised post-war cooperation. This breakthrough for the Soviet Union was something to celebrate. It did, however, present communists in Canada and elsewhere with a dilemma. In one sweep, the fundamental Marxist doctrine of class conflict had been tossed out the window.

When the LPP executive met in January 1944, Tim Buck explained that Canadians weren't ready for socialism.[14] To push for socialism prematurely would be divisive. The correct path to domestic unity and international harmony was to support the government on all substantive issues. Fred Rose and Dorise Nielsen had just a few days to absorb the new message. When Parliament opened the following week, they were to button their lips on a volatile labour situation and look for something in the Throne Speech to support. It would not be easy. Labour unions, some of them led by communists, were threatening a national walkout over the government's refusal to lift its wage freeze.

Dorise needed no one to remind her that, despite her four years in Parliament, when it came to the party, she was still a neophyte. She had never led a strike or even marched on a picket line. She had never gone to prison. She had never attended classes at the famous Lenin School in Moscow or the Rand School of Social Science in New York. She had learned everything about Marxism on her own, from reading books. So when Tim Buck said that the time wasn't ripe for socialism, she was inclined to believe him. But unity with the Liberals was not the type of unity she had ever contemplated. Just a month before, both she and Buck had been promoting unity with the CCF. How she would be able to sell such a policy to her supporters in northern Saskatchewan, she couldn't imagine.

From Toronto, Nielsen, Sam Carr, Tim Buck, and Fred Rose took the show on the road to Montreal. Rose had been elected to Parliament the previous summer from the working-class east side of Montreal. It had been a rough and rowdy election campaign against the Bloc Populaire, a new nationalist party formed over the issue of conscription. The CCF had nominated its own golden boy, David Lewis. Rose had won by a narrow margin (with Lewis coming a far third) and he was about to take his seat in Parliament. Four thousand supporters packed into Baron Byng High School on St. Urbain Street to give him a rousing send-off.[15] For Nielsen, it was an amazing contrast to her visits to Montreal just a few years before, when all the party leaders had been either in prison or underground. Rose was definitely the man of the hour. He spoke of outlawing anti-Semitism, improving wages in the needle trades, and freezing rents. If he advocated supporting Mackenzie King and the Liberals, it was not reported by the *Canadian Tribune*. Still, it was Dorise who delivered the outstanding speech of the evening. She called for a better world after the war and vowed that she and Rose would fight for it in Ottawa. Her address was both tactful and well prepared (noted Sgt. Vaughan), but every bit as fiery as usual, and the audience responded with thunderous applause.[16]

A few days later, Dorise made her way through rain and sleet to Parliament Hill for the opening of the new session, the fifth since her election. Ottawa was rejoicing in the mild weather. It meant that the city's stocks of coal might last through the winter. And there were other reasons for rejoicing. The siege of Leningrad was over at last and, further south, the Allies were at the gates of Rome. On a personal level, Nielsen was living better than she had for years. She had been lucky to snaffle a bachelor apartment close to Parliament Hill. It was only one room, but she had a bathroom all to herself, and for once there was no shortage of hot water.[17]

It is likely Dorise had someone to thank for finding her that apartment. With so many professionals moving to Ottawa to work in the bourgeoning civil service, the pool of "like-minded people" had grown. There was Agatha Chapman, an economist who had been fired from her job at Sun Life in Montreal in 1940 for being secretary of the Civil Liberties Union, an organization in which communists were heavily involved. By 1941 she was in Ottawa, working for the Bank of Canada. She lived on Somerset West and often held study meetings at her apartment.[18] Study clubs abounded late in the war and were open to everyone. Dorise was sometimes asked to speak at them. She was fond of Agatha but, for most of the time, she kept her distance. She had no desire to put anyone's job at risk. Still, her new apartment was a boon—so close to

Parliament she could read the Peace Tower clock from her window. Even though the room was so small that her elbows practically knocked on the walls, she was pleased. Often she walked home and made her own meal during the dinner recess. It was a good break from the endless talk and the need to appear sociable.

The first day of the session, as the only other LPP member in the House, it was Nielsen's duty to introduce Rose. When the time came, she crossed the short distance from her desk to fetch him at the door of the Chamber. Together they proceeded up the aisle to clerk's table. "Mr. Speaker," said Nielsen, "I have the honour to introduce Mr. Fred Rose, the member for Cartier."

They made an odd couple: Dorise, five foot ten (even taller in her pumps), and Fred Rose, five four. At thirty-six, Rose was a slightly built man with a receding hairline and dapper little moustache. A bantam rooster and a crane, side by side. Both were anomalies—Dorise, a woman in a world of men, and Fred Rose, a Jewish immigrant from Poland, in a Parliament where immigrants (other than British) were rare indeed. Four new members were introduced that day and none of them were Liberals. The by-elections the previous summer had been a disaster for the ruling party. There were two new CCF members from the West, and, from Quebec, a communist and a member of the Bloc Populaire.

As another wartime Parliament opened, the *Evening Citizen* once again bemoaned the occasion's "drab, glamourless, formality," but the Speech from the Throne promised a shiny new world after the war. King proposed a comprehensive system of social security, to be administered by three new government departments. The opposition parties, who had listened to such promises for years, were not impressed. They knew that comprehensive social security would require constitutional change (hadn't the Rowell-Sirois Report in 1939 outlined the whole problem?). To express their concerns, both the Conservatives (who had recently changed their name to Progressive Conservatives) and the CCF proposed amendments to the motion to accept the Throne Speech. In a House with an overwhelming Liberal majority, neither amendment had any hope of passing. But for Nielsen and Rose, it was the first test of the LPP's new policy of supporting a "Liberal-Labour coalition."

Nielsen had often voted with the CCF on divisions, and it seems that her inclination was to vote with them again. She agreed with every word of their motion that the government "had failed to propose fundamental social changes and economic planning which alone can hasten the winning of the war and make possible the establishment of a post-war Canada capable of providing full-employment and complete social security."[19] Moreover, voting with the CCF made sense for her political future in Saskatchewan. Yet, Rose insisted they must vote against the amendment. Their heated (and audible) argument went on for two hours.[20] By February 8, when the division on the CCF amendment came, Nielsen had been brought to heel. Both she and Rose lined up on the government side.

A few weeks later, she explained to an LPP national meeting that she had been confused about the CCF amendment but that Fred Rose had discussed it with her for several hours until she "understood the necessity of voting against this amendment." She compared Fred Rose to a great light that illuminated the House of Commons.[21] Did she really believe what she was saying? If not, she was certainly trying hard. And she had the party's well-established process of self-criticism to push her along. In essence, Nielsen was in retreat. No doubt, the party leadership had taken Rose's side and told her to accept his leadership.

Whether relations between Nielsen and Rose ever recovered is hard to say, but it is clear he was the senior partner from the moment he entered the House of Commons in 1944. In the House, Fred Rose and Dorise divided up the work, but when both were given time to speak on a bill, Rose spoke first, and if only one of them were allotted time, it was Rose who took the floor.[22] Nielsen, it seems, was expected to bend her talents to issues of health and welfare, agriculture, and the status of women, while the newcomer took on the weighty portfolios of foreign affairs, banking, and industry and commerce. Although it was a blow to her pride (not the first, and certainly not the last), it's unlikely she raised further objections. Rose was her senior in the party. In fact, everyone else on the party's national executive was her senior when it came to the number of years they had been doing party work. She probably decided not to dwell on the fact that she had two additional strikes against her: she was a woman and she was from the West.

On several occasions near the beginning of the session, Nielsen came to Rose's defence. Some members of the House who had refrained from attacking her, even when her affiliation was clearly known, had no such qualms when it came to Fred Rose. The first blast of disapproval had come from Hanson, the former Conservative leader. He said that the results of the by-elections appalled him. "An extremely radical ... and in my view subversive element in this country had what I hope is only a momentary triumph."[23]

The next day Dorise referred to Hanson's tirade as "unbecoming a senior member of the House" and illustrating "what a thin coating this 'progressive' is on the Conservative Party." She said that the people of Montreal had elected Rose because he was "an honest man and a man of the people ... they elected him because they felt they could trust him" (an ironic statement in light of his later conviction for conspiracy to spy for the Soviet Union). For her own part, she said she was happy to have him and believed he "would do something to relieve that somewhat stuffy atmosphere of this chamber."[24]

In keeping with the communist agenda of national unity, Rose's speeches were usually conciliatory and optimistic, but that didn't matter. He was known as a communist organizer in Quebec and had been one of the fourteen leading communists who had surrendered in September 1942. Here he was, a little over a year later, in the House of Commons, questioning the Minister of National Defence on the role of the army during strikes. Some of the older reservists, he said, "are quite reactionary.... They are jingoes: they do not understand the new spirit of Canada and the world."[25] The old reservists weren't the only ones. There were plenty of reactionaries present in the House. He spoke with a Yiddish accent, which, for some, confirmed his allegiance to another country. The fact that he spoke four languages did not matter. But Rose barrelled on, growing in confidence by the day. Soon he was cracking jokes with journalists and the Liberal brass, dropping the names of VIPs as if they were his bosom buddies.[26]

Despite King's promise of social legislation, he still maintained that his government's first priority was fighting the war. Only after the dust settled, he said, could there be any thought of an election for Canada. Everyone knew the Allied invasion of France would come in the spring. God only knew what the casualty rate would be. Already air force casualties, most of them from bombers pounding the German homeland, took up a full page in the daily papers. Over 90,000 Canadian soldiers were serving in the Italian campaign, which had started the previous summer. Soon the toll in casualties there would reach 24,000, with over 11,000 confirmed dead.[27]

Early in the 1944 session, fresh from the Italian front, came Flight Lieutenant Jimmy Sinclair, Liberal MP for Vancouver North. He had been absent from the House for three years. Handsome with his curly dark hair and his RCAF uniform, he congratulated the government on its magnificent war effort. He had seen first-hand a vast fleet of trucks made in Windsor and Oshawa, ferrying supplies across the Libyan desert. And, at home, the government had managed to feed its population well with very little change in the cost of living. But there was something he could not abide, and that was the government's new Order-in-Council PC #9834. Canadians, he said, did not want a freeze on sweatshop wages for the duration of the war. The government's Order-in-Council had united Canadian labour from coast to coast as never before, and he stood with them. If the government didn't change its policy, he predicted that troops would come home singing "The Red Flag" instead of "Land of Hope and Glory."[28]

When he sat down, Dorise and Fred and members from all parts of the chamber thumped their desks in approval. Seven other Liberals from BC immediately expressed their support, and Mackenzie raced to put out yet another fire. There would be a new labour code, he promised, and it would come within days.

But the brief revolt in the Liberals' ranks and the consequent new labour code that finally guaranteed collective bargaining rights were among the few surprises in the 1944 session. It was clear from the Throne Speech that the King government was proposing a long session with a heavy load of legislation, and everyone settled down to work. Dorise was on three standing committees as well as the ad hoc Committee on Post-War Reconstruction. It would be her busiest session by far. Already a blue-chip extra-parliamentary committee on reconstruction (the James committee) had produced a groundbreaking *Report on Social Security for Canada* (often called the *Marsh Report*). It argued that an effective system of protection against unemployment, sickness, and old age would produce economic stability in post-war Canada. So far, Canada had only unemployment insurance (from which many workers were excluded) and a skimpy old-age pension for those over seventy, based on need. But now it seemed from the Throne Speech that the government was finally willing to implement the *Marsh Report*'s recommendations, provided, of course, that the provinces agreed. There would be a contributory pension scheme for all

Canadian workers, health insurance for all Canadians, and a family allowance for children sixteen and under.

All this legislation, as well as programs for veterans and a national housing act, would be on the table during the 1944 session. Dorise was particularly interested in health insurance, something she had pushed from the beginning of her term in Parliament. Also, she was concerned about post-war employment for women. During the war, the number of women in the labour force had doubled. What would happen to them when the men came home? A subcommittee on the post-war problems of women had just completed its report. She was determined that its recommendations about the continuation of government-funded nurseries, equal pay for equal work, and non-discrimination in all areas of employment be heard and implemented.

Just before the Easter break, an article in *Saturday Night* predicted a bright future for Jimmy Sinclair, the man who had achieved an immediate change in labour legislation. The writer went on to speak of two others whom Dorise knew even better. It described David Lewis and Tim Buck as men of "mental competence, moral courage, and intellectual integrity" who, along with Sinclair, could keep the country from bogging down in "political inertia and reactionary ineptitude."[29] It was good to read something positive, for a change. The CCF had been coming down hard on the LPP (and on Nielsen and Rose) over the new policy of supporting the Liberals and promoting a no-strike pledge in industry. "We know now where the LPP stands in the labour movement," wrote Clarie Gillis in the *Glace Bay Gazette*, "they are the weasels in the hencoop."[30]

All through the two weeks of Easter vacation in 1944, Nielsen worked on a booklet on women's work after the war. By 1944 women were entitled to equal pay for equal work under wartime regulations, but there were a myriad of ways for employers to get around the rules. And too many women regarded their employed status as a temporary wartime measure to cause a fuss. All that had to change, in Dorise's opinion. If some women wanted to retreat to the home after the war, so be it, but they shouldn't be pushed out of their jobs, and they shouldn't accept shoddy wages, either, no matter how much they were hounded to make sacrifices for the war effort.

New Worlds for Women, published by the LPP in November 1944, was a moderate document, with no mention of socialism, no exposition of the Marxist belief that women could never achieve equality in a capitalist system. It urged women to join unions, seek advanced positions in their professions, and demand a living wage whatever their line of work. Although Nielsen was credited as sole author, in the foreword she thanked the women who helped her gather the materials and dedicated the 110-page booklet to the women of Canada. "It is over 150 years since Mary Wollstonecraft wrote her famous treatise *The Vindication of the Rights of Women*," she wrote in the foreword, but "many handicaps still stand in our way."[31]

Nielsen was well aware that her own views on women were considered radical for the times. Housework, she believed, was a vastly overrated activity, designed to stifle the intellect. In her homesteading days, she had fought hard against the endless possibilities for drudgery. Women needed time to themselves; they were not meant to be the slaves of husbands and children. She had had these ideas long before she knew anything about the class struggle, and they had been set in stone when she encountered her Norbury neighbours "working their fingernails to the bone." Occasionally such ideas surfaced in her writing and her speeches. In the *New Worlds*, for instance, she surmised that many women "who have been through the mill" of raising families actually enjoyed working outside their homes during the war and appreciated having some money of their own. She proposed that opportunities for part-time work, designed specifically for mothers working in war industries, should be continued after the war.

But usually Nielsen tried to couch her ideas in terms that would appeal to the majority of both women and men who still believed women's primary duty was to their own household. Women must have choices, she argued. If they have choices, they will be better mothers and better wives. If they have choices, the country will benefit from having the talents of a hitherto-neglected group available to all of society. She was not alone in her arguments—all this had been said before. But seldom had it been so consistently pounded home in Canada's House of Commons.[32]

In addition, the need for women's paid labour during the war gave Nielsen and other feminists hope that equal pay for equal work would soon prevail. When the women's branches of the armed services were initially set up in 1941 and 1942, women were paid two-thirds the basic pay of men holding the same rank and doing the same job. Since they were actually replacing men, the injustice of the pay scale was so obvious that it was soon challenged by the National Council of Women and other groups. In the House Nielsen asked the Minister of National Defence to defend the logic of two-thirds pay. She appreciated logic, she said, but she was sure there was nothing logical about the pay scale. It was simply a relic of the Dark Ages. "We have overcome ... discrimination with regard to religion and race, though not altogether, but we still do suffer in this country from sex discrimination," she maintained. If she, herself, were paid two thirds of male MPs' wages, she promised that she would start a union with the other woman member, not just for their own sakes but on behalf of women who would take their places in Parliament in the future.[33]

By 1944, opposition leaders knew they could count on Nielsen to take up any cause relating to women and children, and they were usually willing to back her up. "When I made way for the honorable member for North Battleford," said Progressive Conservative house leader Gordon Graydon, "I realized she would make a much more eloquent appeal on this matter than I could."[34] The matter in question that day was the practice of cutting off dependents' allowances to the families of enlisted men who had gone AWOL. A plea for women and children was, of course, more effective when it came from a woman, and a woman with children of her own. Nielsen was able and willing to use her status as the only woman in opposition to spearhead a number of issues relating to women. If she were being used as a tool in the Tories' jousting match with the Liberals, so be it—these were issues she cared about, too. Cora Casselman, as a Liberal backbencher, seldom took strong stands on such issues, though once, at the end of a speech on naval estimates, she did say that she could see no reason why women in the armed services did not get equal pay.[35]

Nielsen raised the issue of equal pay again and again. By the end of the war, the pay of women in the armed forces had risen from 67 percent to 80 percent of their male equivalents. She had even less success on several other issues. When the new Department of Health and Welfare was being set up, she proposed an amendment for a separate division on child welfare in which some of the administrative officials would be women. Such an amendment would involve the spending of funds, said Mackenzie King, and was therefore beyond the scope of amendment by a private member. It was not a matter of funds at all, Nielsen argued, with the support of Stanley Knowles (CCF Winnipeg North). But the Speaker ruled with the government and the amendment was dropped.[36]

During the short Easter break in 1944, Dorise had only three days to spend with the children in Winnipeg and she didn't get back to her riding at all. Bob Paul came down to meet her in Regina, where she was slated to speak for the LPP. It was almost certain a provincial election would be called in Saskatchewan that year, but the purpose of her trip was not to help nominate LPP candidates. The party ran only Art Doucet (Meadow Lake) and Nelson Clarke (Saskatoon). In Turtleford, Minerva Cooper had dropped out of the race. There and elsewhere, party members were urged to support the CCF. "The CCF," Dorise said in Regina, "are honest sincere Canadians trying to bring about a better society."[37] These were mild words compared to some of her parliamentary pronouncements on the CCF, and show that she was still hoping for a trade-off with them locally when it came to the federal election. The next day, in Moose Jaw, she preached the party line to 300 people in the Technical School auditorium. "I don't think we've got to have socialism right away," she said. Although it had seemed, during the Depression, that "capitalism was on its last legs," now, as a result of the war, "it has had a blood transfusion."[38] The important thing, she said, was to keep Canadians employed after the war and that would mean the creation of new industries, particularly on the prairies.

Altogether, the spring of 1944 was a hectic and anxious time for Nielsen. Because of the impending federal election, the party's demands on her had increased. Her schedule was so full that she flew for the first time. Towards the end of April, only a week into the spring session, she boarded a plane for Vancouver. In the few days she was there, she spoke for several LPP candidates and addressed an audience of 10,000 at the annual May Day parade.[39] From there she flew back to Toronto and took the train to Ottawa (stopping to speak to the Women's Canadian Club of Sudbury on the way). As usual, she scrambled to keep up on the war news. Every day the papers reported the tonnage of bombs dropped on Germany. It was already April and the invasion of northern Europe was expected to begin any day. On one of her first mornings back in Ottawa, she heard on the eight o'clock news that Britain had forbidden all diplomats, whether allied or neutral, from leaving the country, a move intended to protect the secrets surrounding the coming invasion.[40]

On May 4, 1944, Nielsen made a major speech on the new labour code. All her work on the women's booklet stood her in good stead. The government had finally embraced the principle of equal pay, she acknowledged, but how was it going to be enforced? Even in its own contracts the government was still allowing women to be paid less than men. And what was going to happen to women's jobs after the war? "Are the government and the employers going to say to these women, 'Well girls, you have done a nice job; you look very cute in your overalls and we appreciate what you have done for us; but just run along; go home; we can get along without you very nicely'?"[41] It was time Canadians rid themselves of the old Victorian ideas that women who wanted to work were usurpers, taking men's places.

After the war, she pointed out, there would be even more women who would have no choice about working, for they would have no husband on whom to depend. She made an emotional plea for widows, citing the case of her sister, who, after the last war, had been left a widow with a month-old son: "I have often wondered in the long years since, who paid the greatest price, who made the greatest sacrifice, whether it was the man who died or the woman who went on living."[42]

When Minister of Labour Humphrey Mitchell reiterated that the War Labour Board had already adopted the principle of equal pay, he was hammered by Nielsen with the help of Joe Noseworthy (CCF Toronto) and John Blackmore (the leader of New Democracy). "What has been done about it?" said Blackmore, and he asked for examples. The minister, however, ignored the questions. He ended the debate by paying tribute to the wonderful work women were doing for the war and thanking Nielsen for her constructive suggestions.

But issues other than the status of women interested Nielsen, too. She was studying reports on the feasibility of manufacturing synthetic rubber from grain alcohol. Such an industry, if it took off like the petrochemical industry in Sarnia, could be the key to stemming the exodus from the prairies. Perhaps the family farm could be saved, after all. And the National Film Board was doing some good work in the field of arts and education. On Tuesday and Thursday evenings, members could view short films during the dinner recess. Most of the films could be called propaganda, but they were informative enough. There were several good films on the Soviet Union (too many, according to the Tories) and a very good film on the Group of Seven. She wanted to see such films distributed free to rural schools and community halls. And she liked the idea of a National Arts Board to distribute federal funds for art education, too. Canadians, in their scattered communities, were starved for art and entertainment. Now that the Liberals were willing to spend substantial amounts of money to stimulate the peacetime economy, it was a matter of pushing on several fronts at once and hoping that somehow all the work would help make a better world after the war.

May dragged on and the weather turned hot. Every day Dorise caught herself holding her breath as she tuned in to the news. The invasion still hadn't come. In Ottawa daffodils and then tulips poked up in odd bits of ground not reserved for victory gardens or covered by ramshackle temporary buildings. The Saskatchewan election was finally called for June 15. Tommy Douglas, Saskatchewan's provincial CCF leader, gave up his federal seat to join the campaign. The CCF was hopeful of a breakthrough—they had come so close in Ontario and were still high in the polls. And so tension was high on two counts, but there was nothing she could do about either.

10

VICTORY AND DEFEAT

If we had created a basis of real social and economic equality in the province of Quebec and the rest of Canada we might all of us have accepted conscription.[1]

WHEN DORISE TURNED ON the eight o'clock news on Tuesday, June 6, 1944, she heard that it had been pre-empted by a special nationwide broadcast from the prime minister. So the invasion had begun at last. The Russians had been calling for the opening of a second front for three years and finally it had come. King had received the news in the middle of the night. As expected, Canadian forces were heavily involved.

By the time she walked to the Hill, crowds of silent men and women were already gathering before the bulletin boards at Ottawa's two newspapers. There was no rejoicing. The raid on Dieppe two summers before had shown very clearly the cost of attacking the French coast. The *Evening Citizen* filled its front page with the words ALL GOES WELL, but it didn't take much imagination to know that it was really too soon to tell.

A solemn group met in the House of Commons that day. Most Canadians, having had such long preparation for that day, were more keenly aware of "invasion day" than any previous battle. Members of Parliament listened as King repeated the bits of information that Churchill had given a few hours earlier in the British House of Commons. Four thousand ships had crossed the channel, he said, and everything was proceeding according to plan. But the man of the day was an American, General Eisenhower, Supreme Commander of the invading forces. King quoted his words to the troops as he ordered them in to battle: "The hopes and prayers of liberty-loving peoples everywhere march with you."

After King's speech, the opposition leaders expressed the same hopes for the success and protection of "our boys," and then a young French-Canadian MP asked for permission to sing "La Marseillaise" in honour of the liberation of France. Everyone rose and those who knew the words sang with him, and when it ended, someone else, not wanting to give the French the upper hand, began singing "God Save the King," so they remained on their feet singing. It was a release to sing instead of argue, a rare gesture of unity in a contentious and exhausted House.

When King reminded them, shortly after, that there was a heavy load of legislation yet to come, all parties agreed to longer hours, and the House began to meet from eleven in the morning until eleven at night, five days a week, through June, July, and half of August. A new department of veterans' affairs was set up and a generous package of benefits was approved for the returning troops and for the dependents of those killed. Then it was on to the Department of Reconstruction, its business to oversee the transition from war to peace so that there would be no disruption of employment, and next the Department of Health and Welfare to administer the universal health and pension schemes that were to be negotiated with the provinces, as well as the first universal social program ever approved in Canada, a system of subsidies to each family based on the number of children.

The generosity of the 1944 legislation was unprecedented. The family allowance alone would cost $200 to 250 million a year, almost one half the pre-war federal budget.[2] The government also allotted hundreds of millions to support agricultural prices and to subsidize the construction of new housing. It seemed that at last Mackenzie King believed, like Tim Buck, that if the country could find billions for the war, it could afford a few billion to improve the lives of Canadians. Of course, he had had a number of nudges in the direction of the welfare state, including the growing popularity of the CCF, and finally they had become too painful to ignore.

Dorise was particularly happy about the family allowance bill, a benefit first advocated by J.S. Woodsworth in 1929. Before the advent of medicare and other social programs, family size was a significant cause of poverty. Australia, New Zealand, and Great Britain had family allowances. Now the Canadian government proposed to join the band of progressives states and send each family a monthly allowance of five to eight dollars per child, depending on the child's age, not such a small amount at a time when a good wage was thirty dollars a week.[3]

The Tories argued that this was an insupportable extravagance for a country so heavily in debt, and a bribe to Quebec with its large families, but in the end they voted for it. Indeed, it would have been political suicide to vote against such a measure, especially in an election year.

When the family allowance bill was debated at the end of July, Dorise's main concern was who would get the cheque. It must go to the mother, she said, for there were married women who had very little control over money at all, and it was mothers rather than fathers who were more attuned to the needs of their children. She argued the case head-to-head with Mackenzie King, who refused to commit himself one way or the other. It would depend on the results of consultation with the provinces, he said.

Nielsen was not the only one to raise the issue. It was raised by Coldwell, who spoke before her, and by the young Stanley Knowles, the new CCF member from Winnipeg, and her friend, Victor Quelch (Social Credit), who followed her. Both Quelch and Knowles said they supported the suggestion of "the honorable member for North Battleford." Perhaps Nielsen did a little lobbying, for a few days after her confrontation with King, Knowles took up the matter again in the form of an amendment to the family allowance bill that payments should be sent to mothers "whenever possible." He was seconded by Percy Wright from Saskatchewan, with Nielsen and Coldwell speaking, once again, in favour.[4] But the Liberal majority held fast, and the amendment was defeated seventy-two to fifteen. Cora Casselman felt the need to explain her negative vote. "It's not that I do not trust the mothers to spend the money just as well as the fathers," she said, but she did trust the fathers equally.[5]

In the end, the family allowance cheques did go to mothers, and Nielsen liked to tell her daughters that she had played a role in that decision. She was pleased to think of all the poor women she knew, and she had met many, women who drudged all their lives and hardly ever saw anything but the egg money, if they were lucky. She could see them getting cheques for ten or even twenty dollars, money they could count on every month, the plans they could make to buy boots or a coat for first one child and then another, and maybe something for themselves. Indeed, she was happy to be an MP the summer of '44. So what if the monstrous stones of the building held the heat, and she sweated through long airless evenings and then had to summon the energy to walk home to her room and fall into bed? History was being made and she was part of it.

Nielsen and Rose also teamed up with the CCF and progressive Liberal Arthur Roebuck on the issue of voting rights for Japanese-Canadians. Before the war, nearly all Japanese-Canadians lived in BC, where, under provincial law, they were not allowed to vote. Those few who lived in other provinces did have the vote. Now that the Japanese had been removed from the coast, Roebuck proposed they be allowed to vote under the laws of the provinces in which they presently resided. Dorise spoke immediately after Roebuck. She tore into the racists of BC and Mackenzie King in equal measure. "The Prime Minister's argument about (the Japanese) going to the polls and getting mobbed was one of the weakest I have ever heard him put forward," she said.[6] But once again, when the amendment came to a vote, most Liberals voted with King, and the Japanese who had resided in BC on July 1, 1938, remained disenfranchised.

All these initiatives show that despite the new party line of supporting the Liberals, Nielsen did not become a Liberal patsy, kowtowing on every issue. She remained, on a number of issues, part of a loose progressive group that included the CCF, Social Credit, and the occasional progressive Liberal. If the CCF came into her line of fire more and more often, no doubt she thought they deserved it. In a May Day speech in Toronto, she said the CCF insistence on socialism was causing disunity in Canada.[7] This was, of course, the new party line, and it was beginning to cause a growing rift between Nielsen and her CCF colleagues in the House. Earlier, Angus MacInnis had declared Tim Buck was a "scumbag" for appearing on the same stage with the union-busting Liberal Mitchell Hepburn.[8] Now he and the others sat back, amazed (and sometimes amused) as Nielsen and Rose declared socialism unrealistic.

"What has happened to you?" asked one CCF member when Rose spoke out against a CCF amendment to nationalize the banking system. Rose went on to explain that jobs were what counted to Canadians—it didn't matter who owned the banks. As long as capitalism worked, it could be left alone. "The key issue at the present stage of the war is not to play into the hands of those who want to make an issue of socialism . . . let us collaborate . . . let us be realistic."[9]

Nielsen could be even more blunt in her criticism of the CCF, accusing their leaders of "an utter lack of a scientific approach to the dynamics of social change." How could they assert that "the only alternative for Canada is socialism or depression?" Their thinking, she said was "wishful and utopian" and she wanted, definitely, to disassociate herself from them.[10] Indeed, by the end of the

1944 session Nielsen had taken up the new party line with a vengeance. Later she criticized the LPP strategy of the period, and the part she had played, but for the moment she was fully on board, let the chips fall where they may.

But, at the time, the CCF was riding high, and its members didn't take the communists very seriously. On June 15 they had swept Saskatchewan. Tommy Douglas took his place as premier. George Williams, who had led the party in the 1930s, was appointed Minister of Agriculture. Nielsen had fought the Saskatchewan Liberals long and hard, and even, in her recent Easter meetings there, had advised voters to support the CCF where there wasn't an LPP candidate. However, when she saw the results of Art Doucet's campaign in Meadow Lake, she must have had a few qualms. He had run third and lost his deposit. And, with its stunning victory, the CCF would have little trouble finding a candidate to run against her.

At last, on August 14 after midnight, the longest parliamentary session of the war came to an end. Even if the prime minister had postponed the Dominion-Provincial conference on social security until after the next election (thereby putting the health plan into limbo for the next twenty years), much had been accomplished by a group of legislators who were weary from war, from pushing victory loans, and from answering letters on a host of new government regulations—letters about jobs and transfers and military deferrals, letters about eligibility for this program or that, about rationing and sending parcels overseas, about censorship and daycare for children and labour laws and how much the new health plan would really cost. Though some MPs were more conscientious than others, it was a punishing schedule for all of them, easier to bear, perhaps, because the war required sacrifices of everyone, but still a long march. They would not meet again until January 31, 1945 (unless an emergency arose), and then, if the war were finally winding down, an election would be called at last.

So off they went, first to see their families and then to continue the process of nomination meetings and electioneering. Nielsen had booked a cottage at Lake Edith with Victor Quelch and his family, and this year Christine had agreed to come. Dorise planned to put all the work out of her mind for two weeks and once more become reacquainted with her children. All she wanted for herself was a little time to swim and a few good sleeps.

That year the holiday began well. There was canoeing and swimming, and the spectacle of Dorise getting dunked and laughing so hard that she couldn't manoeuvre her bulk back into the canoe. But soon Christine found friends her own age and wanted to spend her time with them. Then there was an argument, "another blow-up with Mom," and she was sent home to Winnipeg early. For Sally and Johnny, the holiday ended abruptly when Dorise received a telegram a few days after Christine's departure. She had been summoned to Toronto immediately. Victor Quelch drove them through fog and darkness to Banff. There, hungry and tired, they climbed aboard a train crowded with troops. Her children were embarrassed when Dorise hustled them into the dining car and insisted they be fed.[11]

Although Parliament did not assemble again until January 1945, Nielsen's life was as busy as ever. She was as valuable to the party in the pre-election period as she had been in 1940–41. She was a high-profile personality and the best speaker they had. There was even talk of sending Nielsen and Tim Buck overseas. Liberals were touring the front, why not the LPP?[12]

Between meetings in support of other LPP candidates, Nielsen spent her time in Saskatchewan, trying to pick up the pieces from the CCF victory in June. Coldwell had come north for that campaign, and, for the first time, had openly denounced her as a communist fellow-traveller from the beginning. He had cited her record of not supporting the war until the attack on the Soviet Union in 1941, of calling for a second front when it wasn't feasible (he mentioned the unnecessary bloodshed at Dieppe in 1942), and of generally following the line of the Communist Party rather than representing the interests of her constituents.[13] He had wanted to say these things for a long time, but had been restrained early on by members of the Saskatchewan CCF, who feared that any remarks against the popular Mrs. Nielsen could backfire.[14] Coldwell had taken his accusations right into the heart of Nielsen territory at Meadow Lake. She was furious with him.

But that wasn't the worst of it. The CCF had won a stunning victory in Saskatchewan, not only in Meadow Lake, but throughout the province. They had taken forty-seven seats to five for the Liberals. It was a complete reversal of the situation ten years before. As Dorise had predicted, there was no shortage of CCF candidates for the coming federal election. In fact, when the North Battleford CCF met at the end of October 1945 in Medstead, eight men were nominated. It took eight ballots to select the candidate, a well-established farmer named Peter Townley-Smith.[15]

Shortly before the CCF convention, Nielsen had been nominated unanimously at an LPP convention held in Glasyn, a town on the road to Meadow Lake, not far from Medstead. The meeting, described as "well attended" by the *North Battleford Optimist*, was chaired by Gilbert Berg, the reeve of Mildred, and included speeches by a Rev. John Mortimer from Sackville, New Brunswick, and James McPherson, LPP leader of Alberta. The LPP was doing its best to support Nielsen, but no matter what it did, there was far more interest in the CCF. Her only comfort was that Cameron McIntosh had gone down to defeat at the constituency's Liberal convention. Instead of McIntosh, the Liberals had selected John Harrison, a merchant from Glenbush.[16]

The rush of nominations after harvest proved timely, for by November 1944, the King government appeared to be on the verge of collapse. Throughout the summer and autumn, the battle maps in the newspapers showed little change as the Canadian army battled to Caen, then inched its way east along the heavily fortified French coast. Meanwhile, in northern Italy, the Canadian divisions fighting with the British Eighth Army broke through a German defence called the Gothic Line, but at the cost of the heaviest casualties in the Italian campaign.

So far all the Canadians sent overseas had been volunteers. None of the men conscripted under the National Resources Mobilization Act (NRMA) had been sent into combat unless they later volunteered. By 1944 there were thousands of NRMA men (derisively called "zombies) assigned to home defence. The plebiscite in 1942 had given King a mandate to send these conscripts overseas if necessary, but Quebecers had voted strongly against it. Thus he hesitated, fearing further erosion of the Quebec wing of the Liberal party.

In the autumn of 1944, the crunch came. The Minister of National Defence, Colonel James Ralston, fresh from a visit to the front, realized that the number of voluntary enlistments would soon fall short of the need for reinforcements.

He recommended sending the conscripts overseas. King was, as they say, caught between a rock and a hard place. If he sent the NRMA men overseas, he would enrage the French section of the Liberal caucus, and if he didn't, he could lose most of his English support. In a clever but ruthless manoeuvre, King forced Ralston's resignation and replaced him by General McNaughton, a popular World War I veteran who had commanded the Canadian army in Europe during the first part of the war. McNaughton was optimistic that he would be able to raise enough volunteers to fight the final stage of the war. Still, there were others in Cabinet (and in the country) who were not so optimistic. King called Parliament back to explain his policy. He hoped to win a vote of confidence.

Dorise put all thoughts of electioneering on hold and, with other MPs from across the country, made her way to Ottawa. The issue had gone beyond party politics. For most French-Canadians, it was a matter of the solemn promise (made to them at the beginning of the war) of no conscription for overseas service. For most others, it was a matter of "backing the attack." Men on the front lines had to be supported, if not by volunteers, then by conscripts, and it had to happen soon.

When Nielsen entered Parliament for the first day of the session, a long queue of people was already waiting to enter the galleries, and the hallways, too, were filled with hundreds of people, some of them men in uniform. It was being called the "zombie" session of Parliament. The war was almost won, but not quite. To be thrown into the toughest fighting of the war, just before the moment of victory, to die, perhaps a few days before the armistice, this, surely, was the fear of the NRMA men. But it was clear that most of the crowd was in favour of sending the conscripts and that most parliamentarians were, too.

The *Evening Citizen* described the high tension on the opening day as Mackenzie King read Colonel Ralston's letter of resignation. The galleries were packed with people standing three to four deep along the walls. "It was as if the atmosphere was surcharged with electricity or dynamite or as if an unexploded bomb lay on the floor in the middle of the chamber."[17] But as the Tories thumped their desks in support of Ralston's statements, and King played out his role of providing Parliament with a full investigation into the matter, he was already feeling assured that his government would survive. The Liberal caucus had met that morning. King had announced that McNaughton would send conscripts if he found voluntary enlistments insufficient. By clever timing and some luck, King had managed to pull the rug out from under the pro-conscriptionist lobby without causing a major revolt in the Quebec wing of the Liberal party. Essentially, both King and McNaughton had done an about-face. They knew Ralston had been right after all. As Parliament opened, an Order-in-Council to conscript up to 16,000 NRMA men for overseas service was being drafted.[18]

Neverthless, the House sat for two weeks of highly emotional debate and many divisions. When the main motion of confidence finally came on December 7, Rose and Nielsen voted with the government, as did the CCF and Social Credit. Once again, when it came to the debate, Dorise ceded first place to Fred Rose. She did not speak on the motion of confidence until the final evening of the session, just after dinner. She used her speech to deplore the stirring up of racial hatred and "the slanderous attacks against the people of Quebec" by the Tories. The Liberals were not guiltless, she said. "If we had created a basis of real social and economic equality in the province of Quebec and the rest of Canada we might all of us have accepted conscription." But it was the Tories she blamed for the current political crisis over the issue of reinforcements. "It has been said, and truly said, that patriotism sometimes becomes the last refuge for scoundrels."[19] And as far as she was concerned, the Tories were the worst scoundrels of all. Nielsen, by backing the party line and supporting the Liberals, may have been confident in the path she was following, but she was making enemies right and left. Her charges were not lightweight, not the irksome verbal spitballs she'd deplored. They were wounding enough to merit a reply from the next speaker, who asked her where the communists were when Britain had her back to the wall.[20]

Finally, after one in the morning, the vote was taken and the government survived by a healthy margin of 143 to 70. The troops would be reinforced by conscripts. It was only the French-Canadian MPs who had lost significantly in the political game. Still they stood politely as "God Save the King" was sung, then gathered their papers and filed out. The next day Union Station was full of MPs starting home.

Parliament met for one day in January 1945 and was prorogued until spring. There was still no sign of the war's end. The conscription debacle continued. After the November session Minister of National Defence General McNaughton had ordered 14,000 conscripts overseas, but so far only 8000 of these had arrived in Britain. The rest had gone AWOL.[21] When McNaughton himself ran in a by-election, he was defeated by a Tory.

Through the winter and into the spring, the unofficial election campaign continued. In March Dorise flew to Whitehorse to support the candidacy of Tom McEwen (LPP). It was Winter Carnival time and she wore her raccoon coat. During the day, she handed out prizes for dogsled races. At night, she donned a sleeveless evening gown for the trappers' gala. A few days later, her picture appeared in the paper, one long, white arm raised high with the winning ticket for the $2000 grand prize.[22]

At that point the Yukon was flooded with army personnel and crews of young men working on the Alaska highway, and McEwen's chances of winning were high.[23] No one knew precisely when the election would be called, but King had vowed not to go beyond his five-year mandate, which meant an election that summer at the latest, and earlier if the war ended soon. But the war was dragging on. Although Canadian towns and cities had been planning victory celebrations since the fall, German armies ferociously defended their country's western frontier and the Allies made little progress. By spring of 1945, a Gallup poll showed the Liberals had 38 percent voter support, the Tories, 34, and the CCF, only 12 percent. [24]

The Tory menace struck fear in the hearts of Canadian communists. They could imagine nothing worse than another Tory government in Ottawa. The Tories might be calling themselves progressives (wasn't everyone now?) but the iron heel of the Bennett government had left its mark. And, since 1943, Ontario had been governed by a Tory government whose premier, George Drew, had led a campaign against the family allowance bill. Wherever an LPP candidate was not running, the party urged supporters to "give your vote to the best man in the riding, so long as that vote does not go to a Tory."[25]

The fact that the LPP was not even mentioned in the Gallup polls did not keep communists from hoping for a breakthrough. They figured they had enough support to gain several seats in the federal house, and then exert their influence by supporting the expected Liberal minority government. These hopes were not just pipe dreams. In liberated Europe, communists were taking their place in newly constituted coalition governments. In Canada the LPP had surpassed its pre-war electoral successes, and could count on the support of approximately 20,000 active members.[26]

The communists' popularity in Canada would never be greater than in 1945. With all the goodwill engendered by the Soviet war effort, and by the role of communist partisans in the European resistance to the Nazis, the party's stigma of being unpatriotic (and un-Canadian) was abating. Although most of the party still consisted of "the radical foreign element" of first- and second-generation Finnish, Ukrainian, and Jewish immigrants, it was busy recruiting new members from all classes, races, and geographical areas.[27] Its multi-ethnic character and strong stand against racism put it in the forefront of an anti-racist trend that gained ground during the war.

More and more people were speaking out against anti-Semitism, something the communists had been doing for years. The horrifying discovery of Nazi death camps confirmed the righteousness of their cause. The same newspapers that carried precise lists of the camps and numbers of people exterminated featured exhortations to Canadians to end the scourge of racism at home. The new emphasis on equality was part of the need to make all the death and destruction count for something. "Smith? Kelly? Cohen? Svoboda?" read a full-page ad in the *Regina Leader-Post*, "Let's put an end to the foul prejudice fanned by our enemies.... If Smith, Kelly, Cohen, or Svoboda is good enough to die for us, he's good enough to live with us ... as an equal."[28]

For Nielsen, the party's growth and its electoral ambitions meant a hectic five months of campaigning for herself and others, interrupted by two brief interludes in Ottawa. The party ran sixty-seven federal candidates under its own label in 1945 and three as independent or labour candidates. It ran large ads in its own newspaper, seeking a federal election campaign fund of $250,000 "to make sure Tim Buck, Sam Carr, Fred Rose, Dorise Nielsen and others are elected."[29] Because of the number of candidates, the party was granted free air time nationwide. Its broadcasts were shared by Tim Buck and Dorise. Nielsen's task, it seems, was to win the female vote. Her topic: "Women's Stake in This War."[30]

In March, after her excursion to the Yukon, Dorise received notice that King wanted Parliament back to approve the draft resolutions for setting up the United Nations Organization. It was an extraordinary time to be an MP in Canada. The discussion of world affairs occupied huge chunks of parliamentary debate and Canada played a more important role on the international stage than she ever had before or ever would again.

The big difference between the old League of Nations and the new United Nations organization was the participation of both the US and the Soviet Union. It was obvious that the new organization had the potential to be more effective on that ground alone. But what about the influence of the smaller powers and the so-called middle powers like Canada? And what about the role of the British Commonwealth? Should Commonwealth members vote as a block? These were some of the issues discussed in Parliament as winter turned to spring, the Allies finally broke through on the Western Front, and the Canadian First Army liberated Holland.

When Parliament opened, Mackenzie King delivered a speech of 30,000 words, summarizing the plans for international cooperation that had been drafted during conferences at Bretton Woods and Dumbarton Oaks. Then he asked other members to keep their remarks short so that the session could end in good time before the Canadian delegation (yet to be named) made its way to San Francisco for the conference on April 25. No one paid him any heed.

Both Fred Rose and Dorise spoke early in the session. Fred, as usual, had the privilege of speaking first. Along with the Liberals and the CCF, he rejected the idea of the British Commonwealth's acting as a block in the new organization. Otherwise, he expressed unqualified support for the draft plans, emphasizing the importance of peace for Canada's trade-based economy. He asked only that Canada's delegation to the San Francisco conference include a representative of organized labour, that the new organization facilitate plans for setting up a Jewish state in Palestine, and that all its members be encouraged to outlaw anti-Semitism. Then, in a discussion that was supposed to be non-partisan, he went on to attack the CCF leader, Coldwell, for expressing "reservations over secondary and even minor features of the Dumbarton Oaks proposals."[31] The communist policy of supporting the Liberals seemed to be the cause of such nitpicking, for it is almost impossible to find in Coldwell's speech any real cause for offence.

The next day, Nielsen rose to express her own hopes for the post-war world. No longer would hatred of the Soviet Union keep nations divided. Peace and economic development would result in prosperity not only for prairie farmers in Canada, but for millions of long-suffering people in India and China, as well. Then, she, too, turned to attack Coldwell for "damning the conference with faint praise."[32] She said his mild remarks in the House belied what he and other CCFers were saying elsewhere, and went on to quote articles in which the CCF questioned the wisdom of the deals Stalin and Churchill and Roosevelt had made in Tehran and Yalta. Here was the crux of the matter. The communists were determined to support post-war unity between the Big Three and saw any criticism of their "deal making" as divisive. If the detente between the Big Three were to break down, the Soviet Union would be isolated once again and communist parties in the Western world would be out in the cold.

Nielsen's speech ended in a very lively and nasty verbal battle with both Coldwell and Angus MacInnis. The days when she had teamed up with MacInnis to defend the miners at Kirkland Lake were long gone, and the gloves were off. Coldwell and MacInnis kept interrupting her and refused to give up. "You know better than that," said Coldwell. "Just be moral for once!" "Terrible," exclaimed MacInnis. "I'm glad we agree on something," she retorted. "At least I didn't say Canada would be better off under Hitler," said Coldwell.[33]

The battle continued the following day, when Clarence Gillis, a CCFer from Cape Breton who had previously supported Nielsen on several issues, described her as "pathetic," and took pains to distinguish between the program of the CCF, which he said expressed the sentiments of the people of Canada, and the program of Nielsen and Rose, which, he maintained, was drafted elsewhere. Once again, Nielsen's speeches in 1940–41 were quoted to show her lack of patriotism in that period.[34] All this furor over Nielsen's criticism of Coldwell shows that the CCF did not take the communist appeal to the voters lightly. There was a battle going on for the support of organized labour, and the communist idea of a "Liberal-Labour" coalition had been gaining ground.[35]

Finally, the debate on King's resolution of support for the San Francisco conference ended with all, except a few independents from Quebec, voting in favour. But still there was the matter of approving supply so that the government could pay its way until the next Parliament could meet. For the first time, there was no Easter break, just a long weekend spent in Ottawa for those from far away, and then it was back to business in the rush to end the session on Friday, April 13.

The week after Easter, King announced at last the names of the delegates to San Francisco. He included Cora Casselman as the token woman, and Coldwell and Gordon Graydon (Progressive Conservative House Leader) to represent the opposition. There was no representative of organized labour. Currying favour with the Liberals hadn't got the communists very far. It was in this atmosphere of haste and rancour, with the war about to end, the earnest plans for the post-war world, and an imminent election on everyone's minds, that the news came of President Roosevelt's sudden death. The news trickled into the chamber late in the afternoon on Thursday, April 12. It was one of those blows that fall when least expected. What would happen now to the San Francisco conference? To the war against Japan? To the alliance of the Big Three? Roosevelt had been the cornerstone of the alliance between two old enemies, Churchill and Stalin, and all the plans for post-war peace and cooperation depended on this alliance's holding fast.

When MPs took their seats in the chamber at eight o'clock that evening, the leaders paid tribute to Roosevelt, and then the House adjourned. Members rushed to buy evening newspapers. Already, President Truman had vowed to follow the policies hammered out by Roosevelt. The San Francisco conference would continue as planned. That weekend King took the train to Hyde Park in New York for Roosevelt's burial, and the following week Parliament wound up at last with the calling of an election for June 11.

The LPP ran three candidates in Saskatchewan, all women, but only Dorise had any hope of winning and that was slim. "Nobody's heart was in it," remembers Stewart Paul, "but she could still draw a good crowd."[36] One thing in her favour was the number of candidates in her riding. In North Battleford, not only had the CCF nominated, but so had Social Credit and the Progressive Conservatives. Then, at the last minute, Nielsen's old rival, Cameron McIntosh, having lost the Liberal nomination, decided to run as an independent Liberal. Thus, there were six candidates running, more than in any other riding, a situation that may have shaken the confidence of the CCF and have given Nielsen a ray of hope.

Once again it was a matter of travelling dusty roads to meetings in schools and community halls, but this time she had a better wardrobe and was accompanied by a featured speaker whom she had managed to snaffle from the party pool of fellow-travellers so far unsullied by their communist connections. Dyson Carter was a young journalist from Winnipeg with expertise in practical science. He had written features for *Saturday Night* and other magazines, and a novel that had been praised in the *New York Times*.[37] Whether they had heard of him or not, townspeople and farmers flocked to meetings advertised in his name as lectures on "Chemurgy" or "Chemical Engineering for the West," with Dorise's name in small letters.

The arrangements, as usual, had been made by Bob Paul. In each town he had booked the hall and found a local luminary to chair the meeting. Carter would give his lecture and then praise Nielsen for being the first MP to raise the matter of chemurgy for the West in the House. Then it would be her turn to defend her record and explain the LPP goal of keeping the Tories out and making labour a partner in government. Each meeting would end with farmers and their wives gathering round to finger the samples Carter had shown in his lecture—lengths of rope made of nylon, a square of window screening that could not be broken. It was, indeed, amazing that wheat and sunflowers could be transformed into products other than food, and to hear that such products were already being turned out in Germany and Russia, and, more recently, in the United States.[38]

And so Dyson and Dorise and Bob took their show on the road for six weeks with only a pause on May 7 as each town held a prayer service and a parade to celebrate the end of the war in Europe. They went to North Battleford and Meadow Lake and Spiritwood and all the places in-between. If they watched the national polls, they knew that the Liberals, campaigning on the slogan "Opportunities for all. Build a new social order," were gaining ground, but in Saskatchewan, even with the first family allowance cheques due July 1, voters were inclined to be skeptical of the Liberal's late conversion.

Toward the end of the campaign, Nielsen made one desperate attempt to stem the CCF tide by distributing an open letter to Coldwell, charging him with making vicious and unjustified attacks on her, most of them related to her support for a Liberal-Labour coalition. She said he had supported various informal coalitions throughout his career and asked why he was so adverse to a coalition now, when it was vital to prevent the Tories winning. It was his ambition, she said. He didn't care who won the election, as long as he became official leader of the opposition.[39]

But the LPP's fear of a Tory win did not materialize. On June 11 the Liberals won with a reduced majority and the Tories once more formed the official opposition. The CCF jumped from eleven to twenty-eight seats, twenty-one from Saskatchewan. Even Mackenzie King lost his Prince Albert seat to a CCFer in a close race that was finally decided by the service vote. "This town was liberated by the Canadian army," some joker said, and it ended up on a sign along the highway.[40] In southern Saskatchewan, General McNaughton, in his second attempt to win a seat, lost to Gladys Strum (CCF). Once again there would be only one woman in the House, and she would come from Saskatchewan.

Mackenzie King would soon find another seat. For Nielsen it was a different story. She had come third with 2214 votes, compared to 5049 for Townley-Smith (CCF) and 4420 for Harrison (Liberal). It was small comfort that Cameron McIntosh had come a distant last with only 847 votes. She knew that she would not be without a party job, but the question was, where? Dorise and Bob Paul argued that she should stay on in Saskatchewan as a party organizer. The CCF popularity in Saskatchewan, built on the provincial win in 1944, might be a blip. Nielsen wanted to stay in the West, where she knew the people and the issues.[41] But the party had other ideas. Nielsen was too big a fish to be left in the backwaters of Saskatchewan. Down east, there was work to be done. Although the party was down one seat, instead of up, as it had predicted, Rose won again in Montreal, and in Toronto Tim Buck came close, and Sam Carr polled over 10,000 votes.

After arguing her case, Dorise bowed to the wishes of the party and made plans for a move to LPP headquarters in Toronto. It would mean moving the children from Winnipeg. She had already paid John's school fees and was in a dilemma as to whether she should forfeit them or leave him there for another school year. Either way, money would be tight. Her salary would be reduced by more than half, from $4000 a year to $35 a week. There would be no more railway passes, no more holidays in the mountains, and little opportunity to see Bob Paul. But the party needed her and she needed a job. It is unlikely she even thought of refusing. Like all communists, she knew her personal wishes must take second place to her political duty. It had been a nasty campaign and she had done her best. Now it was time to shake the dust off her heels and get out.

TORONTO

11
SPIES

I knew them all but was not involved.[1]

IN MID-AUGUST 1945, as the streets of Toronto's Chinatown filled with crowds celebrating the victory over Japan, the 100-member National Committee of the LPP met in the King Edward Hotel. There was at least one police informant among the group who carefully recorded the criticism and self-criticism that ensued. Buck came under fire for promoting a no-strike pledge during the war, as well as the Liberal-Labour coalition in the election. In the United States, CP leader Earl Browder had been expelled for being soft on capitalism (and the Democrats), but Buck had all his soldiers lined up and he held his ground. His chief critic, Fergus McKean, party leader in BC, was expelled. Nielsen spoke on August 14, towards the end of the plenum. She confessed that she had been influenced by the policy of Browder and that she had been confused before finally coming to the conclusion that Browder was a revisionist. She concurred in the expulsion of McKean, and admitted that she "fully understood she had much to learn in order to become a Marxist." Once again she was elected to the National Executive of the LPP.

For Dorise, confusion followed by confession and a declaration of loyalty was becoming something of a ritual. The last time, she had faltered over the CCF amendment to the Speech from the Throne and then had praised Rose for enlightening her on the issue. Had there once again been a long and heated discussion before she saw the light? "She was a whole-souled person," said Virginia MacLeod. "When she was interested, she was intensely interested and she followed through."[3] It would not be easy for such a person to digest the changes in the party line. Whatever she did, she wanted to give it her all. It seems that, at this point, she was inclined to believe that the fault was hers—that she really was "theoretically under-developed." She hoped to make up for her theoretical deficit by attending the first national party school since the war, to be held in Sudbury the following summer.

Nielsen's start in Toronto was a rough one domestically, too. She had arrived with only her sewing machine and her clothes. After several weeks of living with others, she had found rooms (with shared bathroom) on the second floor of a house on Markham Street near Bloor. It was a working-class area of old houses, on the northern edge of Toronto's garment district, a key sector of party strength. Most of her neighbours spoke Italian or Polish or Yiddish. Provincially, the constituency, called St. Andrew's, was represented by Nielsen's friend and colleague, Joe Salsberg. It was one of two communist constituencies in Toronto. The other, Bellwoods, was represented by her good friend, A.A. MacLeod. The party also had two members elected to city council, two on school boards, and one on the city's Board of Control.

On Markham the family had to make do with two mattresses and several packing crates as furniture until they gradually acquired other people's cast-offs.[4] Dorise used her savings to buy a stove. Once more she registered Christine and Sally in school, and, for the first time, Christine was put back a year. Each provincial system of education had its peculiarities. It was discouraging for anyone who moved province to province, but there was nothing to be done. Both girls dutifully went to school and Dorise hoped for the best. She had decided to leave Johnny in Winnipeg. Boarding schools, she believed, were good for children of a certain age, particularly for boys from all-female families, and, since she had already paid his fees, he would have to manage there for another year. As it turned out, keeping her youngest child in boarding was one of her better moves that year. At least she had one less worry as she awaited the knock on the door.

In a very tight housing market, Nielsen was lucky to have found a place for herself and her two girls. Years of depression, then war, had caused a housing crisis. The situation would grow even worse in 1946 as more and more servicemen came home, followed by contingents of war brides and babies. A landlord advertising a suite for a couple with one child had over 1600 applications. He decided to draw lots. The picture of the winning family was featured on the front page of the *Globe and Mail*.[5]

Nielsen's official title was National Legislative Secretary of the LPP. She was to work up the program for the party's national campaigns on domestic issues. In fact, she had been doing that for the last five years, so it was nothing new. The party counted on her to rouse an audience and pound an issue home. That would be her task, though the issues would change from time to time. Since she was now working from the party's headquarters, she had far more meetings to attend. She was also assigned to a party club, which met every two weeks. Her evenings and weekends were seldom free. That fall she was away for several days, campaigning for Bill Kardash's re-election in Winnipeg and addressing meetings in Montreal.

As far as her colleagues were concerned, Nielsen took up her duties with grace and enthusiasm. If she were longing to be out of Toronto (later she would say that she was never happy there), she didn't let on. But in the fall of 1945, the Cold War had not yet begun and Toronto was not as hostile to communists as it soon became. Dorise lived, almost exclusively, in the company of other party members who looked forward to the increasing success of their movement. All depended, of course, on the wartime alliance holding. If the Soviet Union became, once more, an outcast among nations, Dorise and her friends would lose their tenuous hold on respectability. So they continued to hope that all the knotty problems of the peace, including international control of the atomic bomb, and the disputes between Britain and the Soviet Union over Greece and Poland and Iran, could be settled through the new United Nations organization.

On the personal side, Bob Paul had decided to leave Saskatchewan as soon as he could find a job in Toronto. Dorise looked forward to his arrival, though she knew it could take months. Asking Pete for a divorce was out of the question. The process of proving adultery would be humiliating and the stigma for a person in the public eye too great.[6] But at least she and Bob could be together in the same city, and they might even live together. All her children were fond of him, and no one in the party would blink an eye.

As usual, her personal hopes and plans took second place to work. In December the party decided to launch a national campaign on the housing crisis. Nielsen was in charge. The campaign had her writing articles in the *Canadian Tribune* and *National Affairs Monthly*,[7] planning a cross-country tour for the new year, and gathering a petition to be presented to Parliament in the spring. She got most of the plans in place before Johnny came home for the Christmas holidays. On January 18, 1946, she launched the campaign at the Chateau Laurier in Ottawa. Then off she went to Halifax, Glace Bay, Sydney, and St. John's with several stops in-between. She was well versed in the government's own reports on housing and quoted them freely to prove her points. It was, no doubt, a relief to be on firm ground after navigating the shifting sands of party policy over the past two years.[8] Almost every evening she spoke at a meeting. In some towns she shared the stage with the mayor or other local official. After a week she travelled back to Toronto, then through northern Ontario, and on to points west. Sally and Christine were farmed out to other women in the party who were almost as busy as Dorise. They felt quite deserted.[9]

When Dorise was in Kirkland Lake on February 3, 1946, an American broadcaster, likely acting on a leak from the US State Department, announced that there was a Russian espionage network operating in the US and Canada. He mentioned Ottawa and said that a Russian spy had confessed.[10] It was probably at this point that Dorise began to fear arrest, though she may have known something was in the wind even before the housing tour began. At some time, either at the beginning of the tour or during a stopover in Toronto, Christine remembers her mother's giving her a list of people to call if she were arrested. She also handed over her bank book.[11] She did not want to leave the girls without resources—though what she had in her bank account would not have kept them for long.

In fact, the newspapers had been wrong. It was not a spy who had confessed, but a cipher clerk at the Russian embassy in Ottawa who had defected. Igor Gouzenko sought asylum in Canada in exchange for revealing a list of contacts that the embassy's military attaché, Nicolai Zabotin, had used to gather information during the war. The case had been brewing since Gouzenko's defection in September 1945. Mackenzie King had hesitated to act on the information for fear of disrupting completely the fragile relations between the Western powers and the Soviet Union. In addition, most of the code names on Gouzenko's list were discovered to be federal civil servants. The whole thing was an embarrassment.[12]

By the time King finally acted, Nielsen had reached the prairies and had just finished a series of meetings in Saskatchewan. On February 16, she awoke in Edmonton to the headlines "Atom Secret Leaks to Soviets, Canadians

Suspected." Eleven suspects had been picked up at dawn and were being held incommunicado for interrogation under the War Measures Act. Over the next few days, two more people were taken in. The newspapers said that most of those detained were communists, but the government refused to release any names. It appointed a Royal Commission consisting of two judges to investigate, and said that in time the commission would release a report.

Nielsen continued on her way to BC. In Vancouver her meetings drew 1600 to the Hotel Vancouver and the Boilermakers Hall. She shared the stage with her friend Dyson Carter.[13] It was like the winter of 1941 all over again. The same hat set at a jaunty angle, the same fear. The party was determined to carry on and not flinch under fire, and had put Dorise Nielsen and Dyson Carter in the front lines. When and where would she be picked up for questioning? What would she say? Officially Tim Buck denied that any communists were being held, but that was not true. Dorise knew most of the suspects from her time in Ottawa.[14] She had spoken at meetings in their homes and apartments. Some had helped her mail out copies of her speeches. All were sympathetic to the party, and, as far as she knew, most of them were secret members of the LPP.[15]

For two more weeks, Dorise continued to travel the country, searching the newspapers each day for a hint of what was to come. In the United States, Secretary of State Byrnes denied that any atomic secrets had been stolen. In Ottawa the government confirmed that eleven men and two women had been detained. The Conservative and CCF leaders declared that as soon as the House opened in March, they would question the government's right to detain thirteen people without access to counsel. The *Vancouver Province* predicted that "sensational arrests" would soon be made: "The trail of treason may lead to the door of at least one man in the public eye and two others of prominence."[16]

It wasn't until March 5 that the first suspects were charged, and pictures of four very ordinary people in their felt hats and winter coats made the front pages. There was Kathleen Willsher, Secretary to the British High Commissioner, in her bulky Hudson seal. Everyone in Ottawa (everyone remotely on the left) knew Kathleen. A Brit who had worked in Ottawa since 1930, Kathleen was bright and single and a favourite at dinner parties.[17] The other three, younger than Willsher, were Canadians who had come to work in Ottawa during the war.

When the first charges were laid, Dorise was back in Toronto, preparing for the final rallies of the housing campaign. On March 6 she and Tim Buck and

A.A. MacLeod spoke at Massey Hall. A few days later, she went to Montreal to speak and collect petitions for the housing campaign. Over a thousand people attended that meeting, and Fred Rose, the re-elected MP for Cartier, also spoke briefly.[18] He was not his usual cocky self, and with good reason. He must have realized that his own was one of the "sensational arrests" yet to come. Sam Carr, the LPP's national organizer, whose name was also on Gouzenko's list, had disappeared when the first detentions took place in the middle of February.[19]

Obviously the party's national housing campaign was no way to divert public attention from a spy scandal that was becoming more riveting each day. The LPP decided to blow its budget and run a half-page ad in Canada's daily newspapers. It appeared across the country on Saturday, March 16. "Let's get back to sanity," it pleaded. The spy scare was being "blown up to fantastic proportions" in order to "damage beyond repair our co-operation and friendship with the Soviet Union."[20] Strangely enough, that was just what Soviet Union authorities were saying. Yes, they admitted, their military attaché, Nicolai Zabotin, had gathered some secret information, but it was really quite insignificant stuff, nothing to make such a big fuss about.[21]

The LPP ad ran the day after Rose's arrest. He was picked up at his Beechwood Avenue apartment in Ottawa the evening Parliament opened. In the House, Mackenzie King outlined Rose's role in the spy ring. A week later, at Rose's preliminary hearing in Montreal, Igor Gouzenko took the stand for the first time and testified for four and a half hours. Now it was impossible for Tim Buck to deny the involvement of communists in the spy scandal. The best he could do was say that the LPP did not condone espionage and reiterate the need for unity among the big three.[22]

Like other communists not in the first rank of the party, Dorise was no doubt stunned by Gouzenko's revelations and the pivotal role in the affair played by Fred Rose. Even those detained were surprised to find themselves part of a spy ring. Each had given information to a contact without knowing that others were doing the same. And the information given was not as weighty as the public first believed. The most important secret passed on was the formula for an explosive called RDX that a McGill scientist, Raymond Boyer, shared with Fred Rose in 1943. The Americans actually authorized its release to the USSR a year later, confident by that time that Russian factories producing

RDX would not fall into the hands of the Nazis.[23] Even the seasoned RCMP investigators were amazed at the goings-on, but for entirely different reasons. None of the people detained had passed on secrets in return for money or any other favour. It was because they believed the Soviets should know. They had risked their freedom and their jobs because of their ideology. Now all communists were all viewed as potential spies, and it seemed the civil service was rife with them.

Igor Gouzenko worked very hard that spring and so did the panicked Labour Progressive Party. In rapid succession, those in detention were charged and tried. They were trundled off to each other's trials and sometimes sentenced to an additional time in prison for refusing to testify. But Gouzenko was always there to identify the documents he had rifled and to tell how things worked at the Soviet embassy. Although the party gave those on trial no official support, J.L. Cohen, who had defended the communist internees during the war, served as counsel to Rose and several others.

Meanwhile, the party feared that it would be banned, but continued to carry on as if its political future were assured. In June, in the midst of Rose's trial, the party held its first national convention since the founding of the LPP in 1943. At Columbus Hall in Toronto, Buck gave his opening address. Why, he asked, had Canada not given the Russians the formula for the RDX explosive at a time when the Russians had the only artillery fighting the Nazis? He went on to blame Mackenzie King for creating an artificial plot and expressed the LPP's full support for the Atlantic Charter, the Big Three, and the liberation of the world's colonial people. His speech went for over two hours, and when it ended the delegates rose to sing "We'll keep the red flag flying here. . . . "[24]

Two weeks later, Dorise packed her bag for Montreal. On June 13 the Crown had wrapped up its case against Rose. It had called over fifty witnesses and entered more than 175 pieces of evidence against him.[25] Dorise's role, as witness for the defence, was to answer questions about a certain secret session of Parliament that she and Rose had attended in 1944. She was relieved to find that her testimony itself was taken in secret and that her name did not appear in the newspapers. On Saturday, June 15, it was all over. After conferring less than half an hour, the jury found Rose guilty of conspiring to violate the Official Secrets Act. He was sentenced to six years, the longest of all those convicted. It was a sad day. Nielsen had no love for Rose, but he was a comrade doing his duty and he had paid a very heavy price.

Any way you look at it, the Gouzenko spy case is a story of betrayals. In the end, nineteen people were charged and eleven were convicted.[26] The information gathered may have been insignificant, but those people convicted had violated the oath of secrecy they had taken and they had paid the price. Theirs were the most obvious betrayals. For Canadian communists, there was a second betrayal, one that few wanted to think about: the Soviet Union's cavalier use of their Canadian comrades to gather information, some of which could have been gleaned from newspapers. The USSR had once more put its national goals (some would say its survival) ahead of the needs of its fraternal party, and at least one man in the highest echelon of the Canadian party had complied by asking a score of members to participate. The number of people involved may have been small, and the secrets penetrated not of strategic importance, but the Gouzenko spy case smeared all Canadian communists as potential spies. The Soviets had decided to play with fire, but it was the LPP that got burned.

The third betrayal was obvious at the time, but has taken a while to find its place in the history books. Without the suspension of the civil liberties of those detained, the justice department estimated it would be able to secure only four convictions from the information supplied by Gouzenko.[27] What it needed were confessions and the implication of one person by another—in other words, the naming of names. Thus, the government decided to use the War Measures Act, which allowed it to hold the detainees indefinitely without counsel, and the Inquiries Act, which forced the detainees to answer questions or be charged with contempt. As John Diefenbaker said in the House, the suspects "were held until they incriminated themselves."[28]

As to the names named, they were published in the several widely distributed reports of the commission, even if there was not sufficient evidence to lay charges. Nielsen's friend, Agatha Chapman, who had held meetings in her apartment, was named by the commission as a "cell organizer." She demanded a trial and was acquitted. Still, she lost her job as economist with the Bank of Canada. It was this betrayal of civil liberties that Nielsen and others in the party saw most clearly.

As a result of Gouzenko's revelations, the party's recruiting of new members slowed to a trickle, but very few members chose to leave. The spy scare, they believed, was largely concocted by a reactionary clique in the justice department.[29] The party was under siege once again. It was time to draw in the wagons, take up one's post, and obey orders.

The summer of 1946, Dorise attended a school for party organizers at a Finnish camp near Sudbury. The school was the first since the 1930s. Its ambitious program was to emphasize "the study of Canadian imperialism, social-democratism, socialism in the USSR, the basis of formulation of party policy, and methods of leadership." The instructors were Stanley Ryerson, Tim Buck, and Leslie Morris; J.B. Salsberg, William Kashtan, Paul Phillips, and Stewart Smith were discussion leaders.[30]

Nielsen played the role of student, but her presence was hard to miss. A young union organizer from Quebec remembered that she "spoke an elegant language (a rare occurrence in our circles if you exclude Leslie Morris) . . . and . . . there was no such lovely women in our midst. I had studied drama for four years . . . in Paris . . . and she was to me an artistic pleasure to see and hear. . . . She gave us wonderful performances in the recreational evenings we organized. On one occasion she personified the typical Liberal Lady (Dogooder) at an electoral meeting . . . on another she gave a reading of letters by Karl Marx's wife, as his wife. . . . I can see now that Dorise had much on her mind about the woman question that I did not understand at the time."[31]

Nielsen may have been a notable presence at the party school, but she was also a vulnerable one. "During the school some comrade told her she was using racist language because she had used the phrase 'nigger in the wood pile' and I remember how devastated she was to think that, indeed, she could use such a phrase, perfectly innocently. . . . It was that innocence that moved me at the time. . . . I consoled her by telling her that the French often say 'Ivre comme un Polonais.'"[32] It was a hard lesson for Dorise. Good will was not enough. She must have felt that her own political development was not much better than the "Liberal do-gooder" she had spoofed.

In September Dorise returned to Toronto to pick up the pieces of family life. Sally had spent the summer working at the Jewish Camp Naivelt and John had lived with the Polaski family (now in BC). Christine, seventeen, had spent the summer at home in Toronto and she had fallen in love. In June, during a month-long strike of the Canadian Seaman's Union (when Dorise was billeting crews between their shifts on the picket line), Christine had met a seaman called Jacques. Although Jacques was a party member, Dorise soon decided she did not like his drinking or his manners. She considered him very poor company for her daughter. Her daughters remember her calling him "déclassé," a strange word to come from a committed communist, they thought. For several months that fall the battle raged. Finally Dorise issued an ultimatum. "If you continue to see him, you will have to move out." Christine began to rent a room nearby, but continued to come home for dinner. She had already dropped out of school and worked for an insurance company.

That fall Dorise and the other children moved a few blocks over to Palmerston Avenue, where she rented the second and third floor of a house. Not only was Johnny living at home again, but Bob Paul was coming to Toronto. The party was about to launch a daily paper and he would help with distribution. Stewart Paul, who had joined the merchant navy, stopped to see Dorise before his first round-the-world cruise. She had just moved and was still getting things in order. "Your father is coming," she told him; it was obvious that she was looking forward to Bob's arrival. That was the first word Stewart had that his father, so often absent from home, had finally decided to cut all ties. It was an awkward visit. Dorise, he realized, was trying to welcome him into the family, a gesture for which he was hardly prepared.[33]

Later that fall Tim Buck paid a visit. "I need your permission," he told Sally and Johnny, "to send your mother on a little trip. Do I have it?" Such visits became a ritual. Sometimes, Johnny would deny his permission, and Buck would cajole him into changing his mind.[34] That November and December, Dorise once again toured the West, shoring up support and raising funds for the new daily *Tribune*. Compared to her housing tour the previous winter, the numbers were disappointing. In cities like Edmonton and Calgary, she never attracted more than 300 people. It was in party strongholds like Blairmore and Kamsack and Winnipeg that the crowds still came out and hung on her every word. Where can you read the truth? she would ask. Certainly not in the capitalist press. We must have an expanded paper with daily news from all across the country. Every day, we are besieged with news of the Russian threat, but it isn't the Russians who have the atomic bomb. Then she would give a dramatic account of meeting an American colonel on the train from Winnipeg. He had just come from Churchill, Manitoba, and a military exercise called Operation Muskox. The Arctic, he maintained, would have to be defended. "Against whom?" Nielsen asked innocently. "Are the polar bears being mobilized?" It was the kind of story she loved. She could make a point and get a laugh at the same time.[35]

She arrived home a week before Christmas and dove into the preparations. Bob Paul was there and so were Dyson Carter and his wife Charlotte. Dyson had come to work for the new paper, too. It was a happy time. For the Nielsen children, Bob Paul with his jokes and teasing was like a breath from home, a substitute for the father they rarely saw.

But in the spring of 1947, as Canadian communists launched a daily newspaper, the Americans dug in their heels against communists in Europe, and the Cold War began in earnest. Urged on by the British, the Americans took three initiatives in 1947 and communists viewed them all with alarm. In March, President Truman announced a new policy (soon known as the Truman Doctrine) that the United States would "support free people who are resisting attempted subjugation by armed minorities or by outside pressures." The immediate emergency was in Greece where the royalists (supported by Britain) had been fighting a civil war against the communists. The Americans took over the British role there. In addition, to prevent communism from spreading further, they offered a massive aid program, the Marshall Plan, to any European country that chose to take part, and they created the Central Intelligence Agency to monitor threats from abroad and, in particular, to stir up anti-communist sentiment in Italy and France where communists held a number of seats in newly elected assemblies. As far as Dorise and her friends were concerned, the United States had replaced Germany as the world's most aggressive imperialist power. But for most Canadians tuning into the news of communist coups in Bulgaria, Hungary, and Czechoslovakia, it was the Russians who appeared the aggressors. "Where Will the Russians Strike Next?" read the headlines.[36]

As the events of the Cold War continued to escalate, Nielsen and Paul and their colleagues worked feverishly to keep the new daily paper afloat. Through the spring and summer of 1947, the children rose an hour early to deliver papers on their bicycles, and Dorise pumped out her daily column on the women's page. Her first column appeared on May 14, 1947, between a recipe for pig's knuckles with sauerkraut and an article on women's hemlines. "Simple Test Determines Whether Children Are in the Proper Environment" was its title. She had devised eight multiple-choice questions for mothers ("Do members over five have a share in the household work? Do all members of the family feel free to bring friends into the home? Is the home a democratic society in which the opinions of all are considered?"). The test was an interesting summary of her philosophy of child rearing, if not always of her practice. It was also designed to illustrate the new paper's appeal to the majority of Canadians who still believed that a woman's place was in the home, managing her children, rather than on the streets, agitating for political change.

Nielsen wrote twenty-two columns the summer of 1947. Most of them were not as innocuous as the first one. With the removal of wartime price controls, inflation was reaching unheard-of levels and wages were lagging. In 1947 inflation reached 16 percent and, the next year, 18 percent. Nielsen urged women to join the Housewives' and Consumers' associations, local communist-led organizations that demanded the return of price controls.[37] She interviewed housewives and working women and the owners of several small businesses. She read reports on wages in the textile industry and the price of stockings. Everything became grist for her mill in her campaign to rouse women. Her efforts and those of many others did culminate in a petition with 700,000 signatures, demanding the return of price controls. Despite the numbers, in the increasingly chilly atmosphere of the Cold War, the federal government was able to dismiss the petitioners as communist dupes. In the end, the campaign resulted in only a slight delay in the lifting of some price controls, and a massive increase in police surveillance of individuals involved.[38] By 1949 inflation was less than 5 percent and wages were catching up. Even the ethnic working class, the core of communist support in Toronto and Montreal and Winnipeg, began to prosper and move to the suburbs, dispersing the left-wing vote.

When the daily edition of the *Canadian Tribune* folded in November 1947, Bob Paul got work as a packer and loader in the shipping department of the Canadian Wire and Cable Company.[39] Starting such heavy manual labour at his age was not easy, but it was becoming more and more difficult for communists to find work outside the party and its organizations. And even within these organizations, paid positions were at a premium. At this point, the mass meetings that Nielsen had addressed so eloquently and persuasively were rarely on the party's agenda, but she was kept on salary as a full-time party functionary. Her official title had changed from National Legislative Secretary to Chair of the National Women's Commission.[40] In December 1947, she also became business manager of the party's theoretical journal, the *National Affairs Monthly*. It was not a job she relished, but she was lucky to have a job at all.

Throughout 1947, Bob and Dorise and her two youngest children continued to rent the upstairs at 475 Palmerston Avenue. That summer they acquired a dachshund pup called Sue, who would wait at the top of the stairs to greet the first one home. Because of working on the paper, Dorise travelled less than usual that year and her life had begun to fall into a routine. She would come home to make dinner and then, most evenings, she would go off to a meeting. It was still a very busy life and she was often exhausted by the end of the day. She faced certain problems in her personal life, too, though she was not overwhelmed. Christine had taken off to Montreal with Jacques, and both John and Sally were unhappy at school, but they had not given up. In her relationship with Bob, his ardour was greater than hers. She had too much on her plate most of the time and found him demanding.

Years later, in giving advice to another woman, Nielsen finally told the story of how she ended her relationship with Bob Paul, or, at least, that part of the story that illustrated her point. Her friend, Louise Harvey, was debating whether to end a long-term relationship. In fact, she had met a new man who interested her more, but still she hesitated to break off with the first man. "He claims he wants you still," wrote Nielsen, "maybe he does . . . but you don't need him in the same way. You only need him to tinker with the faucet or the bathroom leak, etc. Somehow you're not the woman I used to know. It doesn't sound honest. I've known this sort of thing to happen to other women and it happened to me." And so she wrote about Bob Paul, but she didn't use his name. She didn't say whether she, too, had become interested in someone else. She was presenting a lesson and doing it as discreetly as possible.

> The man whom I knew back in the old Saskatchewan days was unhappy with his wife. We were genuinely in love with each other for a few years, but my love cooled off. His did not appear to do so. He had always been the stronger in some ways, but as he began to realize that I didn't respond in the same way he cracked.... He was living with me in Toronto and working in the city.... One day I returned home to find the flat full of doctors, nurses and commotion.
>
> He'd had a heart attack! I was told he needed absolute rest and good care. I couldn't afford a nurse so I did everything myself. At midday Sally took him his meal.... Gradually he began to move around in the

> bed a bit, but began talking in terms of how he would write in bed to earn his living and we would make the best of his being a permanent invalid. Already there was no love left and I was horrified at such a prospect. One day I went to see the doctor to ask about his condition. The doctor was a nice old fellow and very frank. Right off the bat he asked if I were married to the guy. I was equally frank and told him no. With a wise smile he told me that the best medicine I could give the invalid would be to throw him out of the house! I was astounded....
>
> To cut a long story short the doctor told me that the heart attack was what is known as a false heart attack ... in other words it was psychosomatic. He said that the human mind has defence weapons. This man realized that my love for him had ended. He had cut loose from his wife—he was stranded. He had no home—no place to lay his head. No job. Subconsciously the false heart attack was a way in which his mind tried to make me take care of him. He would prove by his devotion to me even in illness that he deserved my love.... Well you can imagine how I felt. I was run down and ill myself from nursing him and trying to do a Herculean job on the daily paper and now the doctor told me I had to precipitate a first class emotional upheaval by turning this man out of the house....
>
> I went home that very evening ... without any preliminaries I merely said that because the party work was so exacting he would have to go and find a room to live in and learn to take care of himself.
>
> The night I slept with Sally and locked the door, spending the night in fear, wondering if I'd have a suicide case on my hands the next morning. But he was up and dressed the next day before me. He said he would see the doctor and take his advice. I knew what that would be. When I returned in the evening he was gone, simply leaving a note of the address where he had found a room. Amazing—so simple—just like that, and I'd been half dead with worry![41]

Thus Dorise presented the tale of Bob's heart attack as a lesson in her own sane method of dealing with a man who didn't want to leave. He was the neurotic, she was the sensible one who sought expert advice and acted on it. She wrote that she had come to the conclusion that women are no more monogamous than men. "That you can't be faithful to one man and have fallen out of love with him is nothing special to you ... it happens to millions." In a true communist society, men and women would be free to meet and mate. All children would be love babies, raised by the community. Couples would stay together only if they had interlocking intellects and interests, never because of habit or social pressures. This was Nielsen's ideal marriage. She had taken her favourite Marxist classic, Engels's *The Origin of the Family, Private Property and the State*, and given it a romantic twist. She was looking back (she was sixty-two when she wrote this letter) on a long life, but she had not given up her idea of the ideal mate. No matter how rarely such meetings occur, she believed such a union was the ultimate goal. In the meantime, one had to settle for a series of men with whom one could enjoy, for as long as it lasted, "the condition known as being in love."

But the letter to Louise showed something other than Dorise's persistent romanticism. It showed how seriously she took the party's demand that political work must always come first. It also showed a woman who was exhausted from fetching and carrying for a man confined to bed (just as her father had been, though she had blocked out all memories of him). There was so much else she had to do and she was sure that her entrapment would go on forever. Perhaps she was afraid of "cracking" herself. "I was horrified at the prospect," she wrote. "Horror" is a strong word. I believe that Nielsen's decision to end the relationship with Paul was not all courage and self-preservation and cool logic; it was, at least partly, fear. When life became intolerably dull or draining, her inclination was to make a quick decision to alter the situation. If she hesitated, she feared that she might remain stuck forever.

Bob Paul never told his side of the story, at least not to his sons nor the woman he eventually married, eight years later.[42] His heart attack occurred in March 1948, when he had been living with Nielsen for a little over a year. Whether he had suffered a false heart attack or a true one, he had no further heart problems. After a few months' recuperation, he got a job as a travelling salesman with a pest control firm, where he worked until retirement. He was a popular, hard-working employee. Occasionally he wrote tales of the old Saskatchewan days for the company magazine. He remained a party member until his death from cancer in 1971.

12

WOMEN AND PEACE

The modern individual family is founded on the open or concealed domestic slavery of the wife.[1]

BY THE 1970S, when Nielsen passed on her copy of Friedrich Engels's *The Origin of the Family, Private Property and the State* to her eldest daughter, it was a well-used tome, with a number of paragraphs and phrases underlined in red ink. In the margins were terse, applauding comments and exclamation marks. Obviously Engels's analysis of women's repression had hit a resonant cord. First came matriarchy, then, with settled agriculture (the earliest example of capitalism), patriarchy prevailed. Only under socialism could women and men enjoy true equality.

It is possible that Nielsen first studied Engels at the party summer school in 1946. (Her later columns reflect his ideas.) Before that, her feminism was of her own devising. It had emerged from everything she had thought and read and experienced, but it did not have the firm theoretical base she craved. She believed that women had to be roused to fight for their rights—that men would never simply confer them. In several parliamentary speeches, she cited the struggle of the British suffragettes. And she was firm in her belief that women belonged in the public sphere. At her meetings during the war, she often made a point of welcoming women. "I'm very happy to see so many women here tonight," she would say, and then an RCMP officer would turn around and begin to count, and add a new category to those in attendance.[2] She chose to call her column in the *Canadian Tribune* "Women's Place Is Everywhere," an idea few would contest today, but many still doubted at the time.

But her core belief in equal-rights feminism was, at times, masked by a tactical appeal to women as wives and mothers. Urging other women to become politically active became, as time went on, one of her chief tasks in the party, and she was willing to promote women's activism based on their traditional roles. Women's rights were not a priority in the Communist Party of Canada during the period.[3] Instead, women's issues were used as a tactic to draw women into various party campaigns. As a member of the party's women's commission and a founding member of a new communist-led organization called the Congress of Canadian Women, Nielsen was certainly part of that process.

However, there is some evidence she became increasingly impatient with the low priority given to the status of women in the party itself. In 1949, when she gave the women's panel report to the third national convention of the LPP, it included strong words on the "deeply rooted male chauvinism" of party members and proposed that "bold promotion of women comrades to leading positions in the party is needed."[4] This recommendation, did, however, come last in the report. The women's panel considered its main responsibility was to "attract large numbers of women to active support for our candidates" in the 1949 federal election, and to other party campaigns such as peace and price controls. At the fourth national convention, two years later, Nielsen censured the party for having made no progress on the issue of more women in leadership positions.[5] Still, despite her criticism, she chose not to "vote with her feet." She remained an active and faithful party member as long as she lived in Canada.

In her private life Nielsen was occasionally free with her opinions on gender inequality. During her sojourn in Toronto, she took in several younger women who needed a place to stay and who were willing to supervise her children when she was absent. The first one, Kay Sheldon, left her work with the Wartime Information Board in 1946 when she came to work in the party's Toronto office. She could not afford her own place and was grateful to Nielsen, who charged her only a token rent. Kay was well educated and almost thirty when she met Nielsen, but still she found Dorise's take on women's issues radical for the times. Dorise was the first feminist Kay had ever met. Women had as much right to sexual satisfaction as men, she told Kay, and too many women were settling for less. She was also critical of the way money was raised from women's labour. She thought the work of women in communist-led cultural organizations was burdensome and undervalued. At the Ukrainian Hall, she'd never seen a man working in the kitchen.[6]

Communist men were certainly informed when it came to women's issues, but when it came to equality for women, the party's practice did not always match its rhetoric.[7] Dorise's initial experiences may have been deceptive in this respect. She had been given a very big job in North Battleford, one that matched her abilities, but in the Toronto party centre, with men jockeying for leading positions, she soon discovered that women were assigned secondary roles, usually working with other women. The few female stars of the Toronto scene were the women who won electoral office. There was Edna (Blois) Ryerson on the Toronto School Board, Helene (Anderson) Coulson on the Hamilton Board of Control, and Rae Luckock, who was first an MP (CCF) and then went on to lead both the Housewives' and Consumers' associations and the Congress of Canadian Women. Dorise Nielsen was, as Edna Ryerson would later say, "a woman from the Saskatchewan,"[8] who had no history working with women in Toronto, and few close contacts when she arrived. For an ambitious woman who had started at the top, the situation was designed for disappointment, even without the constraints of the Cold War.

And the larger issue of male chauvinism in the party, which Dorise and other women battled regularly at party meetings and conventions, mirrored the society at large. After the war, progress made by women in the labour force evaporated very quickly. In the long run, the war actually served to reinforce gender roles and stereotypes. Even in the party, finding (party) jobs for the men coming home took priority over gender equality.[9] The popular image of a liberated Rosie the Riveter, wearing trousers and a bandana to her job at the factory, was definitely a temporary phenomenon. Soon government-supported day nurseries were closed, the women's branches of the armed services were disbanded, and everywhere was the idea of woman as mother, housewife, consumer.[10] In her column, Dorise spoke out on issues such as the closure of day nurseries and the exploitation of the unpaid labour of student nurses, but the zeitgeist was not in her favour.

Meanwhile, Nielsen continued to bear the double burden of worker and single parent. In Toronto, despite a constant stream of work, she was more closely involved in her children's problems than at any time since her election. When

John Nielsen left his boarding school in Winnipeg and started school in Toronto the autumn of 1946, he was a good-looking, well-mannered boy on the verge of his twelfth birthday. Once again he faced a number of major changes in his life, and all at once. He had a new home, a new school, and more freedom than he'd had in several years. Before long, it was evident that he was intensely disturbed. At home he got into roaring fights with his sister Sally. At school, where he had little success and was taunted because of his mother's politics, he began to play truant. Dorise, with her firm belief in consulting the experts, took him to a psychiatrist. Johnny is testing your love, the psychiatrist told her. He advised that Sally should continue to live at home (despite her brother's increasingly abusive behaviour) and that Johnny should be encouraged to play sports.[11]

Then, in the spring of 1948, Dorise heard, via the grapevine, that Christine was pregnant. She had left Jacques and was leading a miserable life, but she refused to consider an abortion. And, like her mother twenty years before, she was determined not to run home. Throughout the summer of 1948, she continued to live in Montreal and supported herself by working in a wool shop. That October, seven months pregnant, she was finally let go. She had no choice but to phone Dorise. And she found that it was, after all, a relief. Her mother didn't fly off the handle as she had expected. The words "come home" were the most welcome she had heard in a long time.[12]

In fact, on learning of Christine's pregnancy, Dorise had been distraught with embarrassment. "She was more upset than I'd ever seen her," said Kay (Sheldon) Repka. "She was humiliated. It was a real stigma in those days."[13] If it had been anyone else's daughter, she might have reacted with her usual cool pragmatism, Sally believed, but her own daughter was a different matter. The whole thing was a blow to her pride and her reputation.[14] In the 1940s it was customary for unwed mothers to disappear for their pregnancy and delivery, to either the home of an aunt in the country or an institution. But in this case there was no aunt in the country, and since Chris had decided to keep the child, there was no point in secrecy. The practical problems were even more daunting than the stigma. If Chris went back to work, who would care for the baby? If she didn't, how could Dorise support four people beside herself? A few weeks after Chris's return, Dorise arranged for her to stay with a couple where she could do light housework in return for room and board. It was the best she could do at the time. As usual, she was snowed under with work.

By the summer of 1948, the world appeared to be on the brink of World War III. The former allies had not been able to reach agreement on a peace treaty with Germany. When the Western powers decided to unify their zones of control into a new west German state and took the first step by issuing a new currency, the Soviets responded by blockading land traffic to the Western-controlled zones in Berlin. In the United States, President Truman introduced the first peacetime draft in American history and began negotiations that would lead to the NATO alliance. In the Canadian House of Commons, Minister of Defence Brooke Claxton warned that a thousand Russian planes might bomb Canada, though he admitted "the possibility was slight at the moment."[15]

Not surprisingly, the international situation contributed to growing anti-communism in both the United States and Canada. In July 1948, twelve leaders of the Communist Party of the United States were arrested. Eventually it would become clear that the Canadian government would not follow the same course, but in the summer of 1948, the path ahead was not clear at all. Early in 1948, Quebec reactivated its Padlock Law, which had not been used since 1940, and raids on left-wing organizations began. The Padlock Law prohibited both the use of homes to propagate communism and bolshevism, and the publication and distribution of material to spread either cause. Elsewhere, the LPP members continued to operate openly, though meeting places such as schools were sometimes closed to them and their organizations were watched closely. Increasingly, they met in people's homes and made plans to go underground if necessary.

The fear of persecution and all her family worries did not dampen Dorise's fighting spirit. In the fall of 1948, she began writing her new weekly column, "Women's Place Is Everywhere." In her first column, entitled "The Torch of Anger," she tore apart an article in the leading women's magazine of the day, the *National Home Monthly*. Women were "the all-time flop in politics," said the article.[16] It was not fair, Dorise maintained, to label the five women so far elected to the Canadian House of Commons as failures. The writer would have been far closer to the truth if he had chosen five typical male backbenchers.

Ignoring the writer's comments about her own "great platform presence" and "brave efforts on behalf of women" (before he wrote her off as a "real Red"), Nielsen chose to defend Agnes Macphail and Cora Casselman and then to dismiss the whole article as the "vicious propaganda of a liberal hack writer." But the journalist, Austin Cross, seems to have struck a cord with his contention that women simply were not supporting other women when it came to politics. Nielsen ended her column with the following three questions for her readers: "How can women be convinced that they do constitute a force which can be used in their own interests, and in the interests of the nation? How can they be helped to organize themselves? How can they be helped to overcome the fallacy of their inferiority?" She warned her readers that to fail to recognize the needs of women was to fail as Marxists, and that to fail as Marxists was to fail in the achievement of socialism. She ended with an eloquent call to action: "Here in this column let us light the torch of our anger, and by its light see the way ahead."[17]

If Dorise took even a second glance at Cross's comment that "Mrs. Nielsen could have gone places," she likely buried that thought very quickly as just another example of bourgeois thought. What "places" could she have gone? Become chair of some organization like the YWCA, as Mackenzie King had suggested? That possibility was out of the question now. Just the year before, her good friend Mary Jennison, a social worker for over twenty years, had lost her job as director of a community centre in Hamilton for being a Red. Even when hundreds of parents mounted a protest, the board of the centre did not relent.[18]

By 1948 the priority for Canadian communists had changed from price controls to promoting a widespread peace movement. Eventually, it would be one of their more successful initiatives of the Cold War, but in the autumn of 1948, it was only beginning. Nielsen's task was to engage women in the movement. In her column she warned that Canada was becoming part of the US war machine and could be used as a base to launch an attack on the Soviet Union. In Great Britain, women were already demonstrating for peace, and she suggested Canadian women band together and do the same. She approached a conference of CCF women in Ontario with her proposals but was allowed only to leave her written proposal, not to speak.[19]

Starting any sort of united front action during the Cold War was an uphill battle. Early in 1946, Dorise had attended the founding conference of the Congress of American Women.[20] Later she helped launch the Congress of Canadian Women. Although its purpose was to attract broad popular support, it remained a group of largely communist women supporting yet another cause.[21] Its international affiliate, the Women's International Democratic Federation (WIDF), experienced the same attrition. When it was founded in Paris in 1945, the WIDF had a broad base of socialist and feminist support, but by 1948 it had lost much of its western membership because of the pressures of the Cold War. Nevertheless, attending two meetings of the WIDF and hearing the stories of women from the Third World and from war-ravaged Europe helped sustain Nielsen's faith in Marxism during the anti-communist crusade in North America. Maybe she could have "gone places," as Austin Cross suggested, though her path appeared to have been decided a long time before. But her sojourns in Europe late in 1948 and again in 1949 seem to have assured her that she had chosen the right place, the right work, for the moment.

Late in November 1948, Dorise set out from Toronto for a WIDF Peace Congress in Budapest. She was accompanied by a Mrs. Agnew, who was sponsored by the Congress of Canadian Women. Nielsen represented a committee of the LPP called the Women's Committee for Peace Action. The two women boarded the train for Halifax and then went by ship to Southampton. In London they met their British counterparts and a single delegate from Australia.[22] All of them were to fly to Prague on a Czech aircraft and go from there to Budapest by train.

It was Dorise's first trip home since 1931. Her reaction at seeing the city of London with its heart torn out from bombing is unrecorded and so are any meetings with her family there. By this time the Webber family was dispersed and dwindling. Shortly after her youngest daughter's election, Jessie Webber had died in her sleep.[23] Nielsen's favourite sister, Nell, who had supported Dorise so faithfully with parcels during the thirties, was in ill health from diabetes. On one of her transits through London (either 1948 or 1949), Dorise visited Nell in hospital shortly before her death. In 1948, she certainly had plenty of time. The flight to Prague was delayed for five days on account of dense fog. As for her brother Harry, he "dismissed me altogether when he learned that I'd become a socialist," she wrote later. "That I was a communist I never dared tell my family."[24] If she did meet Harry in the late 1940s, it was for the last time. When she returned to England in the mid-fifties, she did not even let him know she was there.[25]

Eventually the plane took off for Prague, and the delegations from Britain, Canada, and Australia arrived in Budapest to a conference that had started without them. But the event was so impressive, missing a few days hardly mattered. Here was a city in ruins. For three months the Nazis and Russians had fought over it. As the Nazis withdrew to the Buda side of the Danube, they had destroyed every bridge across the river. Now, three years later, the citizens of Hungary were rebuilding. A country that had been in the grip of fascists since the 1930s was being transformed into a socialist democracy, where women would take their place as equals. The problems were great, but, in Nielsen's opinion, the efforts being made to overcome them were even greater.

Every day the 500 women delegates from fifty-six countries gathered in the Hall of Parliament, a huge circular room with two galleries, as lofty as an opera house. Hundreds of Hungarian women came in groups to stand in the galleries and listen. The delegates sat on the main floor, some in national costume. Behind Dorise were women from Israel, and in front of her was the Greek delegation, a group of young guerrillas all in military uniform. To her right, the delegation from Iran included one of the most beautiful women she had ever seen.

Dorise had come to the conference with a definite agenda. She wanted to see that Hungary, one of the "new democracies," was doing well without Marshall Plan aid (no rationing here, she reported, though there is still some in Czechoslovakia) and she wanted to assure her Canadian readers that the so-called Iron Curtain was a myth. For Dorise and other Canadian communists who travelled to eastern Europe after the war, many of them on work parties, it was, indeed, a time of hope. As a man who helped rebuild a village in Czechoslovakia remembered, "Signs of special privilege, ineptitudes of all kinds, were not lacking, but through it all it was impossible not to sense among sizable sections of the population the spirit of self-sacrifice, vigour and moral drive, inspired by Marxism, to create a new kind of social order out of the ashes of the old."[26] And, of course, if you were a communist, you were expected to refrain from criticizing the ineptitudes, and show solidarity with the "new democracies." But Dorise went even further. She reported that on her way home her ship carried hundreds of Hungarians, Poles, and Czechs, some of them travelling to Canada first class. "No doubt ... they will say they fled their countries to escape the terror of the Communists!" she wrote, and then surmised that they had become *persona non grata* in their own countries because of collaborating with the Germans.[27]

The fact that some Nazi collaborators were admitted to Canada in no way mitigates Nielsen's judgment. She saw what she wanted to see and, in her view, dissenters had to be fascists for they had no real cause of complaint. Like the women around her, she believed the cause of communism was worth the fight. In Budapest, she met French women who had fought in the resistance, and an Hungarian woman who had spent years in a concentration camp. Her belief that communism gave women their rightful place was reinforced by what she saw and heard. In Britain and Canada, women were still being dismissed from jobs when they married and their pay was only a fraction of a man's for the same work, but in the Soviet Union and the new democracies, she was told, that was not the case. She came home with the righteousness of her cause reinforced. Soon after she returned, she wrote a pamphlet, *80 Million Speak for Peace*, to kick off the party's official peace campaign, which began the following spring.

Meanwhile, on December 24, 1948, Christine gave birth to a girl and named her Noelle. Sally and Johnny visited her in the hospital. They were inclined to treat the whole thing as a joint enterprise, particularly in their mother's absence. Uncle John, fourteen, had purchased a pack of diapers. It was another example of the Nielsen children's mothering each other. Dorise was somewhere off the coast of Nova Scotia. Her ship docked in Halifax on December 27.

After her trip to Budapest, Nielsen travelled the country, urging women to unite for peace. In February 1949, she set out on a ten-week tour. She began in Montreal, swung through the usual stops in northern Ontario, then went on to BC and slowly made her way east, addressing meetings in the evenings and on Sundays, and speaking on local radio.

It was, for the most part, discouraging work. Too many people feared Soviet intentions. Even the CCF supported rearmament and the North Atlantic Pact. In almost all her meetings (and she estimated she spoke to approximately 15,000 people), she met women she couldn't reach. She concluded that in some homes women are so isolated that "they don't understand the relationship between the world outside and their own security."[28]

Nevertheless, Nielsen was in top form and could not be ignored. "Mrs. Nielsen on the Rampage for Communism," read the *Ottawa Journal*. (The article, a reprint from the *Timmins Daily Press*, went on to say that it was time to put a stop to "this sort of thing.")[29] She had decided, it seems, that the best defence was offence, and opened each meeting by declaring herself a communist and proud of it. Then she would speak for one or two hours on the American menace and the need for disarmament.[30] At some point in the meeting she would make a plea for funds to pay for the hall ("our supply of Moscow gold has not arrived," she would joke) and afterwards she would fall into yet another strange bed. She was no longer a guest at the Bessborough in Saskatoon or any other hotel—it was billets all the way.

On April 7, after seven weeks on the road, Nielsen addressed a meeting in Moose Jaw. There were only fifty-six people present, most of them middle-aged or older, but she was not deterred. Even the RCMP constable, a man who seems to have had a literary bent, was impressed: "Mrs. Nielsen spoke for a solid two and one half hours," he recorded, "in tones that could be heard clear to the back of the hall." He went on to describe her as "a handsome, striking lady built on the rangy lines of a first baseman" and contrasted her "smart black ensemble" to the chairman's tacky brown suit and loud socks.[31] But even looking smart was becoming a problem. The suits she had bought during the war had become worn and shiny. Sally remembers her mother taking a whole suit apart piece by piece, turning the fabric, and restitching it.

Dorise's tour that spring helped lay the groundwork for the peace movement in Canada. While there is little doubt that the post-war peace movement began as an instrument of Soviet foreign policy, it did become an international movement with broad appeal. Stars of the communist left, such as Pablo Picasso, Jean-Paul Sartre, and Pablo Neruda, lent their names to the cause. In Canada the movement was lead by Dr. James Endicott, a former United Church minister and missionary in China. The movement was officially launched at a conference held at Bathurst United Church in Toronto, May 6–8, 1949. In the late 1940s and throughout the 1950s, Canadian communists devoted a great deal of time and money to the peace movement. Endicott estimated that 80 percent of the active workers in the Canadian Peace Congress were communists.[32] Paradoxically, this participation did not translate into votes or new party members. Eventually, however, the peace movement could claim some success, notably the Partial Test Ban Treaty of 1963, which banned the testing of nuclear weapons in the atmosphere.

Shortly after her return to Toronto from her western tour, Nielsen learned that her younger daughter, Sally, was pregnant. She was seventeen. Sally had always played the role of the good daughter, anxious to please Dorise, or at least not be a nuisance to her. She had grown up in awe of her prodigious mother, who, it seemed to Sally, could do everything well. Sally had seen Dorise's initial reaction to the news of Christine's pregnancy and could not bring herself to tell Dorise about her own pregnancy. Instead, she told a friend and finally the news got back to Dorise. This time Dorise kept her cool, and Sally agreed to have an abortion. Abortions were illegal at the time, but Dorise knew of a doctor who was willing, so the two of them went to his office after hours. A week later Sally was back to work. She didn't tell her mother the whole story for twenty years.

The spring of 1949, as a member of the National Federation of Labour Youth, Sally had been busy raising funds for the Canadian Seaman's Union (CSU), which was fighting a losing battle against a rival union, the Seaman's International Union. One evening, a member of the CSU walked her home from a fundraising party, came in the house, and raped her. (The woman staying with the Nielsen children was occupied with her own boyfriend at the time.) The shame of the episode lingered for years.[33] "You should not be feeling sinful for what you did or what was done to you as an adolescent," wrote Dorise, when Sally finally told her the story. Dorise blamed herself. She had left her children alone too much. And she believed she had given them too much freedom, just as her mother had given her too little.[34]

Soon after the founding of the Canadian Peace Congress in May 1949, the federal government, now led by Mackenzie King's successor, Louis St. Laurent, called the first election since Dorise's defeat in 1945. The LPP ran eighteen candidates, all men, a far cry from the sixty-seven candidates it had run in the previous election.[35] Dorise organized women's election work in the constituency of Toronto-Trinity where Tim Buck was running, as well as sending missives to provincial leaders and other candidates on methods of getting out the women's vote. In Trinity women distributed a leaflet outlining the party's stand on peace, housing, prices, equal pay for equal work, old-age pensions, and national health insurance (which was still non-existent). Tim Buck had already announced that he favoured raising the old-age pension to sixty dollars a month, almost twice the current rate. The Women's Commission in Trinity planned to use sound trucks three afternoons a week in addition to canvassing, holding teas with women speakers, and organizing a baby-carriage parade. Nielsen suggested that other constituencies do the same. A parade of women with their babies was less likely to provoke hostility, and "it is quite spectacular if good slogans are used."[36]

On June 27, 1949, Tim Buck came third with 6438 votes and was ahead of the CCF candidate. Joseph Zuken in Winnipeg and Harry Binder in Montreal also made good showings, but were very far from winning. And, for the first time in over twenty-five years, there was not one woman elected to the Canadian House of Commons. The *Canadian Tribune* pointed out that there were 277 women in the Supreme Soviet.[37] In her column, Dorise explained that only when a socialist economy lifted the burdens of child care and housework from the shoulders of individual women would they be able to compete with men on an equal footing. "It is being tied to all the multitudinous tasks of home and family that robs women of the opportunity to compete with men, not her inferiority."[38]

In 1949 Christine Nielsen met the man she would marry. Evan Wong was a student of Chinese origin who had followed his sisters from Guyana to the University of Toronto. His field was chemical engineering. Although he wanted nothing to do with communists, he found that he liked Dorise and he was in love with her daughter. For the next two years, until he graduated and left for Guyana with Christine, he was a regular visitor on Palmerston Street.

By this time the acrimony between Dorise and her most openly rebellious child had subsided. Both women were mothers now, and Christine was a mature twenty. Chris continued to live with the Andersens, doing housework and caring for their toddler as well as Noelle. She could count on Sally to babysit for her on her days off, and, though Dorise was often away, she was a loving grandmother.[39]

According to Evan, Dorise always seemed to be in good spirits: "I never saw her down." On politics they agreed to disagree, but her interests were broad and they had long conversations on a variety of subjects. Sometimes he would buy a bottle of Benedictine (her favourite, though she wasn't much of a drinker) and they would polish it off. He wonders now why an energetic, intelligent woman took such an interest in a twenty-year-old who knew very little, but the reasons are not hard to fathom. Dorise liked men, especially tall, good-looking men, and Evan's intelligence and exotic origins added some spice to the mix. Most of all, he was a great improvement on Jacques. Here was a well-educated man who could give Christine a good life.

Despite her columns urging her women readers to assert their independence, Dorise was concerned for her daughters' security. She had deeply absorbed the party line that capitalism was doomed and that another deep economic depression was just around the corner. Neither of her daughters had finished high school. To have a home and children, they would need dependable men who could earn a good living. Life for a woman alone was not easy and she wished it on no one.

With Evan Wong, Dorise showed the side of her personality that made her most useful to the party. She was able to charm very diverse groups and individuals. Whether it was the wives of miners in Alberta, or a young engineering student in Toronto, she still had the knack of making them all believe she was interested in them and their concerns. Evan believes that her interest in people was genuine, but views her commitment to communism as intellectual rather than emotional. "She was not the preaching type," he maintains. "I never saw her trying to convert anybody to her beliefs."[40] Yet, she preached the communist gospel weekly in the *Tribune* and taught in party schools. Perhaps her determination to separate her work from her private life came into play here. Just as she listened to the Metropolitan Opera those Saturday afternoons on the farm, in

Toronto she would take her dachshund for a long walk in the ravine on a Sunday, or kill a bottle of Benedictine with her future son-in-law. In the party, everyone knew of Dorise Nielsen, but few people knew the private Dorise.

Until 1949, Nielsen had toured Canada regularly and had managed to arrange travel to Europe. She knew very well that her every move was monitored, but so far nothing had prevented her from doing her job. Then, at the end of August 1949, she prepared to accompany James Endicott and Mary Jennison to the Pan-American Peace Congress in Mexico City. The obvious route, and the cheapest, was to drive through the United States. When they arrived at the border, Dorise was refused entry. The other two would have been allowed through, but, instead of leaving her behind, they decided to rearrange the whole trip. They ended up flying to the British West Indies and then on to Mexico from there. For Dorise, it was a very embarrassing experience and not one she would ever try again.[41]

Later, in November, Nielsen had no problems when she attended another conference of the WIDF in Moscow. This time she travelled in the company of Mary Kardash, representing the Association of United Ukrainian Canadians, and Libby Park for the Congress of Canadian Women. Dorise again represented the party's Women's Committee for Peace Action. (Despite the variety of labels, all three women were communists.) It was Mary who had minded the Nielsen children for several years during the war, and the two women were good friends. This would turn out to be the best of the two trips Nielsen made to Europe in the post-war period. The conference was chaired by Dolores Ibarruri (La Pasionaria), a heroine of the Spanish Civil War whom Nielsen had admired for years.

Once more Dorise was impressed with the opportunities open to women in a communist state. She met a woman engineer who had helped plan Moscow's subways and was now the director of the whole system. She learned that 60 per-cent of the Soviet Union's doctors were women and that many of them took particular interest in obstetrics. She visited a maternity clinic on the outskirts of Moscow and was told that all women in the Soviet Union received prenatal care and were eligible for twelve weeks' maternity leave at full pay.[42]

Everywhere, of course, there was still evidence of the war's destruction. In Moscow, goods were in such short supply that their Soviet hosts regretted they could not present their visitors with gifts (if only they had come a few months later, they were told). Stopping in Warsaw after the conference, Dorise witnessed a city rising from the ashes. At the end of the war, only 10 percent of Warsaw had been left standing. Now, five great co-op housing schemes were underway. Each would house 10,000 people in apartment complexes that included schools, shops, daycare centres, and clinics. Dorise pronounced them "the last word in modern beauty" and noted that rents would be geared to wages.[43] None of her observations are surprising. Until later in the 1950s, communist economies were generally growing faster than the western democratic economies.[44]

This time Dorise arrived home in time for Christmas, but a sad Christmas it was. That fall Christine had decided to give Noelle up for adoption and take a job as clerk in the advertising department of the *Toronto Star*. She was no longer willing to continue her strange life as a housekeeper; she wanted something more. She thought of going back to school and maybe going on to university once she had saved some money. And if she decided to marry Evan Wong, she knew there was no way she could take Noelle with her to Guyana. His family would never accept a woman with an illegitimate child. All around her, people assured her that there were many couples wanting to adopt, couples who would be able to give Noelle a better life than she could. It was a very tough decision and one she would later regret.[45]

A year later, in the summer of 1950, both Nielsen daughters married. Evan and Christine had a very small wedding performed by an Anglican priest (at Evan's request) in the chapel of Hart House at the University of Toronto. Dorise embroidered a blouse for the bride and prepared the wedding dinner at her apartment on Palmerston. All went smoothly until the priest, who'd also been invited to the dinner, entered the home and noticed something that offended him (possibly a photo of Tim Buck). He left immediately.[46]

A few weeks later, Sally, who had just turned nineteen, married her boyfriend, Bob McLaren. All she really wanted to do was get away from home. Living with her brother was driving her crazy, and Dorise, she believed, was beyond doing anything about his behaviour.[47] The family that Evan Wong had viewed as normal was going through more than the usual adolescent rebellion and sibling rivalry. All their dislocations and losses, together with Dorise's frequent absences, added up to a very unhappy mix. However, any escape, as they all discovered, would only be temporary.

Alexander Albert MacLeod, a leading public figure for the Communist Party of Canada. He was an Ontario MP from 1943 to 1951. (Archives of Ontario, F126–4–0–1, B–1266)

Dorise in Vancouver, May Day, 1944. (Courtesy: Eva Phelps)

Minerva (Cooper) Miller, Tom McEwen, and Dorise Nielsen, all LPP candidates in the 1945 federal election, Whitehorse, February 1945. (National Archives of Canada, E003894461)

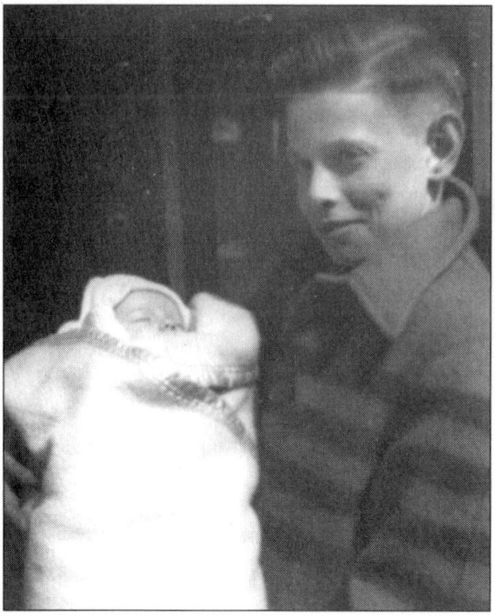

John Nielsen with Noelle, Christine Nielsen's first child, Toronto, 1949. (Courtesy: Robert Wong)

Dorise Nielsen, c. 1953. (Photo: Sylvia Schwartz. Courtesy: Robert Wong)

Louise Harvey, Dorise's faithful friend and correspondent, at a camp in the Laurentians, 1955. (Courtesy: Melanie Cleveland)

Evan Wong and Christine Nielsen on their wedding day, Toronto, 1950. (Courtesy: Robert Wong)

Constant Godefroy and Dorise Nielsen welcome Communist Party of Canada leader Tim Buck to China, Beijing, December 1957. (National Archives of Canada, E003894463)

Constant Godefroy and Dorise Nielsen, making "a toast to absent friends," Beijing, New Year's Eve, c. 1958. (Courtesy: Sally Nielsen)

The apartment block where Dorise and Constant lived in 1957–58, Beijing Foreign Studies University. (Photo: The author, 2003).

Dorise Nielsen and Constant Godefroy at the Ming tombs near Beijing, c. 1958. (National Archives of Canada, E003894462)

The Friendship Hotel (You Yi Bin Guan), Beijing, where Nielsen lived from 1964 to 1980. (Courtesy: Fern Morris)

Sally Nielsen, Beijing, 1963. (Courtesy: Sally Nielsen)

Sally Nielsen's children. Left to right: Alan, Scott, Glen, and Roy McLaren. Beijing, 1963. (Courtesy: Sally Nielsen)

Dorise Nielsen and Sally, Manitoulin Island, 1974. (Courtesy: Vivienne Nielsen)

Dorise Nielsen at the Palace Museum, Beijing, 1979. (Courtesy: Vivienne Nielsen)

Christine Nielsen with Yu Fanqin (Xiao Yu), Nielsen's friend and translator, Beijing (?), 1979

Christine, John, and Sally Nielsen, San Francisco, 1981. (Courtesy: Vivienne Nielsen)

The scattering of ashes after Nielsen's memorial service. Christine holds the ashes, and Yu Fanqin holds a photo of Dorise. Near Beijing, December 1980. (National Archives of Canada, E1913589)

13
FEAR AND DISCONTENT

Justice Department officials say the RCMP is prepared to sweep into a net all known Communists in Canada … the plan is not to drive subversive elements underground, but to intern them.[1]

At THE END OF JUNE 1950, just a week before the first Nielsen wedding, war broke out along the truce line between North and South Korea. Within days the North had overrun the South, and the United States, with the backing of the United Nations, had intervened militarily to support the South Koreans. So began the hottest phase of the Cold War and the most dismal time to be a communist in Canada.

That November, as the Americans swept through North Korea and the first Canadian troops were dispatched to join the fight, Nielsen was once more on the road from Winnipeg to Vancouver and back again. This time she was not promoting the peace movement (though that was still part of her message), but the Canadian-Soviet Friendship Society (CSFS).[2] Nielsen was among the earliest members of the new society and, by 1951, she was working full-time as its executive secretary. According to her daughter Sally, Dorise took the job because she felt it her duty, but she was not happy to leave her work in the party's national office.

Nielsen's transfer may have been due to financial problems in the party, as well as her known capacity to attract a crowd (if anyone could) for the fledgling CSFS. In 1950, there were other cuts in the party's paid staff and some people were left without jobs at all.[3] The CSFS was a separate organization, funded partly by VOKS, the All-Soviet Society for Cultural Relations Overseas. Its president was Nielsen's personal friend, Dyson Carter. Both Nielsen and Carter had recently spent time in Moscow, going on tours and gathering materials to use in their presentations. The fall of 1950, Nielsen repacked her bags and set off. Her first stop was Winnipeg's Playhouse Theatre, where she was greeted by the usual crowd of party faithful, 800 strong, out to hear yet another presentation on "What I Saw Inside the Soviet Union."

But even among the faithful, doubts sometimes came to the surface. At one of her meetings, an elderly man asked her to dispel the rumour that Jews in the Soviet Union were not allowed to emigrate to Israel. "I don't think it's a case of Jews only," she answered, "these are tense times . . . until the international situation eases Russia needs to take certain precautions." If travel restrictions were eased, she went on, people might give undesirable descriptions of the USSR that would be exploited by the Americans and the British.[4] A very strange and unconvincing argument, most people would agree, to restrict travel from a country. Nielsen ended by assuring the elderly man that the Soviet Union "has always respected its minorities." Probably that was what he wanted to hear. After suffering through pogroms in Czarist Russia, he was doing his best to keep the dream of equality alive.

Nielsen, it seems, saw herself as holding back a barrage of vindictive anti-Soviet propaganda by presenting the true picture. At this point she had spent several months in the USSR and eastern Europe. Unlike the elderly Jew, she had seen the Soviet experiment for herself, but, like him, her own hopes and dreams affected her focus. In an interview with the *Saskatoon Star-Phoenix*, she repeated again all the benefits she saw for women and children in the USSR—the day-care centres, maternity leave, and prenatal care, the opportunities for women to have a professional life.[5] At her public meetings for the CSFS, she refused to answer what she called "political questions," saying that the CSFS was a non-political group. It was a sham that few believed. At Brandon University, students shouted her down.[6]

Dorise made one more western tour for the CSFS in the autumn of 1952. Otherwise she worked with Dyson Carter in Toronto. Dyson was in charge of the society's monthly newsletter, *News Facts*. A subscription fee of one dollar would cover twelve issues, mailed in a plain brown envelope. When they opened their plain brown envelopes, subscribers could read about the latest wonders of Soviet science: "famed Soviet scientist finds way to double production of sheep . . . daring new airplane flies with no fuel." They could be assured that they were in good company: that in Britain, Vivien Leigh, Laurence Olivier, and Arthur Rank were members of the British-Soviet Friendship Society. And they could have some of those hard questions answered. Why, for example, had the Soviet Union refused to allow the UN to investigate charges of slave labour camps? No, answered Carter, the Soviets had not refused, they had proposed a commission to investigate prisons in all countries. In the Soviet Union, all physically fit prisoners were required to work, but, according to the Corrective Labour Code, they were to be paid union rates.[7]

As executive secretary, Dorise did most of the organizational work. She arranged to send delegations of Canadians on tours of the Soviet Union and set up speaking engagements for them on their return. She distributed films and books, wrote press releases for CSFS events, and did all the society's correspondence in Canada (it was Carter who reported to VOKS). Her ultimate goal was to set up chapters throughout the country, but progress was slow. It seems people were more willing to receive a newsletter in a plain brown envelope than to invite their non-communist friends to a meeting. In December 1951, a year after her first tour on behalf of the CSFS, Dorise mailed missives to all *News Facts* subscribers, asking for donations, anything at all, "to help promote goodwill and friendship with our Soviet neighbour." She suggested inviting neighbours in for a Friendship evening and promised, "We will send you Soviet pictures, literature, or even a movie.... All films we distribute have passed the Film Censor in your province and are legal to show."[8]

In January 1952, when the society held its first national convention at Bathurst United Church in Toronto, Dorise reported that only British Columbia had a committee that met regularly and that the Maritimes and Quebec had no committees at all. The organization still had no national office. She and Carter were working out of their own homes and using the mailing address of another organization. Nevertheless, she was able to report that a delegation of trade unionists sent to the USSR had addressed scores of meetings on their return, and that, as a result, approximately 10,000 Canadians had heard the true story about life in the Soviet Union. With effort, she believed that *News Facts* subscriptions could increase to 5000 in the next year. Countering anti-Soviet propaganda, she reminded the 250 delegates, was at the centre of the struggle for peace.[9] The highlights of the convention were the showing of a film on the childhood of Maxim Gorky, and a speech by a ranking Soviet diplomat at

Massey Hall. L.F. Teplov, the Soviet chargé d'affaires in Canada, was received by Toronto's mayor on his arrival, and there were no disturbances during the meeting—much to Nielsen's relief.[10]

Apart from chairing the society's national convention in 1952 and going on a western speaking tour later that year, Nielsen played a minor public role most of the time. At meetings and concerts, she might give a brief introduction, or a plea for funds, or remind another speaker that his time was up. There were no more two-hour speeches with her voice reaching to the back of the hall. The role of charismatic leader had been taken up by James Endicott. Canadian Peace Congress rallies continued to attract large crowds of Canadians determined to "ban the bomb" and to prevent the Korean War from escalating into World War III.

Nielsen's low profile may have suited her in some ways. Once more she feared arrest and worried that her phone was tapped.[11] In the United States, the most virulent period of the anti-communist crusade began in the wake of the Chinese communist victory, late in 1949. In February 1950, Senator Joseph McCarthy declared that the State Department was riddled with communists, and soon the House Un-American Activities Committee (HUAC) began its televised hearings. In Canada, the federal cabinet considered banning the LPP and then changed its mind because it wanted to protect all the undercover agents operating within the party.[12] Indeed, the extent of the police surveillance during the period is incredible. In January 1951, during the party's fourth national convention in Toronto, undercover agents produced a full written report on the proceedings, a booklet with twenty-seven still photos and over fifteen metres of movie film.[13]

Under fire from both without and within (for who really knew if so-and-so was a police informant?), party members carried on their usual rituals. They attended biweekly club meetings and gathered to celebrate May Day, the Russian Revolution, and Tim Buck's birthday. They came out to hear Pete Seeger and Paul Robeson and to view Soviet films. They continued to pay their dues based on their incomes. But the LPP attracted few new members, apart from the grown children of supporters. During this period, a group that had once formed a dynamic movement took on some of the characteristics of a sect, set in its ways and cut off from the mainstream of society.[14] When communists gathered in 1952 to celebrate the thirtieth anniversary of the party's founding, it was the struggles of the 1930s they eulogized. A.A. MacLeod, still an MLA in Ontario, was praised for leading the total war effort during the war. Dorise Nielsen was mentioned as playing a major role in organizing the new LPP in 1943.[15]

The early 1950s were not happy years for Nielsen. Whether her unhappiness stemmed from the party's decline, or the decline of her own role in the party, or from more personal reasons, is hard to know for sure. Later, she would say that there had always been two kinds of people in the party, "those who take and those who give." Some people, she believed, never sacrificed anything for the movement and made a better living in the party than they might have done otherwise.[16] Clearly, she saw herself as one of those who gave and got little back. The fact was that Nielsen's star quality was no longer so useful to the party. Her daughter Sally believes that Dorise was ambitious and that she liked being in the limelight. She was disappointed when the leadership of the peace movement fell to James Endicott, not her. Then, she hoped to have some success with the CSFS, but there she ended up playing second fiddle to Dyson Carter. Norman Penner, the party's national youth organizer at the time, believed that Nielsen was as bright as any of the men in the party's leadership, but they valued her only as a speaker and popularizer of the party's message, not as a theorist. "They couldn't seem to find the right job for her and she didn't like it."[17]

William Kashtan, who was on the national executive with Dorise and who went on to become the party's leader, described her as a populist in the western Canadian tradition. "She lived by emotions rather than by knowledge. She was not theoretically developed."[18] In a Marxist party, populists are regarded as rather fuzzy-headed individuals. So Dorise's growing resentment of the party leadership was not baseless. But, for most of the time, she seems to have accepted their assessment of both her talents and her deficiencies. She, too, came to interpret life almost exclusively in political terms, and to place a very high value on theoretical correctness. On the other hand, her particular style (populist, emotional, or however one describes it) was what endeared her to others who found some of the leaders rather humourless and dour. "She was humane," said Kay Repka. "She cared about real issues. Some of those women were steamrollers."[19]

Until she left Canada in 1955, Nielsen continued to support the party in the usual ways. On Sunday evenings, she could be seen at Bathurst United Church, where the National Federation of Labour Youth held a regular forum after the evening sermon. Until March 1951, she continued to write her weekly column, "Women's Place Is Everywhere," for the *Canadian Tribune*. She taught evening classes at the Toronto Labour College on such topics as Women in Society, World Affairs, and the USSR Today.[20] She served as membership convenor of the Congress of Canadian Women and remained a member of the LPP's National Women's Commission. All this was in addition to her main job with the Canadian-Soviet Friendship Society. Obviously, she had not given up the cause.

In the early 1950s, there was little in Nielsen's personal life to raise her spirits, either. She was on her own, growing older, and there was no man in her life, or, at least, not one on whom she could depend. In the summers, she would spend a week or two at Balsam Lake, north of Toronto, where a Finnish couple let her a cabin near the lake. She liked to work up a sweat in the sauna and plunge into the lake. In the evening, she would row out to fish for bass and fry a pan of them for breakfast. But she wanted to have company with her. Sometimes the Carters came, or Johnny drove out with a friend, or Sally and her husband came for a visit. She did not like to be alone for long.[21]

In Toronto, she and John had moved to a smaller flat on the second floor of 308 Robert Street, not far from the old place on Palmerston. John had left school and was happier working in a print shop, but he had his own life now and was not much company. Christine had departed for Guyana with Evan and their infant daughter the summer of 1951. Sally lived far away in the suburbs. By the time Dorise turned fifty, she was a grandmother four times (counting Noelle). But she wasn't ready for her old age yet. She wanted more from life than walking her dog and going to meetings and spending the odd Sunday with Sally and her baby.

In 1953, Dorise Nielsen's political career ended with both a bang and a whimper. In February that year, the CSFS sponsored a visit to Canada by Hewlett Johnson, the Dean of Canterbury. Known as the Red Dean, Johnson had visited Canada on several occasions before. Although he was a controversial figure, thousands of people had come out to hear him. It was a coup for both Dorise and Dyson Carter to have him come once again. But it was soon apparent that the times had changed since his last visit in 1950 and they had a major problem on their hands.

By this time, a number of local branches of the CSFS were operating and one of them was in London, Ontario, the seat of the University of Western Ontario. The dean spoke there—or, he tried to speak there—before his main engagement in Toronto. That night, the Masonic Hall in London was packed with 600 people, most of whom were students out to disturb the meeting. Nielsen and Carter were not prepared for this. They attempted to talk over the sounds of paper bags bursting and shouts of "go back to Russia," and so did the seventy-eight-year-old dean. Eventually they all gave up and tried to leave, but the students followed and surrounded their car.[22] For once, Dorise was grateful for the police.

The next evening at Massey Hall, the meeting was tightly controlled. Admittance was restricted to 3000 supporters and "officials" were in place to keep order. Dorise chaired the meeting and introduced the dean. "Yesterday," she said, "a handful of misled youth befouled our nation's name." She looked over the audience, daring anyone to do the same. "Tonight no ill-mannered interruptions will be tolerated."[23] Only a few hecklers had to be removed in the course of the evening.

A few months later, in the summer of 1953, Nielsen resigned from the CSFS in a huff. She resented her low salary, particularly when she discovered that Dyson and his wife, Charlotte, were drawing more. Dyson Carter, she believed, was managing the organization like his own private fiefdom. When she asked the party's leaders to back her up, she was told they had no jurisdiction over the CSFS.[24] But a year later, she told her friend, Heide Vockeroth, a very different story. "As for myself," she wrote (after giving the news of her children and grandchildren), "things are much the same. Last summer I began to feel quite unwell, and finally had to give up the tough assignment with the Society and take a routine job in the city where I didn't have to travel."[25] What she needed, the doctor said, was a hysterectomy, but she couldn't afford one and had been putting it off. She had a more routine job now, working in a trade union office, and was finding it quite interesting.

In fact, the transition had not been smooth, the new job in the office of the United Electrical Workers' Union was boring her to tears, and her final public performance for the party had been an embarrassing defeat. The party aimed to nominate 100 candidates in the 1953 federal election and all the party stalwarts were called to duty. Dorise ran in the constituency of Brantford, at that time a farming area west of Toronto. The town of Brantford was home to Massey Harris, a manufacturer of agricultural implements. Dorise tried to draw on the working-class vote and made a direct appeal in an open letter to farm implement workers in *The Brantford Expositor* on August 4, 1953.

Her election poster shows her face framed with a volume of thick hair, still long and looped over her ears. She had gained some weight when she stopped smoking, but at fifty-one she was still an attractive woman. The party slogan in that election was "Put Canada First." In her open letter to the workers of Brantford, Dorise made an earnest, though rather contradictory, argument for opening up world trade on agricultural products and cutting imports of American-manufactured farm implements. But it probably would not have mattered what issues she emphasized. Communists had lost most of their influence in trade unions as well as everywhere else. In Toronto-Trinity, Tim Buck gained only 1725 votes as compared with 6438 in the 1949 election. In Brantford, Dorise polled a pitiful 216 votes.

As to her job working in the United Electrical Workers' office, Nielsen didn't find it interesting for long. Later, she warned one of her granddaughters against office work: "The last few years I was in Canada I was forced to do office work and from experience I know there is no worse drudgery. It is stultifying, boring and with no room for originality."[26]

"My private life continues to be very happy," Dorise wrote Heide in 1954, "and that has been the only nice thing about this last year."[27] For several years that happiness remained a very private affair indeed, for her friend, Constant Godefroy, was a married man. Originally from Holland, he had come to Canada many years before to do fieldwork for a degree in mining engineering and had married a Canadian woman from Toronto. They had spent the next twenty years in Indonesia, where Con worked for a Dutch mining company. When Dorise met him at a CSFS event, she saw a man in his mid-sixties, tall and good-looking and energetic, though rather aloof. He had retired on pension, but still did consulting work with various mining companies in Canada.

Before long, Constant Godefroy was smitten. His family still marvels at his recklessness. Dorise, he said, was the love of his life.[28] But perhaps, too, she offered him new adventures, not all of the amorous sort. Certainly Nielsen's life was in the doldrums until she met Con. Possibly his was, too. Perhaps like Tennyson's Ulysses, this aging man with an aging wife was restless. In any case, he was willing to give up both his worldly wealth and his reputation to be with Dorise. The fly in the ointment (as Dorise would say) was that his wife did not want to let him go. As long as Dorise and Con lived in Toronto, they would never be free of her.

They were a strange pair. Both have been described as undemonstrative. Neither had the knack of intimacy with their children. Both had been absentee parents for much of the time (the Godefroy sons had boarded at Upper Canada College). But with each other they had, for a while, the degree of closeness they sought. "Old dogs can learn new tricks, you know," Dorise wrote a friend. She said that when she first met Con, she had found him rather pompous, but she had managed to make a few changes and he had shown her a few things about herself that were good to know. Where there is affection, she believed, anything was possible.[29] On weekends they would go for long walks, striding forth as Sue, the dog, scrambled to keep up. For a while they dreamed of living on an acreage in Nova Scotia or BC, but they didn't have the money. It would be difficult for Con to find full-time work at his age, and Dorise was convinced that she was blacklisted. If she left the United Electrical Workers' office, she was sure she would never find a job anywhere else in Canada.

Although there is no indication she tried looking for other employment, she was probably right. Already she had seen several friends dismissed from the National Film Board when security screening was introduced there in 1949. Later, in one of the most blatant examples of the anti-communist crusade in Canada, six members of the Toronto Symphony Orchestra were fired because they had been prevented from crossing the border for a concert in Detroit.[30] By the end of the 1950s the atmosphere would begin to improve. If Nielsen had remained in Canada another five years, perhaps she might have had a chance of finding decent employment, but by then she would have been almost sixty years old. Timing was not on her side.

Dorise had no intention of leaving the party, and there was exciting work going on in China since the liberation. All sorts of foreign experts were flowing in to help, most of them from the Soviet Union. If you were on the left, China was definitely "in"—if only you could get in! What it took was a formal invitation from the Chinese Party, negotiated through a fraternal party. The situation would take a while to explore and might not pan out at all. In the meantime, Dorise and Con headed for London, where the anti-communist crusade had been less damaging than in North America.

The summer of 1955, Dorise found a home for her dachshund and sold her precious sewing machine and all the rest of her household paraphernalia. Con left the house and his Dutch pension to his wife. Together they boarded a ship for Southampton. They had decided to make do with their savings and whatever they could earn.

The London Nielsen returned to in 1955 was, of course, not the one she'd left in 1927. It may have expanded in size, but in other ways it was a much reduced, less hopeful place. Ten years after the war, the rubble had been cleared from the bombed-out areas but there had been little reconstruction. The fifties were lean years in England. Rationing had just ended but shortages of food and fuel persisted. And a Conservative government was back in power.

At first the joy that Dorise and Con felt at being together may have compensated for the drop in their standard of living. They rented two poorly furnished rooms in southwest London, near Chelsea. To get hot water, they had to put twelve shillings in the meter. Con took a course in x-ray crystallography at London University and ended up working in the research department there. He had hoped to become involved in the exploration for oil, but, in the 1950s, with British geologists flocking to Iran and Iraq, very little was going on in Britain. His work was interesting enough, but the pay was very low. They found all the wages in England low, compared to the cost of living. Dorise worked as a clerk in the Death Claims Department of the Post Office Savings Bank. Her own wage, six pounds per week, was poor enough, but she was appalled to discover that women who worked there for many years earned only one pound more.[31]

On the weekends they took in mostly free entertainment. Dorise found the galleries magnificent, "until you stop to think that they contain the loot of the world that these British people have taken by force."[32] Theatre didn't interest them much ("being mostly American, cheap and nasty"), but they did enjoy several concerts by visiting Soviet artists, and Soviet films. Despite all these economies, they had to dip into their savings just to live.

Then came the winter. It was mild when compared to a Canadian winter and the grass stayed a brilliant green, but there was nowhere to get warm. "For goodness sake," Dorise wrote Christine, "don't come here in winter."[33] In the apartment, pipes froze, then burst, flooding the place and putting the toilet out of action for days. According to Dorise, it was more primitive than living in northern Saskatchewan. She would give anything, anything, she said, to be living in a warm house. Anything for a hot Canadian summer. Her arthritis played up from the dampness and cold, and the two of them had hardly been free of the sniffles all winter.

What they waited for, that miserable winter of chills and colds and burst pipes, was the return of Tim Buck. Late in January he had spent an evening with them on his way to the Twentieth Congress of the Communist Party of the Soviet Union. He was to go on to China after that and promised to see what could be done for them, but they were not hopeful. Still they awaited word from him before booking their passage home. By the time they paid for their passage, they would be just about flat broke. Dorise would have to live with Sally for a while and Con would have to comb his old contacts for work. Dorise regretted selling all her kitchen things—they would be costly to replace.

Still, she was very happy to think about returning to Canada. She didn't like the English people much at all. The upper classes were a bunch of relics, and even the party was a disappointment. She had come with a letter of introduction from Buck to Harry Pollitt, the British leader, but she had not been allowed to join the British Communist Party.[34] As far as they were concerned, she was a foreigner. Altogether, coming to England had been an interesting jaunt, fun at first, but she wouldn't live there permanently if you paid her.

On March 31, 1956, Dorise and Con arrived in Halifax and boarded a train for Toronto. They were back where they started from, with the same problems of how and where to earn a living. Dorise, at least, was eligible to collect unemployment insurance while she looked for work. They spent several months living with Sally, who was pregnant with her third child. Eventually Dorise found work clipping articles in the office of MacLean Hunter Publishing, and they moved into a basement apartment downtown.

By the summer of 1956, like all communists throughout the Western world, Dorise was digesting the news that revered leader Joseph Stalin, dead since 1953, was a mass murderer. At a secret session of the Twentieth Congress of the Soviet Communist Party, the new Soviet leader, Nikita Khrushchev, had reported a long list of Stalin's crimes dating from the 1930s until the last years of his rule. Soon the news of the report leaked out. The text of his address was published in the *New York Times* and later in a special supplement to the *Canadian Tribune.*

The question facing all communists that summer was whether the failure in the Soviet Union was the failure of one man, or whether the whole idea of Marxist-Leninism was flawed. What had gone wrong? Too much power in the hands of one man, said Khrushchev. Tim Buck agreed that it was "the cult of the individual" that had allowed such monstrous crimes to happen. But there were others who believed that such damage could not be the fault of just one man, that it had much deeper and broader roots. When Russian tanks suppressed the Hungary revolt that fall, the doubters had their worst fears confirmed. There had been no true reform in the Soviet Union.

Through the fall and winter of 1956–57, these issues were discussed at all levels of the LPP. Diverse opinions were published in the *Canadian Tribune* and the *National Affairs Monthly*. It was the freest discussion that had ever taken place in the party. Many members openly criticized the Canadian leadership for the first time. They looked back and realized how little democracy there had been in the party, and resented their manipulation. Some of the members of the national executive supported sweeping changes within the party. They wanted a truly democratic party, and one that would be independent of the Soviet Party.[35]

Dorise did not take part in these debates in any formal way. She was disappointed, initially, that Tim Buck had returned from Moscow with so little information (the fraternal party representatives had not been present for Khrushchev's speech),[36] but in the end she supported Tim Buck and the majority of party members who wanted to give Marxist-Leninism and the Soviet Union another chance.[37] Stalin, they believed, had gone off the rails and made mistakes, but he had done some things right, too. What about the improvements in education and health, the daycare centres for children, the status of women? They didn't want to throw the baby out with the bathwater. And they wanted a return to party discipline.

In the end, that is what they got. After the national convention in April 1957, those who had wanted substantial change either resigned or were ousted or gradually drifted away. Most of the Jewish members left, decimating the party in Montreal and Toronto. It was a sad parting for many people and one they didn't care to broadcast. Kay (Sheldon) Repka left, but her husband stayed. Joe Salsberg left dramatically; A.A. Macleod, quietly. Bob Paul was at the April convention and tried to persuade at least one of the rebels to stay.[38]

By the time the defections from the Canadian party had played themselves out, Dorise and Con were no longer in Toronto. In the spring of 1957, Con received an invitation from China's Ministry of Geology to come for three months to explore the possibility of work there. It was the opportunity for which they had been waiting. They gave notice on their apartment and packed a few good things in trunks that Sally could send on to them later, if they decided to stay. In May they flew to London, then on to Prague and Moscow, and finally to Beijing.

BEIJING

14

GUNG HO

The entrance to our Institute looked magnificent and all the children from the Co-op farm came and stared at it in open-mouthed wonder, especially at the three large red hanging lanterns and the red star lit up at night.[1]

ON OCTOBER 1, 1957, the eighth anniversary of Mao's victory in China, Dorise was on the reviewing stand at the Tiananmen Gate, waving her scarf at the long parade of military men, who were followed by even longer columns of workers, students, athletes, acrobats, Buddhist monks, teachers, and on and on, everyone waving banners or huge paper flowers, one group releasing doves. There were more marchers than watchers, as far as she could tell, at least half a million of them. The parade started at ten and the last procession passed the gate at two. She stood the whole time and was so impressed that she didn't realize how tired she was until she climbed aboard the institute bus for the drive home.

The next Sunday she sat at her typewriter and started a letter home. It was another clear day (there had been no rain since August), and her only day off. She and Con had been in China since June and were living on a compound northwest of the city. Just a few years before, it had been a farmer's field. Then the blocks of classrooms, dormitories, dining halls, and teachers' apartments of the Institute of Foreign Languages had taken over. That was the way things were in Beijing—everything was either very new or very old. When the communists took over in 1949, Beijing had a population of two million. By 1957, it had grown to five million.[2]

Dorise called herself Judy Godefroy now. Judy had been her nickname with a few close friends in the party, and it was easier for the Chinese to pronounce than Dorise (they called her Du-lee). The Godefroy was a necessity. How could she explain to the puritanical Chinese that she was living with a man not her husband? They would have been shocked. Not so different from any place else, really. In England she had lived as Dorise Godefroy; in China, it was Judy Godefroy. Only a few other expatriates knew the truth.

The English-speaking expatriate community in Beijing was small. Some, like Rewi Alley, the new Zealander who had introduced the phrase "gung ho" into the English language, had lived and worked in China long before liberation.[3] When the rest of the foreign community had fled, Rewi and a few other ex-pats had opted to stay and work for the new regime. Then there were the members of fraternal communist parties, like Dorise, who had arrived since. Essentially refugees of the Cold War, they were a paltry group compared to the thousands of Russians and east Europeans who provided the bulk of foreign expertise for China's developing economy. But some of them had useful skills to offer and all were enthusiastic supporters of the revolution. China, at this point isolated from much of the Western world, was happy to give them the status of foreign experts and honoured guests for as long as they wanted to stay. The Chinese were particularly happy to have Con's expertise in geology. At first they considered Dorise "the wife" (or "the expert's lady," as one of her early translators remembered).[4] She was very unhappy with that designation. Within a few months of their arrival, she found a position at the Institute of Foreign Languages, replacing David Crook, a British communist who had taken a year's home leave.

Like many workers in China, Con and Dorise were allotted an apartment at Dorise's workplace. They had three rooms plus a bathroom with cold running water. It was Spartan by Canadian standards, but spacious enough and centrally heated. Six mornings a week, Con was driven to his workplace in the city while Dorise walked across the compound to meet her class of future interpreters. Classes started at 7:30 in the summer and 8:00 in the winter. During the week they ate in the dining hall. On Sundays when she cooked breakfast on the coal-burner in the kitchen, she just had to duck out the gates to buy eggs from the Evergreen Cooperative farm.[5]

It was a simple life, but a very busy one, and it seems to have suited Dorise to a tee. Here was the discipline, the sacrifice, and the political correctness that she valued. "Time flies here," she wrote, "and everyday is packed full."[6] In the evenings she was busy producing materials, for there were no textbooks. On Wednesday and Saturday afternoons, classes stopped for political study. Sunday was the only holiday. On Sunday mornings Dorise wrote letters. In the afternoon there was often a group excursion, either by car or bus. The institute was less than half an hour from the Western Hills, where they could hike up to a teahouse, or go boating or swimming on Kunming Lake at the Summer Palace. From the window of her third-floor apartment, Dorise could look out over the fields to the line of marble balustrades marking the old canal that linked the Winter Palace in the heart of the city to the Summer Palace. She could imagine the old dowager empress in her barge and think how the times had changed.

Support for Mao's regime was high in 1957. It was clear to everyone in the country, whether communist or not, that China was being governed better than it ever had been before. In 1949 the communists had taken over a country devastated by twenty years of war, a country where reform had been touted for years, but chaos had reigned. Within a few years the crime-ridden cities had been made safe by a combination of drastic penalties and massive public education rallies, and land redistribution had been carried out in the countryside. At the same time, the Chinese had successfully waged what they saw as a defensive war against the United States in Korea. After the war, under the first five-year plan (1953 to 1958), industrial production had doubled, and agriculture had been collectivized without the enormous economic and human costs that had occurred in the Soviet Union.[7]

By 1956 it seemed that the hardest phase of the revolution had been accomplished and there was room to play a lighter hand. Mao inaugurated a campaign of criticism of the bureaucracy. "Let a hundred flowers bloom," he said. Soon social and political criticism among students and intellectuals grew to a torrent. It was the freest period of expression since Mao took over in 1949. Jazz clubs sprang up in Beijing. Peking University offered courses in Keynesian economics and the philosophy of Bertrand Russell.[8] In the midst of this campaign, just before Nielsen's arrival, Mao issued his famous edict *On the Correct Handling of Contradictions Among the People*. All classes working for socialism, he wrote, whether peasantry, intelligentsia, working class, or the bourgeoisie, must be considered "the people," and all contradictions between them must be settled democratically through discussion, persuasion, and criticism, not through coercion or repression. Coming a year after Khrushchev's revelations, the document could be viewed as an antidote to Stalin's cruel tyranny. It was something Dorise took to heart and mentioned in her letters over the years. Struggle, she believed, was inevitable, but from what she knew of China, the struggle to create a new socialist society there was being conducted in a relatively gentle, constructive way.

It was in such an atmosphere than Nielsen settled into the routines of her life in China. When she snatched a few moments on Sundays to write home before she warmed a pot of water to wash her hair, she presented a view of China that was almost entirely positive and optimistic. The scarcity of teaching materials, the bitter coffee, and even the problem of getting decent writing paper were all minor glitches in the progress of a great revolution in the making. If she had any doubts about her work or her situation, she kept them to herself. She had been a promoter for most of her life. She knew how to get a message out. What she wanted was support for China and for her own efforts there. Thus, she sent out a series of round-robin letters, hoping that they would be read as widely as possible. And she asked for some Canadian reading material for her students. They knew so little about life elsewhere. Two titles she suggested were Farley Mowat's *People of the Deer* and Gabrielle Roy's *Tin Flute*.

Life that first year was not easy. First came the humid heat of the monsoon summer, then the frost and bitter winds of winter. Indoor temperatures were kept low to save coal. The winds blew often and with great ferocity, sweeping in dust from the Gobi Desert. Dorise donned padded trousers and jackets like everyone else, and wished she'd brought a good set of long johns from Canada. She had flu twice and developed an allergy to dust that kept her nose running and her eyes itching.

Nevertheless, Nielsen's enthusiasm for the venture seems genuine in these early letters. Austerity was something she knew well and she bore it lightly at first. She was impressed by the courtesy and warmth of her Chinese colleagues. She loved the lines of students' washing hung over fences each Sunday, the sounds of the flute and the urhu coming from the dorms, the whack of ping-pong games set up in the strangest places (outdoors, indoors, it didn't seem to matter). Her students were adults who worked hard and had very few possessions, but they had great hopes and a deep sense of community. Between classes, they dashed outside for fifteen minutes of exercise done to music blasted out by loudspeakers. She tried it herself for a few days and ended up so stiff she could hardly make it up the three flights of stairs to her apartment.[9]

In the spring of 1958, Mao inaugurated China's second five-year plan, known as "The Great Leap Forward." The country's economic development was to be pushed ahead at a much faster pace and everything was to happen simultaneously. The cooperative farms were merged into larger self-supporting communes. Astronomical production goals were set for everything from steel to wheat to the number of books translated. From her apartment window, Nielsen watched hundreds of volunteers from the city spending their Sundays digging an irrigation canal through the fields adjacent to the institute.

On the campus, all available land, apart from the playing fields, was cultivated in sunflowers and castor beans. Professors who hardly knew one end of a spade from another worked alongside their students, breaking up the rock-hard earth. Then, every afternoon, there was the ritual of watering each patch of earth by hand. Nielsen stood with other volunteers at the only hose on campus, waiting to fill her pail. It was primitive but necessary, and it was something in which she could take part.[10] The idea, Dorise explained to her friends abroad, was to narrow the gap between the intellectual and the labourer. Soon, students had thrown up sheds and, between classes, were producing hydrochloric acid, chemical fertilizer, and building tiles. They were cutting hair in their own barbershop and repairing boots in a new shoe-repair shop.

In the middle of April, just as the lilacs and forsythia and fruit trees began to blossom, and the winter wheat showed green, all the students were ordered out into the fields for three days to eliminate "the four pests"—rats, grain-eating birds, flies, and mosquitoes. "It has been found that certain sparrows eat more grain than insects," wrote Nielsen, "so they're going to be destroyed. (Don't tell the R.S.P.C.A.!)"[11] The method was to keep the birds flying by waving flags and banging on pots. On Saturday Nielsen took up her post on the flat roof of her building, banging her washbasin with a spoon and yelling whenever she spotted a bird.

By this time the freewheeling period of "Let a hundred flowers bloom" had ended with a hunt for "rightists" in each institution, followed by a "rectification campaign." In this great heresy hunt, which anticipated the Cultural Revolution, dissidents both within and without the party were exposed, criticized at public meetings, and branded as counter-revolutionary.[12] For several months, classes came to a halt as students and professors spent hours in political meetings. Everywhere, huge wall posters (*dazhibaos*) appeared containing denunciations, confessions, and promises of improved behaviour.

Foreigners were excluded from the meetings. Nielsen had to rely on Peking Radio's English-language broadcasts and on the young teacher who sometimes served as her interpreter for explanations of what was happening. The whole process, however, seems not to have alarmed her, for she was eager to pass on whatever she could glean to her friends in Canada. About the rightists, she wrote that "only one young teacher was thought bad enough to be sent away for ideological remoulding through labour, and the others will remain here, but with demotions, and opportunities for reforming themselves through discussion."[13]

Her earnest life on campus was a contrast to the occasional foray into the more luxurious world of official hospitality. On October 2, 1957, they attended Premier Zhou Enlai's annual banquet for foreign experts and embassy personnel at the Peking Hotel, and at Christmas Tim Buck paid an official visit. Dorise and Con were part of the welcoming party at the airport and accompanied him on several excursions, including a visit to Norman Bethune's gravesite. Dorise was very happy to see her old friend and share her insights on the Chinese scene. Part of her job, unofficially, was to serve as a link between China and the Communist Party of Canada. Apart from Isabel Crook, who had left Canada many years before, Dorise and Con were the only Canadians in Beijing, and possibly the only Canadians in all of China.[14]

In the spring of 1958, accompanied by a cadre from the Geological Ministry and an interpreter, Con and Dorise took the train south to Shanghai and Hangzhou. This would be the first of several junkets on which, as foreign experts, they were provided with transportation and hotels, and paid only for their food. After that trip, Dorise typed an eight-page letter on her portable Olivetti, making the usual six carbon copies. With so little time to write, she sent copies off in different directions—one to a couple in Wales, one to Masha, a teacher in Leningrad, others to friends in Montreal, Toronto, and western Canada, and one to her daughter, Sally, who was then living in BC. As usual, the people interested her more than the sites. Sometimes in her letters she told the stories of her students' lives. In this letter, she wrote about an interpreter who had run away from home at fifteen to join the People's Liberation Army. Now, she said, he was equally intent on perfecting his English. Every few sentences he would ask her, "Am I pure?"

From Shanghai to Hangzhou, they had travelled second class for the first time, and it was worth the five hours on hard seats. Everyone flocked around them to stare until the ticket collector told them to sit down. Then, through the interpreter, Dorise and Con were able to answer many questions and ask a few of their own. She found "the curiosity of people … terrific and their friendliness very heart-warming." When they arrived in Hangzhou, more than half the people in the full carriage came to shake hands with them.[15]

In Beijing there was very little time to socialize and no time at all for learning Mandarin. On special holidays, they might meet other foreigners and have an interesting conversation. At a Geological Ministry banquet, they met a Russian couple, fluent in English, who had worked for a year in Mongolia, and after the May Day parade—another dazzling extravaganza—they went to the home of George Ma Haide, an American doctor, for a weiner roast.[16] In the summer of 1958, Anna Louise Strong, an American journalist, well known for her pro-communist views, settled in Beijing. Dorise spent an afternoon with her and found that Anna did all the talking![17] But while all these encounters made good stories, because of the distances, the language barrier, and everyone's heavy schedule of work and meetings, the opportunity to make friends was actually quite limited. Isabel Crook, who lived across the hall from the Godefroys, remembered Dorise's inviting her over to listen to a recording of Beethoven one evening, but she didn't go. There was too much work and she had young children, as well.[18]

Dorise was sometimes embarrassed by Con, but he was her only companion. His attitude to the Chinese was fond but rather condescending, she thought. If only foreign workers could be included in the anti-bourgeois "rectification campaign," she was sure Con would benefit. "Con needs help in many ways," she wrote Louise. "He has been an individualist all his life, and is quite conscious of his failings. But how to change … that's another matter!"[19]

When they returned from their trip to Shanghai, Dorise once more lined up in a bucket brigade to water the sunflowers and castor beans, while groups of students took turns excavating a giant irrigation reservoir near the Ming tombs. A rather grandmotherly figure, she was too old to join in anything but the gardening, but she could applaud the efforts from the sidelines, happy to be witness to the evolving revolution. And even if she shook her head when the younger teachers proposed speeding up courses so that students could learn 1000 words in a week, and master phonetics in six days instead of six weeks, she did admire their enthusiasm. Her letters home were full of production statistics she heard on Peking Radio. The aim was to surpass Britain in steel production, and she believed they just might do it. As for herself, there were moments that spring, when the winter dust had settled and before the muggy summer heat set in, that her own life seemed full of possibilities.

By September 1958, the Great Leap was being pushed forward at a frantic pace. At the Institute of Foreign Languages, teachers and graduate students worked all day and half the night to meet deadlines on a number of projects. The English department devised a new curriculum, a new English-Chinese dictionary, and, finally, a series of dialogues for English learners, which had to be composed, rehearsed, and then recorded. Nielsen worked on the third project—a collective process all the way, with hours of meetings over the scripts and then more hours of coaching Chinese students in correct pronunciation, all this in cold rooms with dusty floors. At this point, so many teachers were working late that the kitchen laid on a midnight supper for staff before they staggered home to bed.[20]

Soon Nielsen was so ill that she could no longer endure the rigorous schedule of classes. Her bouts of allergy left her terribly fatigued, depressed, and anxious. Frequently she suffered from insomnia. It was an effort even to write a letter. Her allergy to dust was diagnosed and she began injections to desensitize her system, but they did not work at all. She believed that stress might be at the root of the problem. She told friends at home that her nerves had been frayed by years of stress, in Canada as well as China, and that now she was paying the price. "I've always been one of those fools who work on nervous energy," she wrote, "and now I seem to have run out of that commodity."[21] She believed it was her tendency to take on too much at once that had defeated her. She did not delve more deeply, to wonder why she had such a tendency. Perhaps, in the early enthusiasm of the Great Leap, such interior ruminations would have been sacrilege.

Because of her illness, Nielsen was transferred to the Foreign Languages Press (FLP), where she could work part-time. She told Louise Harvey that she hated to go. "The students wept, I wept, but the Party stepped in and made the decision, that for at least six months I am not to teach."[22] She would work as a "polisher" of an English-language publication, *China Reconstructs*. She and Con would live in an apartment in the FLP compound, which was closer to downtown. Con, whom Dorise described as keeping "on his even keel, happy as a mudlark,"[23] would be within a few minutes' walk of his workplace. He would be able to have a nap at home after his lunch.

Early in December 1958, they packed their few suitcases, their record player and short-wave radio, and Dorise's camera (purchased second-hand from a Russian and costing her one month's salary) into the institute car and drove to the urban compound of the FLP. No more playing fields, no lilacs, no gardens to water, and no students. Polishing texts was not work that interested her, but she hoped, in time, to return to teaching. In the meantime, the FLP complex had certain advantages. Its staff of a thousand was a sort of United Nations. In the dining room they met German, Vietnamese, and Spanish comrades. Con, who spoke both French and German, was in his element. Just across the hall lived Israel Epstein, one of the stars in the community of China's foreign friends. He had written a history of China, *From Opium War to Liberation*, and served as editor-in-chief at *China Reconstructs*. In the FLP library, the latest editions of the *Guardian* and the *New York Times* were available. On Sundays, Dorise's former students sometimes paid a visit.

Thus, Nielsen settled in to her new life, determined to douse any regrets. The five-storey FLP building was a concrete monstrosity and the apartments across the narrow brick courtyard were equally grim. She decided to grow houseplants to brighten the gloom. She reminded herself of the old saying, "to travel hopefully is better than to arrive."[24] It had never made sense to her when she was young, but it did now. She could only manage one day at a time.

Throughout 1959 and 1960, the Great Leap Forward continued. At the Foreign Languages Press, production charts were stuck up in rows on the fence with extravagant promises to translate more words, to proofread more pages. In

Tiananmen Square, two monumental buildings, the Great Hall of the People and the National Museum of the Revolution, were completed by October 1, 1959, the tenth anniversary of the revolution.

Soon, however, enthusiasm gave way to exhaustion, and eventually to a famine. Those years became known as "the difficult years." Like other foreigners in China at the time, Dorise believed the official line that food shortages were caused by a combination of drought and the abrupt withdrawal of Soviet economic aid in 1960. Later, she would admit to a friend that it had been a terrible time. "The marvel was that no one died as they undoubtedly would have in the bad old days," she wrote.[25] But she was wrong. Eventually, after the death of Mao, China would officially declare the Great Leap Forward a failure, and admit that millions had died from hunger.

But, for Dorise, "the difficult years" began even earlier, in the fall of 1958, and extended right through 1962. As soon as she began work in the FLP building, she became so ill from the dust that she made arrangements to work from her apartment. Even then, her health problems continued. Finally, in May 1959, she and Con moved to a huge complex of apartment blocks, built specifically for Russian experts, known as the Druzba. A Spanish colleague at the FLP, who also lived there, delivered Nielsen's work and collected it when she had finished. The Druzba was a self-contained village with its own dining halls, movie theatre, ballroom, and swimming pool. Living conditions were the best in China, but it was located on the outer edge of the city, and the only Chinese people one met were the staff of interpreters and cleaners and cooks. Most foreigners, like Dorise, who were politically minded and considered themselves permanent residents of China, hated their isolation at the Druzba.[26]

That summer, Con and Dorise set off for their first holiday by the sea at a resort called Tsing Tao, a former German (and then Japanese) city with fine bays and bathing beaches, but Dorise quickly developed a skin infection and had to return to Beijing for treatment. When antibiotics failed to work, she had four large carbuncles on her torso removed by surgery. In October she was still going to the hospital daily to have her dressings changed.

She managed to write only two round-robin letters home in 1959, one describing a trip to the ancient capital Xian, taken in April (and cut short because of her allergy), and the other, the tenth anniversary celebrations in October. She had gone to the Great Hall of the People to listen to foreign delegates bring greetings to the people of China. Most of the leaders of the communist world were there, including Khrushchev and Ho Chi Minh. There was Dolores Ibarruri, the heroine of the Spanish Civil War whom Dorise had met in Moscow, and a delegation of three from the Communist Party of Canada, including Nelson Clarke from Saskatchewan. Khrushchev had come straight from his American tour and was given roars of applause. The whole process of delivering greetings took two days. Dorise took in as much as she could, but she was not up to attending the annual state banquet for foreign experts, so Con went by himself.[27]

Living at the Druzba with its hot water, adequate heating, and daily swabbing of floors gave Nielsen some relief from her allergy. She also started a course of acupuncture administered by a doctor who visited her twice a week and whom she nicknamed Confucius because of his benign smile. He believed she had too much "heat" in her system—too much anger and worry and other emotions that were causing damage to her nerves. "Selecting a fine gold or silver needle as fine and flexible as a hair he gently wiggles it in me at various spots."[28] It was not painful, she said, and the doctor was confident the treatment, in time, would cure her allergies.

She continued to work from her apartment through the winter and spring of 1960, and even managed to keep up with "an emulation campaign" in which each department of the FLP competed to publish the most material. She was very proud when her section, which had only two English "polishers," won the red flag. That summer, fearing another skin infection if she swam at the coast, Dorise and Con stayed in Beijing. Then in September, armed with some new antihistamine pills, they travelled south once again to Shanghai and Canton and then further into the Kwangsi area, home of several "national minorities." As usual, the dust from the upholstered fabric on trains and planes caused her symptoms to flare up, but with the antihistamines they were less severe.

When she returned from her trip, Dorise had several notebooks full of her scribbles from visits to communes and factories, and was anxious to put it all down in a letter home. In Shanghai she had paid a visit to a notorious slum that had been transformed into an urban commune, complete with medical facilities, schools, daycare centres, and jobs for women who had formerly worked the streets. In Canton she had visited a maternity hospital and a rural commune. But she would not have time to write that letter until four months later. Shortly after returning from the south, the well-ordered life she had devised was once more disrupted.

In the fall of 1960, after not hearing from Sally for several months, Dorise received a letter saying that she was in poor health and desperate to leave her husband. They were living near Vancouver, trying to raise four children on very little money. Sally said she was afraid to leave her husband and had nowhere to go if she did. In fact, she wrote the letter partly to "get her mother off her back." The letter was her explanation of why she had not written, and why she could not continue to send her mother parcels of paper and tins of coffee. She had enough of her own problems. She was twenty-eight. Her four boys ranged from two to eight years old. She weighed only eighty-nine pounds and was under a doctor's care.[29]

Almost immediately Dorise decided to come to the rescue. She believed that Sally's husband was much like Pete Nielsen—a good-enough fellow when everything was going well, but not a person to count on when the going got tough. Also, she was sure that Sally had suffered more than her other children from "being neglected and left to the not-so-tender mercies of anyone who would take care of them."[30] That was why she had married so young, seeking security. Now she needed help and Dorise was determined to do what she could. Her first thought was that she must leave China and return to Canada. She would become housekeeper and nursemaid so that Sally could go out to work. But when she consulted her contact at the Foreign Experts' Bureau, the woman suggested bringing Sally and her children to China. Soon the matter was settled.

It is clear that guilt played a role in Dorise's decision, but so did hope. She believed that with the quieter life in China, her daughter's health, both mental and physical, would improve. Within a month of writing her desperate letter, Sally received news that all the arrangements had been made. Dorise and Con secured a larger apartment. With their savings and help from the Foreign Experts' Bureau, they bought air tickets for the whole family. Dorise wrote Sally's husband a letter, explaining that she had invited Sally and the children to come for a holiday. In fact, Sally had no intention of returning, at least not to him. She packed only their clothes, a few photos, and a large amount of instant coffee (ordered by Dorise), in order not to give the game away.[31]

Two months after Sally's arrival, Dorise told Louise that her "mind (was) a welter of problems concerning our daily life" and said that she hadn't "read the news or a political magazine since they arrived." None of the children were in school. It was difficult to find food they liked. The weather was not good for playing outside any length of time, and few of the amusements Nielsen could provide appealed to them. Even the Peking Zoo didn't arouse much enthusiasm. "They miss the hurdy-gurdy of TV," Dorise told Louise, "the gangster movies and other capitalist delights to which they have become addicted, and they take little pleasure in the simple things of life."[32]

Nevertheless, on two successive Sundays that winter, Nielsen packed Sally and the children off to skate on Kunming Lake at the Summer Palace, and typed round-robin letters describing her travels the previous fall. After six pages, she ended her second letter cheerfully, saying that she had much more to tell, but in a few minutes "an army of hungry youngsters will come dashing along the corridor."[33] It appears that the initial pandemonium was under some control and that, in small doses at least, Dorise enjoyed her grandsons' exuberance.

At some point that winter, Sally moved to an apartment across the hall. Two of the boys continued to sleep at their grandmother's apartment, but the additional space and the arrival of good weather were a godsend. By April the boys were enrolled in schools and nurseries from which they returned only on weekends, and Sally was studying Mandarin. Every morning she bicycled to the Institute of Foreign Languages, where Dorise had taught on her arrival in China. In the afternoon she studied at home. It was a hard life for Sally. Mainly she missed her children and worried about them, and she resented being treated like a child herself.[34] The relationship between mother and daughter was stormy right from the beginning. Dorise was determined Sally's health and her studies should come first. Women, she believed, should not be slaves to their children. Learning the language would serve Sally well in the long run, she was sure. It was an opportunity she had missed herself—there was never the time.

The food crisis continued through 1961 and 1962. In the Druzba dining room, the food was plentiful but monotonous. Elsewhere, food was rationed and Chinese faces were showing the effects. Many were haggard and thin; others suffered the swellings of edema. But the foreign community was not deprived. The summer of 1961, the family spent three weeks at Beidaihe, a small resort on the Yellow Sea, a day's train ride northeast of Beijing. Dorise once again enjoyed her long swims and splashing in the shallows with her grandsons. The water was cleaner than at Tsing Tao, and she had no problem with infections. When they returned, there was a flurry of activity to get the children outfitted with padded jackets and pants for school.

It is clear from her letters that, despite all the problems, Dorise was proud of her family. On October 1, 1961, Sally and Glen and Alan (the two older boys, aged nine and seven) accompanied Dorise and Con to the annual Liberation Day banquet. Sally had enrolled once again to study Mandarin, this time with a class of students from Africa. By this time, Dorise believed that the boys were adjusting better than Sally. And, indeed, Sally's eldest son has fond memories of his elegant gran who loved to sing and go for a walk after dinner. She insisted he swim in the deep end of the Druzba pool and took him shopping for clothes and taught him how to crack an egg. He found Con strict and very set in his routines, but he did teach the boys to play ping-pong and chess and billiards. He expected them to behave well, but then, so did everyone else.[35] For Sally, the adjustment was not so easy. Her physical health had improved but there were few foreigners her age. She was finding her life of constant study very lonely.

15

ALONE

> So I went in the hospital for five weeks. Had several kinds of electrical treatment for the cortex trouble, drugs for the insomnia, and a starvation diet for the (incipient) diabetes. After leaving the hospital I rested two months and right now I'm only working half a day, but feeling much better.
>
> P.S. Please use my own name, Nielsen, when you write.[1]

WITH HER FOUR GRANDSONS off to school, Nielsen had achieved, by that fall of 1961, a certain calm in her everyday life, but the surface order in no way reflected her inner turmoil. Sally's arrival corresponded with the beginning of two other upheavals in her life that went way beyond the chaos of accommodating four culture-shocked children and her unhappy daughter.

The first was the Sino-Soviet split. Until the summer of 1960, the Russians had been China's chief source of foreign aid and technical assistance. Several thousand Russians had worked in Beijing and most of them had lived at the Druzba. Then, suddenly that summer, within a few days, all the Russians left. Khrushchev's ordering all Soviet advisors out of China was the first major sign of what would become a complete rupture in the relationship between the two communist giants.

For communists throughout the world, the Sino-Soviet split came as a shock. At first they hoped for reconciliation. When that didn't come, they were forced to choose sides. For Nielsen, the choice was a particularly agonizing one. She was still a member of the Communist Party of Canada, which, after a period of deliberation, predictably backed Moscow. If she chose the Chinese side, she would jeopardize her ties with the Canadian party. On the other hand, if she didn't back the Chinese, she would have to pack her bags and go home. Her allegiance to the Canadian party and Moscow was still very strong. Visitors from the Canadian party continued to count on her to brief them on the China scene,[2] and part of her value to China was her Canadian connection. She saw herself as a committed revolutionary who was prepared to follow orders and make sacrifices, but now she was faced with contradictory demands.

In 1961 and 1962 Dorise was involved in a political study group that included Bert Whyte, the *Canadian Tribune* correspondent, his wife, Monica, another young couple, the Mascolas, who had Canadian connections, a Swede, and Bertha Sneck, an American who worked with Dorise at the Foreign Languages Press. Sally was allowed to attend the discussions but not to take part.[3] The Sino-Soviet rift had thrown the group into a dither. All the issues, Dorise maintained, were discussed thoroughly. "Our Chinese comrades have bent over backwards in their efforts to avoid influencing us," she wrote in 1962 (after making up her mind), "but they have been wonderful in making all material available to us so that we've had a chance to know all that was said on both sides."[4]

The roots and ramifications of the Sino-Soviet split are not easy to understand, even in hindsight. The two sides presented their differences as being purely ideological, and it was likely the ideological debate that Nielsen and her cohorts in the study group considered. It is doubtful if they knew about the more practical matter of Russia's request for missile bases along the Chinese coast and radio communication sites inland. These demands had enraged Mao, particularly since Russia had refused to share nuclear technology with China. On the other hand, Nielsen had good access to foreign news and she knew that the Cold War had heated up. In 1960 the first summit meeting on disarmament between the USSR and the United States was scuttled when an American U-2 spy plane was shot down over the Soviet Union. A year later, the Americans attempted to invade Cuba at the Bay of Pigs. And they continued to recognize Taiwan as the real China, and prevent the People's Republic of China from taking a seat in the United Nations. Certainly, from the Chinese point of view, there were many reasons not to trust American intentions in 1961, yet Khrushchev continued to pursue détente with them and to declare the possibility of peaceful coexistence of communism and capitalism. The Chinese, on the other hand, continued to maintain that there could be no compromise: communism and capitalism were incompatible.

In this long debate, Nielsen's inclination (and those of most others in the study group) was to support Moscow. Their discussions were not confined to the once-a-week meetings, either. There were heated arguments in the Druzba dining room, as the sides lined up. Dorise warned Sally on several occasions not to associate with "the wrong people" (though who was wrong and who was right changed dramatically almost overnight).[5] Either late in 1961 or early in 1962, Dorise finally relinquished her allegiance to the Soviet party and made the shift. Soon she was expressing her scorn for Khrushchev's attempts at détente with the United States. According to Monica Whyte, she "tried to push the Chinese line down everybody's throats."[6]

In the spring of 1962, Dorise wrote Louise that she was "seriously thinking of becoming a Chinese citizen."[7] She said nothing of her long night of the soul or her struggle to take others with her. In June she applied for citizenship and tried to have Sally do the same.[8] Her letter of application said she had not been happy during her last few years working in the Canadian party, and realized now that the party's revisionism had been the real basis of her disagreement. She expressed her gratitude to China for allowing her to live and work in a country that was giving "ideological leadership to the progressive forces of the world." Although aware of her limitations, she believed she would be able to work for another ten years or even more. "I do not wish to remain a foreigner," she wrote. "Instead, I wish to share whatever lies ahead in the way of difficulties or struggle, with the Chinese people, with whom I have for a long while felt close and strong bonds of comradeship."[9] Applying for Chinese citizenship was not necessary. Some of the foreigners who remained in China kept their original citizenship and updated their passports regularly. But Nielsen was never into halfway measures.

At the same time, Nielsen made several last-ditch efforts to pitch the Chinese view to the Canadian Party. In the spring of 1962 when her old friend Leslie Morris took over the leadership of the party, she wrote him a warm note of congratulations, together with advice on the party's agricultural policy. Referring to the party's pro-Moscow stance, her words were relatively mild: "I wish, more than I can say ... that I could support your position.... I hope that events will help clarify the ideological questions which face us all."[10] But that summer when Tim Buck visited China, their discussions were long and heated. She "told him frankly that for anyone to say they could lead Canada to socialism by waiting till there was a progressive majority in the House of Commons was ... ridiculous."[11] He said that she had been brainwashed by the Chinese. She stood her ground, but found herself so anxious and agitated that she lay awake night after night.

Her last visitors from the Canadian party arrived the following year. Leslie Morris paid an official visit to China in 1963. He was accompanied by William Kashtan, who would become leader when Morris died suddenly a year later. When Dorise had lunch with them at the Summer Palace, she wanted to talk politics, but it was obvious they preferred to avoid discussing anything serious. She believed they had come to China so they could say that they had listened to the Chinese position, but they were not really interested. The two men must have felt they were walking on a minefield. There sat Dorise, ready for a showdown with the revisionists. There sat the Chinese interpreter, monitoring their every word. Dorise was particularly disgusted at some of William Kashtan's wisecracks. Once she might have laughed, but now she didn't find them funny at all. When asked if he liked his food hot, he said, yes, I like both my food and my women hot. The interpreter, a woman, looked at Dorise and pronounced that Kashtan could do with some "ideological remoulding." Dorise agreed.[12]

After Tim Buck's visit in the summer of 1962, Nielsen's health broke down. She attributed her long illness to allergies, but stress may have played a role, as well. Sally had never seen her mother so ill. Her sociable, hard-driving mother could hardly lift her head from the pillow. She had lost her will to live. The illness went on for several months, and Nielsen's recovery was slow.

When she did recover, one of her first actions was to leave Constant Godefroy. It was a move she had been contemplating for some time. In a long letter to Louise Harvey the previous spring, commiserating with Louise's own problems with a man, Dorise explained her impending separation from Con as the natural end to a relationship that had run its course. She said it was difficult for some women to meet the right man with whom to form "a life-long association," but if the right man couldn't be found, so be it. She and Con had been together for over ten years, and she expected that they would soon part, amiably, she hoped. Some men, she went on, made quite a fuss about leaving, but when the thrill was gone, when ideas diverged to the point where it was impossible to recapture closeness, she believed it was better "to cut the cord decisively." For herself, she would "welcome the break. Freedom is such a sweet thing."[13]

But in the end, the process of separation was not as simple or amiable as Dorise hoped it would be. In the first place, everyone in China except Sally believed that Con and Dorise were married. When Dorise tried to arrange separate apartments, she endured several earnest attempts at mediation and finally she had to tell her Chinese colleagues the truth. Nielsen's belief in a woman's right to engage in what we now call serial monogamy may have been ahead of her time, but she was also a woman acutely aware of appearances and reputation. Having everyone know her private affairs must have been deeply embarrassing. In addition, just had she had anticipated, Con was unwilling to leave. Finally one day she summoned all her energy and simply moved herself out. With Sally's help, she shoved several heavy pieces of furniture across the hall. When Con returned from work, she was gone.

But this time there was really nowhere for Dorise to run. With the Russians gone (and the East Germans, Czechs, Hungarians, etc.), the Druzba was largely deserted. Meeting Con was hard to avoid. At seventy-five, he had grown old and unsteady and was a rather pitiful figure. Dorise thought he played on people's sympathies. She could feel the disapproval every time she walked into the dining room.

But she never wavered in her resolution. It was as if, in opting to live rather than die, she had chosen a new life, free of the stresses that had dragged her down in the first place. Early in 1963, she made a determined effort to have Con removed from China. She wrote Leslie Morris, the new leader of the Communist Party of Canada, outlining her complaints against Con and requesting that the Canadian party give the Chinese party permission to ship him off, either to his sons in Toronto, or to his sister in Holland. He was an old man, she said, and quite useless, but the Chinese would never ask him to leave without clearance from Canada. She said that he was a selfish person who had used her as his ticket to get to China where he could get work and live in relative ease. Moreover, he had "grown lustier with age." Since their separation, he had caused a scandal by taking a woman to his room and attempting to form other liaisons.[14] These revelations, coming from a woman who guarded her privacy and reputation so closely, show how desperately determined she was to rid herself of Con. Once he had been the source of her "personal happiness." Then he had become a man in need of re-education (but still tolerable, even admirable as he slogged along through tough times "as happy as a mudlark"). Now he had become an embarrassment. She may also have believed him to be a political liability. In her letter to Morris, she said that Con had scouted out jobs in eastern Europe, rather than unequivocally opting for China as she had done.

Did Con's behaviour actually jeopardize Nielsen's own position in China? It is likely that she believed it did. Foreigners in China, whether citizens or not, knew they were always under scrutiny. A few years later, Anna Louise Strong hesitated to have a niece come for a visit until she had asked for assurances that the young women would do nothing to embarrass her.[15]

When Nielsen's efforts failed to have Con expelled, she decided to move back to the Foreign Languages Press compound. Later she would explain that she was determined to forgo the privileged atmosphere at the You Yi Bin Guan (or Druzba) for a more authentic revolutionary lifestyle.[16] That may have been true, but she was also anxious to keep her encounters with Con to a minimum. Dorise's move involved a move for Sally, too (which may have been part of her plan). Sally was already working at the Institute of Foreign Languages as an English tutor, but now she began to live on campus. It was a Spartan life for her, living on Chinese wages, while Dorise (with her foreign expert's salary intact) continued to pay the boys' school fees. The rupture between mother and daughter, which had been brewing for two years, was almost complete.

A colleague at the university where she taught remembers Sally as a free spirit, a liberated woman determined to be open and follow her own path.[17] She made friends among the African and Cuban students and some members of the diplomatic corps. For the first time in a long while, she began to have some fun. As far as Dorise was concerned, some of Sally's friends were the wrong people, but there was little she could do except issue warnings. Soon she grew so exasperated that she refused to deal directly with her daughter at all. Their only contact was through a third person, and, for a while, through Sally's boys. And so the China phase of what Sally would later describe as "the love-hate relationship I have always had with my mother" limped to a conclusion.

In the summer of 1964, after almost four years in China, Sally was informed that she had to leave the country within thirty days. It is unlikely the Chinese authorities would have taken this step without her mother's acquiescence. That September, Sally packed up her children and flew from Beijing to Conakry in the African Republic of Guinea. She had been told by one of her African friends in Beijing that she could easily find work teaching English there. She was still afraid to return to Canada and face the fury of her husband.[18]

Although the relationship between Dorise and Sally had been stormy for most of Sally's stay in China, in letters she wrote at the time, Nielsen, with her usual reticence, said very little about it. At one point she said that she and Sally were not close, "but what mother and daughter are?"[19] Later, at the end of a long letter, she mentioned simply that "Sally has left China. Gone to Conakry. I'm sorry for the grandchildren's sake, but I think she'll learn to stand on her own feet much better than being my daughter, as she was here, and trading on it."[20]

In Conakry, there was no job for Sally, after all. She and her children were saved from starvation by some missionaries who listened to her story in amazement and suggested she could support herself by writing a bestseller. They went so far as to put her in touch with a literary agent in New York. None of this produced any cash to get her either to the States, which was her first choice, or back to Canada. Eventually, the Canadian government advanced the money to send the family to Toronto.

The lengths to which Dorise went to have Con and Sally expelled from China are sobering, but not out of character. She was capable of acts of amazing generosity, but she also had a strong instinct for self-preservation. And with both of them, she thought she had done her best. What they needed, in her opinion, was a new start—somewhere else. But there was also, in all this, a matter of saving face. Nielsen was a proud and private woman. Whether Con's behaviour (or Sally's) actually threatened Nielsen's status in China is debatable, but it certainly injured her pride.

The three crises she faced in the early 1960s brought Nielsen low and she fought back with her usual arsenal of tools, which did not include psychiatry or introspection. She made decisions to cut her losses, she acted on her decisions, and then she got back to work. "One thing that has helped me to happiness," she wrote Louise (who was going through an unhappy spell herself), "is to see what has happened to others. There are women here who endured child marriage to brutal men three times their age, who bore numbers of children, most of whom died, and who are now free ... earning their own living ... happy as the day is long. I've met others who saw their own children butchered before their own eyes.... They tuck their pasts behind them and rejoice in what they have now."[21] The Chinese, Dorise knew, scorned psychiatry. They proposed that most diseases could be overcome by leading a consistently balanced life. She was both heartened and discouraged by this advice. She tried hard to follow the example of the wife of Premier Zhou Enlai, who soldiered on despite TB, kidney disease, and a number of other ailments, though, Dorise noted, "having a man like En-lai for a husband was not one of the least of her assets."[22]

After the breakdown in the summer of 1962, Nielsen gradually got back to full-time work at the Foreign Languages Press, but other aspects of her life had changed. Her mail, which had once been very heavy, began to dwindle. She no longer wrote her round-robin letters to friends in the Canadian and British parties, or to her friend Masha in Leningrad. Her audience, she realized, had become unsympathetic to her pro-China views. Her old friend, Dyson Carter, a key pro-Soviet propagandist in Canada, took the lead in denouncing her, and she responded by referring to him as "the highest-paid Soviet agent in Canada."

Since coming to China, Nielsen seldom heard from John or Christine, who spent most of the 1960s in Guyana. She realized any connection with her could jeopardize their careers. Now she was out of touch with Sally, as well. Living alone, she had time on her hands and at last was able to attend political lectures. If they were in Chinese, she took an interpreter and always she took notes. She filled notebook after notebook with her study of Lenin and his thoughts on revisionism. She became highly critical of Khrushchev, whom the Chinese considered a renegade revisionist, and she believed that "poor old Joe" (Stalin), despite his persecution of good revolutionaries, had done some things right. It was an enlightening time, she said, and she wouldn't have missed it for the world.

She continued to write long letters to her friend Louise Harvey in Montreal, many of them full of her gleanings on Marxist-Leninist theory and her thoughts on contemporary world affairs. In the fall of 1962, she lambasted Khrushchev for his "sell out" of Cuba. It was sheer adventurism to send missiles to Cuba in the first place, she wrote, but to back down from a confrontation with the US was disgusting.[23] Like Mao, she believed the US was a paper tiger and would never really use its nuclear arsenal. Louise disagreed. "After JFK made his speech, I was alerted to the imminent call-up of my oldest boy," she wrote, "this could happen so fast we would have no time for even a good-bye tear." Louise declared that at this point she was in a "political fog" and found the word "revisionism" so overused that it had lost all meaning. In Montreal, the party had become so small that "people ... ask in the tones one uses in museums about rare specimens, 'How did this get there?'"[24]

When Louise dropped out of the party early in 1963, the correspondence between the two women increased in volume. On Dorise's side, there were always a few paragraphs of commiseration with Louise's personal problems before getting on to the important business of politics. Soon Nielsen added another dimension. She began to send "little packages" of Maoist literature to Louise. Please pass them on, she would say, to others who have left the party. Nielsen was on a new mission and Louise Harvey was her only contact in Quebec. There were new Maoist groups forming in Canada and Dorise wanted to know who they were. She said she was in touch with a group in BC called the Progressive Workers' Party.[25] At times she grew impatient with Louise, who was not about to jump on the new bandwagon, but then she would apologize, saying that she was out of touch with Canada, that she had grown less diplomatic with age.

Nielsen's own leap appears to be genuine. Just as she embraced the communists over the CCF in the 1930s, saying they were the true brothers of the poor, in the 1960s she saw the Chinese communists as the true leaders of the developing world. The You Yi (Druzba), having been deserted by the Europeans, was filling up again, this time with groups from Africa, Southeast Asia, and Latin America. The three hard years of famine were over, and the war in Vietnam was heating up. The Chinese, who'd supported Ho Chi Minh against the French, continued to support him against the Americans.

Living back at the Foreign Languages Press, Nielsen attempted, once again, to work at the office like everyone else. When dust from the cement floor triggered her allergy, she ordered a can of paint and astonished her co-workers by getting down on her hands and knees to paint the floor.[26] But she soon had to give up going to the office and worked from her apartment with its wooden floor. She was able, for a few years, to live a quiet, predictable life, working as a polisher for a publication called *Chinese Literature*. Because of her love of poetry, she was often asked to polish the poetry section, and she took pride in her re-creations. Her social life, always second to work and study, had narrowed even further since her separation from Con. Together they had attended parties with other foreign experts, but most of them came in couples and she now avoided them.

On the Foreign Languages Press compound lived an American woman called Betty Chandler, about ten years Dorise's junior, who was separated from her Chinese husband and still raising the youngest of her five children. Betty and Dorise became close friends. According to Betty, "She seemed to need one friend, and for a while, I was the one."[27] In the evenings the two of them would go for a walk. Some Sundays they would take a bus into town to shop at the Friendship Store, or hike over to the You Yi for a film or a swim in the hot weather.

Apart from her friendship with Betty Chandler, and her occasional visits to Anna Louise Strong, Rewi Alley, and George Ma Haide, all old China hands whose loyalty to the cause was never in question, Nielsen focussed her attention on teaching a class for graduate students at the Foreign Languages Press. She enjoyed this part of her job much more than polishing English translations. Some of her students were young people, straight from the universities; others were older and had families themselves. What they all needed was more contact with modern English. They had all been trained in the English classics. They could say "A garden is a lovesome thing, god wot" but were puzzled when it came to everyday English expressions. She was anxious to obtain suitable materials for them. English-language books had always come through the USSR, but by 1964, that route was no longer open. Dorise wrote to Heide and Louise, and anyone else she could think of, asking them to sent old paperbacks, anything but the classics, all packages to be wrapped in brown paper, with one end left open. Her apartment became a lending library for many Chinese.

In 1964, with the food shortages over, the annual trips for foreign experts resumed. That spring Dorise travelled to Inner Mongolia with a small group of other foreigners. They ate the Mongolian diet of milk and meat day after day and slept in yurts. ("I nearly said slept with the herdsmen ... but I don't quite mean that ... worse luck," she wrote Heide.)[28] For the spring festival early in 1965, she flew to Shanghai by jet for the first time. It took only two and a half hours instead of the twenty-two-hour journey by train. Her allergy hardly bothered her at all on that trip.

In Beijing, her favourite outing continued to be a trip to the Western Hills, that chain of scrubby mountains northwest of the city, straddled by the Great Wall. Despite arthritis in one hip (for which she took two aspirins a day), she could still manage to hike up to a teahouse on an old estate there and sit over a pot of tea for hours, reading a book or making a sketch that she could later turn into a watercolour. She had come to love the pale palette of the Chinese landscape. Sometimes she had a meal there and felt she had earned it from the long climb. At such times, she could never imagine being back in dull old Toronto. What would she do there? If she could have afforded a place of her own in the country, with a garden and a few pets, that might be a different story.

To others in China, Nielsen may have been an aging woman, out of the action, but that was not how she saw herself most of the time. She was pleased that her hair remained dark, just as her mother's had, and that she was able to keep her weight under control. Her friends at home were all retiring and most had the money to travel. Off they went to Mexico or Hawaii, missing the grim Canadian winter, while she donned her padded pants and two pairs of socks and seldom ventured out when the dusty winter winds blew. But apart from the allergy, she believed her health was sound, and she might live a long time.

Along with accounts from Canada of leisure and travel to exotic places came the news of deaths. Eva (Hunt) Phelps, her old student, wrote that Maynard Woollard, the former communist organizer, had died suddenly of a heart attack.[29] Dorise shed no tears for him, but she was sorry to learn of Agatha Chapman's suicide. Like Louise Harvey, Agatha had suffered for years from rheumatoid arthritis. A brave woman always, thought Dorise, but perhaps if she hadn't lost her faith in communism she might have had the courage to go on.[30] On the other hand, Dorise was beginning to realize that there might come a time when, she, too, would need that option. Anna Louise Strong, at seventy-nine, had difficulty making her way up the stairs to her apartment, and was always desperate for company. "When people get as old as I am," she told Dorise, "there should be some painless way of easing them out of the misery."[31] Anna Louise had arranged to have company every evening. So far Dorise had resisted being allotted a time. She didn't have the energy to make her way downtown and play bridge till all hours of the night.

Dorise, as usual, was determined to spend her energy where it counted. She had her students, her few correspondents in Canada, her collection of magazines and books to lend out, all this in addition to political study, keeping up on the news, and editing whatever the Foreign Languages Press chose to send her. Early in 1965 she attended a massive rally against the American bombing of North Vietnam. Tiananmen Square was packed and it was a wonderful sight to see all the banners waving. "Why doesn't [President Johnson] put his own house in order before he tries to spread democracy in Asia?" she wrote Heide.[32] Already, she believed, the Americans were in over their heads and were about to learn a lesson the hard way. She was happy to have a good income so that she could send money to the North Vietnamese.

Then, in the spring of 1965, Nielsen fell ill again and was off work for many months. Once more she moved back to the You Yi, where she would remain for the rest of her life. That fall she was still too ill to respond to her mail. When she finally wrote to her faithful correspondent, Louise Harvey, in May 1966, she explained in a handwritten scrawl that she had been too sick to care about writing to anybody, "unless it's been important, political and urgent."[33] However, the letter was a long one, and though it was full of complaints about her own health, and Louise's lack of political passion, its length and irascibility show that Nielsen was on the road to recovery, and that her own zeal for living the life of a revolutionary was not quite spent.

16

REVOLUTION

... you want to help change the world, but the kind of activities you are engaged in, although worthy of nice old ladies and others who understand nothing of history or social change, will lead you no where.[1]

IN 1966 NIELSEN AND THE OTHER FOREIGNERS in Beijing found themselves caught up in the swirl of the last and greatest upheaval in Mao's China. If Dorise wanted her revolutionary zeal tested, the time had come. Today, when the Chinese refer to "the revolution," they do not mean the communist victory that brought Mao to power in 1949, they mean the Great Proletarian Cultural Revolution that erupted in 1966 and continued in its various phases until Mao's death in 1976.

There is little doubt that the Cultural Revolution was instigated by Mao himself. His authority within the party had suffered a setback as a result of the Great Leap Forward, and, at seventy-three, he was determined to reform the party and set a course for his successors to follow. He would ultimately fail and the Great Proletarian Cultural Revolution would become a power struggle for the succession, but for its millions of participants, it began with a set of ideals that seemed genuinely relevant in the building of the new society.

From both the Russian and the Chinese experience, it was obvious that party members often became a new elite, replacing the bourgeoisie in a capitalist society. Like the bourgeoisie, they sought security for themselves and their families. Mao believed that such a state of affairs was unacceptable. To prevent it, he advocated a continuous process of criticism from below. Anyone living a bourgeois lifestyle or promoting bourgeois values, no matter how powerful his position, was to be chastised and demoted. In the summer of 1966, Mao appointed the most radical (or sycophantic) members of the party, including his wife, Jiang Qing, and several energetic cadres from Shanghai, to the Cultural Revolutionary Group, which was to guide the revolution. He also assured the complete loyalty of Defence Minister Lin Piao, whom he had chosen as his successor.

Classes ended early that year so that students could study the latest pronouncements of the Cultural Revolutionary Group and act on them. The young were being asked to rebel and they responded en masse. That summer, as usual, most of the foreign community from Beijing, including Nielsen, spent the month of August on the beach at Beidaihe. She first saw a group of student rebels there. They marched down the street wearing army caps and red armbands and called themselves Red Guards.

When she returned to Beijing there were dazhibaos everywhere and Red Guards marching with banners. They had come from great distances and were billeted all over the city. A group of high school students from Shandong were put up at the Foreign Languages Press building. Dorise and all the other employees were asked to supply them with sheets and blankets. Armed with their little red books of *Quotations from Chairman Mao,* the students attended meetings with Red Guards from other parts of the country, and awaited the highlight of the excursion, an opportunity to hear Mao speak in Tiananmen Square. At the press, the most zealous of the Red Guards threatened to cut off women's braids and slit the legs of pants they considered too narrow. Others in the city invaded the homes of the wealthy, destroying everything and parading the owners in dunce caps, a humiliation first meted out to landlords in the days of land reform twenty years earlier.[2]

Soon, in every workplace, a rebel group had formed, and most of the time was taken up by meetings. Foreigners were left with little or no work. Still, they felt a certain exhilaration at being witnesses to a great event. The situation was confusing, but at first it was not threatening. They could feel the earnestness of their Chinese colleagues. Even the You Yi workers, all employees of the Foreign Experts' Bureau, had formed a rebel group and were holding meetings. It seemed that the whole society was in the midst of a change as momentous as the French or the Bolshevik revolutions. A new era of equality and fraternity was about to be born. When foreigners attended "struggle meetings," they did so as guests, but for the first time they were allowed to sit on the floor with everyone else.[3] And if, as with any revolution, things occasionally got out of hand, the incidents of violence were considered an aberration. Hadn't Mao made it clear that people should struggle with reason, not with force?

In September 1966, Nielsen wrote a long, enthusiastic letter describing these early tumultuous days of the revolution. It was, she wrote, "the greatest revolution in the history of mankind, in terms of participants."[4] For the first time in history, there was no reactionary ruling class opposing the revolutionary will of the people. In fact, the ruling party itself had launched the revolution. Everywhere, bourgeois ideas and customs were being cast aside for proletarian values. She explained that women were bobbing their hair (or having it done for them) because, previously, all married women had been expected to wear their hair in a bun. According to Dorise, the whole revolution was about liberation and social justice. An American woman she knew, who had left an abusive husband, was finally vindicated when the Red Guards invaded his thirty-room house and found all the loot he had demanded of his patients. The man was henceforth allotted a two-room apartment. As to the adulation of Mao (how the foreign press sneered at that!), she believed that he was a greater teacher than Marx or Lenin or Engels. The others were all intellectuals, but Mao was a country schoolteacher who wrote simply so that peasants and workers could apply Marxism to their everyday lives.

Later, Dorise would confess that it was difficult to know what was happening and what the issues were—everything was a blur. But, at first, she believed what she was told, and the revolution made sense to her. She had to rely, of course, on a few friends at the You Yi who were in closer touch with the action than she was, either because they understood Mandarin or they went out to work. The best informed of all the foreigners appeared to be Sidney Rittenberg, an American who worked for Radio Peking. Although he didn't live at the You Yi (he had a Chinese wife and lived in the city), he came frequently to the dining room to tell the latest Khrushchev joke and keep everyone up-to-date. When Nielsen first came to China, Tim Buck had warned her to be careful of Rittenberg, who might be an American spy. In 1949 the Chinese had imprisoned him on that charge but in 1955 they released him with an apology for their error. Since then, he had been given more and more responsibility. He was a clever, energetic fellow and obviously the Chinese leadership had confidence in him. In the early 1960s he was part of the team that translated Mao's works into English. During the early stages of the revolution, Rittenberg's briefings became an important source of information for residents of the You Yi.[5]

Six months after the beginning of the revolution, the question of what role foreigners could play in it was finally settled. All the foreign friends in Beijing were summoned to a meeting with Foreign Minister Chen Yi, the night of January 28, 1967. After dinner Dorise dressed in her customary two pairs of padded pants, piled on several sweaters under her jacket, and boarded a bus with the others. Casting off bourgeois customs meant no flashy colours, no jewellery, and certainly no make-up. On the streets of Beijing, they passed the lantern-lit stands where workers bought dough balls and vegetables on their way home from work. The usual stream of bicycles and pedestrians made way for the bus. As they approached Tiananmen Square, there were rows of dazhibaos lining the streets. They could hear the blare of a loudspeaker, but the square itself was deserted except for the buses and cars arriving to deposit the foreign (non-diplomatic) community.

It was such a small group now, not much more than a hundred. Everyone came, even old hands like Rewi Alley and George Ma Haide, who had already made it plain they thought the foreign crowd should keep their noses out of the whole thing. But they were in the minority. Most of the group, including Dorise, were keen to express, somehow, their solidarity with their Chinese comrades. Nielsen, at sixty-four, was among the oldest residents there. She had lived in China almost ten years and felt like an old-timer herself, though to be a genuine old-timer, you had to have arrived before 1949. Still, she was the same age as Chen Yi, who had been with Mao since 1927. And how many times had she stood at a reception, sipping a steaming mug of green tea, waiting for some event or other to begin? Even in the midst of a revolution, there was tea.

Chen Yi's message that night was what most of the foreign experts had hoped for and anticipated. He said that Chairman Mao had learned of a certain dazhibao in which several foreign workers attacked the Foreign Experts' Bureau for providing them high salaries and privileged living conditions. Mao had approved the sentiments in the poster and had agreed that foreigners could join rebel groups, if they chose. They could also choose to stay out. But, in the end, very few of them stayed out. In March 1967, Dorise wrote Sally that she was completely caught up in meetings and discussions. "Many ... like myself realize how bourgeois this place is and how bad it is to live as we do, so far different from the Chinese. So we are doing a number of things voluntarily ... to live more simply. Some are going to live where they work. I'm taking one third of what I used to have."[6]

The same month, a rebel group called the Bethune-Yenan Regiment was formed at the You Yi. To show that support for the Cultural Revolution was international, members elected five leaders, one from each continent. Then the approximately ninety members divided into nine study groups, based on workplace or language.[7] Meetings of the whole group were conducted in English, with translation services provided. Dorise became a member of a study group made up entirely of women called the Communards. Their job, like the Red Guards, and all other rebel groups, was to use the ideas of Chairman Mao to critique the system (in this case, the Foreign Experts' Bureau and the Foreign Languages Press).

Throughout the very hot summer of 1967, study groups met regularly. Occasionally, large public meetings were held at the You Yi and attended by representatives of other rebel groups, and, sometimes, leading members of the foreign community represented the Bethune-Yenan Regiment at outside rallies. Sidney Rittenberg was often prominent at such meetings and other Americans took leading roles. Dorise went everywhere with her notebook. In one letter home she said she had attended "a number of accusation meetings where the most amazing facts (had) been revealed." The culprit at that moment was Liu Shao-chi, the former president of the republic, who had been denounced as a revisionist. Foreign Minister Chen Yi was not far behind. Everyone, she said, was completely immersed in meetings and it would be a long while before the struggle "to ensure that China maintains the dictatorship of the proletariat" was over.[8] What was at stake, she wrote, was a change in people's thinking, and that kind of change would take much longer than land reform or the construction of factories.

Before long, the whole rebel movement had split into factions, each with particular targets, mirroring a power struggle among the Chinese leadership. It was not easy to know which line was correct. Twenty years later, Denise Lebreton, who was a friend of Dorise's and a member of the Communards, remembered the problem of trying to discern just who was who in the storm of the revolution. "Hints were whispered back and forth: this (faction) was recommended by some reliable rebels, that one was conservative, this other one avant-garde. Actually we were rather at a loss. Which forces, which people *really* represented the rightest revisionist danger we were supposed to be fighting?"[9]

That autumn of 1967, the poplar leaves piled up in the gardens at the You Yi and blew around in the dust. In every institution, competing rebel groups continued to hold meetings and marches. On the northwestern outskirts of the city, near the universities, farmers from neighbouring communes complained that the blare of loudspeakers kept them awake. In Beijing, the ultra-left Earth faction, on a rampage against Premier Zhou Enlai, stormed public buildings and rifled through state documents. And at the You Yi, members of Bethune-Yenan also split into factions, many of them following Sidney Rittenberg, whom they believed to be an impartial commentator on events, but who was actually allied to the ultra-left. One night in October 1967, a group of students allied to the Earth faction captured David Crook, a British teacher allied with the opposing Red Flag (Heaven) faction. He was accused of being a British spy and was not seen again for five years. Nielsen had taught with Crook at the Institute of Foreign Languages in 1958 and had lived across the hall from his family.

After Crook's arrest, the tide turned against the ultra-left. Sidney Rittenberg, Israel Epstein, and a number of other foreigners were arrested early in 1968. The Bethune-Yenan Regiment quickly dissolved. Nielsen wrote very few letters home in 1968 and all she said about the revolution was that she could say nothing. To Louise Harvey, she wrote: "In time China will be telling the world much more about what has happened and is happening here, but until then most of us feel we should wait for official statements. At present none of us is writing much, always aware that our letters are subject to examination in the countries to which they are sent."[10] This was her first veiled acknowledgement that she had to be careful what she said in her letters.

An observer of people's reactions to arrests in the Soviet Union in the 1930s noted that "some retreated even further into their shells … while others … shouted 'Treachery and counter-revolution everywhere!'" Such words became a sort of primitive charm to ward off evil spirits, she said, for if perfectly innocent people could be arrested and never seen again, then no one felt safe."[11] It appears that Nielsen reacted to the arrests of foreigners in China in both ways. She ceased her active involvement in the revolution (as did the rest of the foreign community), but her suspicions of those arrested simmered for years.

By the spring of 1968, every foreigner had become suspect and was excluded from all aspects of Chinese life. None of them were invited to May Day celebrations that year. At the You Yi, the halls were lined with packing cases as those on short-term contracts got ready to leave. Several blocks of the largely deserted complex had begun to fill up with high-ranking officers of the People's Liberation Army (PLA) who were being trained to take over investigations of each institution and get the country moving again. After dinner, the officers would stroll through the leaf-strewn garden, nodding politely at the foreign guests and watching with delight and amazement as a group of foreign children shouted to each other in Mandarin.[12]

Later that year, the PLA contingent assigned to the You Yi asked Dorise for a report on the Bethune-Yenan Regiment. She quickly typed out six pages of notes. There had been a conspiracy, she implied, right from the beginning. The whole thing had been managed by a certain group of foreigners for their own purposes. She was not reluctant to name names. In this case, her suspicions were never passed on. At the top of the first page, she later scrawled, "Long-winded—prepared in a great hurry, then never asked for!" But she did write to Zhou Enlai several times, providing information on certain people, which she hoped would "stimulate further investigation."[13] It seems that Nielsen thought there was, indeed, treachery and counter-revolution everywhere.

By 1969, the Cultural Revolution had entered a new phase. No longer was there the beating of drums and din of loudspeakers as rebel factions fought their battles in the streets. Now the political leaders struggled for power behind closed doors while the army conducted its investigations. But restoring normalcy was not simple. Even if salaries were paid and the buses ran and thermoses of boiling water continued to appear each morning, the atmosphere had been poisoned and the toxicity of fear and suspicion lingered.

In her letters Dorise explained that thousands of students were going to the countryside to do *laodong* (manual labour). The exodus, she said, was designed to end ideas of intellectual superiority. She compared the phenomenon to the pioneer days in America, except that the youngsters were being better cared-for. The son of a friend "had gone out to the edge of beyond, no electricity, no running water, only peasant huts to live in at first," but he had returned for the spring festival full of enthusiasm and raring to go back.[14]

Before long, each institution was also sending a portion of its workforce to the countryside—that portion deemed to be most in need of re-education. Anyone who had been educated abroad or had come from a wealthy family was targeted. At the Foreign Language Press, this included approximately half its editors and translators not already dead or in prison.[15] Among them was Nielsen's friend Betty Chandler, who is still reluctant to talk about those times. "Ten years of chaos" is how she describes them—words that echo the Communist Party's official assessment of the Cultural Revolution. Several times, when Betty returned to the city, Dorise put her up for the night. She remembers how wonderful it was to have a hot bath.[16]

In her letters that year, Nielsen said little about her own situation, except that she was in greater need of reading material than usual. The library at the FLP was closed, so she had no access to current periodicals or books. During a long winter illness, someone lent her new translations of the *The Iliad* and *The Odyssey*, and a copy of Gibbon's *Decline of the Roman Empire*. For news, she relied on her radio. If anyone could send her paperbacks, old magazines, or copies of the *Canadian Tribune*, she would be very grateful (just wrap in brown paper with string and leave one end open). She stayed inside most of that winter. By this time she had covered every upholstered surface in plastic and always donned a gauze mask when she swept the floor.

In the spring she planted a garden, just a small square of earth in the courtyard near her building. Two Nepalese students helped with the digging.[17] Perhaps she was trying to show that she, too, knew something about manual labour. In any case, she was relieved to know that she would not be shipped out to live in a dusty peasant hut with no running water. At first she thought laodong was compulsory and everyone would have to go, but then, one of the gentler emissaries from the FLP (where the rougher and less educated seemed to be taking over) informed her that no, she did not have to go, the whole thing was voluntary.[18] She chose to believe that. She knew she would not be able to lift her head off the mat if she had to live in a peasant hut.

A Pakistani journalist working at the FLP recalled this period as a time when "everybody had become mute ... people usually avoided foreigners ... we were living right in the heart of China, yet our sole sources of information about her were the foreign media, gossip, and rumours."[19] Denise Lebreton, who worked in the French language section of the FLP, remembered it as "a very painful period when we lived from day to day. Work was thrown to me like a bone and I continued to gnaw on it for this was my life."[20] Nielsen, too, was thrown a few bones of work. Sometimes it was brought to the door by a man whose rudeness appalled her. It was an effort to remain polite. It was a challenge to correct the increasingly poor translations without giving offence.[21]

During this time, Nielsen began to write what she called "reminiscences." She sat at her old Olivetti day after day, and, eventually, to her amazement, she had typed almost 400 pages, single-spaced, and she had only reached the year of 1928. But she was not inclined to go further, in any case. She said that she wrote the story for her children, so they would know something about her life before they came into the picture. What came after, they knew well enough and she had no inclination to go through that again.

But Nielsen had several reasons for writing her reminiscences, and letting her children know the family history on their mother's side was probably the least of them. First of all, she needed an occupation, something to keep her mind busy, as she would say, but not too busy. Something to keep herself sane. There was not much to read, no outings, no entertainment at all. She was writing very few letters and seldom had company. And so she began to spin a tale, using her own life history as the starting point, but pushing it, in places, far beyond that. She had written fiction before and had polished the works of others. She knew something about pacing and dialogue, and building suspense, and she drew upon everything she knew as she ground out a story of how her own life had been derailed by World War I. As she wrote, day after day, stopping sometimes to sketch an illustration or recall the words of an old rhyme, the piece became a very strange hybrid, part vividly realized memoir, part Marxist diatribe, part romance novel. In the long middle section, with the story of Dee's two summers with Laurie Gilchrist and then his tragic death on his first solo flight, romance takes over completely. But even before that, she enhanced the story by inventing Roland, the brother she always wanted. He was artistic and university-educated. He made his living as a buyer for Christie's art auction. He was seldom home but when he did appear he always brought a beautiful gift for his mother (often an artefact from China). He was completely unlike the stolid Harry with his beer bottling, golf, and Masonic dinners. But Roland was too good to last. In 1915 he died on the Western Front.[22]

In 1972 Nielsen had to put aside her reminiscences. Suddenly there was work again and lots of it. In 1971 China had resumed talks to normalize relations with the United States. The American president, Richard Nixon, looking for a way out of the Vietnam War, was particularly receptive. The US Secretary of State, Henry Kissinger, made several secret visits, and Nixon announced his intention to visit China in 1972.

On October 5, 1971, before Nixon's visit, Premier Zhou Enlai called a meeting with the English-speaking foreigners remaining in Beijing and asked them to help promote friendly relations with the West.[23] There was a rush to train English interpreters and to provide written materials in English. Once again the skills of China's foreign friends were in demand. In rapid succession, China established diplomatic missions with Canada and the United Nations and began to negotiate with the Americans.[24] Soon, agreements for trade and cultural exchanges were signed, and foreign businessmen and students and tourists began to make their way to China.

On both sides, the rapprochement was a matter of realpolitik rather than ideology. The Chinese needed trade and aid to develop their economy. The Americans needed peace in Asia so they could withdraw from Vietnam. As usual, Nielsen understood the American motives better than the Chinese. "Nixon has come and gone," she wrote Louise. "Although the U.S. press tried to make as much fanfare as possible . . . there was no excitement here at all. We all knew that the desperate state of affairs in the U.S. was the reason for the visit."[25]

She was far more receptive to Canada's prime minister, Pierre Elliott Trudeau. Had Canada finally found someone who would stand up to the Americans? she wondered. Was there any hope that Canada could curb American control of her resources as Chile had done?[26] When she was invited to the Canadian ambassador's for a barbeque on Canada Day, she refused to go, but when Trudeau visited China in 1973, she attended a banquet he gave for his

Chinese hosts in the Great Hall of the People. "(He) spoke modestly about Canada as a third world nation and mentioned how it was dominated by the U.S."[27] Nothing could have pleased Nielsen more. And the banquet was well done, too. Even the favours were tasteful. She was pleased to take home sweets made of maple sugar and a pretty ceramic ashtray to give to her attendants.

Nielsen continued to work at home, polishing texts, but, sometimes, she attended trade shows and cultural events with Chinese interpreters to help them with vocabulary. By this time her life was back to normal. After a five-year hiatus, she was once more going on guided outings and taking her notebook along so that she could write detailed reports on such things as the use of acupuncture in a maternity hospital and the workings of a street committee. Once again she sent off reports of her visits to friends and attempted to renew contacts with party members who had dropped out. Zhou Enlai had asked all the foreign friends to help promote friendly relations with the West, and Dorise was determined to do her bit.

In the summer of 1972 she returned to Beidaihe for the first time since 1966. She swam a kilometre in the morning and another in the afternoon. She turned seventy that summer. Arthritis in one hip and in her spine made walking any distance painful, but she could still swim with ease.

The spring of 1973, on International Women's Day, all foreign friends were invited to the Great Hall of the People. A year earlier, the premier had greeted President Nixon there. This time the ailing Zhou came from his hospital bed to extend an apology to the foreign community for their treatment during the Cultural Revolution. He said that the spying charges against some of them had been trumped-up. Unknowingly and in good faith, they had become involved with the wrong people.[28] He went on to exonerate all the foreigners except Sidney Rittenberg, who was held in prison for five more years. The others were released and immediately took up their work again. China still needed them. They had heard the call long before, and there was no way they would give up the cause. The Chinese leadership may have been playing games of realpolitik, but its old foreign friends (those who had endured) were still bent on building utopia.

17

COMING HOME

I find this a mad society! The waste astounds me. ... The large food stores are like a Disney fantasia.[1]

NIELSEN HAD JUST WATCHED her youngest grandson polish off his third bowl of ice cream and return the empty carton to the freezer. He gave her a conspiratorial look that she didn't find funny at all. It was the summer of 1974, and, after almost twenty years away, she was once more in downtown Toronto, staying in Sally's apartment on Wellesley Street East. She hated Toronto more than ever and thought Sally should crack down on her kids, but she was trying very hard not to say anything.

Dorise knew that Sally had gone to a great deal of trouble to have her. She removed the carpets and covered her mother's mattress and pillows in heavy plastic. And she had made all the arrangements for renting a cottage, far from the city (just as Dorise instructed) so they wouldn't have to cater to a lot of visitors. Dorise wanted to see no one but family on this trip. "Whatever you do, don't tell the Nicholsons when I'll be coming," she wrote. "He will be organizing evening talks and afternoon pink teas and to hell with all that."[2] What she really wanted was time at a lake. It was Sally who had made all this possible, so for a few more weeks in the city, Dorise would keep her mouth shut and try her best to be gracious.[3]

Despite all the acrimony between the two of them over Sally's expulsion from China, Dorise and her younger daughter were seldom out of touch for long. At Christmas in 1965, a year after her departure, Sally had received a letter from a friend in China, telling her that her mother had been very ill and that perhaps a letter from Sally might cheer her up. And so correspondence had begun once more, cool at first, then quickly becoming warm and confessional. Some party members in Toronto, Dorise warned Sally, should not be trusted. They might use her to get back at Dorise (for her Maoist propagandizing). But there were several women whose kindness and wise advice she could trust.[4]

After being rescued by a group of fundamentalist missionaries in Africa, Sally had finished high school in Toronto and begun to study nursing. For a while, she'd taken up religion as zealously as her mother had communism. At first Dorise tried not to be critical. If Sally needed the moral support she was getting from the local congregation, so be it. These early letters show Dorise at her wisest and most compassionate. Once again she thought of coming back to Canada to play housekeeper so that Sally could devote herself to her studies and her work, but she realized they would soon get into the old hassles again and gave up the idea.[5]

But when Sally mailed her mother a subscription for a religious magazine, Dorise could not resist firing off a long letter to its head office in the States. She wrote that she "had long ago given up the idea that just one man died to save the world." She went on to give a long list of the names of philosophers and scientists who had been persecuted as heretics, and added the Soviet troops who had fought at Stalingrad to save the world from fascism and the Vietnamese peasants who were "holding down the most powerful aggressor nation in the world today, like David and Goliath."[6] Then she wrote Sally a letter to tell her how religion came into existence among primitive peoples and was used by the state "to keep peoples' minds in subjection and make them turn the other cheek."[7] Sally had been chastised, again. And thus the volatile relationship between the two of them continued. Dorise still loomed as a powerful force in Sally's life, even at a distance. And Dorise's sympathy for the hard life her daughter was living did not prevent her from asking for parcels to be sent, airmail, please, and as soon as possible.

In China, Nielsen is remembered differently by different people. For Betty Chandler, she was the lively friend who turned out amusing sketches, often making fun of herself. She was the woman who decorated the walls of her apartment with art and crafts, all sorts of odds and ends, but always a pleasure to see. When they walked together, Dorise used to stride along, her head held high, and Betty would rush to keep up. To several young people, she was Judy, the eccentric lady who walked the grounds of the You Yi Bin Guan, humming to herself. She refused to look at them because she believed their parents to be spies. Yet, when they first met her in 1958, she had been friendly.[8] Her interpreters, Chinese women who also worked as translators and editors for the Foreign Languages Press, recall her kindnesses to them, but she was isolated from most of the English-speaking community. She was suspicious, they say, and she liked to be alone, even during her annual holiday at the Beidaihe.[9]

Despite her continued activities, it is clear that after 1968 Nielsen's life in China was not a happy one. The roots of that unhappiness were surely multifaceted. Her serious allergy to household dust, as well as her poor command of Mandarin, were limiting factors, and so was her pursuit of political correctness. The trauma of living through the Cold War in Canada and then the Sino-Soviet split and Cultural Revolution had left her wary and impatient. After the Cultural Revolution she retreated from most of those around her, even from her old friend, Betty Chandler. But with her children, the opposite was true. As she aged, she made a greater effort to connect with them.

Her means from afar were letters and gifts and sometimes money. She would offer money for a coat, or for a down payment on a car, or order a sewing machine sent from Hong Kong. For Christmas and birthdays and sometimes in-between, she would send a length of silk for a dress or skirt, or a batik to hang on the wall. To Christine, who, she believed, was happily married, she sent a pair of carved mandarin ducks, symbols of a lifelong union, and other traditional Chinese gifts. Christine's husband, after all, was Chinese, even though he'd never seen China. It was her grandsons, and she had eight of them, who gave her the most trouble when it came to gifts, but she always sent them something.[10]

As Dorise grew older, her letters to friends became shorter and rather perfunctory. She would write to wish them a happy new year and send a little gift, and she would dutifully respond to their letters. But letters from her children and grandchildren were important events and elicited long replies. Even in the intervals when she was exasperated with Sally (and Sally with her), she still sent her a card and gift at Christmas and remembered her birthday. On the other side of the equation, her daughters dutifully shipped off books and other items Dorise could not obtain in China, such as large-sized bras and bathing suits, and inhalers for her asthma. As the years went by, they became increasingly concerned about what would become of Dorise in her old age. They were prepared to help her come home, though none of them really had the financial means. In 1970 Christine's husband, who had been the most prosperous of the lot, lost his job in Guyana and moved the family first to Hawaii, then Boston, and finally San Francisco, in pursuit of work. Sally and John were strapped just supporting their own families.

But in 1974, their concerns about Dorise were only beginning. Apart from her allergy, she was in good health and she had expressed no desire to move home. This was to be a holiday, a reunion with Sally and her children, and Christine and John if they could come. Plans started early in the year. Letters flew back and forth between Sally and Dorise about flights, the cottage rental, and the amount of foreign exchange Dorise would need to finance the excursion. Dorise shopped for gifts and sewed a new summer skirt to spiff up her wardrobe. She bought her ticket to fly Beijing to Karachi to Paris to Montreal and back again. She wrote Louise Harvey, asking if she could spend a few days with her at her cottage near Montreal before taking her return flight. And Dorise wasn't the only one writing letters. Sally was in touch with Christine in Hawaii, who was in touch with John in Vancouver.

But the whole visit turned out to be a minefield. For the first few weeks, Sally was working and Dorise was home with her teenaged grandsons, whose industry and manners did not meet her standards. (How could they? Her expectations were more Chinese than Canadian.) When Sally took her shopping, she found Dorise tired quickly. Even in China she had had to run to keep up with her mother, but now walking the length of the Yorkdale Mall was too much. Then, at the end of July, John and Christine surprised Dorise when they arrived in time for her seventy-second birthday. That day there was such a hubbub that Dorise embarrassed herself by not recognizing her own son.[11] She tried to make a joke of it, said he looked so slim and handsome that she'd thought he was her granddaughter's boyfriend, but she knew he'd been hurt and there was no time to make it up. Perhaps it didn't matter. He'd hardly ever written to her, and she didn't expect they'd ever be close again. She realized he'd become an alcoholic, just like his father.

Christine stayed on at the cottage on Manitoulin Island for a few weeks, but things there did not go as Dorise had planned, either. She found herself sitting on the verandah every morning, having breakfast by herself. Her girls were consistently late risers. They stayed up most of the night, drinking and talking (far too much drinking, as far as Dorise was concerned), and slept half the day. They hardly ever swam and never used the boat. All her money, she felt, had been wasted, and she had had a pretty dull time, too. There was little to do except read. Sally wanted to talk about China, to catch up on all that had happened since she had been there, to figure out, finally, why she had been ordered to leave, but Dorise refused to say anything. It was all far too complicated—who was in, who was out. What if she said something that got back? Who knew how it would be interpreted?

And so there was a tension in the air about things said and unsaid. When Dorise presented her manuscript of reminiscences, Sally read a few pages and threw it down. More preaching, and she didn't believe half of it. Christine could see Sally's point, but she read the manuscript through anyway, and was fascinated. She realized how little she knew about her mother's life and thoughts and she wanted to know more.

Christine was at a crossroads in her own life. She had chosen, very early, to devote herself to her family, but soon her youngest son would leave for college. Her marriage was faltering. She was forty-five years old and was worried about her drinking. Perhaps there was something she could learn from her mother, after all, some clue about being a woman in a man's world, about carrying on when things fall apart. She had rejected her mother's politics early and knew little about the philosophy that seemed to rule her life. She was willing to listen, but Sally was not, so when the evenings came, they buried themselves in their books until Dorise went to bed.

Then the sisters caught up on twenty years. They reminisced about life long ago back on the farm, and often, at some point, they talked of their father. They agreed that he was much more affectionate than their mother and they felt guilty that no one was with him when he died. Sally was the only one who'd kept in touch with him at all. When she'd received news of his death in 1956, she phoned Dorise. "Are you crying?" her mother had said. "Don't. He wasn't worth it." Those words were impossible to forget and hard to forgive. But before the two of them fell into bed, they would sometimes have a few good laughs about their mother, what an exasperating woman she was, how determined she was to get her way, how even on this holiday she was the one calling the shots. She didn't have to say a word—just a look would do.

To others on that trip, Dorise was sometimes indulgent, but more often distant. She did have dinner with Sandy Nicholson[12] and his wife, after all, and saw her good friends Heide Vockeroth and Louise Harvey. But when they finally met again after so many years of exchanging letters, there were no confidences, no long conversations. At Louise's Dorise had an excuse: the place was so dusty she was constantly drowsy from taking antihistamines, but with Heide, her lack of interest was clear. She ignored her, choosing instead to have an animated talk on world affairs with her son, who was surprised to find Dorise so well informed.[13]

Dorise's granddaughter, Jennifer Wong, then a twenty-one-year-old university student, was intrigued by her unconventional grandmother. She remembers finding her "a bit forbidding, like a rhinoceros, somewhat lumbering and awkward, although she sat with a length of gracefully crossed leg. Her voice was both ringing and mellifluous, and she wore a beautiful, unusually striped skirt which I found decidedly bohemian for a woman her age."[14] Dorise explained that she had made the skirt herself from material used to cover mattresses in China, and that it shocked her Chinese friends to see her "looking like a walking mattress." She gave Jennifer, the first granddaughter she had met, a pair of heavy coral and silver earrings that she had worn herself and invited her to lunch at the Town and Country Club in Toronto. But when Jennifer asked Dorise questions about her life and opinions, she deflected them with a joke or a pat phrase. The rhinoceros metaphor was apt in more ways than one. Even when Dorise sought a closer relationship, as she seems to have done with Jennifer, her layers of armour got in the way.

In mid-September Dorise scrambled to purchase souvenirs for her Chinese friends and helpers, and to stock up on medicine and food supplements for herself. She had read the advice of the nutritional guru, Adelle Davis, and had decided to give her regime a try. She was also interested in the new feminist movement, though she qualified her interest by saying that she wasn't a "women's libber" because she didn't hate men! A calendar collective in Saskatchewan had featured excerpts from several of her speeches in its 1974 calendar. She was pleased to give a copy of it to Jennifer. She also gathered the addresses of Canadian women's groups to pass to the Chinese Women's Federation, and looked for a copy of *The Feminine Mystique* by Betty Freidan. It was, she said, the only feminist book that really interested her. (It is likely that Nielsen knew of Friedan's left-wing connections.)[15]

By the time she got to Louise Harvey's home on Lake Orford, she was exhausted and needed a rest more than anything. Then, after a few days, she took off once again, dreading the nine-hour layover in Paris.

Was the trip worth all the trouble? She had her doubts at the time, but, after a few months back in Beijing, she began to change her mind. She received several long letters from Christine, the best she had had in years, and the next year the letters kept coming. Thus, the revisionist history of the holiday began. Apparently, her girls had become reacquainted during those long, boozy nights. And, according to Sally, the weeks of sleeping in had done her a lot of good. Perhaps the whole effort had been worthwhile, after all, and, if alcohol had aided the process, then maybe that was all right, too.[16]

For China, 1976 was a year of seismic shifts. In January Premier Zhou Enlai died after a very long battle with cancer. He had undergone seven surgeries and over a hundred blood transfusions.[17] Many people, both in China and abroad, believed that Zhou had been a moderating force in the Cultural Revolution and that he had deliberately prolonged his suffering to devote himself to the public good. It was Zhou who had guided the opening of China to Western trade and diplomacy and who had lobbied for the rehabilitation of old comrades ousted during the Cultural Revolution. If, as many people believed, it was Zhou who had saved the country from a group of ambitious radicals surrounding the ailing Mao, how would the country manage without him?

Beijing's foreign community had always revered the urbane Zhou more than Mao. Even Dorise, who had questioned Zhou's judgment about his blanket amnesty for "foreign spies," felt the blow. She believed he set a noble example right to the end of his life. He ordered that no memorial be erected to him. He wanted, instead, that his ashes be strewn over the mountains and rivers of his country. Still, millions of citizens, including Dorise, filed past his body as it lay in state and then lined the roads as it was taken to the crematorium at Babaoshan, the cemetery for revolutionary heroes and high party cadres.[18]

For Dorise, standing in line was a painful experience. By this time, she suffered from osteoporosis as well as arthritis in her right hip and spine. After standing too long or walking too far, she would have to spend weeks at home, lying down until the pain subsided. She had added calcium to her arsenal of pills. Otherwise, her life had taken on a rhythm that suited her well enough. Officially, she was retired on full salary, but, like other long-time foreign experts in China, she was still attached to her workplace and could be called upon to do tasks when there was a rush and no one else was available. She also continued to assist Chinese interpreters who worked at the You Yi.

If work were delivered, she did it right away. If there was no work, she had other projects on the go. She sewed and read and kept up on the news, though she wasn't sure which printed worse bilge, *Time* or *Newsweek*. In the winter, she read the seed catalogues Christine sent her and chose something new for her balcony. In the summer, she rose early to do housework or write letters or make a batch of jam while it was cool, then donned her bathing suit and headed for the pool. In the fall, she baked fruitcakes for her New Year's visitors. Most of the time she cooked herself simple meals to save going up and down three flights to the restaurant. On special occasions like Spring Festival, she went out for a good dinner with her colleagues from *Chinese Literature*, but most of the time she stayed home, and let people come to her.

At the You Yi, Nielsen had become a fixture. For the new foreigners who arrived on short-term contracts, she could provide clues on where to shop and what to buy. Sometimes they dropped in or offered to share a taxi into town. But most of them were young and apolitical and didn't interest her much. Of the old-timers, she sometimes saw Rewi Alley and George Ma Haide. Neither of them lived at the You Yi, but she had them to tea occasionally and they exchanged books. (Anna Louise Strong had died in 1970 in the midst of the revolution.) The people closest to Dorise and those she saw most often were the half-dozen Chinese she assisted and who assisted her. She was rarely invited to their homes, which were tiny, sparse places, compared to hers. She understood, perfectly. That was just the way things were. It was not a bad life, she told Louise, all she needed was a new skeleton.

Politically, she continued to believe the official version of events. In April of 1976, for the old festival of Qing Ming (remembering the ancestors), the people of Beijing heaped wreaths around the Monument to the Martyrs of the Revolution in Tiananmen Square to commemorate Zhou. It was an extraordinary move of protest against the radicals who surrounded Mao and it made the news around the world. When the wreaths were removed overnight, half a million people gathered to protest. They were dispersed with force and hundreds were arrested. A few days later, on her way to the hospital for a heat treatment on her back, Dorise's taxi was caught up in a parade of victors waving their red banners. It was a lovely sight to see. "There has been another little attempt by the reactionaries to stir up a spot of trouble," she wrote Christine, but the people had triumphed once more. One of the reactionaries, Vice Premier Deng Xiaoping, whom Zhou had designated as his successor, immediately lost all his posts, but, according to Dorise, he was only being chastised in the usual Chinese way. "In some other countries he'd either be shot or imprisoned, but not in China."[19]

Soon the instability of the political situation took second place to an earthquake of gigantic proportions. In July 1976, Dorise went to Beidaihe as usual. Early one morning, not long after her arrival, she awoke to a terrible roar, followed by shaking so severe that she became tangled in the sheets and was unable to get out of bed until it stopped. The building held, but its residents spent the next two nights sleeping on deck chairs on the road. They learned that the earthquake had killed over 200,000 people and injured millions in the nearby city of Tangshan. It had caused damage to buildings as far away as Beijing. After a few more nights in tents, the foreigners at Beidaihe were flown back to Beijing, where they again slept in tents because of the aftershocks. Lying on a wooden bench aggravated the pain in Dorise's hip and she hardly slept at all. Nevertheless, she was soon back at her typewriter, bashing out a seven-page report on her experience, determined to assure family and friends that China was handling the emergency with its usual efficiency.[20]

In September Beijing was still reeling from the aftershocks and earthquake alerts, with most of its residents prepared to abandon their buildings at a moment's notice, when the news came that Mao had died. Shakespeare himself could not have constructed a more ominous scenario. Officially, there was a month of mourning for the old chairman, with everyone mouthing the words of mourning, some feeling relief and others, genuine sorrow. Behind the scenes it appeared that the radicals surrounding Mao had taken charge. But after the month of mourning, four leading radicals, including Mao's wife, Jiang Qing, were swiftly arrested. By the end of October, the new party line was established: the Gang of Four had been responsible for the crimes of the Cultural Revolution. Deng Xiaoping was restored to all his party positions. Within two years he was China's supreme leader. The man who had been called a "capitalist roader" and vilified for putting results ahead of ideology ("Black cat, white cat, what does it matter as long as it catches mice?") finally put his pragmatic approach into practice, and did, indeed, start China on the capitalist road. But by the time all this played out, Dorise was no longer an observer.

After the arrest of Jiang Qing and the Gang, there was widespread spontaneous rejoicing. Nielsen was unable to attend the rally in Tiananmen Square because it meant standing for so long, but she watched it on the coloured TV in the clubroom. From her balcony, she heard the cracking of fireworks and saw the waving banners as the parades and celebrations went on for days. All those people who had been criticized and beaten and sent to the countryside from 1966 to 1969 were at last vindicated. Dorise said that she was astonished to learn "how many good revolutionaries [the gang] had destroyed in one way or another."[21]

Whether she ever repented of her suspicions of the score of foreigners arrested during the Cultural Revolution is debatable. She continued to keep herself apart, perhaps through shame. As for the party, she had never said it was perfect, and neither was Mao. He was an old man, and, in his weakness, had made some errors. This is what Nielsen wrote in her letters before she went on to other things. The struggle would continue, she was sure, long after her death. It was all about giving opportunities to those who had had none. She had seen socialism's first faltering steps, but they were enough to give her confidence that it would triumph in the end. Then her letters would go on, at greater length, to discuss family matters, sometimes from a Marxist perspective, but more often from the perspective of a distant grandmother trying to cope with her Christmas shopping.

By this time, Nielsen was writing long and frequent letters to her eldest daughter, Christine. During Nielsen's first ten years in China, the two had not corresponded at all. Christine's husband, Evan, was sure that letters coming from Communist China would jeopardize his career in Guyana. In 1967, when the letters began, Christine was spending the summers in Canada. In the winters, she sent her letters to Heide Vockeroth, who forwarded them to Dorise, and Dorise did the same. After Nielsen's trip to Canada in 1974, where she met Christine for the first time in twenty-three years, the correspondence grew greatly in volume. They began to exchange twenty to forty letters a year until

Nielsen's death. It was a detailed and intimate correspondence. Christine had more patience with her mother than Sally and was not inclined to call her to account for past grievances.

In a way, Nielsen's life had come full circle. Her oldest daughter, the child she had spent the most time with before entering the political storm, became the one close friend she seemed to need. The ups and downs of the Nielsen-Wong household in a suburb of Boston became as familiar to her as the ins and outs of the Chinese communist hierarchy, and, as far as Nielsen was concerned, they were just as important. Until this time, Dorise had never worried about Christine. Unlike Sally, she had a hard-working professional husband and enough money to send her children to good schools. But gradually, Dorise learned that Chris's life was not so happy, after all. Her attempts to help Sally had failed. Now she realized she was being given a second chance. She hoped to do a better job this time.

At first Dorise thought Chris's unhappiness stemmed from the emotional and economic adjustments to middle age. "Middle age is a difficult enough time for most married people," she wrote, "unless they're vegetables (as so many are!)."[22] She advised Christine to find interests of her own, but, at the same time, to try to work things out with her husband. "Blow your stack, girl," she wrote, "but meet the guy half way."[23] When Christine said she felt trapped like Nora in Ibsen's play *A Doll's House*, Dorise cautioned her : "Keep your pecker up woman and forget Norah. One thing old Ibsen didn't do was tell what happened to her after she did a flit.... That's not so easy to contemplate, is it?"[24]

It is strange how determined Nielsen was to somehow save Christine's marriage, when she, herself, had been so decisive about ending three long-term relationships and had several times advised her friend Louise to turf out a lover. But by 1976, Dorise had been living alone for fourteen years. She had never forgotten Bob Paul (during the Cultural Revolution she twice asked Sally to pass books on to him, without saying they came from her),[25] and she may have had second thoughts about the man she now referred to as "my poor old Con." For a long time, she urged Christine to make compromises. Behind this advice was not only her current loneliness, but also her earlier experience of struggling to make a living. She didn't want that sort of life for Christine. Evan Wong, for all his faults, was a well-educated man who had provided for his family. Surely the rest could be worked out.

When Chris started psychotherapy, Dorise was dubious. She had never had much use for head-shrinks, she said, wouldn't it be better to take up swimming?[26] But she came round when she realized her daughter was benefiting from the sessions. Sometimes, Chris confessed, she had hated her mother. That's only natural, wrote Dorise—sometimes I hated my mother, too. For her own children, she knew the problems had been much worse. "Your young hates and troubles were accentuated ... because, besides the fact that I'm not a very demonstrative person, I was also caught up in a terrible political tangle ... and had to consider how I was going to live and take care of the two younger ones."[27] She seems to have realized that Chris was working through her own guilt at giving up her first child for adoption.[28] Guilt was something she knew all about. It was guilt that had made her bring Sally to China, and look at how that had turned out. Somehow, she believed, Chris must rid herself of guilt and get on with her life. After all the work of raising five children, her best years were still ahead.

These long epistles were, in a sense, Nielsen's legacy to her daughter and she knew it. She was happy to answer any questions, and loved to pass on her favourite recipes for such things as lemon curd and carrot pickles (why waste those little carrots when you thin your garden?). Would she ever see her children again? The trip in 1974 had not been an easy one. Still, she was willing to come again, if only she didn't have to wait too long. But when she began to discuss the possibility of another trip home, the question, as usual, was where to go. Her children were so scattered. She wasn't sure if any of them wanted her for two months, or if she had the money or the energy to traipse from one to the other, or whether she could even get a visa to visit Christine in Boston. It was all very complicated.

Soon she decided that the best plan would be for Christine to come to China. All she would need was the airfare to Beijing. From there on, Dorise would pay all the expenses. She proposed a trip to see all the most important sights. In Xian the terracotta warriors had just been unearthed. Everyone was coming to China now. Even an old Spanish comrade who'd fought in the civil war was about to see his daughter after all these years. Surely it was just a matter of persuading Evan to let her come. Dorise vowed not to speak a word about politics. She sent Christine the invitation she had received to the Canadian Embassy Christmas party. Show it to Evan, she said, so he will know "I'm persona grata.... I'm not getting any younger, don't wait too long.[29]

By Christmas 1976, Nielsen was back in her own bed after another earthquake alert. For several weeks she had slept downstairs, sharing an apartment with a Japanese woman on the first floor. Finally she was able to hang her pictures again and to take her precious porcelain lamps from the floor of the closet. Between Christmas and New Year, she had three groups of Chinese comrades in for drinks and Christmas cake, and went out to dinner with Swedish and Greek friends. In January she received quite a long letter from Sally, thanking her for the Christmas presents. Altogether the year got off to a good start. She was still hoping that Christine would come to China in September, and, in the meantime, she was wracking her brain to think of a suitable wedding gift for Sally. She had finally met a good man and was to be married in June.

The winter of 1977 was exceptionally mild. Nielsen had not one cold. By mid-March she was able to sit on her balcony and enjoy the sun. It had been her best winter in a very long time. George Ma Haide was living at the You Yi because his house had been damaged by the quake. They talked about books and she borrowed records from his jazz collection, some of them tunes she remembered from her dancing days in the 1920s. One day she baked a raisin walnut spice cake and had Rewi and George to tea. She was almost seventy-five and not doing so badly.

When she realized that Christine would not come to China that year, Dorise began to think about going to Vancouver. What did Chris think of that idea? she wondered. Would it put John's wife, Vivienne, in too much of a tizzy? She might go in August, stay a month, and then go on to Montreal.

Meanwhile, the Foreign Languages Press was planning a very special trip for old foreign friends in April, and Dorise decided to go. The highlight of the trip would be a visit to Yunnan, China's southernmost province bordering Burma and Laos. They would be the first foreign visitors allowed in. Nielsen managed to get a few rolls of coloured film from someone who been to the States and trekked downtown to a camera shop to find out how to twiddle the three knobs of the camera she'd bought second-hand from a Russian years before. Her last exotic trip had been to Inner Mongolia in 1963.

It turned out to be an unforgettable holiday, full of marvellous sights, great food, and warm people. When she got back, she typed out twenty-four pages and sent them to her family in three instalments. Later, she typed a synopsis for her friends.[30] The group had flown from Beijing to Kunming by jet. From there they boarded a Russian twin-engine plane from pre-liberation days for the trip further south. Dorise eyed the plane with reservations and was alarmed when a young man she'd thought was the baggage handler turned out to be the pilot. However, they lifted up with the greatest of ease and "alighted as softly as a butterfly on a flower" at the smallest airport she'd ever seen. The tarmac was marked out as a basketball court and it was only just big enough! The next day they took five hours to go 250 kilometres by car to Shishuangbanna, the home of the Tai people, one of China's many national minorities. The road wound up and down forested hillsides, around hairpin turns, with never as much as fifty metres of straight, level road. Dorise craned her neck to look up at the giant tapalacas and rocks "covered with masses of white or pink blossoms hanging over them like waterfalls." She wished Christine were there to see it all. When they arrived, finally, a beautiful wide valley stretched before them, green and yellow with ripening crops. In the town the streets were lined with palm trees and there were flowering hibiscus bushes everywhere.

The group stayed in Shishuangbanna almost a week, venturing out to visit farms and a horticultural institute, and to view the dragon boat races that were part of the Tai new year's celebrations. In one village, the mayor asked that the foreigners parade up and down the town's main street so that everyone would have a chance to see them. People stood six deep along the way. There were Dorise, Denise Lebreton, a Japanese couple, and a woman from Australia, all on display, like animals in a zoo. Too bad, they joked, that the first foreigners viewed in these parts were no longer young and beautiful. Dorise thought Chris, with her blonde hair, would have caused a sensation. Another day in another village, they watched people dunk each other with basins of water to celebrate the new year. Before long, Dorise and several others joined in and no one showed them any mercy. It was great fun, she said, and good to cool off. Her hip bothered her on the trip as she lurched from side to side in the car, climbed the steps to a farmhouse (all were on stilts, with the chickens and pigs occupying the first floor), and tried to squat for the toilet, but it was all worth the trouble. In the evenings, back at their compound in Shishuangbanna, they ate well, enjoying fresh vegetables and sweet bananas picked ripe from the trees. By the time they'd finished eating, the tropical night had fallen, and they'd take their chairs outside and talk until late under the velvet sky. There were no mosquitoes to bother them, "only an orchestra of the local cicadas scraping away in the trees."

From Yunnan the group went to Chengdu and then to Chongqing, where they boarded a boat and travelled through the Yangtze Gorges to Wuhan. It was Nielsen's third trip through the Gorges. By this time she was anxious to be home. They'd had no foreign news the whole trip, and, of course, no letters. They flew from Wuhan and were back in Beijing for May Day.

The trip had been tiring, but not exhausting enough to discourage Nielsen from going ahead with plans for a Canadian holiday in August and September. She began to shop for gifts, and packed her suitcase well in advance in case her building was once more evacuated because of an earthquake alert. She had shipped off ping-pong bats and several other things ahead of time, but still her suitcase was so crammed she had hardly any room for clothes. She looked forward to shopping for some new ones as soon as she arrived, some light wash-and-wear stuff not yet manufactured in China.

Then the waiting began. For some reason, there was a snarl in getting both her Canadian and American visas and she didn't leave in August after all. The time stretched out. Through August she kept hoping to reach Vancouver in time for John's October birthday. She had so often missed being with him on his birthday. She thought it would "be nice to make a fuss about it for once in a lifetime."[31] September came and still no visa. The pool at the You Yi had closed. Her office, having made arrangements for her absence, sent her no work. It was increasingly difficult to fill the days. For the first time in her life, she knew what it meant to be a pawn in a game. Always, before, there had been something to keep her busy, but now there was nothing. She couldn't read all the time. Then, just as she was about to give up on the whole trip and try again the following year, the Canadian visa came at last.

When Dorise left China at the end of September 1977, she was prepared to make the best of what seemed, already, to be a botched vacation. Vancouver in the autumn is notable for its rain and fog, and it was her son's busiest time of year at work. Almost everything Nielsen knew about John and his family had come either from Christine, or from letters written by his wife, Vivienne, or thank-you notes from the two grandchildren she had never met. Her meeting with John in Toronto three years before had been brief and unsatisfactory, and he seldom wrote. What she wanted most on this visit was to re-establish the connection and help out his family if she could, and, at least, not be too much of a nuisance. She hoped to buy the groceries and help with the cooking, and, if she didn't go east, she would give them a cheque to help with the son's orthodontic work. She had discussed all this with Christine in her letters.

Christine, in a way, had been John's second mother. In 1953 he had come to her home in Guyana, a tall, gangly, eighteen-year-old. She and her husband had helped him get settled in a job, had been there at his wedding. Like Christine's, John's spouse was of Chinese descent. He and his family had been living in Vancouver since 1964. Both he and Vivienne had steady jobs and they had been able to buy a house on Phillip Street in North Vancouver. Her boy, who had dropped out of school early, wasn't doing so badly, thought Dorise, though she was concerned about his drinking.

It is interesting that on this trip Nielsen is not remembered as an imposing presence. There had been a change, either a deliberate effort to blend in on her part, or a diminution of her energy. Her grandson, Doug, who was twenty, took her around in his hot rod. They went to Stanley Park, the planetarium, and the zoo. He remembers that she was tired and walked with some difficulty, but she was determined to make up for lost time with the family. "She wanted to know us," he says. At first, his father had little to do with her, though Doug didn't believe there was any antagonism. Doug himself had several things in common with Dorise. Both suffered severe allergies and both loved to draw. He gave her a sketch he'd done of a macaw. When Dorise returned to Beijing, she consulted a doctor who suggested bee jelly for Doug's allergies, so she boxed up some and shipped it off to him.[32]

Vivienne, who'd been apprehensive about Dorise's visit, found her not at all intimidating. "She made me feel good. She knew exactly what was happening with John—he didn't try to hide it from her."[33] Most days John went to the pub after work and came home late for dinner. Dorise watched his wife put his meal aside. She admired Vivienne's patience, but her heart ached. It seemed to her that John had withdrawn from his family, as well as from her. There was no breakthrough in the impasse between mother and son until near the end of her visit. One night he came in quite drunk and Dorise called him to her room. They talked for a long time and he ended up weeping and saying how sorry he was for giving her so much trouble in Toronto. For a few moments, the tough woman, who feared tears more than anything, and the stoical man, who'd faced life without his parents at such an early age, let their barriers down. But what was the point? Dorise wondered later. If only John could remember his own adolescent problems when he dealt with his son. The boy needed him, she thought, but perhaps it was already too late.[34]

The highlight of the visit was Christine's arrival. She managed to get a cheap flight to Seattle and came for three weeks. She took her mother out every day and helped her buy clothes as well as books. Dorise had come with a long list of books for friends and organizations in China. She purchased most of them at the UBC bookstore. For herself, she bought a twelve-inch coloured television. Christine helped with the packing up and shipping off of all the boxes, and the Christmas shopping for John's family. The day before she left Vancouver, Dorise presented John and Vivienne with a large box and instructions not to open it until Christmas. It was a microwave oven, something to help Vivienne warm up all those dinners.

Every Friday night for the two months Dorise was in Vancouver, she shared the family's weekly outing to a Chinese restaurant. It always amazed her that two of her children had Chinese spouses. She had ended up with seven Eurasian grandchildren, but she knew more about China than they did! On those nights everyone was together, Dorise would sometimes talk about life in China, but she said little about politics. When Christine arrived, this shorter but livelier version of her mother became the centre of attention. Dorise was content to sit back and watch. She was pleased that at least two of her children got along well, and that all of them were adept with chopsticks. "After you graduate," John told his daughter, Judy, who was in high school, "I'll send you to China to visit Gran."[35]

Nielsen returned to Beijing thoroughly worn out but in good spirits. She was met by three staff from *Chinese Literature*, and her old friend Gao Liduan, who worked for the Foreign Experts' Bureau at the You Yi and who had once been her student. Before long she had distributed gifts and written detailed letters to Chris and John to tell them about the journey home. In Tokyo she had had to stand for hours in line before finally catching a bus to her hotel. By then she was in such pain from her hip that she couldn't sleep at all. "Now old Dante had some ideas about the Inferno," she wrote, "but believe me, he'd never been to the Tokyo airport."[36]

Soon she made trips downtown for Doug's bee jelly and a very special silk robe for Christine. "You will look sensational in it," she wrote, "you will dazzle all eyes."[37] In Vancouver she had been overwhelmed by Christine's many kindnesses to her. She had also realized that Christine, like John, was an alcoholic. Nielsen hoped the robe might help rekindle some of the romance in her marriage, though she was beginning to wonder why Chris was hanging on to a man who was so critical of her weight problem. Surely "love is not love that alters when it alteration finds?"[38]

It wasn't until after Christmas that Nielsen fell into the doldrums. She had felt the same after her 1974 trip, but this time it was much worse. She had little work and not much energy to do the little that came. And, although she hated to admit it, she was very lonely. Several couples she'd known for years were about to leave. George Ma was seriously ill. She began to think of how her life might have gone if she and "poor old Con" had gone to BC instead of coming to China. With Christine about to move to California, two of her children would have been close to her. Perhaps she could have scraped by on the old-age pension. But it was too late now. She wasn't even a Canadian citizen. In any case, she did not want to be a burden to her children. And the blues would pass—they always did.

In April, still very tired and down in the dumps, Nielsen noticed that her ankles were swelling. A liver function test showed that she had hepatitis. Nothing very serious, the doctor said. She would not have to be sent to an isolation hospital. All she had to do was rest and eat well.

18
THE LAST ACT

I've thought for a long while now of asking you to do me one last kindness—that is to buy, beg, borrow or steal a full bottle of Nembutal. I might not use it yet, but to know I had it on hand would be a great comfort.[1]

NIELSEN WATCHED FROM HER WINDOW as the busloads of tourists arrived and departed from the You Yi. They came in the heat of summer, rising early to climb the Great Wall, sweating their way through the days. Even in November, when the winds blew the leaves from the poplars and the gingkos, the tourists kept coming. They were surprised by the cold and rushed out to buy sweaters. The lawns and ivy beds had been dug up so that new electrical cables could be installed for all the appliances the tourists toted with them. In the dining room, Coca-Cola was selling for one dollar a bottle (only American funds accepted!).

Dorise was not altogether happy with the new developments. She knew that China needed to catch up on education and technology—everything modern had been sabotaged by the Gang of Four during the Cultural Revolution. What she didn't like was the emphasis on profit. It was rumoured that soon China would be producing her own Coca-Cola and other useless things. And very few of the new foreign experts living at the You Yi had come to bolster the cause of socialism. They were out for adventure or for money. Still, despite the influx of newcomers, there was a shortage of English teachers and interpreters. Dorise had work, almost more work than she could handle.

In the autumn of 1978, she rose in the dark three days a week to have a fast breakfast before the long ride to town. She had been engaged to train teachers for the Academy of Sciences (medical section). So began her busiest year since the Great Leap. Hundreds of doctors were being sent overseas for further training and they needed some preparation in English. It was up to Nielsen to devise a curriculum, train three groups of teachers, and periodically lecture the doctors themselves on cultural topics. The preparation was massive. She wrote to Christine for medical texts and dictionaries. She rummaged in her stacks of magazines for information on topics ranging from space exploration to cults. She finally located a bible (hidden away in the FLP library) for her lectures on the history of religion. She hired an aiyi three hours a day to do ironing and cleaning and other housework. Still, she wasn't sure how long she could keep up the pace.

Somehow, she did keep going that year. The previous spring, she had been laid low by a bout of hepatitis, but after a few months of rest, her swollen ankles were back to normal and she was able to carry on. Hepatitis was a common ailment in China and not one that alarmed her.[2] She was more bothered by her arthritis and the cataracts that were clouding her eyes, one particularly badly. She could not imagine life without reading and had not a clue what to do about it. When Louise Harvey visited China in May 1979, she noticed the cataracts and began to cry. Forget the weeping, wrote Nielsen later, but if you find anything out, let me know.[3]

Harvey's tour stopped in Beijing for only a few days. She came twice to Nielsen's apartment, accompanied by several other women from Montreal. Nice women, Dorise thought, except for one who was determined to interview her and make a tape recording for broadcast in Canada. She was in the midst of the teaching term then, and far too tired to be bothered. In any case, if someone wrote about her, she hoped it would be her granddaughter, Jennifer.

Beijing was hot and rainy the summer of 1979, even worse than usual. The cockroaches flourished, and drawers and doors swelled and stuck in their frames. The washing hung in the bathroom day after day. Nielsen stayed in the city that summer, still teaching two classes, and preparing for the long-awaited visit of Christine. The year before, when Chris had stopped drinking, her husband had promised her a trip to China. She would come in September, one of the best months, and stay for six weeks. Dorise wanted everything to be perfect. She planned an itinerary for travel south, and ordered a Polaroid camera and ten rolls of film from Hong Kong. People loved having their pictures taken, and few Chinese had cameras of any sort. Photos were really the best gift. But in

June, China Travel informed her that they would be unable to supply an interpreter for only two people. Her plans to take Christine outside Beijing crumbled. At the end of August, her liver function tests were poor, and she started another round of vitamin B12 injections.

When Christine arrived, however, Dorise was determined to show her as much of China as she could. She arranged for her students to take turns accompanying them on local outings to the Summer Palace for lunch, to the Palace Museum in the old Forbidden City, to the zoo and the Temple of Heaven, and, of course, the Great Wall. In the end, she also managed to get permission for a trip to Xian and Chengdu and then a cruise through the Yangtze Gorges. Their interpreter would be Xiao Yu (Little Yu), the woman who had been Nielsen's liaison with the Foreign Languages Press for many years and who had accompanied her to one medical appointment after another.

The trip was difficult for Nielsen. Some days she did not have the energy for an excursion and stayed back at the hotel, resting. Occasionally her temper was short. "Who are you?" asked a Canadian tourist. "None of your bloody business," she answered.[4] Christine was glad to have Xiao Yu along for company, as well as translation. Like her mother, she was a note taker. She had studied Chinese art and history and had a good base for appreciating what she saw.

During her visit, Christine met most of her mother's friends. It was a rather small circle, she discovered. In Wuhan, she met an old professor of botany. For years, Dorise had been sending him articles from her magazines and occasionally seeds. In Beijing, apart from an Australian woman called "Steve" (Mrs. Stevenson), Dorise had few friends among the foreigners. She explained to Christine that she wanted nothing to do with the other "ancient creatures" who were remnants of the old community of foreign experts. She believed they were all reactionaries and had disassociated herself from them years before. "The truth is," Dorise confided, "I'm the sore thumb that sticks out among the rest of them."[5] She seemed to be closest to several interpreters working at the You Yi, including Gao Liduan, who had once been her student and had worked there ever since. It was Gao and Xiao Yu and several others whom Dorise invited to a farewell dinner for Christine on the eve of her departure. Most of the dishes were provided by the You Yi kitchen. It was a sumptuous feast—the best of the best food in the world. Dorise believed the trip had not gone badly after all. It had been a tremendous effort, and she had not said all she had to say (either she was exhausted, or Christine was busy taking her notes or out with Xiao Yu). But so what? There would always be letters.

At the airport she said one of her stoical goodbyes. "I'm glad you didn't spout tears," she wrote Christine. She hated people who "wore their hearts on their sleeves."[6] Shortly after Christine's departure, Nielsen wrote her last letter to Louise Harvey. She admitted she felt as if she'd been "hit by a tornado." As well as being exhausted, she was in pain from her arthritis. She had walked far too much on the trip and now she could hardly make it up and down the stairs.[7]

A month later Nielsen was put on prednisone for her arthritis. It was a miracle drug. For the first time in years, she was free of pain. She asked Christine to send catalogues and weekend editions of newspapers. If she were to teach again, after Christmas, she wanted to have some lessons ready. And, at last, she had the energy to invite her former students, the teachers from the Academy of Sciences, to pay her a visit. It had to be a Sunday, the only day they had free, and she would need to feed them well because they all came from a distance. Eight of them accepted her invitation, arriving at ten in the morning and not leaving until eight in the evening. Before lunch they listened attentively to tapes of Joan Baez, but they were disappointed and declared that her enunciation was very poor. The rest of the day went better. For lunch Nielsen had cooked spareribs and ordered apple pie from the kitchen at the You Yi. She had stocked her fridge with beer and soft drinks. After eating and drinking well, they all took the usual Chinese nap, with the men lying on the floor, using their padded jackets as pillows. The hit of the day was a game of Monopoly. Dorise read the rules and acted as banker. The game went on and on. Finally she excused herself and made a supper of bread and cold cuts and salad. After the meal, the students, all men and women around thirty, helped clean up before they donned their coats and scarves to catch buses home. The day had been a great success and Dorise was pleased.[8]

That Sunday late in November 1979 was Nielsen's last party. By New Year's, she was not up to receiving her usual guests. It was a bleak holiday. The miraculous effects of the prednisone had diminished. She simply had no energy. Her feet had begun to swell and the liver function tests were poor. But that had happened before and she had recovered. It was just a matter of time, she thought.

She managed to keep typing her letters to the family, reading, and watching TV. China had begun to receive world news by satellite. She was pleased to know that she was seeing some of the same news as Christine. She sympathized with American President Jimmy Carter. In Iran a group of students had taken over the US embassy and were holding a number of Americans hostage. Poor Carter—what a bind he was in—all because of previous US policy and the fiascos of the CIA. Since she had no news of her own (she was going nowhere and doing almost nothing), she had little else to say.

At the end of February, her friend and interpreter Gao Liduan went to the States with a delegation to select teachers for posts in China. He was sent off, like the others, with a new suit and a spending allowance of fifteen dollars. While in San Francisco, he would visit Christine and Evan. You must not give him too much, Dorise warned Christine, or he will be embarrassed. She suggested a typewriter ribbon. Dorise wanted to send a little gift for Christine with him. What an effort it was to go downtown by taxi to the gift shop at the Peking Hotel—and then she couldn't find what she wanted. Going up the stairs to her apartment, she had to stop every two steps to get her breath. She had been doing nothing but rest for over four months and was growing worse, not better.

It was a long, cold winter that year. By mid-March there were still no catkins on the poplar trees. Dorise was typing her letters home a paragraph at a time, sometimes only a paragraph or two each day. She was awaiting Gao's return, hoping she would have the energy to take her friends out to dinner then. They would sit around the table, six or seven of them, and hear all about his impressions of America. Perhaps the dinner did happen, but Nielsen never recorded the event. In April she awoke one morning with a badly swollen abdomen and sharp pain in her right side with every breath. She was hospitalized twice that month. A flare-up in the hepatitis was the diagnosis. Apparently the prednisone had aggravated her liver problems.

By this time Dorise had begun to think about suicide. A few months before, she had clipped an article about the Exit Society from the *Guardian*. At the end of May she wrote to Christine, requesting "one last kindness." There was no way she could get enough sleeping pills in China. They were doled out by the doctor at the You Yi clinic six at a time. What she needed was a whole bottle of Nembutal. Seventy capsules would do the trick. "I might not use it yet, but to know

I had it on hand would be a great comfort." Sometimes the liver regenerates, but she was sure hers was growing worse, not better. There was nothing more she could do for her children and nothing they could do for her. She hoped that Christine would look at the whole matter sensibly, not emotionally. "For six months now I have existed not lived." Once Christine obtained them, the pills were to be labelled vitamins and sent airmail.[9]

At this point Christine made a concerted effort to bring her mother back to Canada. Sally and John agreed, Dorise must come home. Vancouver would be the best place. Christine would come up from California to help her get settled. When Dorise heard the plans, she hit the roof. "You must be bonkers!" she wrote. Why should Christine leave her husband to care for "an irritable, bad-tempered old biddy like me, in pain and having so little interest in continuing to live?" In any case, Dorise said, she did not want to return, not at this point. "Even the thought of such a journey fills me with the heebie-jeebies." She promised not to do anything impulsively. She planned to dispose of her possessions little by little so that she would not alarm her Chinese helpers.[10]

This letter, written at the end of June, was a great effort, but she wanted to make everything clear. Chris had already discovered that obtaining a quantity of barbiturates was not easy. She was trying to get in touch with an uncle of Evan's, an old doctor who was ill himself. "All I can hope is that you can encourage him to do his Scout's good deed before he flips off himself!" wrote Dorise.[11] At this point she had been taken off her arthritis medication, as well as the antibiotics she had been receiving on account of a low-grade fever (all these drugs, it was decided, had aggravated the hepatitis). The arthritis pain was back in full force and so was the fever.

Early in July she was admitted to hospital with a severe lung infection. Then "all the beastly business" she had hoped to avoid began: drips, blood transfusions, antibiotic injections. She continued to scrawl notes to Christine. All she wanted was some word from the old uncle. It was her own fault, she believed, for not starting the process sooner. Now she was stuck in an impossible situation, where there was no room for action even if she had her vial of pills.

In Beijing the air was very hot and humid but no rain fell. In the hospital Dorise could sleep only when drugged; otherwise, the heat, the pain, and the mosquitoes kept her awake. Don't waste your money coming here, she wrote

Christine, let us just hope the old uncle comes through. In August she was given a liver scan. No cancer, the doctors told her, but the hepatitis had become chronic, her liver was showing signs of cirrhosis, and she was severely anaemic. Dorise immediately wrote Christine to give her the diagnosis. "The main result of the doctor's verdict takes the pressure off the old uncle," she wrote. "If he can manage twenty (pills) for the next three months I shall be more than happy." She was about to go home with twenty-four-hour care. She would, at last, be able to manage her life, and her death, as she wished.[12]

In fact, Dorise did have liver cancer, but the doctor decided she should not be told the truth. All this was explained in a letter Xiao Yu wrote to Christine. The immediate crisis, the lung infection, had been treated. There was no need for Christine to come to China at that time. If she did, her mother might suspect the truth. Xiao Yu promised to keep Christine informed of Dorise's condition.[13]

If Christine had not known Gao and Xiao Yu and trusted their care of her mother, she might have gone to China that fall. But it would not have been easy to find the money, and she had her hands full caring for her mother-in-law, who lived with her and suffered from Parkinson's disease. So she decided to bow to Xiao Yu's advice and await developments. However, she was determined to get the pills as soon as possible, no sending them bit by bit. She quickly wrote another letter to the old uncle, explaining the new situation and asking for help.

Late in August 1980, Nielsen was carried up the stairs to her apartment in a wheelchair. She knew that she was being sent home from the hospital not because she was getting better, but because she was getting worse. There was nothing more the doctors could do to help her. Everyone urged her to eat. Sometimes she felt hungry for something, but when it came, she was too nauseated to eat it. All she could manage was a glass of milk or a bit of custard or jelly. In the mornings she tried to sit for a while in a chair placed near the balcony door. The rest of time she spent in bed. With great effort and the assistance of her aiyi, she hobbled to the bathroom.

All through July and August, letters had arrived, but, apart from a few scrawls, she had not written a real letter herself since the end of June. She had still been part of the world then, and had something to say. She had cheered the federal victory in the Quebec referendum. She hoped that Trudeau would make good his promise to "bring that ridiculously old-fashioned constitution up-to-date," and that, in the States, "that grinning fool Reagan" would not win the fall election.[14] Now she wrote many letters in her mind, but was too weak to put them to paper. She had become so thin her arms were like sticks, and just about as useless.

Still, a week after her homecoming, possibly bolstered by her last blood transfusion, she wrote Christine a coherent three-page letter. It took her two days. She was thinking of this time the previous year, when she had been so happily awaiting Christine's arrival. Now Beijing was experiencing the longest drought in many years. "It is the year of the monkey," wrote Dorise, "and he is showing his malicious side."[15] There were no fresh vegetables in the markets and workers were being given extra breaks on account of the heat. And here she was unable to do anything for herself, relying on the aiyi, who, though very willing, couldn't understand a word of English.

However, the main reason for the letter was not to voice her complaints, or to ask, once again, for news of the old uncle. She had some advice for her daughter, who, she believed, was on the verge of a nervous breakdown. What Christine needed, said Dorise, was a month or so in Mexico with her husband. Put the old mother-in-law in a nursing home. Tell the kids (all in their twenties at this point) that you simply are not available. Forget all the Christmas falderal and just go. They might get a shock but they will survive. You've put off your own needs too long. Children, she believed, should not be dependent forever. It was time for Christine's children to stand on their own two feet.[16] The advice was typical of Nielsen: tough and practical, but definitely not for the faint-hearted. Somehow, she believed, a break from all her responsibilities would revive both Christine and her marriage. It was worth a try.

But Christine was not like her mother. Her survival instincts were not so strong and she was not about to abandon anyone. She had just received a letter from the old uncle and with it a vial of Valium. "You mother will die a very long way from home," he had written, "and you must brace yourself for the end of her life." Deaths from liver cancer, he said, were not usually painful unless the cancer invaded the spine. He was sending a bottle of tranquillizers in case they were not available in China. "Be sure to tell her not to take all of them at the same time, unless she wants to hasten the end."[17]

"There are so many things to thank you for I don't know where to begin," wrote Dorise later that month. Her handwriting was so shaky it is barely legible. "Now about the vitamin C pills that came a few days ago. You must thank the old man but they are not what I asked for and I would have no faith in them."[18] It was Nembutal she had read about. She was not sure tranquillizers would do a proper job.

At the end of September, too weak to wash herself or get to the bathroom, Dorise returned to Beijing Capital Hospital. She wrote no more letters. On several occasions, she asked Gao Liduan and Xiao Yu to write brief messages on her behalf. After a month, she returned home again with arrangements made for a night nurse to relieve the aiyi. Soon after her return, she dictated a short letter to Christine, "I have counted the days in September and October waiting for the little parcel that the old uncle took to England by mistake.... It would have been used long before this."[19]

A death from cancer is seldom easy, but Nielsen's death was lonely and prolonged beyond imagining. Why wasn't she told the truth? Why did she not place her trust in the old uncle's advice? Why did she not tell her daughter, I want you here, please come? A combination of custom, good intentions, and her own stubbornness all conspired against her. She knew that Christine was beset with her own problems. It was not practical for her to come to China. Suicide, Dorise believed, was a sensible solution, but she was not prepared to take the risk of botching it. And underlying all this was the misrepresentation of her true condition. If her resolve wavered, if she did her best to eat and down glass after glass of milk, she did so on the advice of a doctor who knew that no matter what she ate or drank, her liver would never regenerate.

It wasn't until mid-November, when she began to experience acute pain, that Nielsen knew for sure she was dying. "The quicker the better," she told Xiao Yu. Then she ordered her personal correspondence destroyed and asked one of her helpers to deposit her bonds for safe-keeping with the Foreign Experts' Bureau.[20] Her small estate she left to the people of China, who had given her the best care they could for many years.

On December 7, Christine received a cable from China asking her to come immediately. The request came not from Dorise, but from the Foreign Experts' Bureau. Dorise's Chinese colleagues were extremely distressed to watch her die without a member of her family present. Their pragmatism obviously did not match Nielsen's own. The cable said that Christine should take the first plane available and that her fare would be reimbursed when she reached China. She managed to leave the following day. After enduring an overnight stay in Toyko, she reached Beijing on December 9 in the evening, shortly after her mother's death.

EPILOGUE

FROM THE TIME OF HER ARRIVAL in Beijing, Christine was immersed in a series of rituals she only half-understood. Three carloads of people met her at the airport, but they avoided answering her questions about her mother's condition. You must have a good sleep, they said. She was almost sure that Dorise had died, but, in view of her hosts' reluctance to talk, she decided not to press for an answer that night. In the morning Xiao Yu came to tell her that Dorise had, indeed, died the previous day. Xiao Yu had left her vigil by the body to fetch Christine from the airport.

Soon Christine realized she was dealing with the grief of others as well as her own. When she visited the You Yi kitchen to order a dinner to follow the funeral, the old cook met her, his face streaming with tears. He had been at the You Yi many years. He had baked the apple pie for Dorise's last party for her students and cooked a farewell dinner for Christine the previous year. He would do his best, he said, to make this final dinner very special.

As was customary in China, Dorise's workplace took responsibility for conducting the funeral and paying the costs. The funeral committee included staff from the FLP and the Foreign Experts' Bureau, as well as Nielsen's friend, George Ma Haide. They all came to see Christine the day after her arrival. She had just settled into her mother's apartment, which had been sealed when Nielsen was taken to the hospital and then unsealed and disinfected in Christine's presence. Each member of the committee wept openly as they paid their condolences. Then they quickly settled down to the business of arranging the funeral.

Because of Nielsen's long service to China, the memorial service would take place at Babaoshan, the cemetery for revolutionary heroes. With Christine's approval, it would follow the standard format, beginning with a moment of silence, followed by funeral music and a eulogy. The same format, the same music, was used for everyone from Mao to the lowliest of cadres. In Dorise's case, her boss, the director of *Chinese Literature*, would read the eulogy. Christine, as a representative of the family, was also asked to speak and she agreed. The only delicate matter was the scattering of the ashes. Like Zhou Enlai, Dorise had asked that her ashes be scattered on Chinese soil. She had suggested they be sprinkled beneath the maple trees in the Western Hills, where she liked to walk. But it was wintertime. The ground was hard and the ashes would soon blow away. Would Christine, perhaps, agree to another plan? they asked. Judy had loved to swim in the sea. If her ashes were scattered into a canal, they would return, eventually, to the sea.[1]

Christine consented to everything, but her own speech worried her. She feared she would break down delivering it. And she had to compose it right away for translation the following morning. What would her brother and sister want? she wondered. What could possibly be said about such a complex character as their mother? She was no saint. Self-righteous, domineering, she had wanted her own way, right until the end. When Xiao Yu told her that Christine was on her way, Dorise had not looked pleased.[2] Hadn't she told Christine to be sensible and not to waste her money? And yet Christine admired her mother's stubborn striving to act on her beliefs. She had never given up, never.

At first Christine composed a long, meandering speech full of fancy phrases. In the morning, she scrapped it. Too pretentious, she realized. Dorise would have hated it. She would leave the eulogizing to Luo Jun, the director of *Chinese Literature*. In a few minutes, sitting at her mother's typewriter, she decided what really needed to be said.

A few days later, Nielsen's friends and former colleagues (some of them, like Israel Epstein and Isabel Crook, the very people she had avoided for years) queued under a canopy in front of the Babaoshan memorial hall, waiting to sign the funeral book. Then they stood shoulder to shoulder while the short procession made its way to the front of the hall. Christine carried her mother's ashes; Xiao Yu, a photo; and the translator, a wreath of chrysanthemums. The photo of Dorise had been taken the previous year during Christine's visit. It showed a woman with dark hair wearing thick, dark-rimmed glasses. You would be hard-pressed to guess her age. The thin face and magnifying glasses spoke of illness and failing sight, but the hair showed no strands of white.

"Comrade Judy had a deep love of China and her people," began Luo Jun. "Her feelings for the socialist reconstruction of the Chinese people were profound. She taught and worked painstakingly, assiduously, conscientiously and meticulously.... Even when she was ill she carried on.... She lived a very simple life and was never extravagant." It was a straightforward homily, and it was true, though there was much left out.

Christine came next. She took a deep breath and read in as firm a voice as she could muster, "Much has been said of my mother's contribution to China. I would like to add this to the record. This country and the Chinese people gave a great deal to my mother, too." China gave her a home, she said, it gave her work, and friends and "the excitement and challenge of being part of a great country realizing the potential of its people."[3]

What Christine said was true, as well, but not the whole truth. At the moment of Nielsen's memorial service, the Gang of Four was on trial. "I was Mao's dog," testified Jiang Qing. "If he told me to bite, I bit." Dorise had been a dedicated supporter of a cause that had gone seriously awry. She had tried to understand the right path, but her understanding had been frustrated by lack of information and possibly by her own preconceptions. In her mother's apartment, Christine had found seventeen notebooks, the last of them dating from the previous year. They were full of notes Nielsen had taken on books she read and lectures she attended. Sometimes she had copied verbatim a snippet that she found particularly enlightening. Dorise had been a student right to the end of her life. If she had failed to find the truth, it wasn't for lack of effort. And she had striven, always, to act on what she knew—imperfect as her knowledge was—for she believed that knowing the truth was nothing without action.

Her mother, Christine decided, had been a woman in process. She had willingly set out on unexplored paths. She had arrived several times at destinations she never anticipated, but she had managed to make a life and to make a contribution to the lives of a very diverse group of people. For several months after Dorise's death, the letters continued to arrive. From Saskatchewan: "Your mother was with my husband in the House.... I shall miss dear Judy's letters—she was a trump." From BC: "She wrote me five or six letters a year ... from which I learned a great deal of political history." From Australia: "How I admired her and how grateful I will always be to her for her kindness in my perplexities." From a former student: "She was always enthusiastic and kind in doing things ... attending her course was not only learning but enjoyment." Every one of these people knew and appreciated whatever aspect of herself Nielsen had chosen to reveal. To those who knew her better, she would remain a much more puzzling character. Heide Vockeroth, who had known Dorise longer than any of the others, perhaps came closest to the truth: "the pattern of Judy's life was a most unusual and remarkable one," she wrote. "Since this was the type of existence her strong and remarkable character demanded and carried out—her life was indeed a success."[4]

For me, there remain several disconcerting aspects of Nielsen's life. How could a smart woman uncritically follow the party line all those years? Her own explanation—that she may have left the party had she stayed in Canada, but China had renewed her faith—is too simple. I think Nielsen's whole identity, her vision of herself, was that of a good communist fighting for the underdog. Only by clinging to that vision could her life, her sacrifices, make sense. To admit that she had been wrong, even in the details, threatened the whole structure of her identity.

Like a number of her cohorts in northern Saskatchewan, including Bob Paul, Willard Block, Wass Turple, Bill Polaski, and Minerva (Cooper) Miller, Nielsen had experienced a great awakening in the 1930s. She had suffered first-hand from the Depression and, all around her, saw others whose suffering was even worse than her own. Nielsen and her friends became highly critical of a worldwide system they had grown up accepting. Together, they went on to unite the left and defeat a powerful and well-entrenched political machine. That first great awakening followed by an initial political success was enough to keep all of them in the party for a lifetime.

Another hook for Nielsen was that the party gave her a big job to do. I first heard the phrase "big job" from Minerva Miller, who worked alongside Nielsen in northern Saskatchewan. Minerva had first campaigned for the CCF. Then the communists won her support. "They gave me big jobs," she told me, and I thought of all the support roles women played in the period (and still do). Being given a big job to do is an acknowledgement of one's ability. It is a heady thing. Nielsen was given one big job after another in those early years. And it was only when her use to the party waned that she expressed any discontent.

I believe, also, that Nielsen was not as confident as she appeared to be. She knew little about Marxism, yet was thrust to the top of the party almost immediately. She was awed by the greater knowledge of most of her comrades. This may explain all those political notebooks she stashed away. The party valued members who were theoretically developed, and Nielsen strove, for the rest of her life, to fit the model. In fact, the party's values became her values: the emphasis on correct theory, the subordination of one's personal life to the demands of party work. For better and for worse, she began to see all of life in political terms. There were wrong people and right people; there were some books that should be read and others that should be thrown in the trash.

But I say "for better and worse" because there were both positive and negative sides to life in the movement. Nielsen was never part of an elite, grabbing more than she needed. "In China," writes her grandson, Glen McLaren, "we were taught to help for the sake of the common good, if you have two apples always give the big one to the other person." These were values of which Nielsen approved. Her stoicism, her discipline, her activism, all were characteristics of Nielsen that the party used and nurtured. These were not, unfortunately, traits that enabled her to draw closer to her children, or to maintain enduring relationships with the men in her life, but these same traits did allow her to "tuck her past behind her" (like the Chinese women she so admired) and carry on an independent life.

It is meaningless to speak of Nielsen's courage and independence without acknowledging the fear and isolation she lived with for long periods in her life. When I travelled to Beijing in the spring of 2003, I met four women who had known her, and all of them said, "She was here at a bad time." But whether it was the thirties in northern Saskatchewan, Ottawa in the early years of the war, Toronto during the Cold War, or China during the Great Leap and the Cultural Revolution, Nielsen lived for years under severe stress. During the thirties, isolated from intellectual stimulation and companionship, she feared for her sanity and for the welfare of her children. Then, in China, she feared expulsion during the Sino-Soviet split, and arrest or re-education through labour during the Cultural Revolution.

Her fears, as well as her ideology, made her increasingly intolerant of what she perceived to be the weaknesses of others. The woman whom so many had seen as warm and human in the 1940s showed that face to fewer and fewer people as her life wound down. To others she was aloof, judgmental, and difficult.

In her final years Nielsen wrote very little about politics (though she continued to read and make notes). She channelled her dwindling energy into her teaching and maintaining close contact with her eldest daughter. Although she was loath to admit it, her enemy became loneliness. If she had any last thoughts on the political project that had structured most of her adult life, and finally landed her in China, we will never know.

ENDNOTES

PROLOGUE

1. *Chatelaine* (June 1940): 16.
2. *Spiritwood Herald,* 26 March 1935, p. 1.
3. A.F. Cross, "Parliamentary Personalities," *Canadian Business* (April 1945): 15.
4. *Globe and Mail,* 15 December 1980, p. 15.
5. Dorise Nielsen to Heide Vockeroth, "Friday night, in the Chamber" (March 1944?), Heide Vockeroth Papers, National Archives of Canada (NAC) MG32–F7.
6. Agnes Macphail (1890–1954) was the first woman elected to the House of Commons (1921–1940). She fell in love with another MP but chose never to marry because she did not wish to give up her political career. (See her biography *Ask No Quarter* by Margaret Stewart and Doris French.) Martha Black (1866–1957) replaced her husband, George Black (who was ill) as MP for the Yukon (1935–1940). Although she was seventy at the time of her election and "was keeping the seat warm for George," she was a feisty, independent woman, originally from Chicago, who had left her first husband during the Klondike gold rush. (See *My Seventy Years* by Martha Black.)
7. Dorise Nielsen to Christine Wong, 26 May 1977, Christine Wong Papers, vol. 1, National Archives of Canada (NAC) MG32–G11.
8. Dorise Nielsen to Louise Harvey, 17 May 1962, Louise Harvey Papers, National Archives of Canada (NAC) MG32–G18.
9. Stewart Paul, interview by author in Oakville, Ontario, October 2002.

CHAPTER ONE COMING TO CANADA

1. Eline Morrow, interview taped by Georgina Taylor, July 1981, Saskatchewan Archives Board R8142–3.
2. According to the 1901 census, Maude, twenty-two, was a shop assistant; Florry, seventeen, a stenographer; and Nellie, twenty, was not employed. It seems that Maude married first and left the home. It is always Florry and Nell whom Dorise mentions in her memoir.
3. Dorise Nielsen Papers, vol. 1, Memoir, 85, National Archives of Canada MG27–111C30. Referred to hereafter as Memoir.
4. John D. Webber, 43 Defoe Road, is listed as a builder in a 1903–04 commercial directory for the Clapton area.
5. In 1918 when women over thirty were given the vote in Great Britain, the electoral rolls for 44 Kyverdale Road show Jessie Webber and an Arthur Benjamin Trewinnard (absent military voter). From 1919 to 1924, the registered voters for that address include Elizabeth and Henry Starr as well as Jessie. Elizabeth and Henry were the parents of Alfred Starr, who married Dorise's sister Nellie. The Starr family also came from Defoe Road.

6. Memoir, 91.
7. The 1901 census lists William Woodgate, fifty, living in Beer, Devon; occupation: fisherman.
8. In a letter to her daughter Sally, written several years before the memoir, Nielsen mentioned "having two fine cousins killed, both young men of whom I was very fond. My sister's husband was killed and then towards the end of the war my own sweetheart, learning to fly, came down 1,000 feet in flames!" In the memoir, written a few years later, she seems to have converted one of the cousins into a brother, who, she says, was her youngest and favourite brother, Roland (Ro). There is no record of such a brother in the census of 1891 or 1901, and no record of a Roland Webber dying in combat. Dorise Nielsen to Sally Nielsen, 5 January 1967, Sally Nielsen Papers, National Archives of Canada (NAC) MG32G10.
9. Clapton County Secondary School for Girls no longer exists, but a composer, Minna Keal, who graduated from Clapton County a few years after Nielsen, said she was fortunate to win a scholarship to such a progressive school, run by a Fabian socialist (http://www.musicweb-international.com/keal/).
10. An article on Judiasm in Hackney (of which Stoke Newington is a part) notes that at the turn of the century, the Hackney synagogue served a district "thickly populated by the better class of Jewish working man."
11. According to the 1901 census there was, indeed, a Laurence Gilchrist who lived on the southeast coast of England where Dorise spent her summers. He was seven years older than Dorise. However, a search of the War Graves Commission Web site produced no evidence of his death in 1918.
12. Memoir, 96.
13. Both the death of Alfred Starr and the birth of Geoffrey Starr are recorded in the fourth quarter of 1918.
14. Dorise Nielsen to Sally Nielsen, 5 January 1967, Sally Nielsen Papers, NAC.
15. Memoir, 276.
16. Nielsen mentions the course on Paul in a letter to her daughter, Christine, 15 September 1978. At that time Nielsen was giving a series of lectures to Chinese scholars going abroad and several lectures were on religion. She regretted she had not paid more attention in class years before. Christine Wong Papers, vol. 1, NAC.
17. Memoir, 296.
18. The 1901 census lists a Jack Trevethick, twelve years old, whose father is a Cornwall farmer. In the memoir, Nielsen calls the suitor Jim Trevethic.
19. Memoir, 301.
20. Nielsen to Wong, 27 November 1974, Christine Wong Papers, vol. 1, NAC: "I wrote reams of poetry and threw it out before I left England. Having always been a rolling stone I've never kept much of anything."
21. Memoir, 315.
22. Eva (Hunt) Phelps, interview by author in Saskatoon, August 2003.
23. In her memoir Nielsen gave detailed descriptions of picnics and dances. In the winter of 1953, she had a short story, "The Dance," published in *New Frontiers*.

24. When Dorise saw Mary, she thought she had scarlet fever. However, no one else in the family or the community fell ill.
25. Memoir, 391.

CHAPTER TWO SLAVERY OR FREEDOM

1. Dorise Nielsen to Christine Wong, 23 November 1966, Christine Wong Papers, NAC.
2. At first most of Dorise's books were sent by her sister Nell. Later on they may have come from the Wheat Pool Library, or from her friends, Bob and Cecil Paul. Sally Nielsen also remembers a man she thought was a peddler coming to the house with books for Dorise (e-mail, March 2005).
3. Memoir, 400.
4. The quarter section where the house was built was proved up in 1925, and the other quarter section in 1929. Nielsen mortgaged the home section for $1000 in 1931. Sally Nielsen, private papers.
5. Morrow, taped interview, SAB.
6. Charles Szasz, interview by author in Spiritwood, July 2002.
7. Memoir, 408. The couple Dorise boarded with in 1927 had a baby.
8. Dorise Nielsen, "Twelve Years Homesteading." (Toronto) *Star Weekly*, 31 August 1940.
9. The picture was taken just after Sally's birth in the summer of 1931. The occasion is conjecture. However, Dorise did have all her children baptized.
10. Nielsen, "Twelve Years Homesteading."
11. Ibid.
12. Infant mortality rates in Canada were high generally and even higher in poor and isolated areas. See Cynthia Comacchio, "Saving Mother and Babies: Motherhood, Medicine, and the Modern State, 1900–1945," in *Framing Our Past, Canadian Women's History in the Twentieth Century* (Montreal: McGill-Queen's University Press, 2001), 139–46.
13. Morrow, taped interview, Saskatchewan Archives Board (SAB). Eline Morrow remembered that Dolly "stiffened her spine and dried her tears."
14. It is possible that Jessie Webber bought tickets for Dorise and Christine to travel to England after the baby's death, but Pete Nielsen may have bought the tickets himself. It was at that time that he mortgaged his farm for $1000. Sally Nielsen, private papers.
15. (Hunt) Phelps, interview.
16. The quotations in this paragraph are all from Nielsen, "Twelve Years Homesteading."
17. Christine Wong, interview taped by Georgina Taylor, July 1987, SAB.
18. Sally Nielsen, interview by author, March 2005.
19. Both photos are from Robert Wong's private collection.
20. Approximately 45,000 refugees from the south moved to northern Saskatchewan from 1930 to 1936. See Bill Waiser, *Saskatchewan, A New History* (Calgary: Fifth House, 2005), 298–99. I interviewed one of these refugees, Bill Burchill, by phone in September 2002.

21. Figures are taken from Gary Fairbairn, *Prairie Roots, The Remarkable Story of the Saskatchewan Wheat Pool* (Sasktoon: Western Producer Prairie Books, 1984).
22. Waiser, *Saskatchewan, A New History*, 313–14.
23. George Davidson (campaign manager, Meadow Lake) to Georgina Mathers (secretary to CCF leader, George Williams), April 1936, CCF Papers, Provincial Constituency of Meadow Lake 1934–36, 52991, Saskatchewan Archives Board B7IV–60.
24. Morrow, taped interview, SAB.
25. M.J. Coldwell Papers, Memoir #31, 31 August 1964, National Archives of Canada. Did Dorise ever deliver a baby? Her own daughters doubt it. But people did call on her in emergencies and she would go and do what she could. In this case she obviously wanted to impress Coldwell with the neediness of the community and she succeeded.
26. Dorise Nielsen to Frank Eliason, 5 October 1934, CCF Papers, North Battleford Federal Constituency, 1931–36, 41772–4, Saskatchewan Archives Board B7111–41.
27. Ibid.
28. Nielsen, "Twelve Years Homesteading."
29. Doris Shackleton, *Tommy Douglas* (Toronto: McClelland and Stewart, 1975), 159.
30. Social Credit won fifty-six of sixty-three seats, defeating the United Farmers of Alberta, which had been in power since the 1920s. In his book *Off the Record* (Toronto: McClelland and Stewart, 1968), 54, Saskatchewan journalist C.H. Higginbottom remembers the appeal of Social Credit: "To some in Saskatchewan Social Credit seemed more CCF than the CCF itself. It was against banks, mortgage companies, newspapers, and other vested interests; interest on debts was to be abolished … there were to be no foreclosures on farmers' land … not only did it advocate everything proposed by the CCF, but it was not associated with socialism or communism."
31. Results: McIntosh (Lib) 7039, Robert Watson (SC) 4412, Hill Hamilton (CCF) 4168.
32. Robert Paul to George Williams, 4 May 1936, CCF Papers, Meadow Lake 1934–36, 52994, SAB.
33. Robert (Doc) Savage, telephone interview by author, August 2004. Doc Savage said three died: a man called Alfie, shot through the windpipe; another called Shumanski; and another chap from Montreal. He remembers seeing them and a number of wounded on the floor of a building with a big arched doorway. Unfortunately, the trekkers scattered and did not become the prime witnesses at the subsequent inquiry. Doc Savage escaped arrest in Regina but he was picked up during a demonstration in Calgary shortly after and served eleven months in prison. The other demonstrators got off with fifteen days. See also Victor Howard, *We Were the Salt of the Earth* (University of Regina: Great Plains Research Centre, 1985); Ronald Liversedge, *Recollections of the On-to-Ottawa Trek*, ed. Victor Hoar (Carleton Library, Toronto: McClelland and Stewart, 1973); and Bill Waiser, *All Hell Can't Stop Us* (Calgary: Fifth House, 2003).

34. Savage, telephone interview.
35. Stewart Paul, interview.
36. Stewart Paul, private papers.
37. Stewart Paul, interview.
38. Ibid.
39. Life outline, 1968. Dorise Nielsen Papers, vol. 2, NAC.
40. There is a mention of Bob Bowie in *The Selected Writings of Walter Wiggins* (ed. Cathy Fisher, intro. William Beeching [Regina: n.p., 1985], 55–56). Wiggins was a farmer from Sturgis, Saskatchewan, who became a communist in the 1920s. He was a leading member of the United Farmers of Canada (Saskatchewan Section), and chief organizer of the Farmers' Unity League in Saskatchewan. He wrote that when he travelled to Spiritwood in the early 1930s, Bob Bowie chaired a meeting for him.
41. Life outline, 1968. Nielsen dated her coming to Canada as being 1924 instead of 1927, and her becoming a member of the CCF executive (Meadow Lake) as 1934 instead of 1937. As to her statement that she was communist from the beginning, it may be true, but we will never know for sure. In China it was certainly prudent to say that. Also, from the evidence of one of Nielsen's comrades, Minerva Cooper, it was common practice for communists to court CCF activists whom they viewed as useful. She herself began as a genuine supporter of the CCF candidate, Sandy Nicholson, in his campaign for Parliament in 1935. Soon she was recruited by communists she met and, like Nielsen, was told to retain her CCF membership. She was actually hired by the CCF in 1937 to organize women's clubs. Minerva (Cooper) Miller, telephone interview by author, November 1988.
42. Williams's report was published in a booklet called *The Land of the Soviets, A Western Farmer Sees the Russian Bear Change Its Coat* (Saskatoon: The United Farmers of Canada, Saskatchewan Section, 1931), 86. The tone of the book is one of good-natured curiosity. We have nothing to fear, he says. Let the Russian experiment take its course. "If it can give more satisfaction than our present system it deserves to succeed."

Chapter Three The United Progressives

1. Dorise Nielsen to Alexander (Sandy) Nicholson, 24 September 1975, Alexander Nicholson Papers, National Archives of Canada MG27111–C26.
2. Ivan Avakumovic, *The Communist Party in Canada, A History* (Toronto: McClelland and Stewart, 1975), 90.
3. *Regina Leader-Post*, 13 July 1936.
4. *Saturday Night* (24 October 1943): 1.
5. It is very unlikely that either Nielsen or Paul attended the 1936 convention. Neither were constituency officers that year. The CCF files for Meadow Lake 1934–36 (SAB) show that the area held an open convention because the polls were not sufficiently organized to elect delegates. In a letter to George Williams, T. Ransom of Robinhood, the constituency secretary, explained that there was more interest in the Social Credit than anything (file 53013).

6. Quoted in *Regina Leader-Post*, 15 July 1936.
7. *Daily Clarion*, 18 July 1936.
8. Copy of Organizational Resolution by District of Saskatchewan, 18 February 1936, and Circulation of *The Clarion*, September 1937, Comintern Fonds, National Archives of Canada, MG10K3 K219. Circulation of the *Clarion* reached 1099 for Saskatchewan by September 1937, with five copies going to Rabbit Lake.
9. (Hunt) Phelps, interview.
10. *Spiritwood Herald*, 6 August 1937.
11. Ibid., 29 October 1937.
12. RCMP report on the Communist Party of Canada, Rabbit Lake District, Sask., 18 January 1938, Records of the Canadian Security Intelligence Service, vol. 1039–41, Dorise Nielsen, part 1, 153, National Archives of Canada RG146.
13. Ibid., 21 December 1938, 149.
14. Dorise lists this as one of her early activities. Life outline, 1968. Dorise Nielsen papers, vol. 2, NAC.
15. *Spiritwood Herald*, 10 December 1937: "A good crowd turned our Wednesday evening to the CCF study club meeting at the home of Mr. L. Wakefield. The next meeting will be at Mr. Hunt's on Wed., January 5th."
16. Willard Block, interview by author in Canwood, Saskatchewan, July 2003.
17. Nielsen quotes this letter from "Old Timer" in her 9 December 1937 letter to the *Western Producer*.
18. *Western Producer*, 25 February 1937.
19. Ibid., December 1935.
20. Ibid., 22 April 1937.
21 Ibid., 9 September 1937.
22. *Spiritwood Herald*, 4 June and 17 September 1937.
23. Ibid., 29 July 1937.
24. Circular to all polls, 7 June 1937, CCF Papers, Meadow Lake constituency 1937–39, 53042, Saskatchewan Archives Board B71V–61.
25. David Lewis returned from England in 1935 and became the first national secretary of the CCF in 1936. In his autobiography, *The Good Fight* (Toronto: Macmillan of Canada, 1981), he admits that during his first few years back in Canada, he vacillated about cooperation with the communists (149). Nielsen certainly changed her opinion of Lewis but she recalled her first impression of him in a letter to Louise Harvey, dated January 1973. Louise Harvey Papers, NAC.
26. Report of the Provincial Council to the Second Annual Convention at Saskatoon, 15 July 1937, CCF Papers, Provincial Council 1937–39, 23441–42, Saskatchewan Archives Board B711–236.
27. Bob Paul to George Williams, 22 March 1938, CCF Papers, Meadow Lake constituency, 53133, SAB.
28. In 1936 the Liberal government abolished the relief camps for single men and replaced them with a farm labour scheme. Under the scheme a farmer could hire a

man or a woman. The government paid the farmer five dollars a month for board and room, and the worker, five dollars a month for their labour. Dorise and Pete gave Eva the whole amount. (Hunt) Phelps, interview.

29. Nielsen mentions in her memoir meeting an old settler called Mrs. Tipton, who taught her this.
30. Bruce Hutchison, *The Incredible Canadian* (Toronto: Longman's, Green and Co., 1953), 226.
31. *Regina Leader-Post*, 5 July 1938.
32. Turple to Williams, 25 March 1938, and Williams to Turple, 1 April 1938, CCF Papers, Meadow Lake, 1937–39, 53131–32 and 53143, SAB.
33. Williams to Bob Paul, 22 December 1938, CCF Papers, Meadow Lake, 1937–39, 53105, SAB.
34. *Spiritwood Herald*, 2 March 1938: "Mr. P.O. Nielsen has been quite sick this past week." Later, on April 22, the *Herald* noted that he had gone to Prince Albert to see a doctor, and a week later it said that he had undergone an operation and was doing well. None of my sources remembered what ailed him.
35. Also elected were two members of Social Credit and two Unity candidates. The Unity MLAs, Alan Stewart of Yorkton and Herman Warren of Benough, caucused with Social Credit. Both had formerly run as Conservatives.
36. The final count in Meadow Lake was Liberal 3184, Social Credit 2434, and CCF 1800. "Sorry we didn't make the grade up here," Paul wrote to George Williams, "but we could not check the Social Credit prairie fire." CCF Papers, Meadow Lake, 1937–39, 531189, SAB.
37. Georgina Mathers to Wass Turple (campaign manager), 19 April 1938, CCF Papers, Meadow Lake, 1937–39, 53149, SAB.
38. "BP" to "Dear Friends," undated, Dorise Nielsen Papers, vol. 2, NAC. This letter was probably retrieved from Bob Paul by Christine Nielsen in the 1960s, along with several pieces of poetry, some written by Dorise. The letter was written in the early 1940s as the communists prepared for the next provincial election in Saskatchewan (preparations began in 1942 although the election took place late, in 1944). In it Bob Paul analyzed the reasons for Nielsen's win in 1940 and advised against a similar united front campaign provincially.
39. As quoted in Friedrich Steininger: "George H. Williams: Agrarian Socialist," MA thesis, University of Regina, 1976, p. 320.
40. Maynard Woollard to George Williams, 10 October 1938, CCF Papers, Meadow Lake, 1937–39, 53228, SAB. Also, *Regina Leader-Post*, 13 October 1938.
41. Dorise Nielsen to Violet McNaughton, 23 November 1938, Violet McNaughton Papers, Saskatchewan Archives Board, A1D53.
42. Ibid., 6 August 1938.
43. Christine Wong, interview. Stewart Paul, interview.
44. Dorise Nielsen to Christine Nielsen, 5 October 1974, Christine Wong Papers, vol. 1, NAC.

45. Heide Vockeroth, interview by Elizabeth Smillie, November 1980, as quoted in Smillie's thesis, "Dorise Nielsen, Prairie Populist and Feminist," Trent University, Peterborough, 1981.
46. Bob Paul to George Williams, 23 December 1938, CCF Papers, Meadow Lake, 1937–39, 53293, SAB.
47. Resolution of the Meadow Lake CCF executive, 7 January 1939. Ibid., 53309.
48. Stewart Paul, interview.
49. J.H. Brockelbank reports on meetings held at Spiritwood, Mildred, Belbutte, and Bapaume, 11–14 April 1939, CCF Papers, North Battleford federal constituency, 1937–40, 41974–75, Saskatchewan Archives Board B7III–42.
50. Text of radio address by George Williams, 26 April 1939, CCF Papers, Communist Party, 4687, Saskatchewan Archives Board B7II–48.
51. S*askatoon Star-Phoenix*, 19 July 1939. The CPC candidate was Arthur Doucet; the Social Credit candidate, I. Soderberg.

CHAPTER FOUR A MIGHTY EFFORT

1. Dorise Nielsen to Violet McNaughton, 31 July 1939, Violet McNaughton Papers.
2. *North Battleford News*, 20 July 1939.
3. *Spiritwood Herald*, 8 March 1940.
4. *Regina Leader-Post*, 22 March 1940.
5. Dorise Nielsen to Sandy Nicholson, 24 September 1975, Nicholson Papers, NAC, as quoted in Smillie, "Dorise Nielsen, Prairie Populist and Feminist."
6. Stewart Paul, interview.
7. Bob Vockeroth, telephone interview by author, January 2003.
8. Christine Nielsen, interview.
9. Sally Nielsen, private collection.
10. *Regina Leader-Post*, 26 August 1939.
11. RCMP report on a meeting at Meadow Lake, 22 March 1939, (CSIS) Dorise Nielsen, part 1, 133–34, NAC.
12. T.C. Douglas, *The Making of a Socialist, The Recollections of T.C. Douglas*, ed. Lewis H. Thomas (Edmonton: University of Alberta Press, 1983), 113.
13. W.D. Herridge, *What Kind of Revolution?* (Boston: Little Brown and Co., 1943), 86.
14. *Regina Leader-Post*, 26 August 1939.
15. Ibid., 7 August 1939.
16. Steininger, "George Williams: Agrarian Socialist," 346.
17. *Regina Leader-Post*, 24 August 1939.
18. Douglas, *The Making of a Socialist*, 125.
19. *Winnipeg Free Press*, 5 March 1940.
20. *Regina Leader-Post*, 11 November 1939.
21. Ibid., 28 November 1939.
22. Avakumovic, *The Communist Party in Canada*, 140.
23. "BP" to "Dear Friends," undated, Dorise Nielsen Papers, vol. 2.

24. For an account of Brown's campaign see J.M. Pitsula, "W.G. Brown: 'Righteousness Exalteth a Nation'," *Saskatchewan History* (Spring 1980).
25. Bob Vockeroth, telephone interview.
26. Richard Vockeroth, telephone interview by author, December 2002.
27. Although both daughters knew their father was a binge drinker, they seldom saw him drunk. Only the oldest daughter, Christine, remembered a terrifying incident when Pete threatened to shoot the whole family. Living like this is not fit for a human being, he said. Dorise handed the two girls out the bedroom window and told them to run to a neighbour's. Sally Nielsen, correspondence.
28. Most of these are memories of the oldest child, Christine, taped by Georgina Taylor, SAB. Some are from interviews by the author in 1986.
29. *Regina Leader-Post*, 8 February 1940.
30. *Western Producer*, 22 February 1940, as quoted in Smillie, "Dorise Nielsen, Prairie Populist and Feminist," 24.
31. George Williams to Dorise Nielsen, 16 February 1940, CCF Papers, North Battleford, 42028–29, SAB.
32. Williams to Nielsen, 13 March 1940. Ibid., 42036.
33. Nielsen to Williams, 5 April 1940. Ibid., 42041.
34. "MAG" to "Dear Friends," 3 January 1940, CSIS, Dorise Nielsen, part 1, 121–27, NAC. This letter was apparently seized on the arrest of a CP member in the summer of 1940, and was the government's chief evidence that Mrs. Nielsen was indeed a communist. "MAG" may have been Gerry McManus, leader of the Saskatchewan branch of the party at the time.
35. *Saskatoon Star-Phoenix*, 1 April 1940.
36. Nielsen to Macphail, 5 April 1940. Agnes Macphail Papers, correspondence 1940, 1314–16, National Archives of Canada MG27–111C4.
37. Coldwell, M.J. Coldwell Papers, Memoir #31, NAC.
38. Norman Penner remembered MacLeod's coming through Winnipeg shortly after the election and passing on the news. Telephone interview by author, May 1988.

Chapter Five Fighting for the West

1. Mackenzie King diary, 23 May 1940, National Archives of Canada, on-line.
2. Nielsen to McNaughton, 14 May 1940, Violet McNaughton Papers, SAB.
3. The information about Muriel Kerr is from Margaret Stewart and Doris French, *Ask No Quarter* (Toronto: Longman's, Green and Co., 1959), a biography of Agnes Macphail. The Nielsen daughters remembered the name Kerr.
4. Nielsen to McNaughton, 10 June 1940, Violet McNaughton Papers, SAB.
5. *Regina Leader-Post*, 14 May 1940, p. 1.
6. John Archer, *Saskatchewan, A History* (Saskatoon: Western Producer Prairie Books, 1980), 217.
7. *Debates*, 20 May 1940, 59.
8. Ibid., 61.

9. Cross, "Parliamentary Personalities," 15.
10. *Debates*, 17 May 1940.
11. Mackenzie King to Dorise Nielsen, 23 May 1940, Sally Nielsen Papers, NAC.
12. King dairy, 23 May 1940, NAC.
13. Mackenzie King's diary gives an account of this meeting, but not of the offer of a job as national director of the YWCA. Nielsen mentioned the offer to her daughters. She was proud she had refused it.
14. Copy of *Industry and Humanity* inscribed by Mackenzie King, Sally Nielsen Papers, NAC.
15. Richard Vockeroth, interview.
16. *Debates*, 23 May 1940, 146–47, and 6 June 1940, 555–56.
17. Nielsen to McNaughton, 10 June 1940, Violet McNaughton Papers, SAB.
18. *Debates*, 5 June 1940, 550.
19. Ibid., 30 June 1940.
20. Ibid., 28 May 1940.
21. Ibid. George Castleden mentions the number of Liberal absentees on May 28 and again on May 31. The Liberals held 184 of 245 seats.
22. Nielsen to McNaughton, 10 June 1940, Violet McNaughton Papers, SAB.
23. Jessie Taggart, *Toronto Star*, 15 May 1940.
24. Avakumovic, *The Communist Party in Canada*, 144.
25. Tim Buck, *Yours in Struggle* (Toronto: NC Press, 1977), 298.
26. *Debates*, 6 June and 12 June 1940.
27. Avakumovic, *The Communist Part in Canada*, 143.
28. Louise Harvey saved Nielsen's letters from 1955 until Nielsen's death in 1980. These letters were deposited in the National Archives on the request of Nielsen's daughter, Christine Nielsen Wong.
29. *Debates*, 2 July 1940, 1260.
30. Ibid., 1264.
31. Tommy Douglas to Elizabeth Smillie, 18 November 1980, Elizabeth Smillie private collection.
32. Jimmy Gardiner, former premier of Saskatchewan, was in charge of the Liberal machine in that province.
33. King diary, 20 June 1940, NAC.
34. Christine Wong, interview by author in Ottawa, March 1986.
35. Stewart and French, *Ask No Quarter*, 259. Macphail was probably referring to Nelson Clarke, Minerva Cooper, and Harold Miller.
36. Ibid.
37. Carlyle King, "A Beginning in Politics," *Saskatchewan History* (Autumn 1983): 107.
38. Willard Block, interview. Willard was a neighbour of Nielsen's and a member of the study club. He joined the Communist Party in 1939. (Not all members of the club were willing to take that risk but he remembers all being sympathetic.) Willard's house was searched the summer of 1940 when the RCMP was looking for Maynard

Woollard. They confiscated *Red Star over China* by Edgar Snow, which he had purchased with Dorise.

39. RCMP report, Rabbit Lake detachment, 6 July 1940, CSIS, Dorise Nielsen, part 1, NAC.
40. *Canadian Tribune*, 28 September and 26 October 1940.
41. "Speech of Mrs. Nielson," A.A. Macleod Papers, Edmonton East Election file, Public Archives of Ontario (PAO), mu7592.
42. *Western Producer*, 12 September 1940.
43. RCMP report, Biggar detachment, 10 October 1940, CSIS, Dorise Nielsen, part 1, NAC.
44. *Saskatoon Star-Phoenix*, 15 October 1940.
45. *Winnipeg Free Press*, 23 October 1940.
46. "Speech of Mrs. Nielson," A.A. Macleod Papers, Edmonton East election file, PAO.
47. D'Arcy Hande, "Strike," *Saskatchewan History* (Autumn 1985).
48. *Debates*, 14 November 1940.
49. Comintern Fonds K292, NAC.
50. Ibid.
51. Editorial, *Canadian Tribune*, 11 January 1941.
52. Sally Nielsen, correspondence, 2005.

CHAPTER SIX ESCAPING THE NET

1. Assistant Commissioner LaNauze to the officer commanding North Battleford sub-division, 17 October 1940, CSIS, Dorise Nielsen, part 2, 161, NAC.
2. John Kolasky, *Shattered Illusion, The History of Ukrainian Pro-communist Organizations in Canada* (Toronto: Peter Martin and Associates, 1979), 143.
3. Report to the Director of Criminal Investigation, 21 October 1940, CSIS, Dorise Nielsen, part 2, NAC.
4. Dorise Nielsen to Charles Burnford, Edmonton, CSIS, Dorise Nielsen, part 2, 274, NAC.
5. *Debates*, 18 November 1940.
6. Ibid., 12 November 1940.
7. *Globe and Mail*, 20 November 1940.
8. Memorandum from Sgt. Pepper to Insp. Drysdale, 9 November 1940, CSIS, Dorise Nielsen, part 4, 422–23, NAC.
9. Report on Civil Liberties Union, Montreal, 7 December 1940, CSIS, Dorise Nielsen, part 6, 813, NAC.
10. *Canadian Tribune*, 14 December 1940.
11. *Toronto Daily Star* printed large chunks of her speech on 7 December 1940. *Canadian Tribune* printed its account on 14 December 1940.
12. Norman Penner, telephone interview, and Virginia MacLeod, telephone interview by author, June 1988.
13. See A.A. Macleod papers, PAO.

14. Virginia MacLeod, telephone interview.
15. "Re: A.A. MacLeod," Records of the Canadian Security Intelligence Service, A.A. MacLeod, 2333–34, National Archives of Canada RG146, vol. 1094.
16. This impression of Nielsen's visits to the MacLeod household is based on the memories of Jean Buck, A.A. MacLeod's eldest daughter, who was sixteen in 1940. Jean Buck, interview by author in Sydney, BC, March 2003.
17. Sally Nielsen, correspondence.
18. The memories of Christine Nielsen Wong used in this chapter are from author interviews 1986–88, and from tapes recorded by Georgina Taylor, SAB.
19. RCMP report on mass meeting held at the Walker Theatre, 7 February 1941, CSIS, Dorise Nielsen, part 6, 625–27, NAC.
20. The details of the western tour in the winter of 1941 are from the CSIS file of A.A. Macleod, NAC.
21. RCMP report, Edmonton, 7 February 1941, CSIS, A.A. MacLeod, 2314, NAC.
22. Assistant Commissioner LaNauze to the commissioner, 18 February 1941, CSIS, Dorise Nielsen, part 6, 593–94, NAC. In the margins, the commissioner has scrawled "no" to each of LaNauze's suggestions.
23. Nielsen to Vockeroth, "Monday evening in the Chamber," Heide Vockeroth Papers, NAC.
24. *North Battleford News*, 9 October 1941, p. 2 (a reprint of the James Hatton letter).
25. The list of 503 names was typed out in alphabetical order and went on for pages. Several copies of it appear in Nielsen's CSIS file, parts 8 and 8a, NAC.
26. *Debates*, 27 February 1941, 1069–70.
27. Ibid., 24 February 1941, 949.
28. Ibid., 27 February 1941, 1072–73.
29. Ibid., 23 March 1941, 1888.
30. *Regina Leader-Post*, 19 March 1941.
31. *Debates*, 4 March 1941, 1208.
32. Ibid., 1216.
33. Ibid., 5 March 1941, 1250.
34. Ibid., 1252.
35. Nielsen to Lapointe, 8 March 1941, CSIS, Dorise Nielsen, part 8, 960, NAC. Of course, Lapointe had not really offered to show Nielsen her file at all. She was essentially throwing his remarks in the House back at him.
36. Editorial, *Winnipeg Free Press*, 7 March 1941.
37. McNaughton to Nielsen, 29 March 1941, Violet McNaughton Papers, SAB.
38. See CSIS, Dorise Nielsen, part 8: 951, 952, 976, 987; and part 9: 1304, NAC.
39. *Debates*, 14 March 1941, 1538–39.
40. Ibid., 24 March 1941, 1809.
41. King diary, 8 May 1941, NAC. King asked another potential candidate to step aside and let Casselman's widow run and he urged other members of the Liberal caucus to do the same.

Chapter Seven Supporting the War

1. Assistant Commissioner LaNauze to Commissioner Wood, 17 October 1941, CSIS, Dorise Nielsen, part 11, 1587, NAC.
2. RCMP report on meeting at the Alberta Avenue Community Hall the evening of 27 May 1941, CSIS, A.A. MacLeod, 36–37, NAC.
3. Editorial, *North Battleford News*, 17 July 1941.
4. *Winnipeg Free Press*, 14 July 1941.
5. Ibid., 23 July 1941.
6. Buck, *Yours in Struggle*, 299.
7. Ibid., 298.
8. A.E. Smith, *All My Life* (Toronto: Progress Books, 1949), 205.
9. *Western Farmer*, 21 July 1941, SAB. The *Western Farmer* was a publication of the Saskatoon communists, including Bob Paul.
10. (Hunt) Phelps, interview.
11. Sally Nielsen, correspondence. Sally believes that the children were Cecil's main concern.
12. *Canadian Tribune*, 31 August 1941.
13. RCMP report on meeting in Vancouver's Burrard Hall, 1 October 1941, CSIS, Dorise Nielsen, part 11, 1607, NAC.
14. RCMP report on strike at Acme Screw and Gear Co., 30 August 1941, CSIS, Dorise Nielsen, part 10, 1389, NAC.
15. Assistant Commissioner LaNauze to Commisioner Wood, 17 October 1941, CSIS, Dorise Nielsen, part 11, 1587, NAC.
16. RCMP report, St Catherine's, 27 October 1941, CSIS, Dorise Nielsen, part 11, 1579, NAC.
17. RCMP report on meeting of the People's Victory Committee, Civic Auditorium, Winnipeg, 18 September 1941, CSIS, Dorise Nielsen, part 10, 1356, NAC.
18. Rudolph Hess, Hitler's deputy, maintained that he was on a solo mission to end the war and had hoped to land on the estate of the Duke of Hamilton, which was nearby. There is other evidence that Hitler was anxious to make peace with Britain before he invaded the Soviet Union, but the true reason for Hess's flight is still a mystery.
19. RCMP report on meeting at the Empire Theatre, Edmonton, 26 September 1941, Records of the Canadian Security Intelligence Service, Dorise Nielsen Club, 265–67, National Archives of Canada (NAC) RG146, vol. 3473.
20. *Vancouver Daily Province*, 29 September 1941.
21. *Regina Leader-Post*, 22 September 1941.
22. *North Battleford News*, 9 October 1941.
23. This figure is taken from Laurel Sefton MacDowell, *Remember Kirkland Lake, The Gold Miners' Strike of 1941–42* (Toronto: University of Toronto Press 1983), xiv (attributed to Canada, Department of Labour, *Labour Organizations in Canada, 1974–1975).*
24. *Regina Leader-Post*, 26 September 1941.

25. The TLC held its convention in Calgary that September. Nielsen mentions attending both conventions in *Debates*, 14 November 1941.
26. MacDowell, *Remember Kirkland Lake*, 123. The meeting took place Sunday, 2 November 1941, in the afternoon. Later in the day Nielsen addressed the miners themselves. Another account of these meetings: CSIS, Dorise Nielsen, part 11, 1570–71, NAC.
27. S.P. Lewis, *The Life of Grace MacInnis* (Vancouver: Harbour Publishing, 1993), 153.
28. *Regina Leader-Post*, 20 October 1941.
29. Smith, *All My Life*, 206.
30. *Debates*, 14 November 1941, 4442.
31. Ibid., 10 February 1942. When Nielsen originally presented the petition on 14 November 1941, it was ruled that she could not read its contents (4401).
32. *Debates*, 23 February 1942, 803.
33. *Ottawa Evening Citizen*, 25 February 1942, p. 16.
34. *Canadian Tribune*, 7 February 1942, p. 2.
35. From reports in the *Canadian Tribune*, 2 February 1942, and in the *Regina Leader-Post*, 31 March 1942.
36. Nielsen to Vockeroth, 2 March 1942, Vockeroth Papers, NAC.
37. See the *Ottawa Evening Citizen*, 22 January 1942, and *Debates*, 20 February 1942, 743. Many telegrams either to or from Nielsen were copied by the war censor and sent to the RCMP.
38. Lewis, *The Life of Grace MacInnis*, 155.
39. *Ottawa Evening Citizen*, 24 February 1942.
40. Smith, *All My Life*, 208.
41. She was probably referring to the growing agitation against conscription since King's announcement that there would be a plebiscite on the issue.
42. *Ottawa Evening Citizen*, 24 February 1942, p. 13.
43. *Debates*, 19 February 1942, 706.
44. Desmond Morton, *Working People* (Montreal: McGill-Queen's University Press, 1998), 160.
45. Smith, *All My Life*, 208.
46. Irving Abella, *Nationalism, Communism and Canadian Labour* (Toronto: University of Toronto Press, 1973), 89.
47. MacDowell, *Remember Kirkland Lake*, 211.
48. Nielsen to Vockeroth, 2 March 1941, Vockeroth Papers, NAC. Internal evidence shows that the letter was actually written in March 1942.
49. Shackleton, *Tommy Douglas*, 103.
50. Frank Park, who worked for the Wartime Information Board, remembered Nielsen and Quelch as good friends. Interview by author, July 1987.
51. *Debates*, 10 February 1942.
52. Ibid., 23 March 1942, 1508.
53. The Windsor rally was announced in the *Canadian Tribune*, 15 March 1942.

54. As late as July 1942, J.B. Salsberg and two others were picked up in Toronto (*Canadian Tribune*, 11 July 1942).
55. Irene Brereton to Sally Nielsen, 8 October 1984: "I suggested she leave Christine with Nelson (Clarke) and I, but she said since you weren't able to be with your parents she didn't want you separated." Sally Nielsen private papers.
56. Sally Nielsen, correspondence.
57. Stewart Paul, interview.
58. F.C. Williams to M.J. Coldwell, 5 January 1942, as quoted by Smillie, "Dorise Nielsen, Prairie Populist and Feminist," 73.
59. *Debates*, 10 February 1942, 466.
60. The ad is reproduced in J.L. Granatstein, *Mackenzie King: His Life and World* (Toronto: McGraw-Hill Ryerson, 1977), 162.

Chapter Eight Parenting

1. A.S. Byatt, *Writers and Company*, CBC, 2 November 2003.
2. "Things We Agree Upon," Christine Wong Papers, vol. 6, NAC.
3. Sally Nielsen, correspondence.
4. Bob Paul to Roy Reid, 7 September 1955. Sally Nielsen private papers.
5. *North Battleford News*, 27 August and 10 September 1942.
6. BP to Dear Friends, Dorise Nielsen Papers, vol. 2, NAC. Also, Nielsen to Vockeroth, 8 February 1943, Heide Vockeroth Papers, NAC: "I have received the verdict that we were correct and the Sask. group incorrect. We now have the control of the constituency in our hands."
7. McNaughton to Nielsen, 20 August 1942, Violet McNaughton Papers, SAB.
8. Ibid.
9. Buck, *Yours in Struggle*, 309.
10. *Canadian Tribune*, 17 October 1942.
11. The only female communist interned was Gladys Macdonald, secretary of the Saskatchewan branch of the CPC. She was held first in Battleford and later at the Kingston Penitentiary. Annie Buller, Ida Corley, Margaret Miller, and Ella Gehl were charged with offences under the DOCR and imprisoned in the Women's Jail at Portage la Prairie, Manitoba. See Michelle McBride, "The Curious Case of Female Internees," *Enemies Within* (Toronto: University of Toronto Press, 2000), 163–64.
12. "Turtle Lake," Dorise Nielsen Papers, vol. 2, NAC. It is likely that Bob Paul saved the poetry he received from Nielsen and later gave it to her daughter Christine. The poem is undated, but, given Nielsen's schedule, the visit to Turtle Lake must have taken place in the autumn of 1942.
13. Nielsen to McNaughton, 17 October 1942, Violet McNaughton Papers, SAB.
14. *Debates*, 4 February 1943, 148–51.
15. *Canadian Tribune*, 26 December 1942.
16. Nielsen to Vockeroth, 8 February 1943, Heide Vockeroth Papers, NAC. In the same letter, Nielsen described Christine as worldly-wise and said that Mrs. Dixon's criticism was probably well founded.

17. Ibid.
18. Based on the Gallup poll cited in Robert Bothwell, Jan Drummond, and John English, *Canada 1940–1945* (Toronto: University of Toronto Press, 1987), 326.
19. Nielsen to Vockeroth, 8 February 1943, Heide Vockeroth Papers, NAC.
20. Ibid.
21. *Debates*, 4 February 1943.
22. *Toronto Star*, 5 February 1943.
23. Nielsen to Vockeroth, 8 February 1943, Heide Vockeroth Papers, NAC.
24. *Debates*, 1 July 1943, 4236.
25. Ibid., 4239.
26. Nielsen to McNaughton, 1 July 1943, Violet McNaughton Papers, SAB.
27. Ibid., 14 September 1943.
28. Nielsen to Vockeroth, "In the Chamber, Friday night" (March 1944?), Heide Vockeroth Papers, NAC.
29. The Kardashes and Virginia MacLeod were aware of some of the problems. Interviews.

CHAPTER NINE WORKING FOR A NEW WORLD

1. Dorise Nielsen, *Debates*, 4 May 1944, 2629.
2. Untitled poem, Dorise Nielsen Papers, vol. 2, NAC.
3. This was likely the occasion of Tim Buck's first visit to Spiritwood, when he was remembered by Nielsen's neighbour, Eline Morrow, as a man so persuasive "he could talk your arm off." Morrow, taped interview, SAB.
4. Avakumovic, *The Communist Party of Canada*, 152–53.
5. RCMP report on the Communist Party of Canada constituent convention, Toronto, 21–22 August 1943, CSIS, Dorise Nielsen, part 13, 1785, NAC.
6. *Ottawa Journal*, 23 August 1943, p. 6.
7. Nielsen to McNaughton, 14 September 1943, Violet McNaughton Papers, SAB.
8. Untitled poem, Dorise Nielsen Papers, vol. 2, NAC.
9. *Saturday Night* (28 November 1942): 12.
10. *Saturday Night* (7 November 1942): 26.
11. *North Battleford Optimist*, 21 October 1943.
12. Ibid., 25 November 1943.
13. *Canadian Tribune*, 1 January 1944; *Regina Leader-Post*, 6 December 1943.
14. *Canadian Tribune*, 29 January 1944, gives an account of Buck's speech to the National Committee of the LPP on 23 January 1944. In the United States, Communist Party leader Earl Browder went even further. He replaced the party with a political association allied to the Democratic Party.
15. The meeting took place on Friday, 21 January 1944. It is referred to in the *Canadian Tribune*, 22 January and 29 January.
16. RCMP report on meeting at Baron Byng High School, 21 January 1944, CSIS, Dorise Nielsen, part 14, 2238, 2240, NAC.

17. Nielsen to Vockeroth, "Friday evening" (March 1944?), Heide Vockeroth Papers, NAC.
18. Despite the declared openness of the new LPP, there were still secret factions of professional members in Montreal and Ottawa. According to Gordon Lunan, who was a member of a secret communist group when he lived in both cities, you only really knew the allegiance of those in your group. In other activities such as study clubs and campaigns, you might suspect someone's allegiance but you would never ask. Telephone interview by author, November 2004.
19. *Debates*, 31 January 1944, 50.
20. Extract from an RCMP report, 4 March 1944: "It seems the argument in the Federal House was over the speech from the throne.... Rose said that the amendment was too far advanced." CSIS, Dorise Nielsen, part 14, 2177, NAC.
21. RCMP on the National Plenum of the LPP, Toronto, 12–14 February 1944, CSIS, Dorise Nielsen, part 14, 2205, NAC.
22. Rose spoke first in reply to the Speech from the Throne, on the budget, on the Bank Act, and on a bill to set up the Department of Reconstruction. Of the two, he was the sole speaker on aviation policy, veterans' affairs, mutual aid to the Allies, and external affairs.
23. *Debates*, 2 February 1944, 122.
24. Ibid., 3 February 1944, 162.
25. Ibid., 14 February 1944, 467.
26. Merrily Weisbord, *The Strangest Dream* (Toronto: Lester and Orphen Dennys, 1983), 129–30.
27. *Regina Leader-Post*, 6 April 1944.
28. See *Debates*, 7 February 1944, 211–12, for Sinclair's speech and the *Ottawa Evening Citizen*, 8 February, for the reaction to it.
29. *Saturday Night* (18 March 1944): 2.
30. RCMP report on the LPP in Cape Breton, 16 March 1944, CSIS, Dorise Nielsen, part 14, 2166, NAC.
31. Foreword, *New Worlds for Women*, Communist Party of Canada papers, vol. 64 (National Archives of Canada MG28–IV4).
32. Agnes Macphail also spoke for equality in the labour force. See Terry Crowly, "Agnes Macphail and Canadian Working Women," *Labour/Le Travail* (Fall 1991).
33. *Debates*, 25 May 1943, 3024.
34. Ibid., 17 February 1944, 612.
35. Ibid., 16 March 1944, 1515.
36. Ibid., 14 July 1944, 4865–70.
37. *Regina Leader-Post*, 13 April 1944.
38. *Moose Jaw Times-Herald*, 14 April 1944.
39. RCMP reports, CSIS, Dorise Nielsen, part 14, 2127, 2134, NAC.
40. *Ottawa Evening Citizen*, 18 April 1944, p. 13.

41. *Debates*, 4 May 1944, 2629.
42. Ibid., 2630.

CHAPTER TEN VICTORY AND DEFEAT

1. Dorise Nielsen, *Debates*, December 1944, 6918.
2. Granastein, *Mackenzie King, His Life and World*, 180.
3. Ibid.
4. *Debates*, 1 August 1944, 5747–50.
5. Ibid., 5750.
6. Ibid., 17 July 1944, 4928.
7. *Globe and Mail*, 5 May 1944.
8. Norman Penner, *Canadian Communism: The Stalin Years and Beyond* (Toronto: Methuen Publishers, 1987), 201.
9. *Debates*, 8 May 1944, 2743.
10. Ibid., 10 July 1944, 4666.
11. Sally Nielsen, correspondence.
12. The possibility of such a trip is mentioned in Nielsen's CSIS file, part 14, 1994; in the *Canadian Tribune*, 13 January 1945; and in the *Globe and Mail*, 10 January 1945.
13. On 1 June 1945, Dorise wrote an open letter to Coldwell in which she cited his criticisms of her and refuted them. Coldwell Papers, vol. 34, file: Nielsen, NAC.
14. F.C. Williams to Coldwell, 5 January 1942, CCF Papers, SAB.
15. *North Battleford Optimist*, 2 November 1944.
16. Ibid., 21 September 1944.
17. *Ottawa Evening Citizen*, 23 November 1944.
18. This account of the second conscription crisis in the war is from J.L. Granatstein, *Canada's War, The Politics of the Mackenzie King Government 1939–1945* (Toronto: Oxford University Press, 1975), chapter 9.
19. *Debates*, 7 December 1944, 6918–22.
20. Ibid., 6922.
21. *Winnipeg Tribune*, 20 January 1945.
22. *Canadian Tribune*, 31 March 1945.
23. An RCMP report written 28 March 1945 states that McEwen's chances had been extremely good, but had recently experienced a blow as workers were being shipped out daily. CSIS, Dorise Nielsen, part 15, 2541, NAC.
24. *Winnipeg Tribune*, 4 April 1945.
25. RCMP report on Leslie Morris's address to an LPP meeting at the Chateau Laurier, Ottawa, 10 April 1945, CSIS, Dorise Nielsen, part 15, 2520, NAC.
26. Avakumovic, *The Communist Party in Canada*, 173–75.
27. Ibid., 155.
28. This ad was placed in the *Regina Leader-Post* by a citizens' group as part of a victory loan campaign, 14 April 1945.
29. *Canadian Tribune*, 2 April 1945, p. 13.

30. The broadcast was 15 May 1945 for fifteen minutes. *Canadian Tribune*, 5 May 1945.
31. *Debates*, 21 March 1945, 97.
32. Ibid., 22 March 1945, 142.
33. Nielsen had never said Canada would be better off under Hitler, but, when heckled with the question from Paul Martin, "Do you think you'd be better off under Hitler?" she had answered, "I don't know."
34. *Debates*, 23 March 1945, 173-74.
35. Avakumovic, *The Communist Party in Canada*, 156.
36. Stewart Paul, interview.
37. Carter's novel, *Night of Flames* (1942), went into a second printing in the United States. Once he revealed his allegiance to the communists in 1946, his ability to make a living from fiction and journalism in North America suffered, but his novel *Fatherless Sons* (1955), set in Cold War Canada, became popular in the Soviet Union. See James Doyle, "Science, Literature, and Revolution, the life and Writings of Dyson Carter," *Left History* (Fall 1999).
38. *Canadian Tribune*, 2 June 1945.
39. The full letter was published in the *Canadian Tribune*, but the letter itself did not reach Coldwell until after the election, which he took as further evidence of Mrs. Nielsen's perfidy. Letter dated 1 June 1945, Coldwell Papers, vol. 34, file: Nielsen, NAC.
40. Shackelton, *Tommy Douglas*, 128.
41. In interviews with the author, both Stewart Paul and Norman Penner remembered Nielsen's desire to stay in the West. Interviews.

CHAPTER ELEVEN SPIES

1. Life outline, 1968, Dorise Nielsen Papers, vol. 2, NAC.
2. RCMP report on the LPP national conference in Toronto, 10–15 August 1945, CSIS, Dorise Nielsen, part 15, 2484–85, NAC.
3. Virginia MacLeod, interview.
4. Sally Nielsen, correspondence.
5. *Globe and Mail*, 7 February 1946.
6. Until 1968 divorce law in most provinces (except Newfoundland and Quebec, where there was no divorce law at all) allowed men to divorce their wives on the grounds of adultery, and women to divorce their husbands on the grounds of adultery coupled with cruelty or desertion. In either case, one party had to prove the other guilty.
7. *National Affairs Monthly* (January 1946); *Canadian Tribune*, 5 January 1946.
8. Kathleen Repka, interview by author in Ottawa, June 1989: "Dorise was concerned about real things—the lack of doctors—not so concerned about theory." Kathleen worked with Dorise in the party's national office from 1946 to 1948. She lived with Dorise for several months in 1946.
9. Christine went to live with Edna Blois (later Ryerson), who was a member of the Toronto School Board. At some point, either during the housing tour or later, Sally lived with Mary Jennison, who worked for a community centre in Hamilton.

10. Reg Whitaker and Gary Marcuse, *Cold War Canada, The Making of a National Insecurity State 1945–1957* (Toronto: University of Toronto Press, 1994), 56.
11. Wong, taped interview, SAB.
12. Information on the Gouzenko spy scandal is from Whitaker and Marcuse, *Cold War Canada*; Merrily Weisbord, *The Strangest Dream* (Toronto: Lester and Orpen Dennys, 1983); Gordon Lunan, *The Making of a Spy* (Montreal: Robert Davies Publishing, 1995); and Amy Knight, *How the Cold War Began, the Gouzenko Affair and the Hunt for Soviet Spies* (Toronto: McClelland and Stewart, 2005).
13. *Vancouver Province*, 22 February 1946.
14. Life outline, 1968, Dorise Nielsen papers, vol. 2, NAC: "I knew them all but was not involved." This may have been an exaggeration. Gordon Lunan, one of those charged, worked in Ottawa during the final years of the war, but he never met Nielsen. However, during his interrogation by the RCMP, Edward Mazerall, one of those charged and convicted, said he heard Fred Rose and Dorise Nielsen speak at a meeting in Agatha Chapman's apartment (CSIS file of Agatha Chapman, 81, National Archives of Canada RG146, vol. 1229).
15. Weisbord, *The Strangest Dream*, 91. Some of the accused in the Gouzenko spy scandal were members of a secret communist branch that originated in Montreal with Fred Rose as organizer and Stanley Ryerson as mentor. The group had included Norman Bethune and other middle-class professionals the party had relied on earlier to lead various popular front organizations such as the Civil Liberties Union and the Committee to Aid Spanish Democracy.
16. *Vancouver Province*, 22 February 1946.
17. Lewis, *The Life of Grace MacInnis*, 134, describes a dinner party in the winter of 1939. The hosts were Angus and Grace MacInnis. The guests were Sophie and David Lewis, Islay Johnston (Department of Agriculture), Kathleen Willsher, Bob Inch (Secretary of the League of Nations), Jack Pickersgill (secretary to Mackenzie King), and Muriel Kerr, the teacher with whom Dorise and her children stayed on their arrival in Ottawa in May 1940.
18. *Canadian Tribune*, 16 March 1946.
19. On 7 June 1946, the *Globe and Mail* said there was speculation that Carr's failure to respond to a subpoena meant he had fled to Russia. In fact, he was in the United States, where he was arrested in 1949, tried in Canada for conspiracy to obtain a false passport, and sentenced to six years (Whitaker and Marcuse, *Cold War Canada*, 432).
20. *Regina Leader-Post*, 16 March 1946.
21. *Globe and Mail*, 21 February 1946.
22. Ibid., 19 March 1946.
23. It seems that Boyer knew that C.D. Howe, Canada's minister of munitions and supply, was ready to give the process to the Russians but was prevented from doing so by the Americans. During his interrogation, Boyer willingly told the whole story, thinking his explanation would clear up any misunderstandings. In fact, his testimony was the basis of the case against Rose and himself (Whitaker and Marcuse, *Cold War Canada*, 72–73).

24. *Globe and Mail*, 3 June 1946.
25. Ibid., 13 June 1946.
26. These figures are from Whitaker and Marcuse, *Cold War Canada*, 432. They do not include Alan Nunn May, a British physicist who had been working in Canada but who was charged and convicted in Great Britain.
27. Ibid., 66.
28. As quoted in ibid., 69.
29. This analysis is taken from Stewart Smith, *Comrades and Komsomolkas* (Toronto: Lagus, 1993), 194. Smith was one of the LPP's central figures in the 1930s and the 1940s.
30. LPP National Training School, Program of Studies, June 7–Sept. 1, 1946, Communist Party of Canada, vol. 2, file 12, National Archives of Canada MG28–1V4.
31. Danielle Dionne to Sally Nielsen, 11 February 1986, Sally Nielsen private papers.
32. Ibid.
33. Stewart Paul, interview.
34. Sally Nielsen, interview.
35. Operation Muskox, which involved the Canadian army and air force and observers from both the US and Great Britain, took place from February to May 1946. During the exercise, a dozen snowmobiles made their way over 5000 kilometres of Arctic terrain, making an arc from Churchill to Edmonton. Meteorological stations and airstrips were constructed in advance. Nielsen first mentioned her encounter with the American colonel in Montreal, 17 May 1946. She repeated it on her next western tour in November and December that year. See CSIS, Dorise Nielsen, part 16, 2650–51, and part 17, 2865, NAC.
36. *Winnipeg Free Press*, 5 June 1947.
37. The upsurge of protest against rising prices was, at first, spontaneous, but soon members of both the CCF and the Communist Party sought to direct it. It is described as the most militant action by women in Canada since the suffrage campaign. See Julie Guard, "Canadian Citizens or Dangerous Foreign Women? Canada's Radical Consumer Movement, 1947–1950," in *Sisters or Strangers*, ed. Marlene Epp, Franca Iacovetta, and Frances Swyripa (Toronto: University of Toronto Press, 2004), 161–189; and Dan Azoulay, "'Ruthless in a lady-like way': CCF Women Confront the Post-War 'Communist Menace," *Ontario History* (March 1997): 23–51.
38. Guard, "Canadian Citizens or Dangerous Foreign Women?"
39. The exact dates of Paul's employment were sought by the RCMP in 1950 when surveillance of communists and their activities seems to have increased. CSIS, Dorise Nielsen, part 21, 3233, NAC.
40. Presumably the LPP no longer needed a National Legislative Secretary because after Rose's arrest it had no members elected to Parliament. At this point, Bill Kardash was still an MLA in Manitoba, and Joe Salsberg and A.A. MacLeod sat in the Ontario legislature.
41. Nielsen to Harvey, 30 August 1964, Louise Harvey Papers, NAC.
42. Irja Paul, telephone interview by author, April 2004.

CHAPTER TWELVE WOMEN AND PEACE

1. Friedrich Engels, *The Origin of the Family, Private Property and the State* (New York: International Publishers, 1942), 65. Christine Wong private papers.
2. CSIS, Dorise Nielsen, part 10, 1433 and 1436; and part 14, 2171, NAC. The meetings referred to here took place in Saskatchewan in 1941 and in Montreal in 1944. They are not the only examples of references to the number of women at her meetings.
3. Joan Sangster, *Dreams of Equality: Women on the Canadian Left 1920–50* (Toronto: McClelland and Stewart, 1989), 252. Ruth Frager, *Sweatshop Strife, Class, Ethnicity, and Gender in the Jewish Labour Movement of Toronto 1900–1939* (Toronto: University of Toronto Press, 1992).
4. *National Affairs Monthly* (March 1949).
5. RCMP report on LPP Fourth National convention, 25–28 January 1952, CSIS, Dorise Nielsen, part 23, 3797, NAC: "The address of Dorise Nielsen was not political. She criticized the party members for the way female members were being treated as unequal to men in the party ranks. She called on the convention to see that this sectarianism be corrected."
6. Kay (Sheldon) Repka, interview by author in Ottawa, June 1988. Kay had attended the University of Alberta on scholarship in the 1930s. One of her professors, Malcolm Ross, introduced her to Marxism. She joined the party in Ottawa during the war.
7. It is probable that many of the women in the party and its related organizations also put class and ethnic issues before gender issues. See Frager, *Sweatshop Strife,* chapters 2 and 7. Also, Sangster, *Dreams of Equality*, chapter 6.
8. Edna Ryerson, telephone interview, December 1988.
9. Sangster, *Dreams of Equality*, 182.
10. See Ruth Roach Pierson, *'They're Still Women After All', Canadian Women and World War II* (Toronto: McClelland and Stewart, 1986).
11. Sally Nielsen, interview. Johnny did play hockey for several seasons.
12. Christine Wong, taped interview.
13. Kay (Sheldon) Repka, interview.
14. Sally Nielsen, interview.
15. *Winnipeg Free Press*, 25 June 1948.
16. Austin Cross, "Women—The All-Time Flop in Politics," *National Home Monthly* (August 1948).
17. *Canadian Tribune*, 11 September 1948.
18. Marcuse and Whitaker, *Cold War Canada*, 292. The story was carried by the *Toronto Daily Star*, 25 July 1947. Nielsen's daughter Sally had stayed with Mary Jennison for several months in 1946.
19. *Canadian Tribune*, 4 October 1948, p. 11.
20. *Daily Worker* (New York), 3 April 1946.

21. Dorise's name is not mentioned in an article on the founding of the CCW published in the *Canadian Tribune*, 8 February 1947. It is likely that she worked behind the scenes to set up the organization. She told a Marxist journal that she had been involved in founding the CCW. See the *Canadian Revolutionary Patriot*, 20 December 1980 (published in Guelph, Ontario).
22. *Canadian Tribune*, 11 October and 20 December 1948.
23. Sally Nielsen remembers receiving the traditional one-pound note from her grandmother for her birthday the summer of 1940 in Ottawa, and being told by Dorise that it would be the last one.
24. Nielsen to Harvey, 2 April 1975, Louise Harvey Papers, NAC.
25. Nielsen to Wong, undated (1957), Christine Wong Papers, vol. 1, NAC. Dorise had just spent a year in England and was about to leave when she wrote: "Do not send my brother my address please. Will explain later."
26. Stephen Endicott, "The People's World of 1948," in *Walden 3* (Ontario: Masterpress, 1984), 65.
27. Dorise Nielsen, *80 Million Speak for Peace*, Communist Party of Canada Papers, vol. 66, 19, National Archives of Canada (NAC), MG28–IV429.
28. *Canadian Tribune*, 25 May and 16 May 1949.
29. *Ottawa Journal*, 25 February 1949.
30. For accounts of these meetings, see CSIS, Dorise Nielsen, parts 18 and 19, NAC.
31. RCMP report on meeting in Moose Jaw, 7 April 1949, CSIS, Dorise Nielsen, part 19, 2970, NAC.
32. Whitaker and Marcuse, *Cold War Canada*, 366.
33. Sally to Dorise, 25 November 1966, Sally Nielsen private papers.
34. Dorise to Sally, 5 January 1967, Sally Nielsen Papers, NAC.
35. *Canadian Tribune*, 6 May 1949. The party ran candidates in all provinces except the Maritimes. There were seven in Ontario.
36. Dorise Nielsen to provincial leaders, 19 May 1949, Communist Party of Canada Papers, vol. 2, NAC.
37. *Canadian Tribune*, 26 September 1949, p. 11.
38. Ibid., 3 April 1950. Dorise was responding to an article by Kate Aiken in the *Montreal Standard*, 25 March 1950.
39. Evan Wong, telephone interview by author, July 2004.
40. Ibid.
41. RCMP report on a meeting in Ottawa, 5 October 1949, CSIS, Dorise Nielsen, part 20, 3080–81, NAC. Endicott told the story of the delay.
42. *Canadian Tribune*, 26 December 1949, p. 3.
43. Dorise's daughters remember this conference as being one of the highlights of her career, and her particular delight in meeting Dolores Ibarruri. Accounts of the conference, some of them written by Dorise, were carried in the *Canadian Tribune*, 21 November, and 12 and 26 December 1949. On 9 January 1950, Dorise wrote about the building of apartment blocks in Warsaw, contrasting it with the shortage of low-rental housing in Montreal.

44. Eric Hobsbawm, *The Age of Extremes* (London: Abacus, 1995), 400.
45. Christine Wong, taped interview, SAB.
46. Dorise to Sally, 20 September 1966, Sally Nielsen Papers, NAC.
47. Evan Wong, telephone interview. "I don't know what he saw. It wasn't a portrait of Stalin."
48. Sally Nielsen, interview.

CHAPTER THIRTEEN FEAR AND DISCONTENT

1. *Regina Leader-Post*, 10 November 1950.
2. The CSFS replaced an earlier organization with a similar title that had formed during World War II with widespread Canadian support.
3. One of these cuts was Roland Penner, a young organizer in Winnipeg. Roland Penner, interview by author, April 2005.
4. RCMP report on a meeting at the Hebrew Sick Benefit Hall, Winnipeg, 4 December 1950, CSIS, Dorise Nielsen, part 23, 3867, NAC.
5. *Saskatoon Star-Phoenix*, 9 November 1950.
6. Press clippings taken from the *Brandon Daily Sun*, 6 December 1950, CSIS, Dorise Nielsen, part 22, 3512, NAC. Dyson Carter reported on the same meeting in "General Report on Society, June 20th, 1951," from Canadian-Soviet Friendship Society files held at the State Archives of the Russian Federation, available at the Centre for Research on Canadian-Russian Relations (CRCR), Carleton University.
7. *News Facts*, January 1950 and September 1956, National Library of Canada.
8. "Dear reader," 12 December 1951, CSFS, file 36, CRCR.
9. Report on organization, 26 January 1952, CSFS, file 36, CRCR.
10. RCMP extracts from the *Pacific Tribune* and the *Canadian Tribune* on the national convention of the CSFS, Massey Hall, 25–27 January 1952, CSIS, Dorise Nielsen, part 24, 3923–24, and 3927–28, NAC.
11. Sally Nielsen, correspondence.
12. Whitaker and Marcuse, *Cold War Canada*, 200. The cabinet considered amending the criminal code to include seditious conspiracy so that merely belonging to a certain organization could make an individual guilty of conspiracy.
13. RCMP reports on the fourth national convention of the LPP, Toronto, 25–28 January 1951, CSIS, Dorise Nielsen, part 23, 3795, 3806, NAC.
14. Whittaker and Marcuse, *Cold War Canada*, 214.
15. RCMP report on the thirtieth anniversary of the Communist Party of Canada, Massey Hall, 24 February 1952, CSIS, Dorise Nielsen, part 24, 3911, NAC. Becky Buhay spoke on the party's history.
16. Nielsen to Harvey, 21 November 1958, Louise Harvey Papers, NAC.
17. Norman Penner, telephone interview by author, May 1988.
18. William Kashtan, telephone interview by author, August 1988.
19. Kay Repka, interview.

20. Clippings from the *Canadian Tribune* on course offerings for the summer, 1950, 1951, CSIS, Dorise Nielsen, part 32, 3704 and 3738, NAC.
21. Sally Nielsen, correspondence.
22. RCMP extract from *London Free Press*, 24 February 1953, CSIS, Dorise Nielsen, part 26, 4186, NAC.
23. RCMP report on meeting at Massey Hall, 24 February 1953, CSIS, Dorise Nielsen, part 26, 4178–89, NAC.
24. Sally Nielsen, interview.
25. Nielsen to Vockeroth, 2 June 1954, Heide Vockeroth Papers, NAC.
26. Nielsen to Wong, 16 July 1969, Christine Wong Papers, vol. 1, NAC.
27. Nielsen to Vockeroth, 2 June 1954, Heide Vockeroth Papers, NAC.
28. Information about Constant Godefroy and impressions of him are from Muriel Godefroy (daughter-in-law), telephone interview, January 2003; Hugh Godefroy (grandson), telephone interview, January 2003; and Isabel Hodge (granddaughter), correspondence, May 2005. Con was born in 1886, retired from Indonesia in 1934, and died in Holland in the 1970s.
29. Nielsen to Harvey, 30 February 1959, Louise Harvey Papers, NAC.
30. Avakumovic, *The Communist Party in Canada*, 207.
31. Nielsen to Harvey, 9 February 1956, Louise Harvey Papers, NAC.
32. Ibid.
33. Nielsen to Wong, undated (March 1956?), Christine Wong Papers, vol. 1, NAC.
34. Life outline, 1968, Dorise Nielsen Papers, vol. 2, NAC.
35. Penner, *Canadian Communism, The Stalinist Years*, 237–49. This is an insider's view of what happened in the Canadian party. Penner was one of the "rebels" on the National Executive Council.
36. Sally Nielsen, correspondence.
37. When she left for China in 1957, Dorise continued to pay dues to the Canadian party. For three years she wrote a series of round-robin letters to party friends in Toronto and Montreal. William Kashtan (interview) said that she was not involved in 1956–57, but while in Canada she was always very loyal to the party.
38. Norman Penner, telephone interview. It was Penner whom Bob Paul tried to persuade to stay.

Chapter Fourteen Gung Ho

1. Nielsen, round-robin letter, 5 October 1957, Louise Harvey Papers, NAC.
2. Ibid., 22 December 1958.
3. After the Japanese invasion in 1937, Rewi Alley had joined a group of Chinese and foreigners in setting up cooperatives to employ refugees in China's western provinces. These co-ops were known as Gung Ho, an abbreviation of their full Chinese title. The term entered English usage after 1942 when an article on the co-ops was published in the *Saturday Evening Post*.
4. Tang Sheng, interview by author, Beijing, March 2003.

5. For descriptions of Dorise's environment in China, I have used not only her own letters, but also an anthology of first-person accounts of living in China (as foreigners) from 1949 to 1979, *Living in China* (Beijing: New World Press, 1982).
6. Nielsen, round-robin letter, 5 October 1957, Louise Harvey Papers, NAC.
7. It is estimated that approximately two million people died from 1949 to 1952, some of them landlords executed during land reform. The later collectivization occurred rapidly and with little resistance, since the old landowning class had already been eliminated. Maurice Meisner, *Mao's China and After* (New York: Simon and Schuster, 1986), 80.
8. Ibid., 169–80.
9. Nielsen, round-robin letter, 12 March 1958, Louise Harvey Papers, NAC.
10. Ibid., 18 April 1958.
11. Ibid.
12. Some speculate that the Hundred Flowers campaign was Mao's deliberate method of smoking out dissidents. Others think he did not expect such vehement criticism of the system and was not prepared to accept it. Meisner, *Mao's China and After*, 198.
13. Nielsen, round-robin letter, 20 February 1958, Louise Harvey Papers, NAC.
14. By the autumn of 1958, Sydney Gordon, another Canadian communist, had come to Beijing to research a biography of Norman Bethune. He stayed on to report for the *Canadian Tribune* and was succeeded in 1960 by Bert Whyte.
15. Nielsen, round-robin letter, 6 May 1958, Louise Harvey Papers, NAC.
16. Ibid., 13 May 1958. George Hatem was most often called by his shortened Chinese name, George Ma.
17. Ibid., 21 November 1958. Dorise had met Anna Louise when she'd come to speak in Toronto and Ottawa during the war, but Anna did not remember her. "She talked steadily to me for a whole hour without pausing for breath, and then complained that she simply hadn't begun to get anything out of me, which is so typical of her I had to laugh, and promise to go in and spend an afternoon with her sometime soon. (God give me strength!)"
18. Isabel Crook, interview by author in Beijing, March 2003.
19. Nielsen to Harvey, undated, spring, 1958, beginning: "My dear Louise, Your lovely long letter, link with a land I still love, was so very welcome." Louise Harvey Papers, NAC.
20. Isabel and David Crook, from *Living in China*, 459.
21. Nielsen, round-robin letter, 22 December 1958, Louise Harvey Papers, NAC.
22. Ibid.
23. Nielsen to Harvey, 21 November 1958, Louise Harvey Papers, NAC.
24. Ibid., 6 November 1959. Nielsen attributed the quotation to Robert Louis Stevenson.
25. Nielsen to Vockeroth, 16 July 1964, Heide Vockeroth Papers, NAC.
26. Sidney Rittenberg and Amanda Bennett, *The Man Who Stayed Behind* (New York: Simon and Schuster, 1993), 206.
27. Nielsen, round-robin letter, 2 October 1959, Louise Harvey Papers, NAC.

28. Nielsen to Harvey, 6 November 1959, Louise Harvey Papers, NAC.
29. Sally Nielsen, correspondence.
30. Nielsen to Harvey, undated (January 1961?), Louise Harvey Papers, NAC.
31. Sally Nielsen, correspondence.
32. Nielsen to Harvey, undated (January 1961?), Louise Harvey Papers, NAC.
33. Nielsen, round-robin letter, 22 January 1961, Louise Harvey Papers, NAC.
34. Sally Nielsen, correspondence.
35. Glen McClaren, correspondence with author, July 2005.

CHAPTER FIFTEEN ALONE

1. Nielsen to Harvey, 28 November 1962, Louise Harvey Papers, NAC.
2. Floyd Williston, interview by author, June 2002.
3. Sally Nielsen, correspondence.
4. Nielsen to Leslie Morris, 29 March 1962, Dorise Nielsen Papers, vol. 2, NAC.
5. Sally Nielsen (correspondence) believes that her mother was influenced by the expulsion from China of two foreigners who had been openly pro-Soviet.
6. Monica Whyte, telephone interview by author, May 2004.
7. Nielsen to Harvey, 17 May 1962, Louise Harvey Papers, NAC.
8. Sally objected. She did not want to lose her Canadian citizenship.
9. Application for citizenship, 7 June 1962, Dorise Nielsen Papers, vol. 2, NAC.
10. Nielsen to Morris, 29 March 1962, Dorise Nielsen Papers, vol. 2, NAC.
11. Nielsen to Harvey, 28 November 1962, Louise Harvey Papers, NAC.
12. Ibid., 14 May 1963.
13. Ibid., 17 May 1962.
14. Sally Nielsen (correspondence) confirmed that Con did take an interest in other women after his separation from Dorise, although Sally's portrait of Con is much more sympathetic than Dorise was in her letter to Leslie Morris. He was a lonely old man, she said, not a womanizer.
15. Tracy B. Strong and Helene Keyssar, *Right in Her Soul, The Life of Anna Louise Strong* (New York: Random House, 1983).
16. Life outline, 1968, Dorise Nielsen Papers, vol. 2, NAC.
17. Isabel Crook, interview by author in Beijing, March 2003.
18. Ralph Shellrude to Christine Wong, 28 September 1964, Christine Wong Papers, vol. 6, NAC.
19. Nielsen to Harvey, 28 November 1962, Louise Harvey Papers, NAC.
20. Ibid., 30 August 1964.
21. Ibid.
22. Ibid., 30 May 1966.
23. Ibid., 28 November 1962.
24. Harvey to Nielsen, 11 December 1962, Louise Harvey Papers, NAC.
25. She was also in touch with a group in Guelph, Ontario, that put out a paper called the *Canadian Revolutionary Patriot*. Her correspondence with the group was noted in an article printed after her death, December 1980.

26. Betty Chandler, interview by author in Beijing, March 2003.
27. Ibid.
28. Nielsen to Vockeroth, 15 February 1965, Heide Vockeroth Papers, NAC.
29. Ibid. "I never had any use for that chap. He is where he belongs right now, I imagine."
30. Nielsen to Harvey, undated (August 1964?), Louise Harvey Papers, NAC.
31. Ibid., 30 August 1964.
32. Nielsen to Vockeroth, 15 February 1965, Heide Vockeroth Papers, NAC.
33. Nielsen to Harvey, 30 May 1966, Louise Harvey Papers, NAC.

CHAPTER SIXTEEN REVOLUTION

1. Nielsen to Harvey, 17 February 1965, Louise Harvey Papers, NAC.
2. Denise Lebreton, *Living in China*, 114.
3. David and Nancy Milton, *The Wind Will Not Subside* (New York: Pantheon, 1976), 214. Americans Nancy and David Milton worked for the Institute of Foreign Languages from 1964 to 1969 and lived at the You Yi part of that time.
4. Nielsen to Harvey, 18 September 1966, Louise Harvey Papers, NAC.
5. Rittenberg, *The Man Who Stayed Behind*, 262. Rittenberg describes the isolation of the foreigners living at the You Yi. He says the Chinese party assigned him the task of keeping the remaining foreigners onside, after the Soviets left.
6. Dorise to Sally Nielsen, 4 March 1967, Thelma (Sally) Nielsen Papers, NAC, MG32–G10.
7. In 1968 Nielsen composed a list of all the study groups and members involved in Yenan-Bethune, Dorise Nielsen Papers, vol. 2, NAC.
8. Nielsen to Harvey, 24 April 1967, Louise Harvey Papers, NAC.
9. Lebreton, *Living in China*, 118.
10. Nielsen to Harvey, 24 June 1968, Louise Harvey Papers, NAC.
11. Nadezda Mandelstam, *Hope Against Hope* (New York: Atheneum, 1976), 26.
12. Milton, *The Wind Shall Not Subside*, 351.
13. Nielsen to Fong Huan, 23 March 1973, Dorise Nielsen Papers, vol. 2, NAC.
14. Nielsen to Wong, 24 February 1969, Christine Wong Papers, vol. 1, NAC. Other accounts say the same. The exodus to the countryside was amazingly well organized, considering the numbers of people involved.
15. According to Jan Wong's *Red China Blues* (Toronto: Doubleday, 1996), 157, there were a dozen deaths at the FLP.
16. Betty Chandler, interview by author in Beijing, March 2003.
17. Nielsen to Harvey, 16 April 1969, Louise Harvey Papers, NAC.
18. Both Yu Fanqin and Tang Sheng, who served as interpreters to Nielsen in the period, mentioned her confusion and her fear about whether she would have to go to the countryside. Interviews by author in Beijing, March 2003.
19. Rashid Butt, in *Living in China*, 146.
20. Lebreton, in *Living in China*, 120.

21. Yu Fanqin, interview. During Dorise's long illness in 1965, Yu Fanqin had accompanied her to the hospital. Later, she remembered, Dorise was so appalled at the rudeness of a man sent to her from the FLP that she said, "Don't ever send that man again." Yu Fanqin became her liaison with the FLP from then until Nielsen's death in 1980.
22. Neither the 1891 nor the 1901 census shows a Roland in the Webber household. Before writing the memoir, Nielsen mentioned in a letter to Sally that she had two cousins who died in 1915. It seems she decided to change one of them to a brother, to emphasize the devastating effect of the war on her family. Dorise to Sally, 5 January 1967, Sally Nielsen Papers, NAC.
23. Anne-Marie Brady, *Friend of China—The Myth of Rewi Alley* (London: Routledge Curzon, 2003), 115.
24. Canada established diplomatic relations with China in 1970. With the Americans, negotiations dragged on until 1979.
25. Nielsen to Harvey, 4 April 1972, Louise Harvey Papers, NAC.
26. Ibid., 27 September 1972.
27. Ibid., 24 October 1973.
28. Isabel Crook, interview.

CHAPTER SEVENTEEN COMING HOME

1. Nielsen to Harvey, 18 July 1974, Louise Harvey Papers, NAC.
2. Dorise to Sally, 18 March 1974, Sally Nielsen Papers, NAC.
3. Most of the details of Nielsen's stay in Toronto are from later letters to Christine Wong and Sally Nielsen (both in the NAC).
4. Dorise to Sally, 11 January 1966, Sally Nielsen Papers, NAC. Dorise referred to Hazel Wigdor, Margaret Fairley, and Kay Repka.
5. Nielsen to Wong, 17 July 1967, Christine Wong Papers, NAC.
6. Ibid.
7. Ibid.
8. Paul Crook, correspondence, June 2002: "I recall visiting her and Con in their flat opposite ours when I was a small child in the fifties, when she seemed quite a kindly lady while Con was a little frightening.... I don't remember seeing much of her after she left the campus until the Cultural Revolution. She seemed pleasant but remote initially, but after my father was arrested ... she always made a point of looking the other way when I walked or cycled by."
9. Tang Sheng and Yu Fanqin, interviews.
10. An exception to this occurred on Dorise's trip to Toronto, when she gave her three grandsons there watches, leaving out the youngest (the ice-cream-eater), whom she thought badly behaved and undeserving. Sally Nielsen, interview.
11. Vivienne Nielsen (John's widow), telephone interview by author, May 2004.
12. Sandy Nicholson had been an MP (CCF) for Mackenzie, a constituency in northeastern Saskatchewan, when Dorise was in Parliament, and had visited her in China.

13. Bob Vockeroth, telephone interview.
14. Jennifer Wong, correspondence, November 2002.
15. Betty Friedan (Goldstein) was a journalist in the left-wing press from 1943 to 1952. She attended the founding meeting of the Congress of American Women in 1946 (so did Dorise) and she wrote articles on women for the United Electrical Workers' newsletter. See Daniel Horowitz, *Betty Friedan and the Making of the Feminine Mystique, The American Left, The Cold War, and Modern Feminism* (Amherst: University of Massachusetts Press, 1998).
16. Nielsen to Wong, 8 January and 8 February 1975, Christine Wong Papers, NAC.
17. Han Suyin, *Eldest Son* (New York: Hill & Wang, 1994).
18. Nielsen to Wong, 7 February 1976, Christine Wong Papers, vol. 1, NAC.
19. Ibid., 23 April 1976.
20. Ibid., undated. The long description of the earthquake and its aftermath was likely composed in August 1976.
21. Ibid., 2 December 1976.
22. Ibid., 8 February 1975.
23. Ibid., 22 February 1976.
24. Ibid., 9 May 1977.
25. Dorise to Sally, 26 March and 6 October 1967, Sally Nielsen Papers, NAC.
26. Nielsen to Wong, 21 November 1975, Christine Wong Papers, vol. 1, NAC.
27. Ibid., 2 December 1976.
28. Christine sat down with each of her grown children at this time and told them that they had a sister, Noelle. Jennifer Wong, correspondence.
29. Nielsen to Wong, 7 February 1976, Christine Wong Papers, vol. 1, NAC.
30. Nielsen to Harvey, 6 June 1977, Louise Harvey Papers, NAC.
31. Nielsen to Wong, 10 September 1977, Christine Wong Papers, vol. 1, NAC.
32. Doug Nielsen, telephone interview by author, May 2004.
33. Vivienne Nielsen, telephone interview.
34. Nielsen to Wong, 25 June 1980, Christine Wong papers, vol. 1, NAC. Vivienne Nielsen also remembered the incident.
35. Judy Nielsen, telephone interview by author, May 2004.
36. Nielsen to Wong, "Home Sweet Home" (December 1977?), Christine Wong Papers, vol. 1, NAC.
37. Ibid., 16 December 1977.
38. Ibid.

Chapter Eighteen The Last Act

1. Nielsen to Wong, 30 May 1980, Christine Wong Papers, vol. 1, NAC.
2. Hepatitis B becomes chronic in a small percentage of adults affected. Once the disease becomes chronic, it will lead to death from either cirrhosis or liver cancer in 15 to 25 percent of cases.
3. Nielsen to Harvey, 2 August 1979, Louise Harvey Papers, NAC.

4. Christine Wong, interview by author in Ottawa, 1986.
5. Nielsen to Wong, 5 March 1980, Christine Wong papers, vol. 1, NAC.
6. Ibid., 17 October 1979.
7. Nielsen to Harvey, 17 October 1979, Louise Harvey Papers, NAC.
8. Nielsen to Wong, 29 November 1979, Christine Wong Papers, vol. 1, NAC.
9. Ibid., 30 May 1980.
10. Ibid., 11 June 1980.
11. Ibid., undated (June 1980).
12. Ibid., a scrawled note, dated "I don't know."
13. Xiao Yu to Wong, 14 August 1980, Christine Wong Papers, vol. 1, NAC.
14. Nielsen to Wong, 20 May 1980, Christine Wong Papers, vol. 1, NAC.
15. Ibid., "end of August" (1980).
16. Ibid. Nielsen even drafted a letter Christine could send all her children, telling them she would be unavailable for the next few months. In a scrawled postscript, she added, "If Evan won't go, why not go alone?"
17. Basil Wong to Christine Wong, 28 August 1980, Christine Wong Papers, vol. 1, NAC.
18. Nielsen to Christine Wong, 19 September 1980, Christine Wong Papers, vol. 1, NAC.
19. Gao to Christine Wong, undated, Christine Wong Papers, vol. 1, NAC.
20. Xiao Yu to Christine Wong, 28 November 1980, Christine Wong Papers, vol. 1, NAC.

EPILOGUE

1. Wong to Barbara et al., 26 January 1981. Christine Wong Papers, vol. 1, NAC. Christine gave a full account of her experience and thoughts in a letter to friends.
2. Ibid.
3. Both Luo Jun's speech and Christine's are in Christine Wong Papers, vol. 1, NAC.
4. The letters of condolence mentioned here are from Mary MacIssac, Stan Gratton, "Steve" (Mrs. Stevenson), Juning Wang, and Heide Vockeroth. Christine Wong Papers, vol. 1, NAC.

BIBLIOGRAPHY

ARCHIVAL SOURCES

Centre for Research on Canadian-Russian Relations
The Canadian-Soviet Friendship Society, 1950–54 (copies of files held at the State Archives of the Russian Federation)

National Archives of Canada
M.J. Coldwell Papers MG27 111 C12
Comintern Fonds MG10 K3 K219, K292
Communist Party of Canada MG28 1V4
vol. 2, 64, 66
Louise Harvey Papers MG32 G18
W.L. Mackenzie King Papers MG26 J (diary on-line)
A.M. Nicholson Papers MG27 111 C26
Dorise Nielsen Papers MG27 111 C30
Thelma (Sally) Nielsen Papers MG32 G10
Records of the Canadian Security Intelligence Agency RG 146
vol. 1229 Agatha Chapman
vol. 1094–95, A.A. MacLeod
vol. 1039–41, Dorise Nielsen
vol. 3473 Dorise Nielsen Club
Heide Vockeroth Papers MG32 F7
Christine Wong Papers MG32 G11

Provincial Archives of Ontario
A.A. MacLeod Papers mu7592

Saskatchewan Archives Board
CCF Papers, M.J. Coldwell, correspondence B711 237
Communist Party (1936–39) B711 48
Meadow Lake (1934–36) B71V 60
Meadow Lake (1937–41) B71V 61
North Battleford (1931–36) B7111 41
North Battleford (1938–40) B7111 42
Provincial Council (1937–39) B711 236
Violet McNaughton Papers A1 D53
Eline Morrow, interview taped by Georgina Taylor (July 1981) R8142–3
Christine (Nielsen) Wong, interview taped by Georgina Taylor (July 1987) R1255–62

Private Collections
Sally Nielsen
Elizabeth Smillie
Christine Wong

PUBLISHED SOURCES

Abella, Irving. *Nationalism, Communism and Canadian Labour*. Toronto: University of Toronto Press, 1973.

Archer, John. *Saskatchewan: A History*. Saskatoon: Western Producer Prairie Books, 1980.

Avakumovic, Ivan. *The Communist Party in Canada, A History*. Toronto: McClelland and Stewart, 1975.

____. "The Communist Party of Canada and the Prairie Farmer: The Interwar Years." In *Western Perspectives, Papers of the Western Canadian Studies Conference, 1973*, ed. D.J. Bercuson. Toronto: Holt, Rinehart and Winston, 1974.

Azoulay, Dan. "'Ruthless in a lady-like way': CCF Women Confront the Post-War Communist Menace." *Ontario History* (March 1997): 22–51.

Black, J.L. *Canada in the Soviet Mirror*. Ottawa: Carleton University Press, 1998.

Black, Martha. *My Seventy Years*. London: Nelson, 1938.

Bothwell, Robert, and J.L. Granatstein, eds. *The Gouzenko Transcripts*. Ottawa: Deneau, 1982.

____. Jan Drummond, and John English. *Canada 1940–1945*. Toronto: University of Toronto Press, 1987.

Brady, Anne-Marie. *Friend of China—The Myth of Rewi Alley*. London: Routledge Curzon, 2003.

Brennan, William J. *Building the Cooperative Commonwealth*. Regina: University of Regina, 1985.

Broadfoot, Barry. *Ten Lost Years 1929–39*. Toronto: McClelland and Stewart, 1973.

Buck, Tim. *Yours in Struggle*. Toronto: NC Press, 1977.

Callwood, June. *Emma*. Toronto: Stoddart, 1984.

Canada's Party of Socialism. Toronto: Progress Books, 1982.

Carter, Dyson. *So That Man May Prosper*. Winnipeg: Contemporary Publishers, 1943.

Comacchio, Cynthia. "Saving Mothers and Babies: Motherhood, Medicine and the Modern State 1900–1945." In *Framing Our Past, Canadian Women's History in the Twentieth Century*. Montreal: McGill-Queen's University Press, 2001.

Cross, A.F. "Parliamentary Personalities." *Canadian Business* (April 1945): 15.

Crowly, Terry. "Agnes Macphail and Canadian Working Women." *Labour/Le Travail* (Fall 1991): 129–48.

Douglas, T.C. *The Making of a Socialist, The Recollections of T.C. Douglas*, ed. Lewis H. Thomas. Edmonton: University of Alberta Press, 1982.

Doyle, James. "Science, Literature, and Revolution, the Life and Writings of Dyson Carter." *Left History* (Fall 1999).

Dyck, Betty L. *Running to Beat Hell, A Biography of A.M. (Sandy) Nicholson*. Regina: Canadian Plains Research Centre, University of Regina, 1988.

Endicott, Stephen. *James Endicott, Rebel out of China*. Toronto: University of Toronto Press, 1980.

____. "The People's World of 1948." In *Walden 3*. Toronto: Masterpress, 1984.

____. *Red Earth, Revolution in a Sichuan Village*. Toronto: NC Press, 1989.

____. *Bienfait, The Saskatchewan Miners' Struggle of '31*. Toronto: University of Toronto Press, 2002.

Engels, Friedrich. *The Origin of the Family, Private Property and the State*. New York: International Publishers, 1942.

Fairbairn, Gary. *Prairie Roots, The Remarkable Story of the Saskatchewan Wheat Pool*. Saskatoon: Western Producer Prairie Books, 1984.

Finkel, Alvin. *The Social Credit Phenomenon in Alberta*. Toronto: University of Toronto Press, 1989.

Frager, Ruth. *Sweatshop Strife, Class, Ethnicity, and Gender in the Jewish Labour Movement of Toronto, 1900–1939*. Toronto: University of Toronto Press, 1992.

Frank, David. *J.B. McLachlan*. Toronto: James Lorimer, 1999.

Frazer, Chris. "From Pariahs to Patriots: Canadian Communists and the Second World War." *Past Imperfect* (1996): 3–36.

Gerus, Oleh, and Denis Hlynka, eds. *The Honourable Member for Vegreville, The Memoirs and Diary of Anthony Hlynka, MP*. Centre for Ukrainian Studies, University of Manitoba. Calgary: University of Calgary Press, 2005.

Gonick, Cy. *A Very Red Life: The Story of Bill Walsh*. St. John's: Canadian Committee on Labour History, 2001.

Gould, Emily. "Dorise Nielsen, M.P." *Chatelaine* (June 1940): 16, 67.

Granatstein, J.L. *Conscription in the Second World War 1939–1945*. Toronto: Ryerson Press, 1969.

____. *Mackenzie King: His Life and World*. Toronto: McGraw-Hill Ryerson, 1977.

____. *The Politics of Survival, The Conservative Party of Canada 1939–1945*. Toronto: University of Toronto Press, 1967.

____. *Canada's War, The Politics of the Mackenzie King Government 1939–1945*. Toronto: Oxford University Press, 1975.

Guard, Julie. "Canadian Citizens or Dangerous Foreign Women? Canada's Radical Consumer Movement 1947–1950." In *Sisters or Strangers? Immigrant, Ethnic and Radicalized Women in Canadian History*, ed. Marlene Epp, Franca Iacovetta, and Frances Swyripa. Toronto: University of Toronto Press, 2004.

Han Suyin. *Eldest Son*. New York: Hill and Wang, 1994.

Hande, D'Arcy. "Strike." *Saskatchewan History* (Autumn 1985).

Haynes, John E. *Red Scare or Red Menace?* Chicago: Ivan R. Dee, 1996.

Healey, Dorothy Ray, and Maurice Isserman. *California Red, A Life in the American Communist Party*. Champaign, Illinois: University of Illinois Press, 1993.

Herridge, W.C. *What Kind of Revolution?* Boston: Little Brown and Co., 1943.

Higginbottom, C.H. *Off the Record*. Toronto: McClelland and Stewart, 1968.

Hobsbawm, Eric. *The Age of Extremes*. London: Abacus, 1995.

Horowitz, Daniel. *Betty Friedan and the Making of the Feminine Mystique, The American Left, The Cold War, and Modern Feminism*. Amherst: University of Massachusetts Press, 1998.

Howard, Victor. *We Were the Salt of the Earth*. Regina: University of Regina, Great Plains Research Centre, 1985.

Hutchison, Bruce. *The Incredible Canadian*. Toronto: Longman's Green and Co., 1953.

Kimmel, David. "The Spirit of Canadian Democracy: Margaret Fairley and the Communist Cultural Worker's Responsibility to the People." *Left History* (Spring 1993).

King, Carlyle. "A Beginning in Politics." *Saskatchewan History* (Autumn 1983).

Kinsman, Gary, Dieter Buse, and Mercedes Steedman. *Whose National Security? Canadian State Surveillance and the Creation of Enemies*. Toronto: Between the Lines, 2000.

Klehr, Harvey. *The Heyday of American Communism, The Depression Decade*. New York: Basic Books, 1984.

Knight, Amy. *How the Cold War Began, The Gouzenko Affair and the Hunt for Soviet Spies*. Toronto: McClelland and Stewart, 2005.

Kolasky, John. *Shattered Illusion, The History of Ukrainian Pro-Communist Organizations in Canada*. Toronto: Peter Martin and Associates, 1979.

Laxer, James. *Red Diaper Baby, A Boyhood in the Age of McCarthyism*. Vancouver: Douglas and McIntyre, 2004.

Levesque, Andrée. *Scènes de la vie en rouge, l'époque de Jeanne Corbin 1906–1944*. Montreal: Les éditions de rémue-mènage, 1999.

Lewis, S.P. *The Life of Grace MacInnis*. Madeira Park, BC: Harbour Publishing, 1993.

Lewis, David. *The Good Fight*. Toronto: Macmillan of Canada, 1981.

Liversedge, Ronald. *Recollections of the On-to-Ottawa Trek*, ed. Victor Hoar. Toronto: Carleton Library, McClelland and Stewart, 1973.

Living in China. Beijing: New World Press, 1982.

Lunan, Gordon. *The Making of a Spy*. Montreal: Robert Davies Publishing, 1995.

MacDowell, Laurel Sefton. *Renegade Lawyer: The Life of J.L. Cohen*. Toronto: University of Toronto Press, 2001.

____. *Remember Kirkland Lake, The Goldminers Strike of 1941–42*. Toronto: University of Toronto Press, 1983.

Mandelstam, Nadezda. *Hope Against Hope*. New York: Atheneum, 1976.

Manley, John. "'Audacity, audacity, still more audacity': Tim Buck, the Party, and the People, 1932–1939." *Labour/Le Travail* (Spring 2002).

Martin, Paul. *A Very Public Life*. Vol. 1. Ottawa: Deneau, 1983.

McBride, Michelle. "The Curious Case of Female Internees." In *Enemies Within, Italian and Other Internees in Canada and Abroad*, ed. Franca Iacovetta, Roberto Perin, and Angelo Principe. Toronto: University of Toronto Press, 2000.

McEwen, Tom. *The Forge Glows Red*. Toronto: Progress Books, 1974.

Meisner, Maurice. *Mao's China and After*. New York: The Free Press, 1986.

Mills, Ivor J. *Stout Hearts Stand Tall*. Vancouver: Evergreen Press, 1971.

Milton, David, and Nancy Milton. *The Wind Will Not Subside*. New York: Pantheon, 1986.

Monod, David. "The Agrarian Struggle, Rural Communism in Alberta and Saskatchewan, 1926–1935." *Social History* (May 1985).

Morris, Leslie. *The Story of Tim Buck's Party (1922–1939)*. Toronto: New Era Publishing, 1939.

Morton, Desmond. *Working People*. Montreal: McGill-Queen's University Press, 1998.

Nielsen, Dorise. "Twelve Years Homesteading." (Toronto) *Star Weekly*, 31 August 1940.

Park, Frank, and Libbie Park. *Moscow as Two Canadians Saw It*. Toronto: The Canadian-Soviet Friendship Society, 1951.

Penner, Norman. *Canadian Communism: The Stalin Years and Beyond*. Toronto: Methuen Publishers, 1987.

____. *From Protest to Power: Social Democracy in Canada 1900–Present*. Toronto: James Lorimer, 1992.

Pierson, Ruth Roach. *'They're Still Women after All', Canadian Women and World War II*. Toronto: McClelland and Stewart, 1986.

Pitsula, J.M. "W.G. Brown: 'Righteousness Exalteth a Nation.'" *Saskatchewan History* (Spring 1980).

Prentice, Alison, Paula Bourne, Gail Cuthbert Brandt, Beth Light, Wendy Mitchison, and Naomi Black. *Canadian Women: A History.* Toronto: Harcourt, Brace, Jovanovich, 1988.

Power of the People, 1921–1971. Toronto: Progress Books 1972.

Rittenberg, Sidney, and Amanda Bennett. *The Man Who Stayed Behind.* New York: Simon and Schuster, 1993.

Sangster, Joan. *Dreams of Equality: Women on the Canadian Left 1920–1950.* Toronto: McClelland and Stewart, 1989.

Scott, Jack. *A Communist Life: Jack Scott and the Canadian Workers Movement 1927–1985,* ed. and intro. Bryan D. Palmer. St. John's: Committee on Labour History, 1988.

Shackleton, Doris. *Tommy Douglas.* Toronto: McClelland and Stewart, 1975.

Shapiro, Sidney. *An American in China, Thirty Years in the People's Republic.* New York: New American Library, 1979.

Sher, Len. *The Un-Canadians.* Toronto: Lester Publishing, 1992.

Sinclair, Peter. "The Saskatchewan CCF and the Communist Party in the 1930s." *Saskatchewan History* (Spring 1973).

Smith, A.E. *All My Life.* Toronto: Progress Books, 1949.

Smith, Doug. *Joe Zuken.* Toronto: James Lorimer, 1990.

Smith, Stewart. *Comrades and Komsomolkas.* Toronto: Lagus, 1993.

Spence, Jonathan D. *The Search for Modern China.* New York: Norton, 1990.

Spiritwood, Mildred, and Norbury Historical Society. *Tapestry of Time, A History of the Spiritwood, Mildred and Norbury Districts.* The Author, 1984.

Starobin, Joseph. *American Communism in Crisis.* Boston: Harvard University Press, 1972.

Stewart, Margaret, and Doris French. *Ask No Quarter: A Biography of Agnes Macphail.* Toronto: Longmans, Green and Co., 1959.

Stewart, Walter. *M.J., The Life and Times of M.J. Coldwell.* Toronto: Stoddart, 2000.

Strong, Tracy B., and Helene Keyssar. *Right in Her Soul, The Life of Anna Louise Strong.* New York: Random House, 1983.

Strong-Boag. *The New Day Recalled, Lives of Girls and Women in English Canada 1919–1939.* Toronto: Penguin Books, 1988.

Sullivan, Pat. *Red Sails on the Great Lakes.* Toronto: Macmillan, 1955.

Taylor, Georgina. "'Shall I Drown Myself Now or Later?' The Isolation of Rural Women in Saskatchewan and Their Participation in the Homemakers' Clubs, The Farm Movement and the CCF 1910–1967." In *Women, Isolation and Bonding—The Ecology of Gender.* Toronto: Methuen, 1987.

Waiser, Bill. *All Hell Can't Stop Us.* Calgary: Fifth House, 2003.

____. *Saskatchewan, A New History.* Calgary: Fifth House, 2005.

Watson, Louise. *She Never Was Afraid, The Story of Annie Buller 1896–1973.* Toronto: Progress Books, 1976.

Weisbord, Merrily. *The Strangest Dream.* Toronto: Lester and Orpen Dennys, 1983.

Whitaker, Reg, and Gary Marcuse. *Cold War Canada, The Making of a National Insecurity State 1945–1957.* Toronto: University of Toronto Press, 1994.

Wiggins, Walter. *Saskatchewan, the Land and Its People, Selections from the Writings of Walter Wiggins*, ed. Cathy Fisher. Regina: The Author, 1985.

Williams, George. *The Land of the Soviets, A Western Farmer Sees the Russian Bear Change Its Coat.* Regina: The United Farmers of Canada, Saskatchewan Section, 1931.

Wong, Jan. *China.* Toronto: Doubleday, 1999.

____. *Red China Blues.* Toronto: Doubleday 1996.

UNPUBLISHED SOURCES

Johnston, Faith. "Dorise Nielsen, The Life and Ideas of a Canadian Woman in Politics." MA thesis, Carleton University, 1989.

Monod, David. "Soldiers of the Plough: Popular Protest and Insurgency in Alberta and Saskatchewan." MA thesis, McGill University, 1983.

Smillie, Elizabeth. "Dorise Nielsen, Prairie Populist and Feminist." Honours thesis, Trent University, 1981.

Steininger, Frederich. "George Williams: Agrarian Socialist." MA thesis, University of Regina, 1976.

Taylor, Georgina. "'Equals and Partners,' An Examination of the Roles of Twelve Women Active in the CCF 1932-37." MA thesis, University of Saskatchewan, 1983.

INTERVIEWS AND CORRESPONDENCE

Beeching, Elsie. Telephone interview, July 2003.
Block, Willard. Interview in Canwood, July 2003.
Boyd, John. Telephone interview, May 2004.
Buck, Jean. Interview in Sydney, BC, March 2003.
Burchill, William. Telephone interview, September 2002.
Chandler, Betty. Interview in Beijing, March 2003.
Cleveland, Melanie. Correspondence, November 2004.
Crook, Carl. Correspondence, June 2002.
Crook, Isabel. Telephone interview, August 2002. Interview in Beijing, March 2003.
Crook, Michael. Correspondence, June 2002.
Crook, Paul. Correspondence, June 2002.
Endicott, Stephen. Interview in Toronto, October 2002.

Godefroy, Hugh. Telephone interview, January 2003.
Godefroy, Muriel. Telephone interview, January 2003.
Harvey, Mark. Telephone interview, July 2004.
Hodge, Isabel. Correspondence, May 2005.
Kardash, Bill and Mary. Interview in Winnipeg, August 1987.
Kashtan, William. Telephone interview, August 1988.
Lunan, Gordon. Telephone interview, November 2004.
MacLeod, Virginia. Telephone interview, June 1988.
McLaren, Glen. Correspondence, July 2005.
Martin, Paul (senior). Correspondence, August 1988.
Miller, Minerva (Cooper). Telephone interview, November 1988.
Nielsen, Doug. Telephone interview, May 2004.
Nielsen, Judy. Telephone interview, May 2004.
Nielsen, Vivienne. Telephone interview, May 2004.
Nielsen, Sally. Interviews in Gravenhurst, August 1988, and in Lakefield, June 2005. Correspondence, March to August 2005.
Park, Frank. Interview in Ottawa, July 1989.
Paul, Douglas. Telephone interview, November 2003.
Paul, Irja. Telephone interview, April 2004.
Paul, Stewart. Interview in Oakville, October 2002.
Penner, Addie. Interview in Winnipeg, October 2003.
Penner, Norman. Telephone interview, May 1988.
Penner, Roland. Interview in Winnipeg, June 2005.
Phelps, Eva (Hunt). Interview in Saskatoon, August 2003.
Polaski, Marion. Telephone interview, May 2003.
Repka, Kay (Sheldon). Interview in Ottawa, June 1989.
Ryerson, Edna (Blois). Telephone interview, December 1988.
Ryerson, Stanley. Telephone interview, September 1989.
Savage, Robert (Doc). Telephone interview, August 2004.
Szasz, Charles. Interview in Spiritwood, July 2002.
Tang Sheng. Interview in Beijing, March 2003.
Turple, Alan. Telephone interview, August 2002.
Vockeroth, Bob. Telephone interview, July 2003.
Vockeroth, Richard. Telephone interview, December 2002.
Whyte, Monica. Telephone interview, May 2004.
Williston, Floyd. Interview in Winnipeg, June 2002.
Woollard, Tim. Telephone interview, December 2003.
Wong, Christine. Interviews in Ottawa, February 1986 to April 1988.
Wong, Jennifer. Correspondence, November 2002 to May 2004.
Evan Wong. Telephone interview, July 2004.
Yu Fanqin (Xiao Yu). Interview in Beijing, March 2003.

INDEX

M

N

O

P